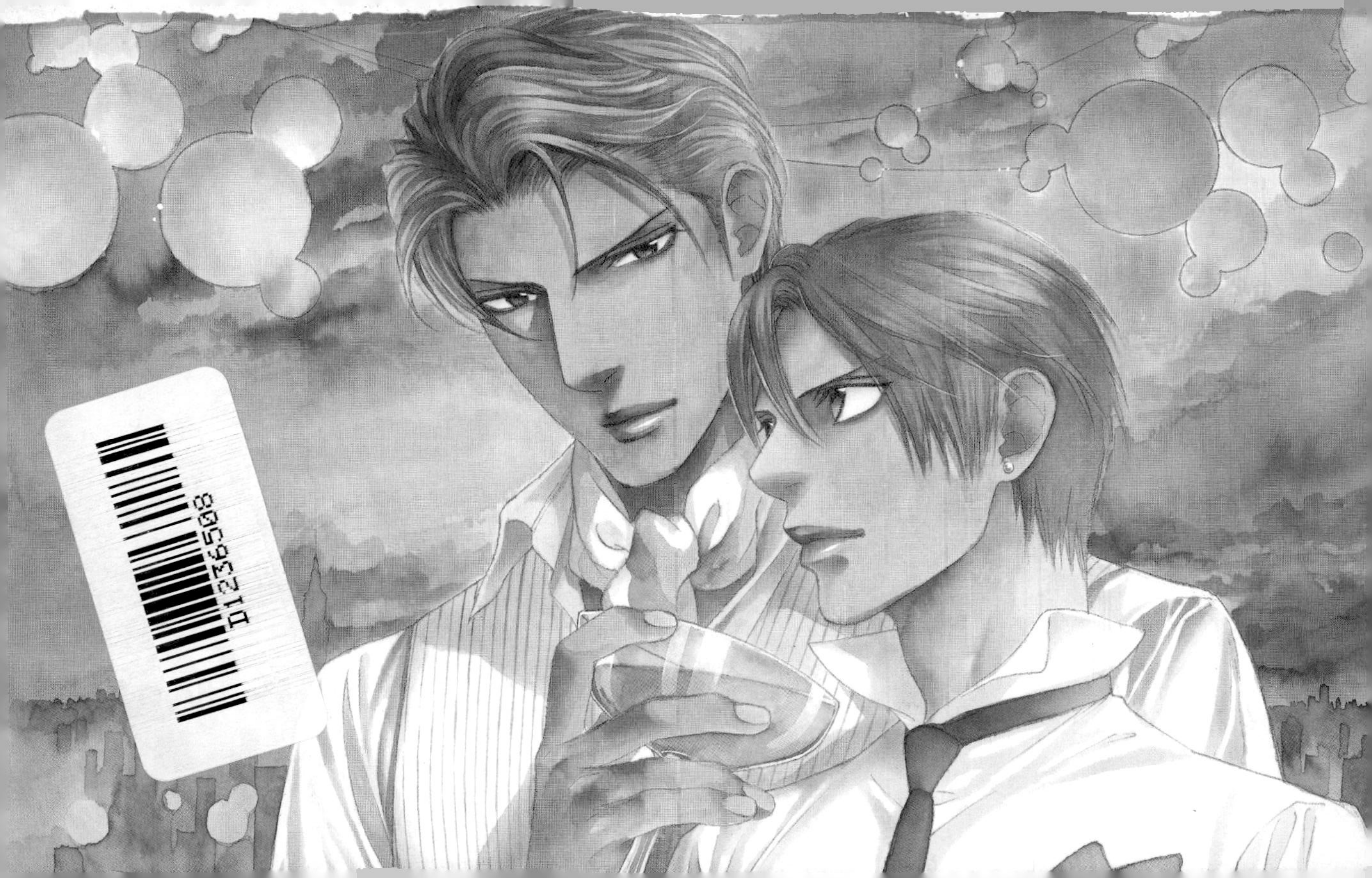

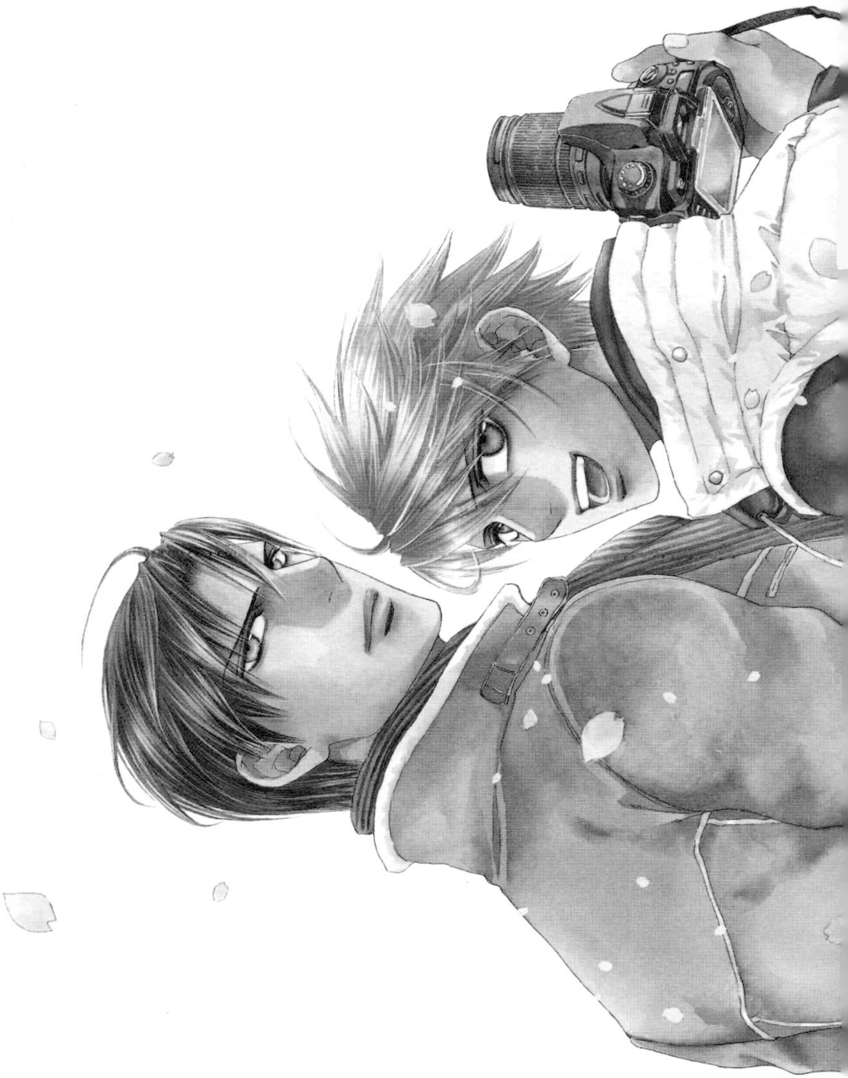

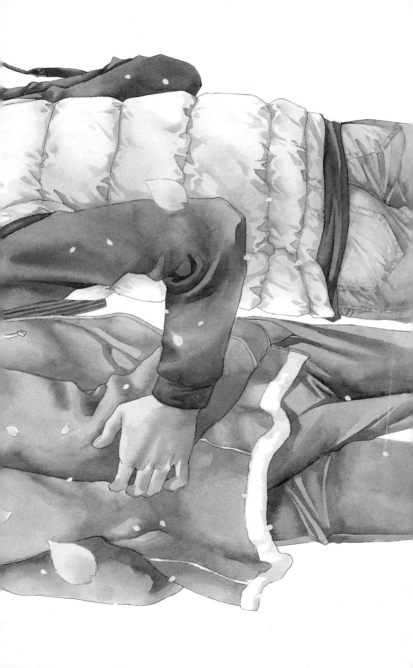

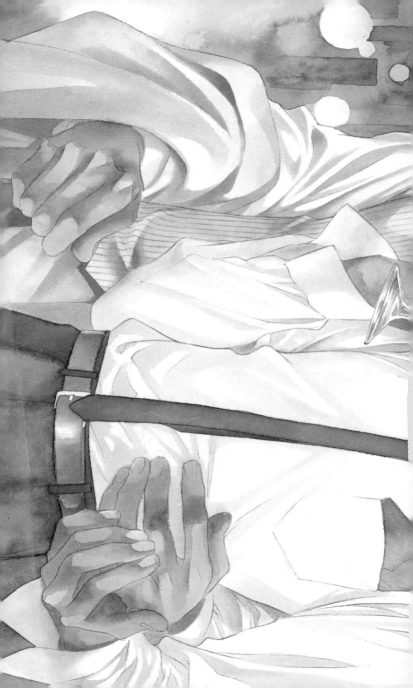

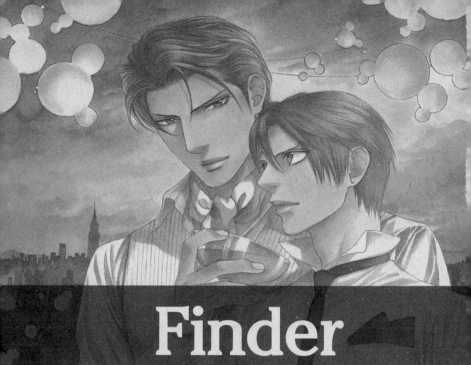

Finder

Story and Art by Ayano Yamane

volume 9

CONTENTS

SUBLIME
SuBLime Manga Edition

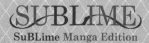

Pray in the Abyss

Finder Series Character Introduction

Akihito Takaba

Akihito Takaba, a freelance photographer, was chasing a scoop on a dirty politician when he first met Asami. Routinely employed by a weekly magazine, Akihito spends his time hunting for news stories. Outgoing and determined, he refuses to back down or lose hope, even in the toughest of situations. After getting caught up in an idol-stalker incident and subsequently hounded by angry fans, he winds up crashing at Asami's place and taking care of most of the household chores. He is very confident in his cooking.

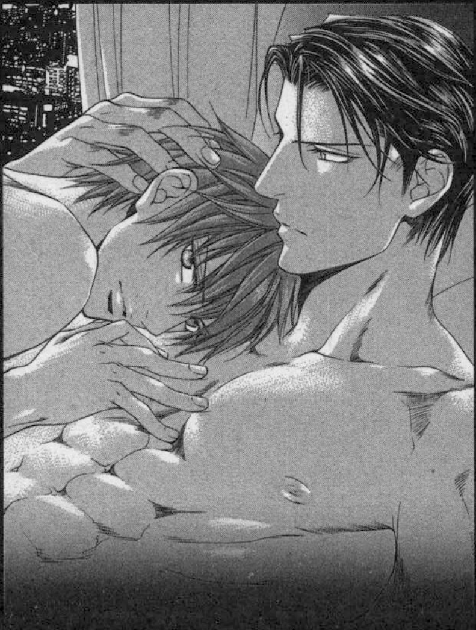

Ryuichi Asami

On the surface, Ryuichi Asami is one of Japan's brightest young businessmen, owning several highly successful luxury hotels and nightclubs. But under this facade lies a cunning and powerful crime lord with influence among not just the wealthy elite but also international movers and shakers. Where he came from and how he got to his current position remains unknown. While generally cold and calculating, he has been known to go out of his way to protect loyal subordinates. He is known for both his intelligence and his cool good looks.

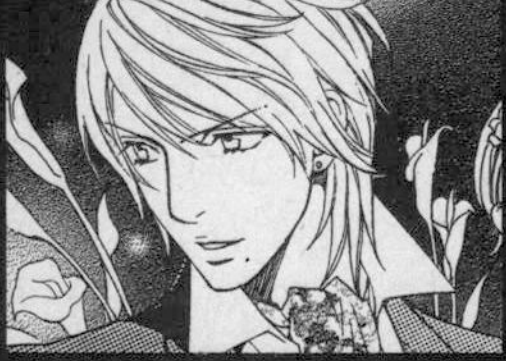

Shu Sudo

The manager at Club Dracaena, one of the luxurious members-only nightclubs Asami owns. He has feelings for Asami, but when he realizes they will go unrequited, he betrays Asami out of desperation.

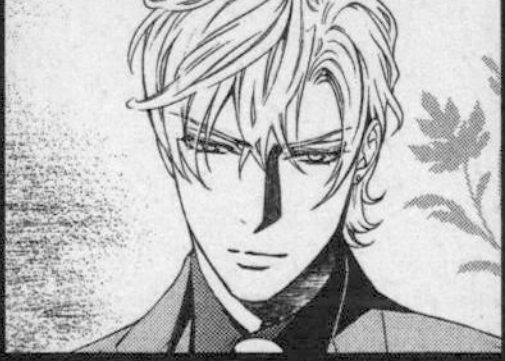

Mikhail Arbitov

One of the top players in the Russian mafia, he once clashed with Asami and Fei Long in Hong Kong over the rights to a Macao casino. Now he's come to Japan looking for Asami's traitorous underling Sudo.

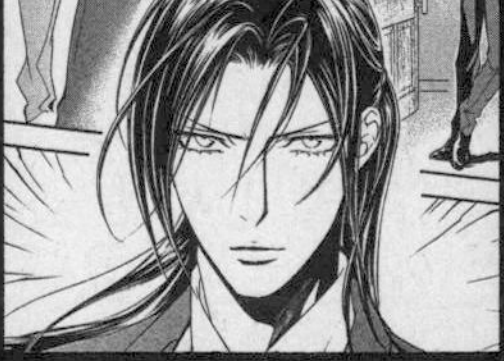

Fei Long Liú

The young leader of Báishé (White Snake), one of Asia's largest mafia syndicates. He seems more the intellectual type, but he's also handy in a fight. At one point he kidnapped Akihito, but now the two are friendly.

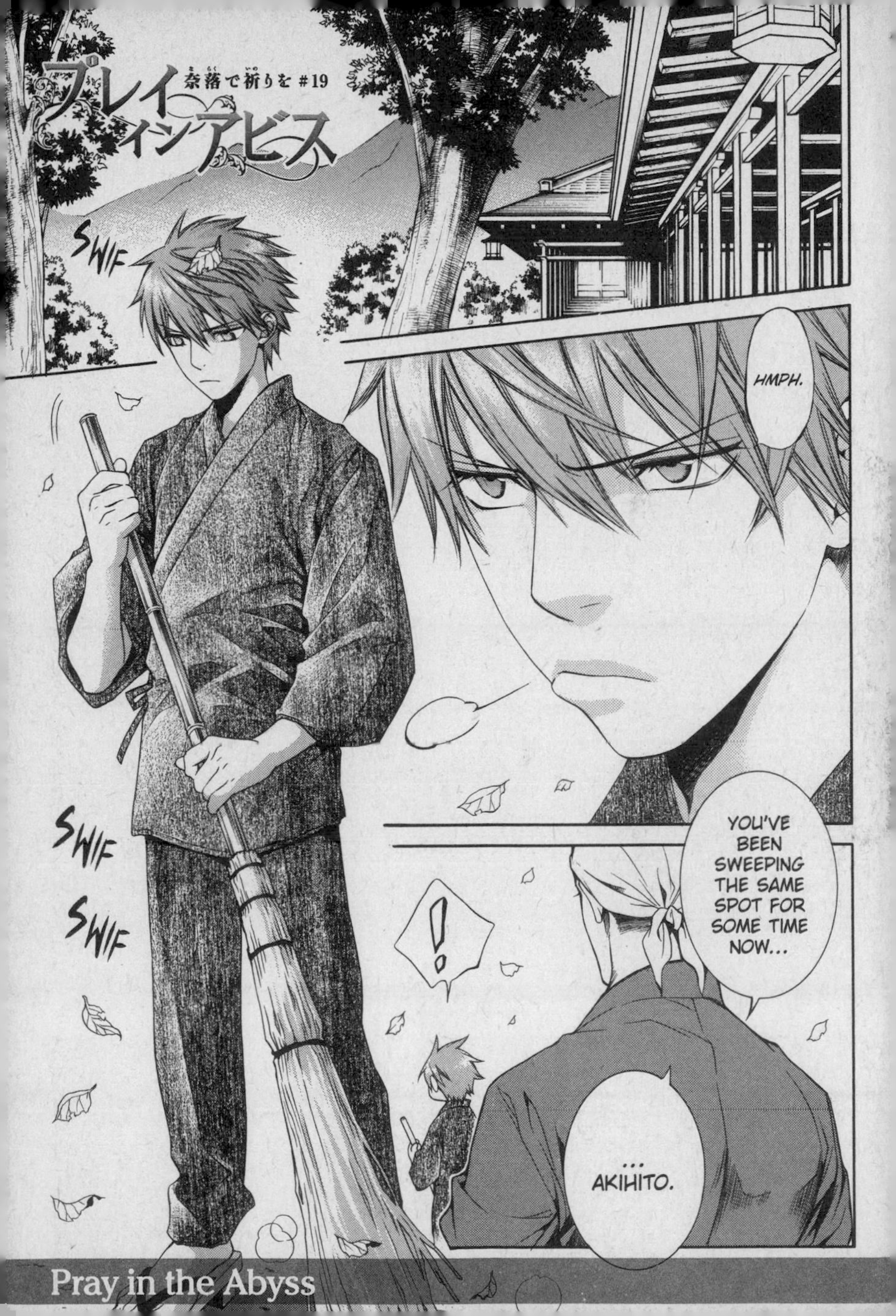
プレイ イン アビス
奈落で祈りを #19
HMPH.
YOU'VE BEEN SWEEPING THE SAME SPOT FOR SOME TIME NOW...
!
... AKIHITO.
SWIF
SWIF
SWIF
Pray in the Abyss

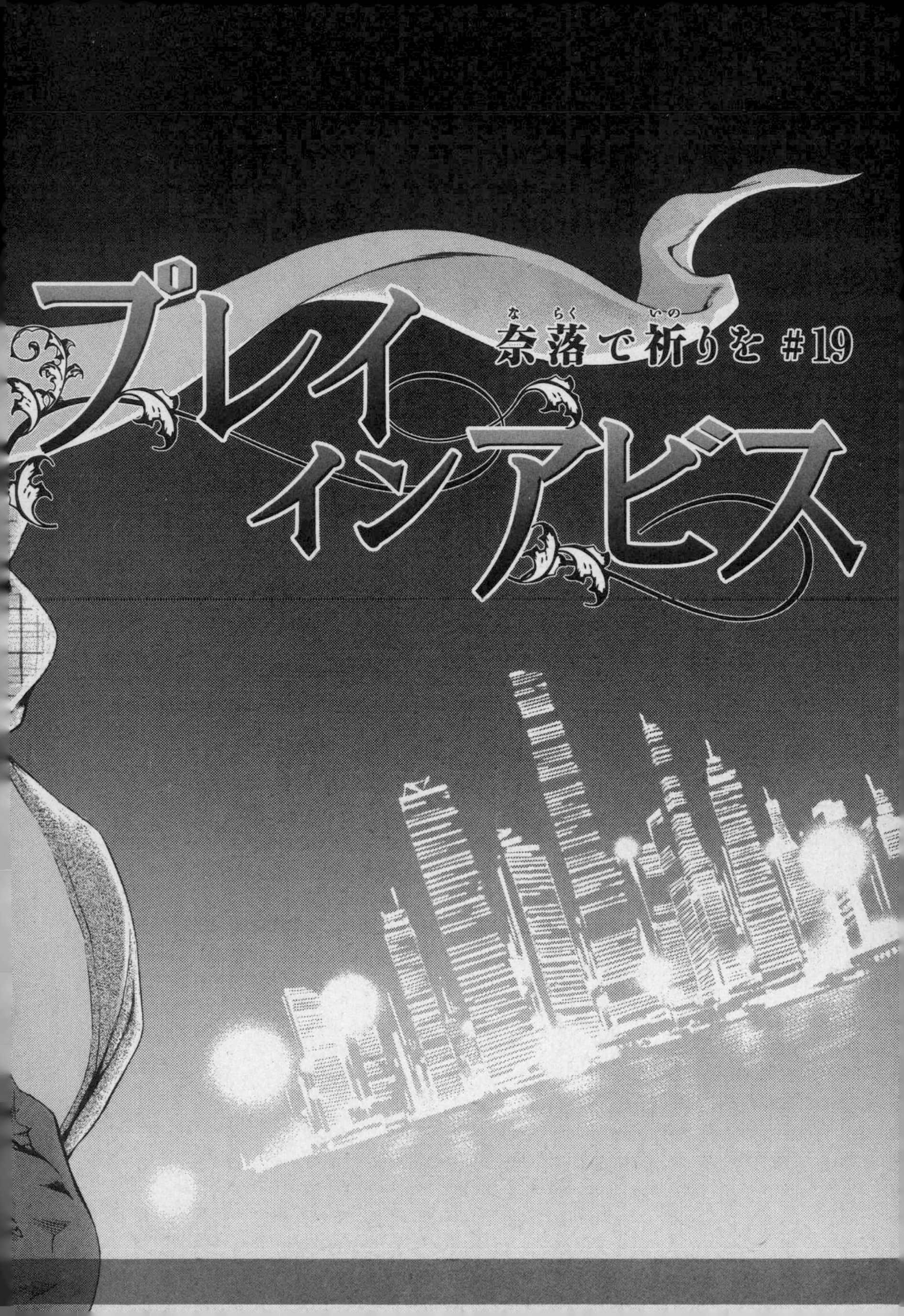
プレイ インアビス
奈落で祈りを #19

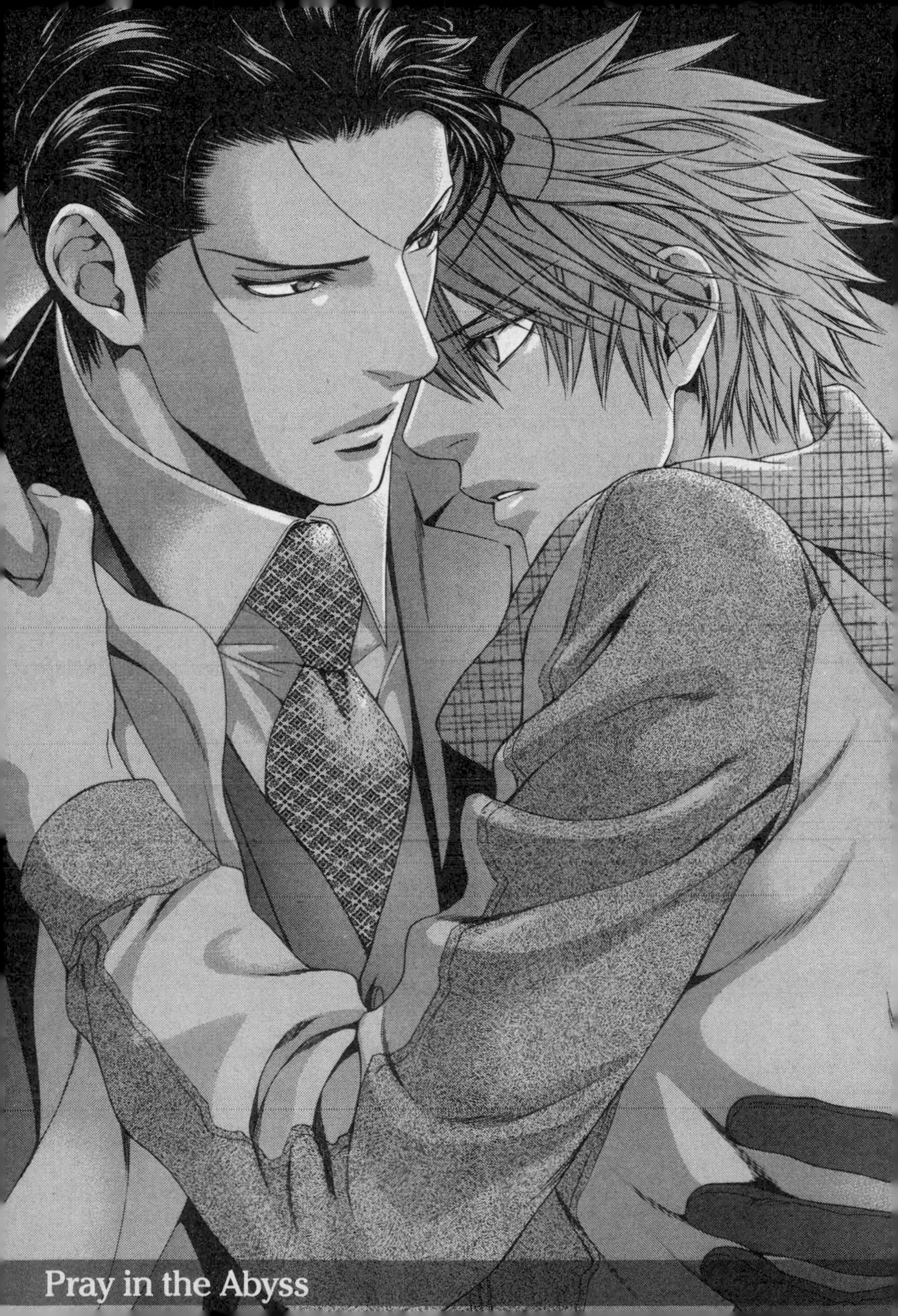
Pray in the Abyss

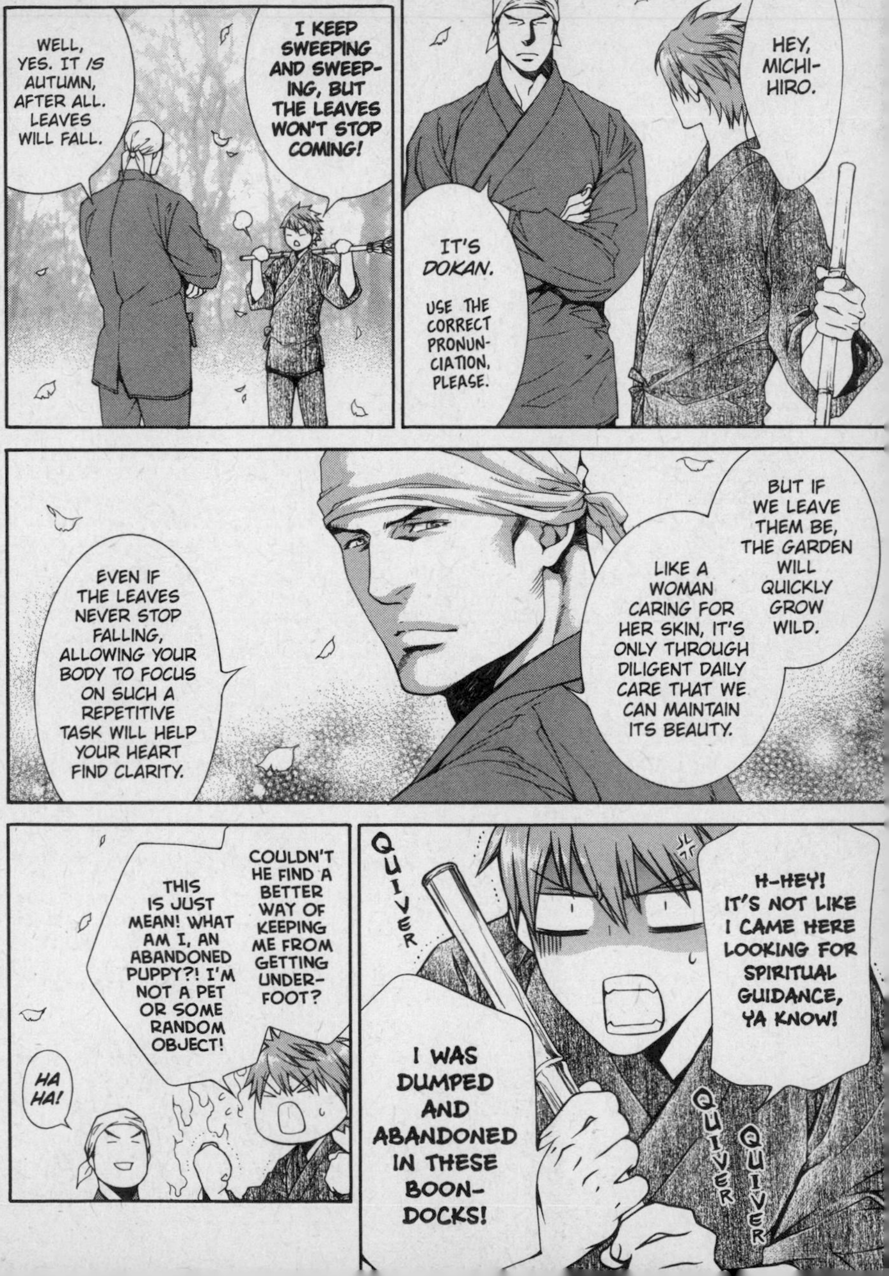
HEY, MICHIHIRO.
IT'S *DOKAN*.
USE THE CORRECT PRONUNCIATION, PLEASE.
I KEEP SWEEPING AND SWEEPING, BUT THE LEAVES WON'T STOP COMING!
WELL, YES. IT *IS* AUTUMN, AFTER ALL. LEAVES WILL FALL.
BUT IF WE LEAVE THEM BE, THE GARDEN WILL QUICKLY GROW WILD.
LIKE A WOMAN CARING FOR HER SKIN, IT'S ONLY THROUGH DILIGENT DAILY CARE THAT WE CAN MAINTAIN ITS BEAUTY.
EVEN IF THE LEAVES NEVER STOP FALLING, ALLOWING YOUR BODY TO FOCUS ON SUCH A REPETITIVE TASK WILL HELP YOUR HEART FIND CLARITY.
QUIVER
H-HEY! IT'S NOT LIKE I CAME HERE LOOKING FOR SPIRITUAL GUIDANCE, YA KNOW!
I WAS DUMPED AND ABANDONED IN THESE BOONDOCKS!
QUIVER
QUIVER
COULDN'T HE FIND A BETTER WAY OF KEEPING ME FROM GETTING UNDERFOOT?
THIS IS JUST MEAN! WHAT AM I, AN ABANDONED PUPPY?! I'M NOT A PET OR SOME RANDOM OBJECT!
HA HA!

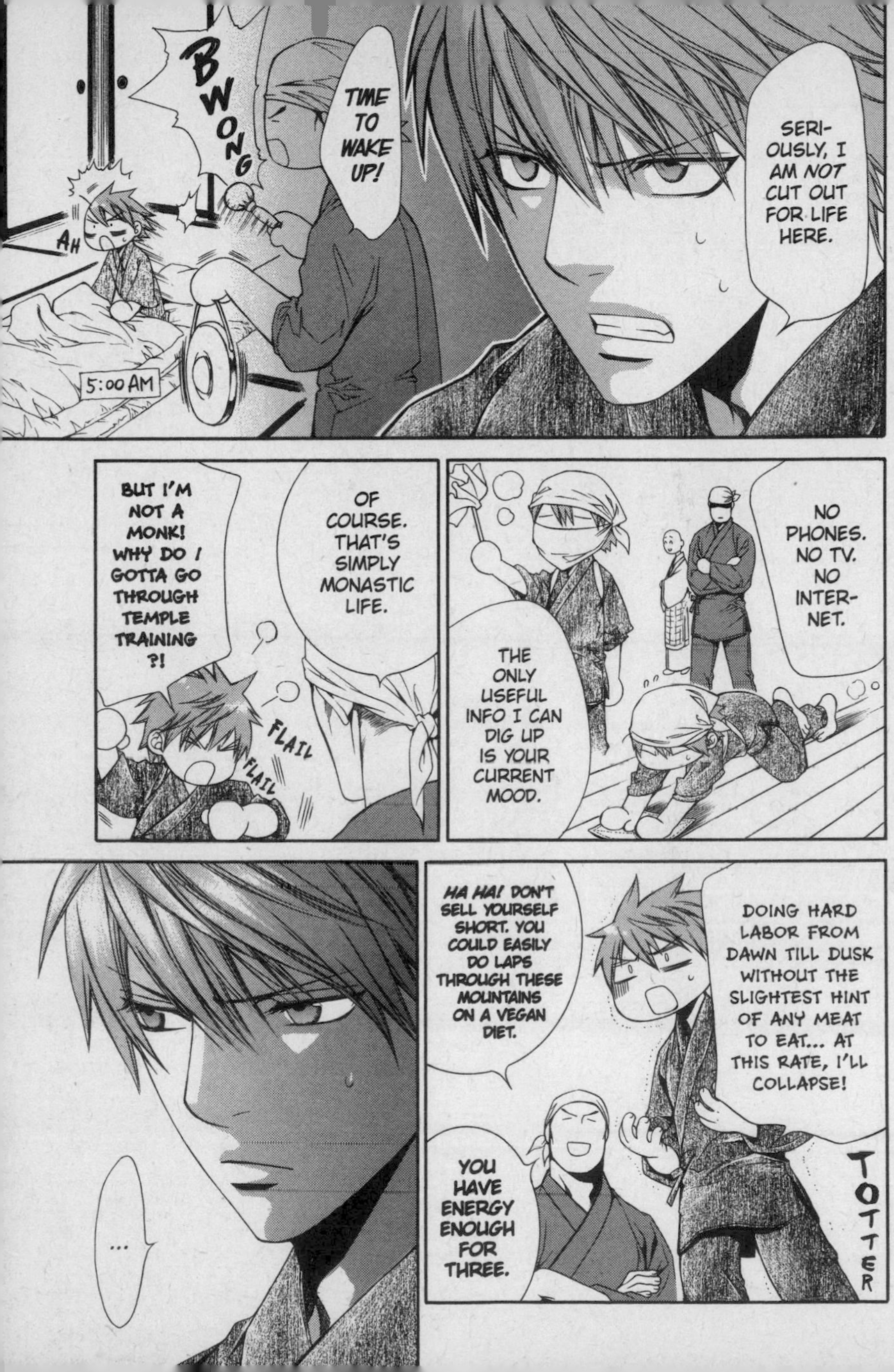
SERIOUSLY, I AM *NOT* CUT OUT FOR LIFE HERE.
TIME TO WAKE UP!
BWONG
AH
5:00 AM
NO PHONES. NO TV. NO INTERNET.
THE ONLY USEFUL INFO I CAN DIG UP IS YOUR CURRENT MOOD.
OF COURSE. THAT'S SIMPLY MONASTIC LIFE.
BUT I'M NOT A MONK! WHY DO *I* GOTTA GO THROUGH TEMPLE TRAINING?!
FLAIL
FLAIL
DOING HARD LABOR FROM DAWN TILL DUSK WITHOUT THE SLIGHTEST HINT OF ANY MEAT TO EAT... AT THIS RATE, I'LL COLLAPSE!
HA HA! DON'T SELL YOURSELF SHORT. YOU COULD EASILY DO LAPS THROUGH THESE MOUNTAINS ON A VEGAN DIET.
YOU HAVE ENERGY ENOUGH FOR THREE.
TOTTER
...

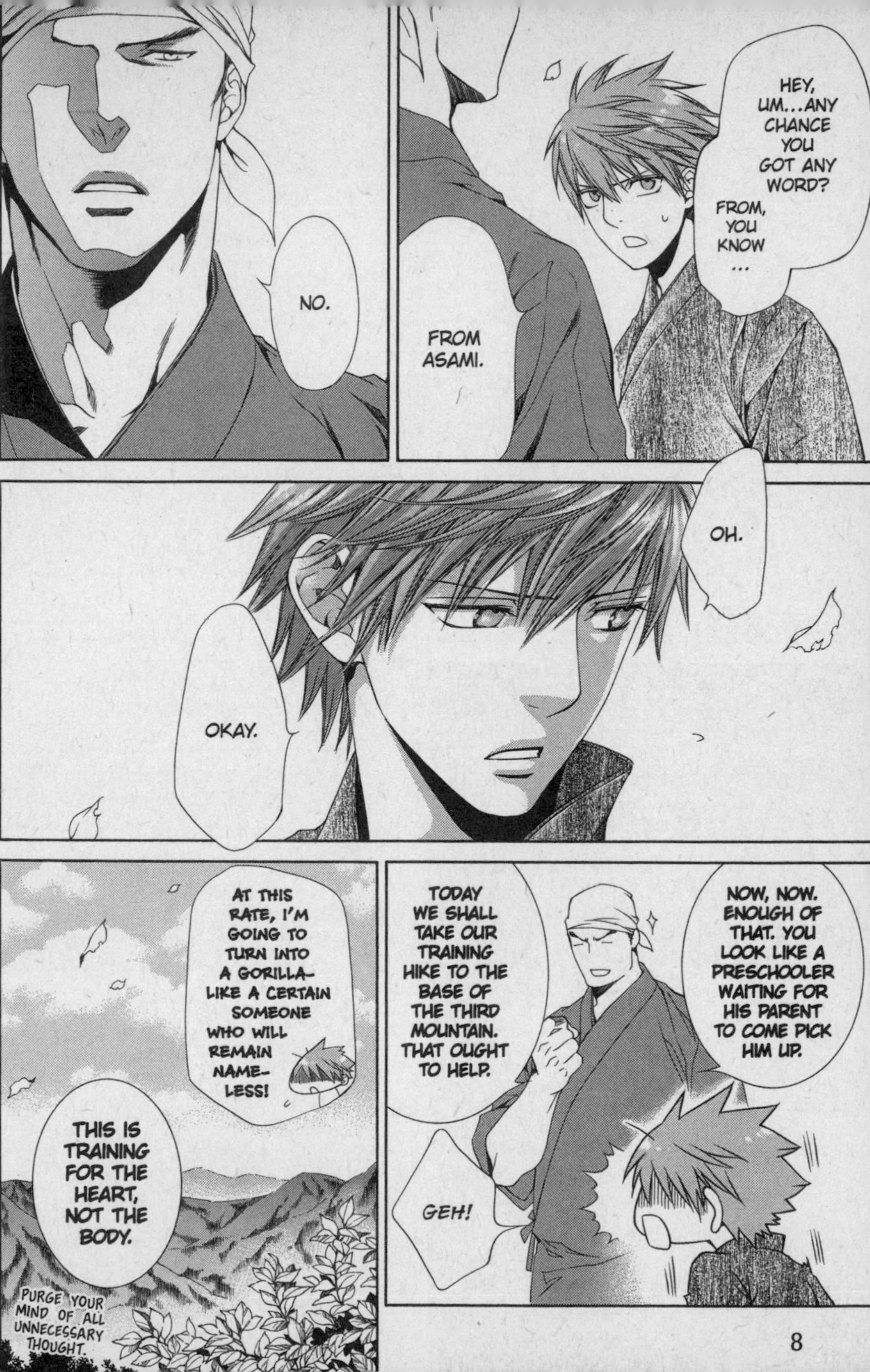
HEY, UM...ANY CHANCE YOU GOT ANY WORD?
FROM, YOU KNOW ...
FROM ASAMI.
NO.
OH.
OKAY.
NOW, NOW. ENOUGH OF THAT. YOU LOOK LIKE A PRESCHOOLER WAITING FOR HIS PARENT TO COME PICK HIM UP.
TODAY WE SHALL TAKE OUR TRAINING HIKE TO THE BASE OF THE THIRD MOUNTAIN. THAT OUGHT TO HELP.
GEH!
AT THIS RATE, I'M GOING TO TURN INTO A GORILLA-LIKE A CERTAIN SOMEONE WHO WILL REMAIN NAME-LESS!
THIS IS TRAINING FOR THE HEART, NOT THE BODY.
PURGE YOUR MIND OF ALL UNNECESSARY THOUGHT.

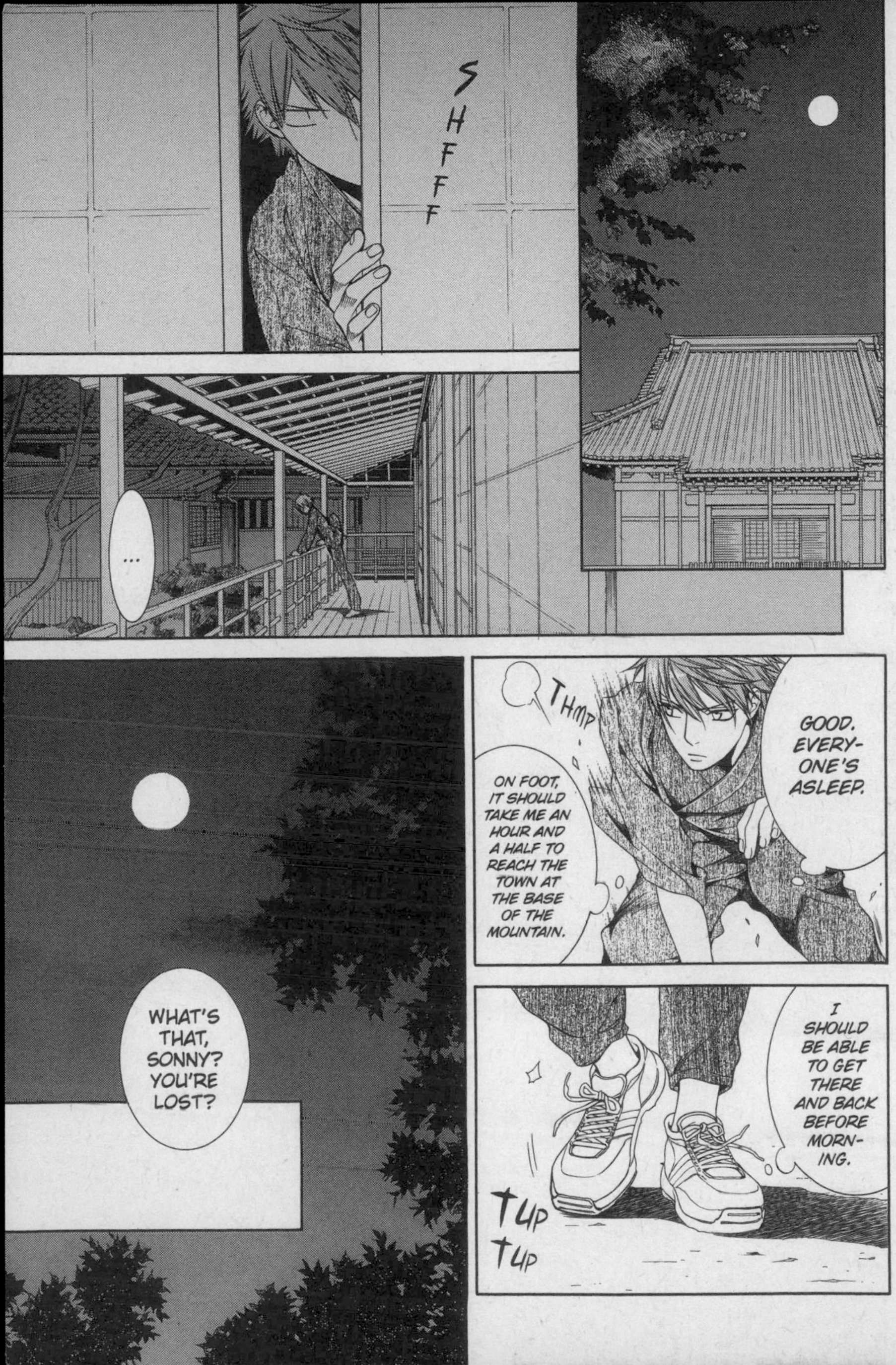
SHFFF
...
GOOD. EVERYONE'S ASLEEP.
THMP
ON FOOT, IT SHOULD TAKE ME AN HOUR AND A HALF TO REACH THE TOWN AT THE BASE OF THE MOUNTAIN.
I SHOULD BE ABLE TO GET THERE AND BACK BEFORE MORNING.
TUP TUP
WHAT'S THAT, SONNY? YOU'RE LOST?

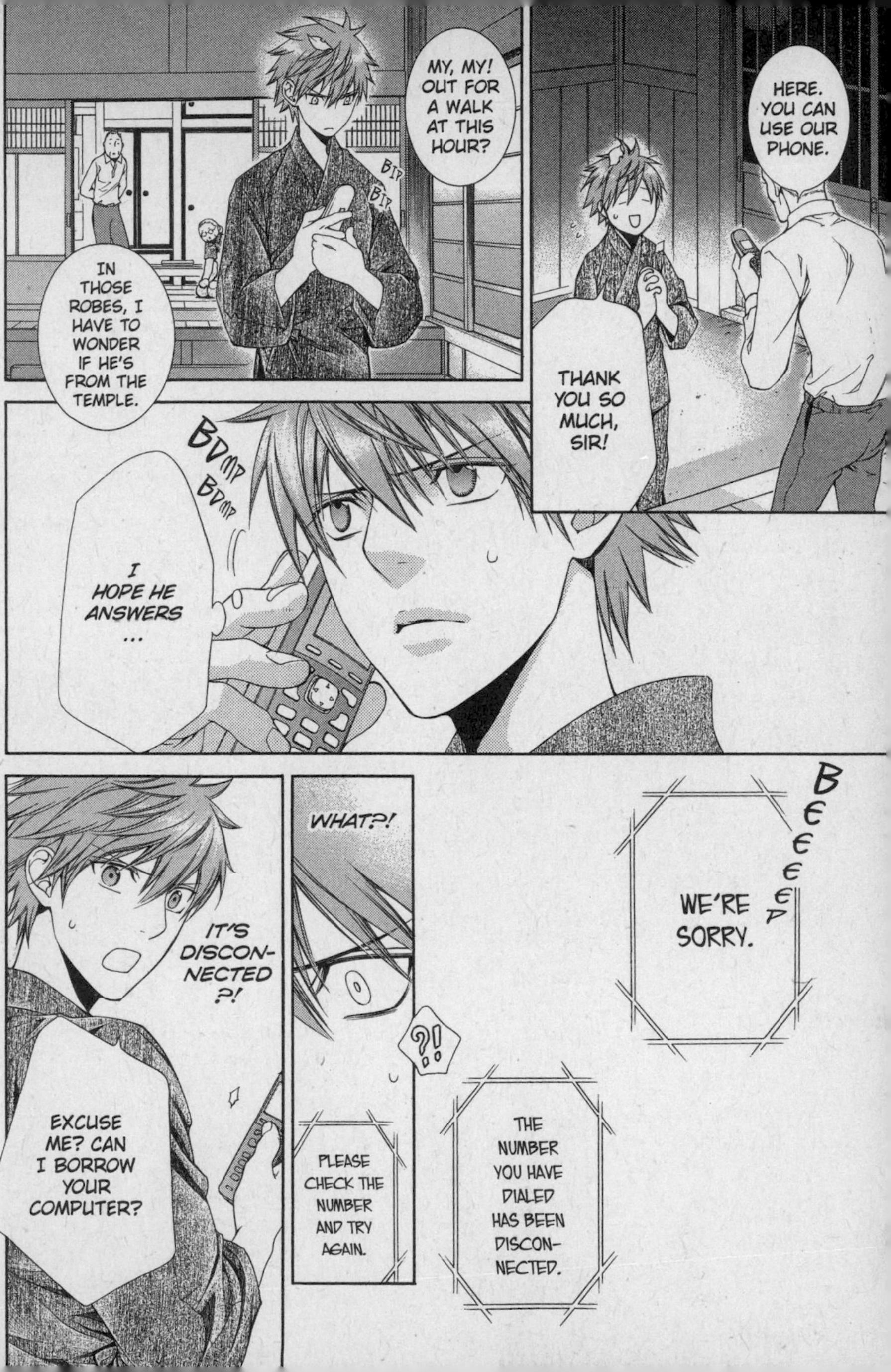
HERE. YOU CAN USE OUR PHONE.
THANK YOU SO MUCH, SIR!
MY, MY! OUT FOR A WALK AT THIS HOUR?
BIP BIP
IN THOSE ROBES, I HAVE TO WONDER IF HE'S FROM THE TEMPLE.
BDMP BDMP
I HOPE HE ANSWERS...
BEEEEP
WE'RE SORRY.
THE NUMBER YOU HAVE DIALED HAS BEEN DISCONNECTED.
WHAT?!
?!
PLEASE CHECK THE NUMBER AND TRY AGAIN.
IT'S DISCONNECTED?!
EXCUSE ME? CAN I BORROW YOUR COMPUTER?

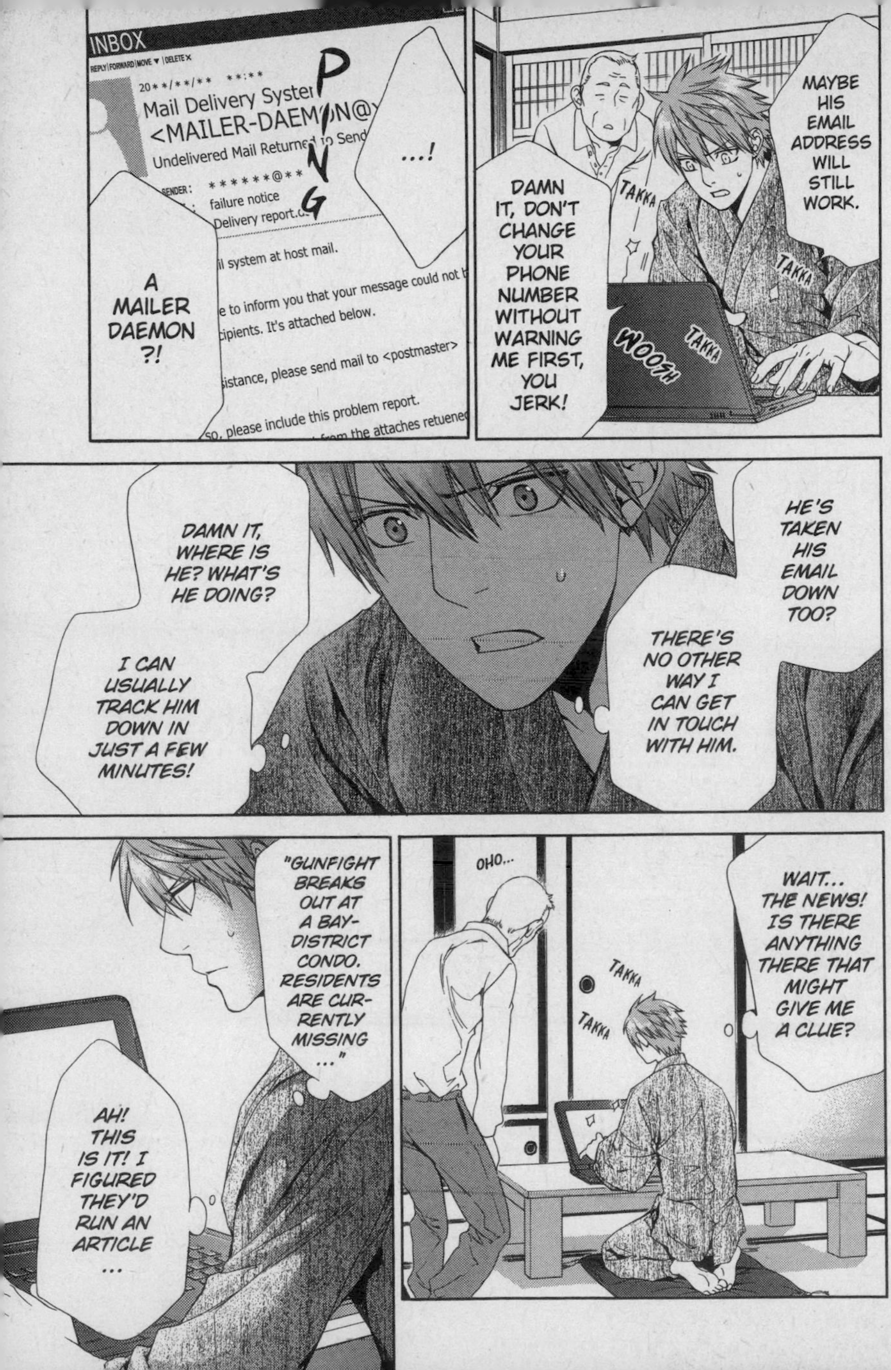
MAYBE HIS EMAIL ADDRESS WILL STILL WORK.
DAMN IT, DON'T CHANGE YOUR PHONE NUMBER WITHOUT WARNING ME FIRST, YOU JERK!
TAKKA
TAKKA
TAKKA
WOOSH
INBOX
REPLY | FORWARD | MOVE ▼ | DELETE ✕
20**/**/** **:**
Mail Delivery Syster
<MAILER-DAEMON@
Undelivered Mail Returned to Send
SENDER : ******@**
failure notice
Delivery report.
il system at host mail.
e to inform you that your message could not b
cipients. It's attached below.
sistance, please send mail to <postmaster>
please include this problem report.
so, please include
from the attaches retuened
PING
...!
A MAILER DAEMON ?!
HE'S TAKEN HIS EMAIL DOWN TOO?
THERE'S NO OTHER WAY I CAN GET IN TOUCH WITH HIM.
DAMN IT, WHERE IS HE? WHAT'S HE DOING?
I CAN USUALLY TRACK HIM DOWN IN JUST A FEW MINUTES!
WAIT... THE NEWS! IS THERE ANYTHING THERE THAT MIGHT GIVE ME A CLUE?
OHO...
TAKKA
TAKKA
"GUNFIGHT BREAKS OUT AT A BAY-DISTRICT CONDO. RESIDENTS ARE CURRENTLY MISSING..."
AH! THIS IS IT! I FIGURED THEY'D RUN AN ARTICLE...

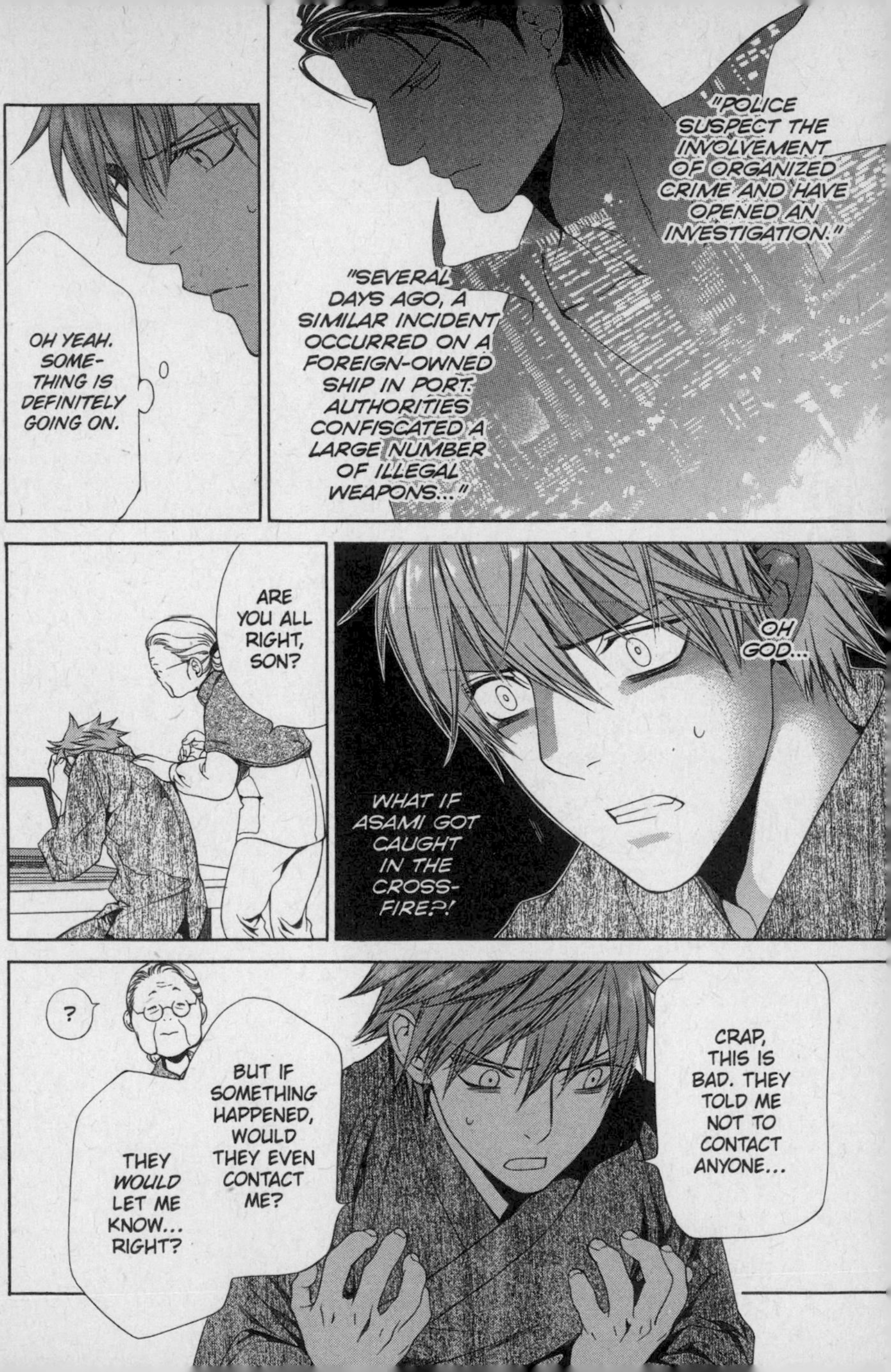
"POLICE SUSPECT THE INVOLVEMENT OF ORGANIZED CRIME AND HAVE OPENED AN INVESTIGATION."
"SEVERAL DAYS AGO, A SIMILAR INCIDENT OCCURRED ON A FOREIGN-OWNED SHIP IN PORT. AUTHORITIES CONFISCATED A LARGE NUMBER OF ILLEGAL WEAPONS..."
OH YEAH. SOME-THING IS DEFINITELY GOING ON.
OH GOD...
WHAT IF ASAMI GOT CAUGHT IN THE CROSS-FIRE?!
ARE YOU ALL RIGHT, SON?
CRAP, THIS IS BAD. THEY TOLD ME NOT TO CONTACT ANYONE...
?
BUT IF SOMETHING HAPPENED, WOULD THEY EVEN CONTACT ME?
THEY *WOULD* LET ME KNOW... RIGHT?

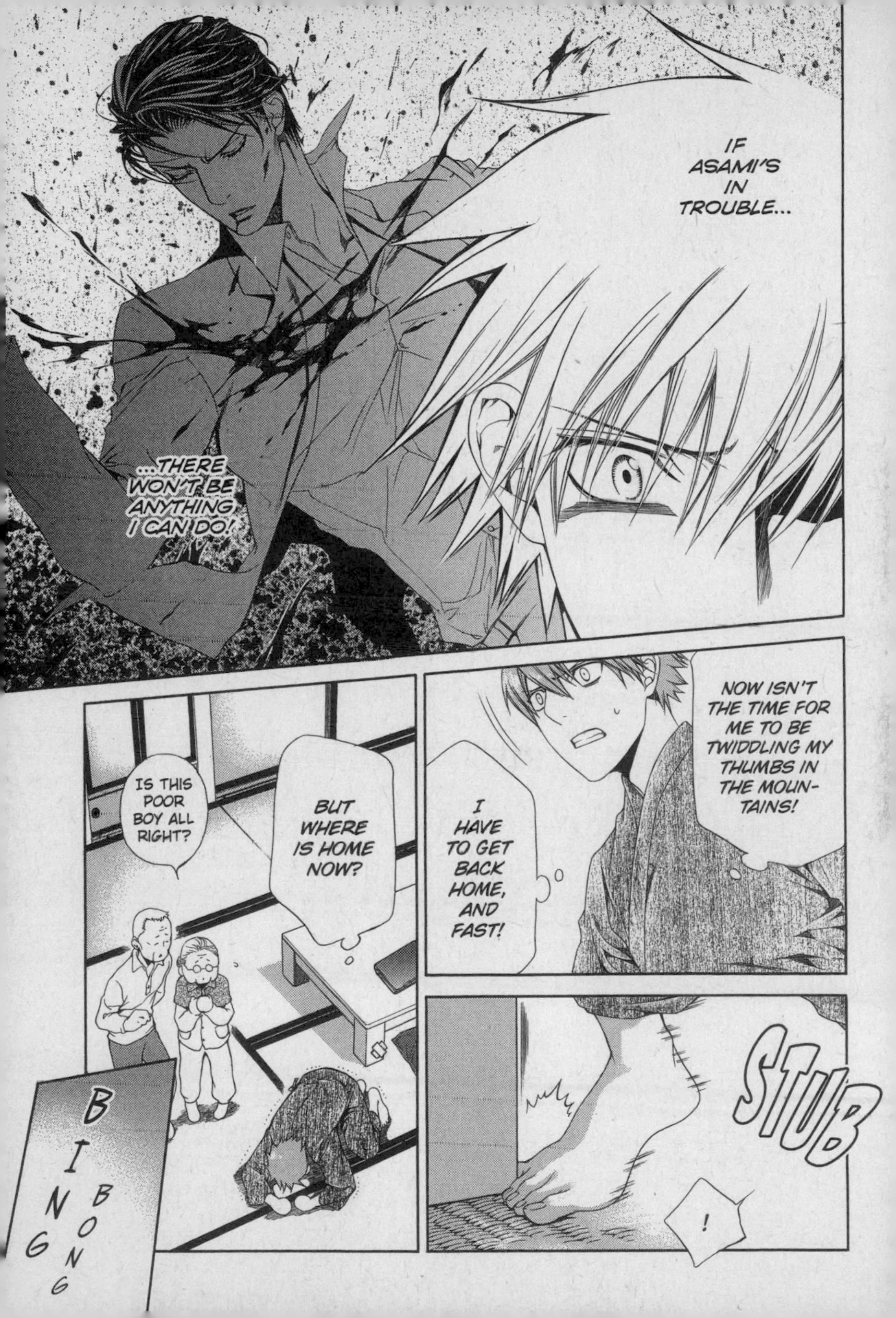
IF ASAMI'S IN TROUBLE...
...THERE WON'T BE ANYTHING I CAN DO!
NOW ISN'T THE TIME FOR ME TO BE TWIDDLING MY THUMBS IN THE MOUN-TAINS!
I HAVE TO GET BACK HOME, AND FAST!
STUB
!
BUT WHERE IS HOME NOW?
IS THIS POOR BOY ALL RIGHT?
BING BONG

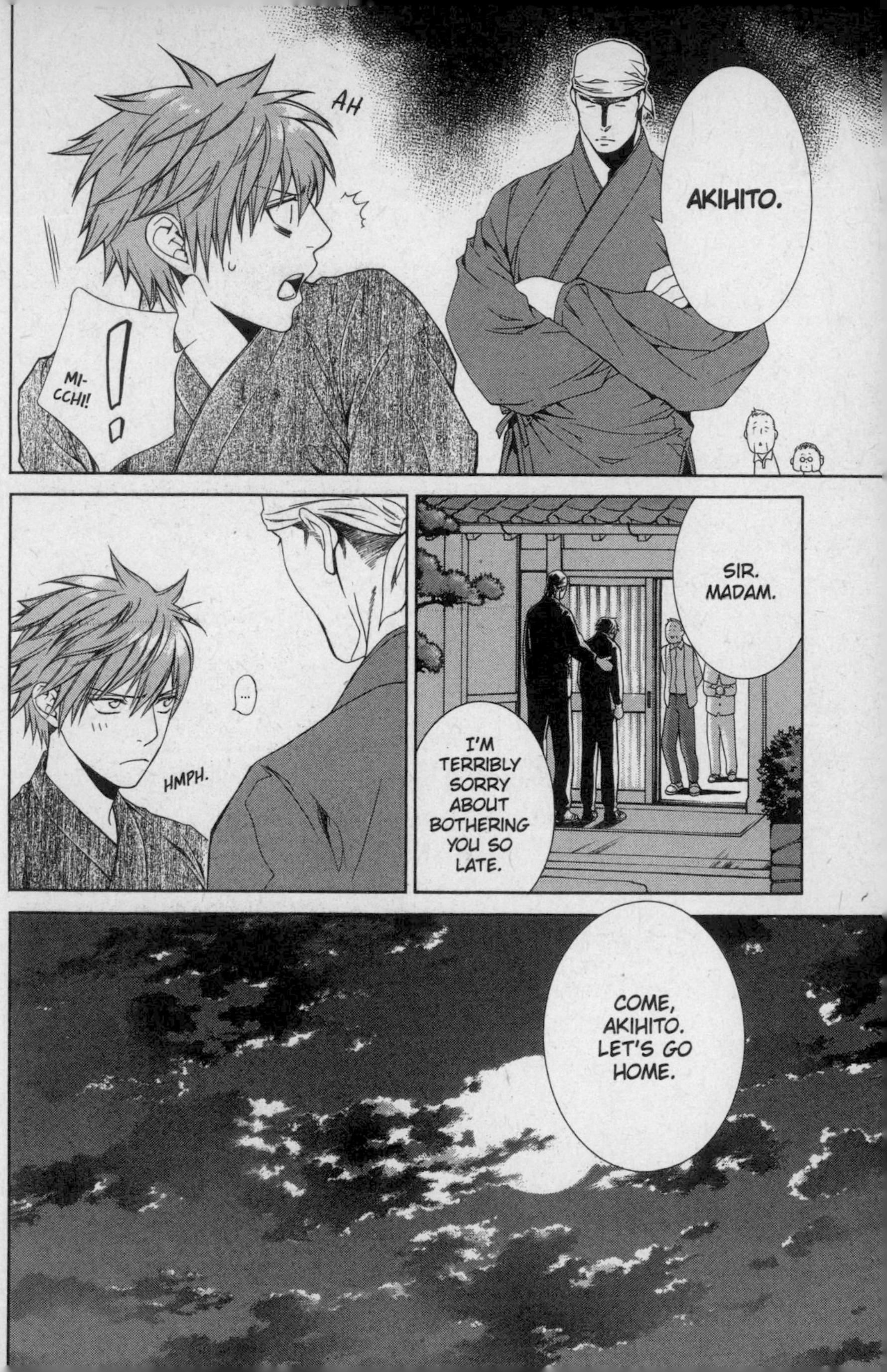
AKIHITO.
AH
MI-CCHI!
SIR. MADAM.
I'M TERRIBLY SORRY ABOUT BOTHERING YOU SO LATE.
...
HMPH.
COME, AKIHITO. LET'S GO HOME.

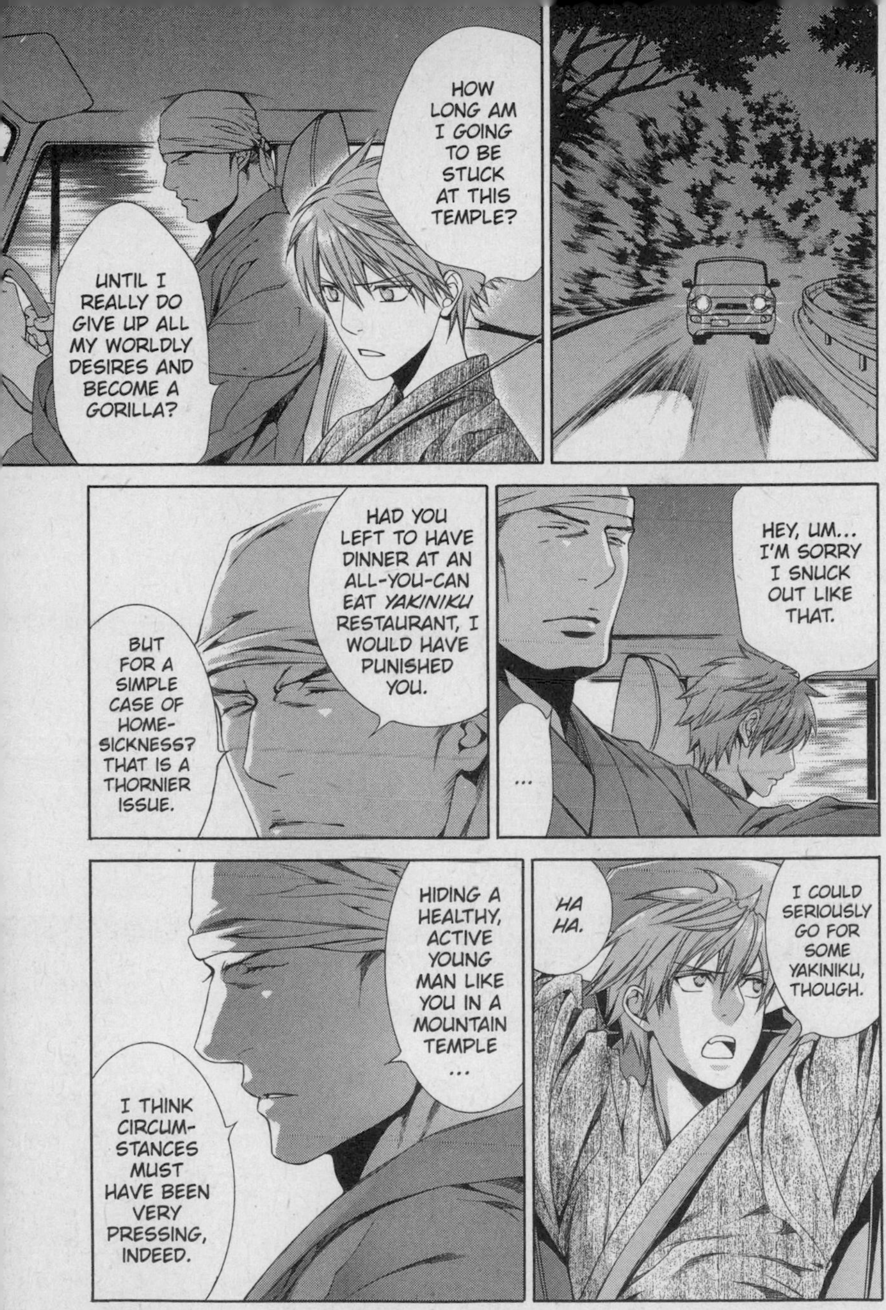

HOW LONG AM I GOING TO BE STUCK AT THIS TEMPLE?
UNTIL I REALLY DO GIVE UP ALL MY WORLDLY DESIRES AND BECOME A GORILLA?
HEY, UM... I'M SORRY I SNUCK OUT LIKE THAT.
...
HAD YOU LEFT TO HAVE DINNER AT AN ALL-YOU-CAN EAT *YAKINIKU* RESTAURANT, I WOULD HAVE PUNISHED YOU.
BUT FOR A SIMPLE CASE OF HOME-SICKNESS? THAT IS A THORNIER ISSUE.
I COULD SERIOUSLY GO FOR SOME YAKINIKU, THOUGH.
HA HA.
HIDING A HEALTHY, ACTIVE YOUNG MAN LIKE YOU IN A MOUNTAIN TEMPLE ...
I THINK CIRCUM-STANCES MUST HAVE BEEN VERY PRESSING, INDEED.

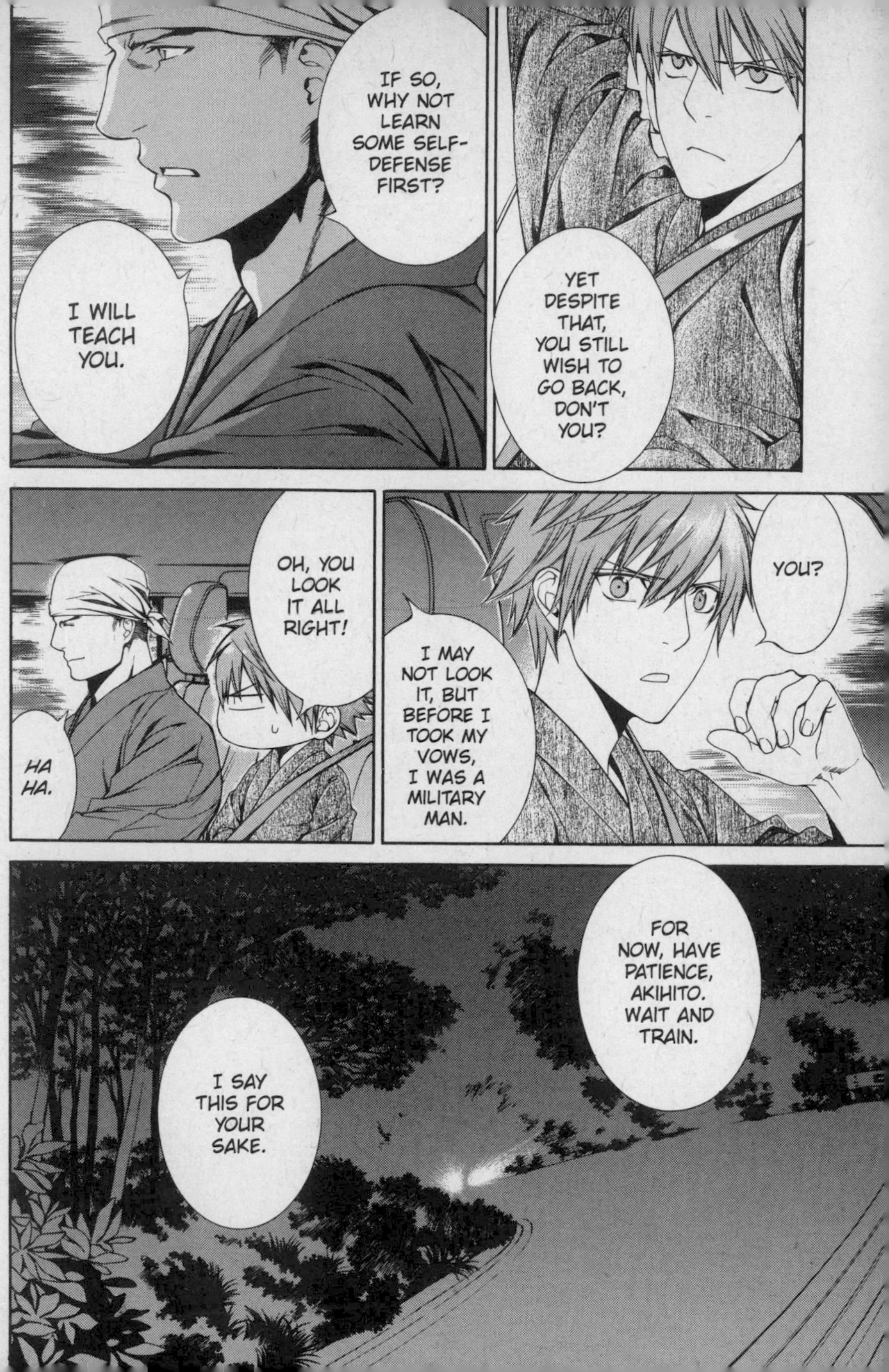
YET DESPITE THAT, YOU STILL WISH TO GO BACK, DON'T YOU?
IF SO, WHY NOT LEARN SOME SELF-DEFENSE FIRST?
I WILL TEACH YOU.
YOU?
I MAY NOT LOOK IT, BUT BEFORE I TOOK MY VOWS, I WAS A MILITARY MAN.
OH, YOU LOOK IT ALL RIGHT!
HA HA.
FOR NOW, HAVE PATIENCE, AKIHITO. WAIT AND TRAIN.
I SAY THIS FOR YOUR SAKE.

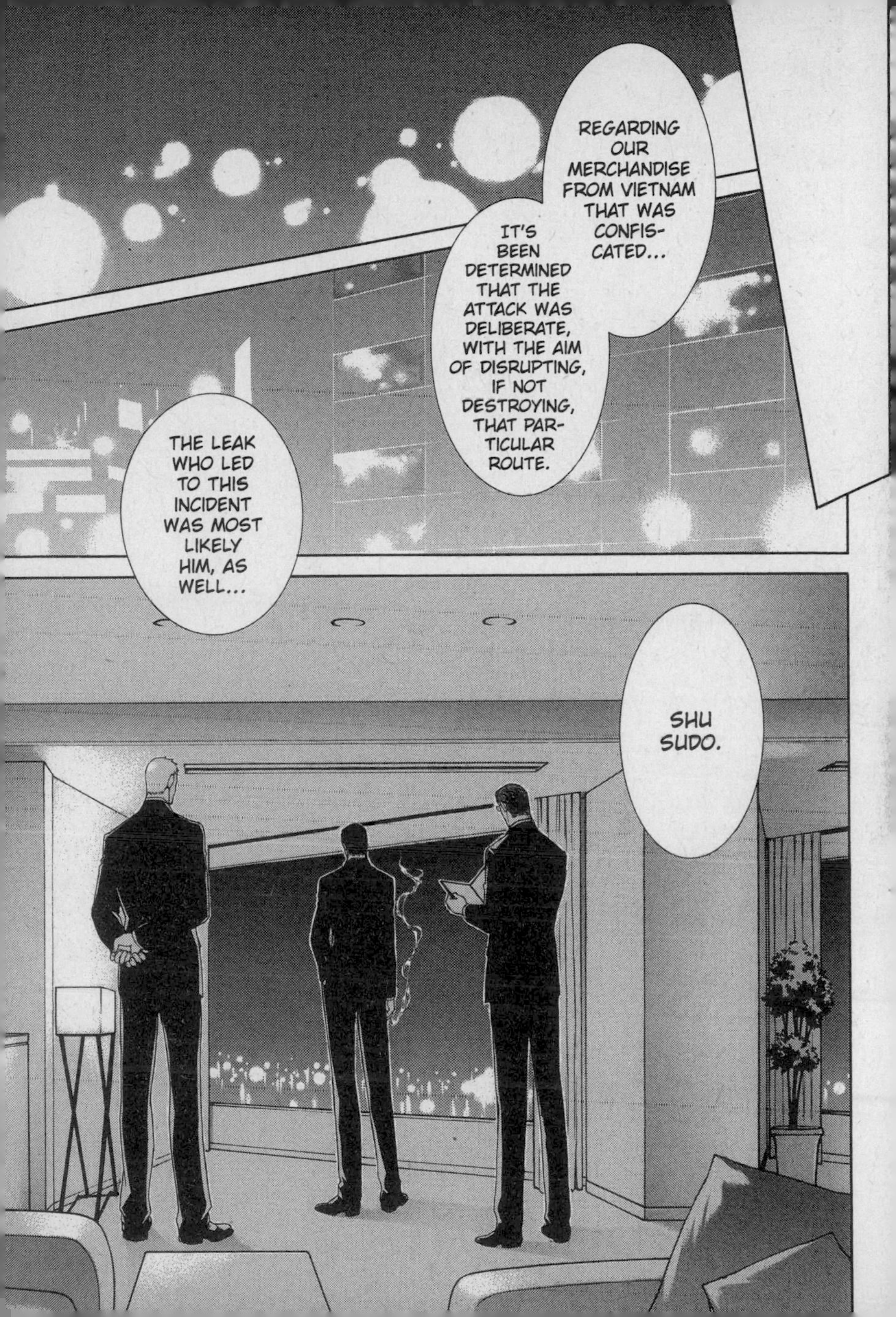
REGARDING OUR MERCHANDISE FROM VIETNAM THAT WAS CONFIS-CATED...
IT'S BEEN DETERMINED THAT THE ATTACK WAS DELIBERATE, WITH THE AIM OF DISRUPTING, IF NOT DESTROYING, THAT PAR-TICULAR ROUTE.
THE LEAK WHO LED TO THIS INCIDENT WAS MOST LIKELY HIM, AS WELL...
SHU SUDO.

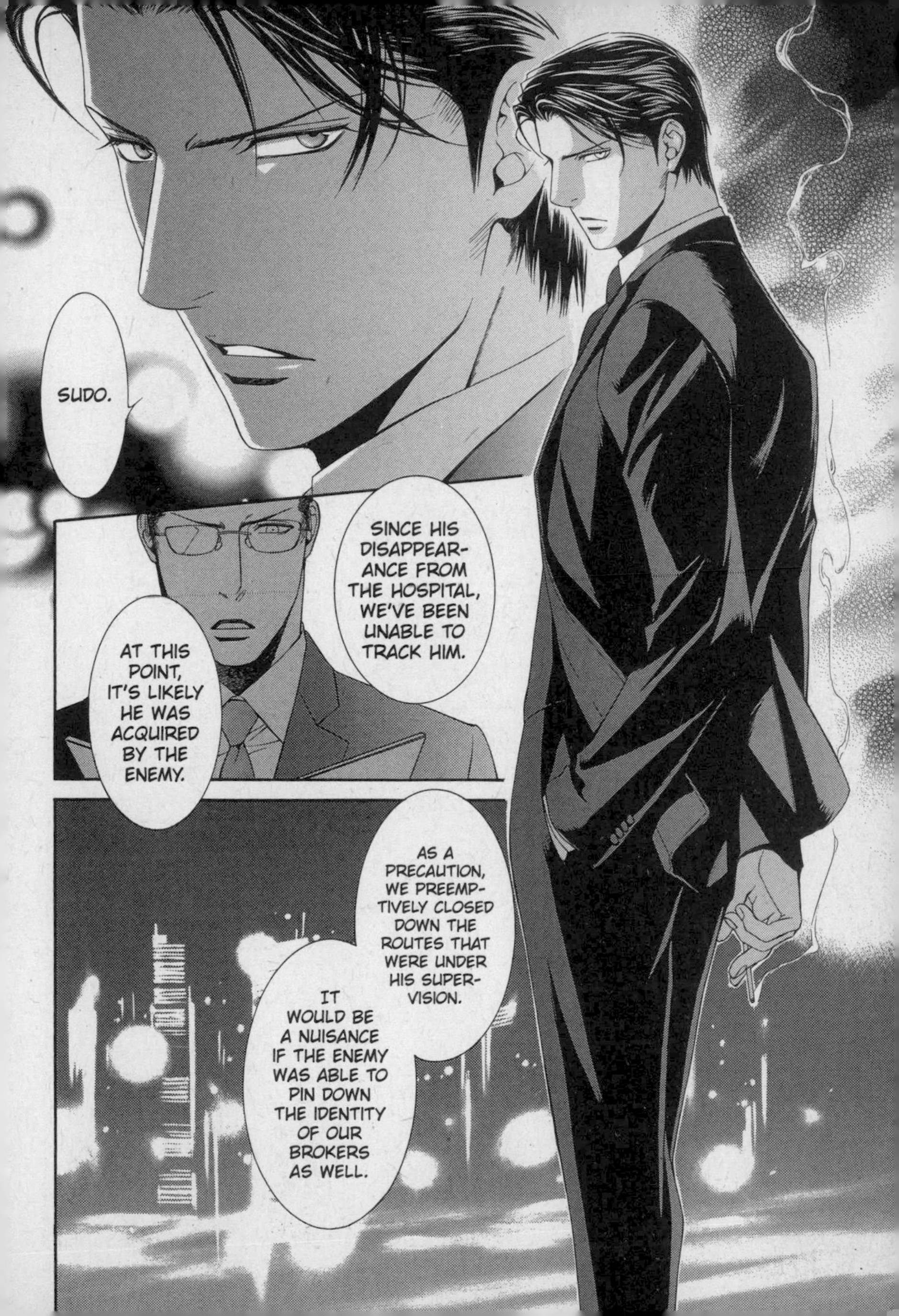
SUDO.
SINCE HIS DISAPPEAR-ANCE FROM THE HOSPITAL, WE'VE BEEN UNABLE TO TRACK HIM.
AT THIS POINT, IT'S LIKELY HE WAS ACQUIRED BY THE ENEMY.
AS A PRECAUTION, WE PREEMP-TIVELY CLOSED DOWN THE ROUTES THAT WERE UNDER HIS SUPER-VISION.
IT WOULD BE A NUISANCE IF THE ENEMY WAS ABLE TO PIN DOWN THE IDENTITY OF OUR BROKERS AS WELL.

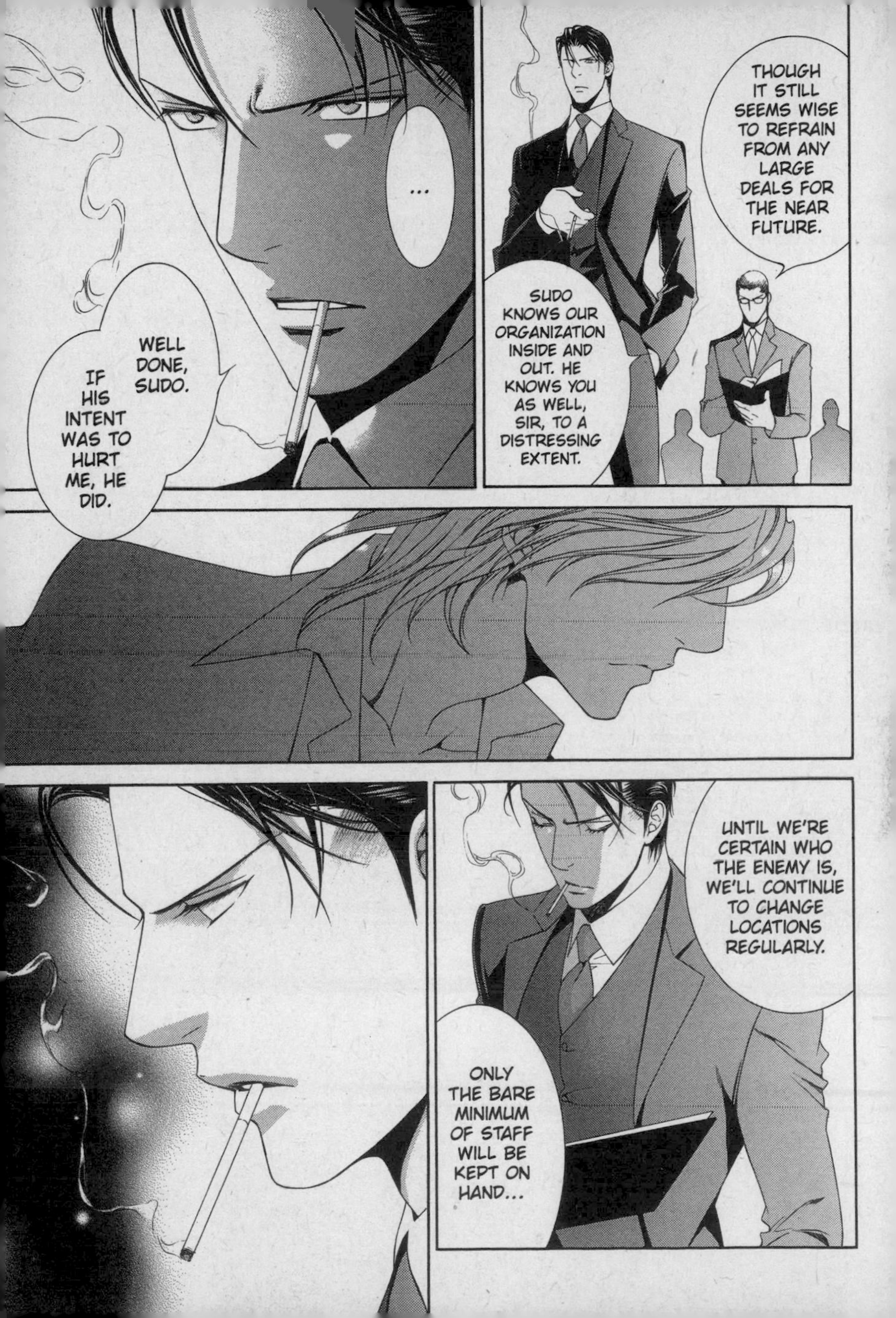
THOUGH IT STILL SEEMS WISE TO REFRAIN FROM ANY LARGE DEALS FOR THE NEAR FUTURE.
SUDO KNOWS OUR ORGANIZATION INSIDE AND OUT. HE KNOWS YOU AS WELL, SIR, TO A DISTRESSING EXTENT.
...
WELL DONE, SUDO.
IF HIS INTENT WAS TO HURT ME, HE DID.
UNTIL WE'RE CERTAIN WHO THE ENEMY IS, WE'LL CONTINUE TO CHANGE LOCATIONS REGULARLY.
ONLY THE BARE MINIMUM OF STAFF WILL BE KEPT ON HAND...

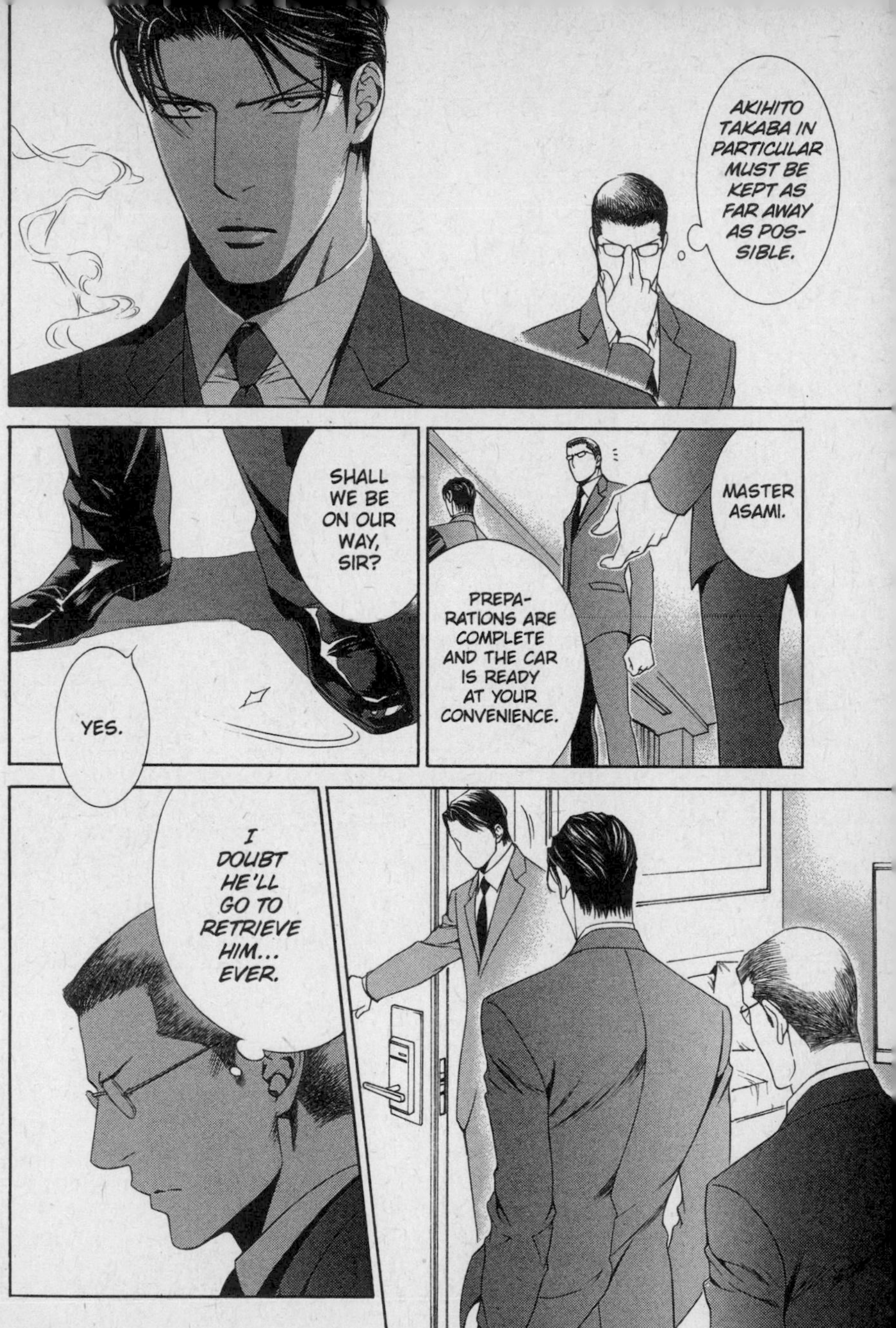
AKIHITO TAKABA IN PARTICULAR MUST BE KEPT AS FAR AWAY AS POS-SIBLE.
MASTER ASAMI.
PREPA-RATIONS ARE COMPLETE AND THE CAR IS READY AT YOUR CONVENIENCE.
SHALL WE BE ON OUR WAY, SIR?
YES.
I DOUBT HE'LL GO TO RETRIEVE HIM... EVER.

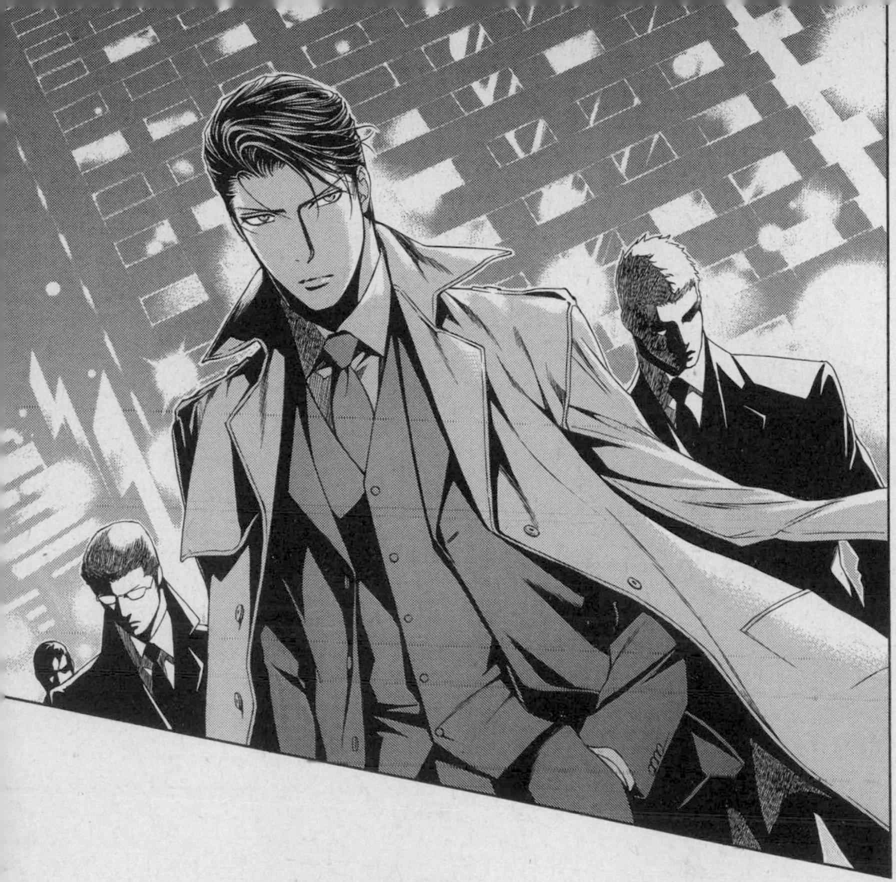
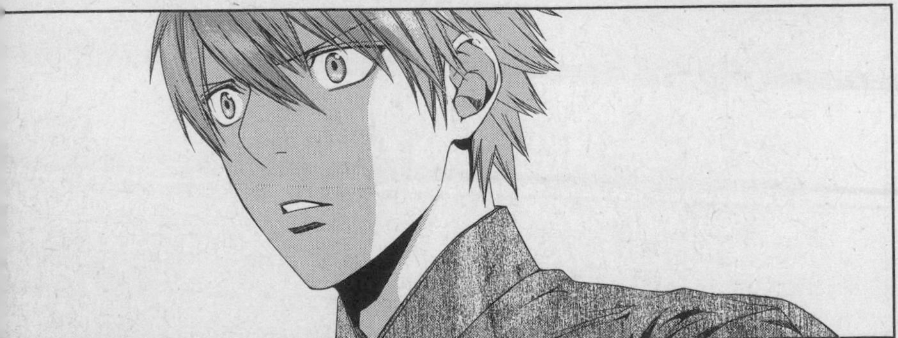

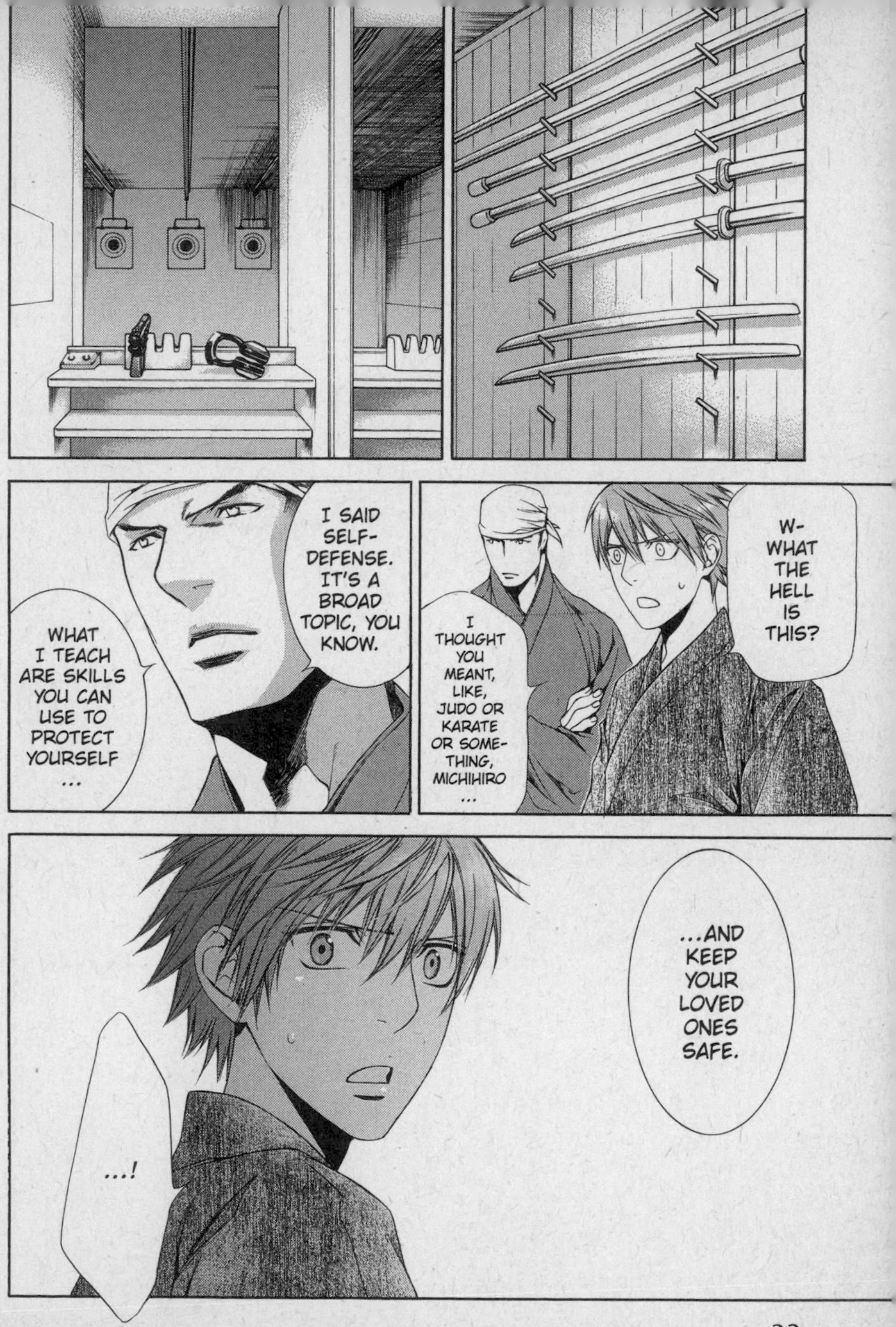
W-WHAT THE HELL IS THIS?
I THOUGHT YOU MEANT, LIKE, JUDO OR KARATE OR SOMETHING, MICHIHIRO...
I SAID SELF-DEFENSE. IT'S A BROAD TOPIC, YOU KNOW.
WHAT I TEACH ARE SKILLS YOU CAN USE TO PROTECT YOURSELF...
...AND KEEP YOUR LOVED ONES SAFE.
...!

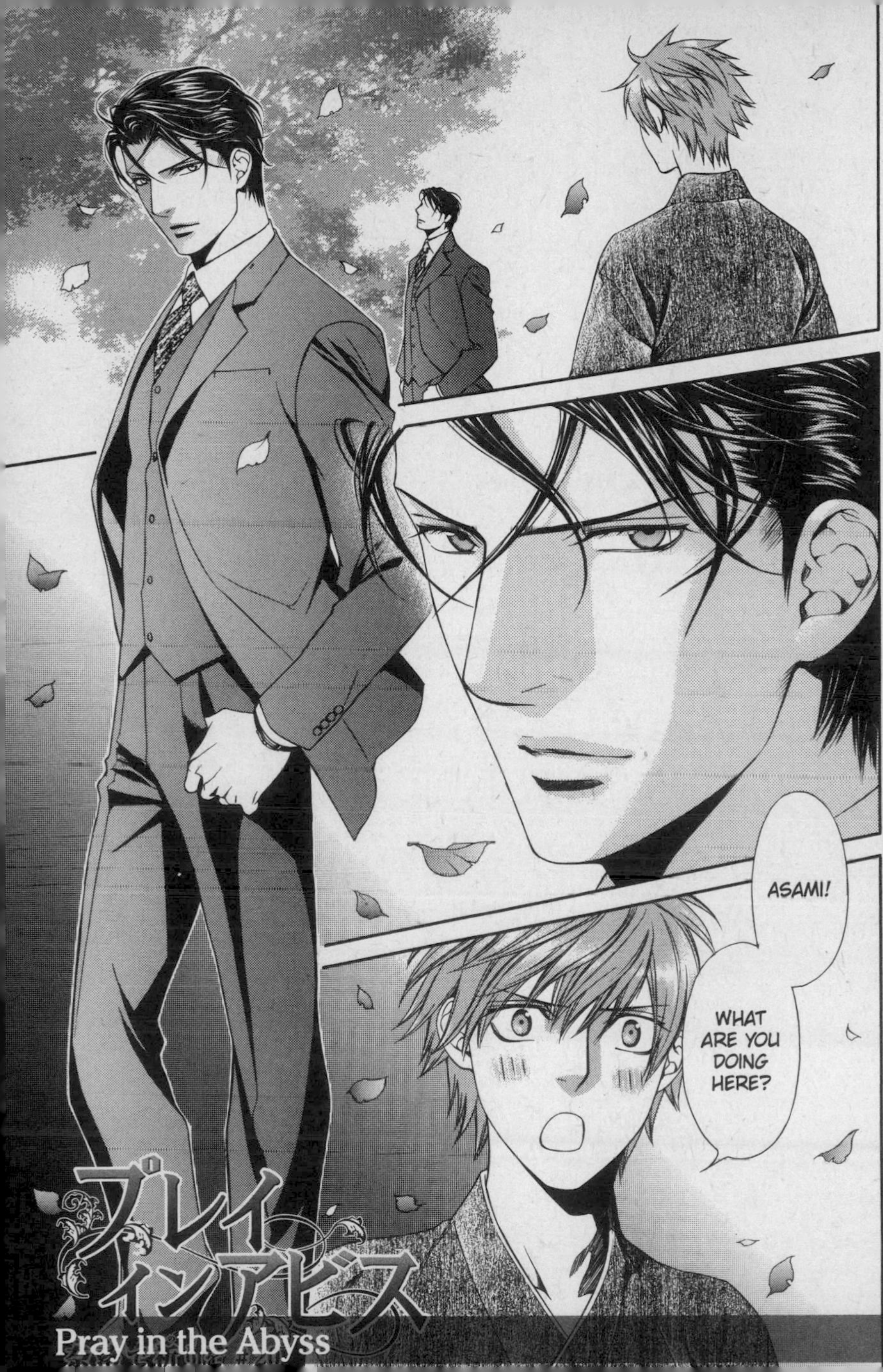
ASAMI!
WHAT ARE YOU DOING HERE?
プレイ インアビス
Pray in the Abyss

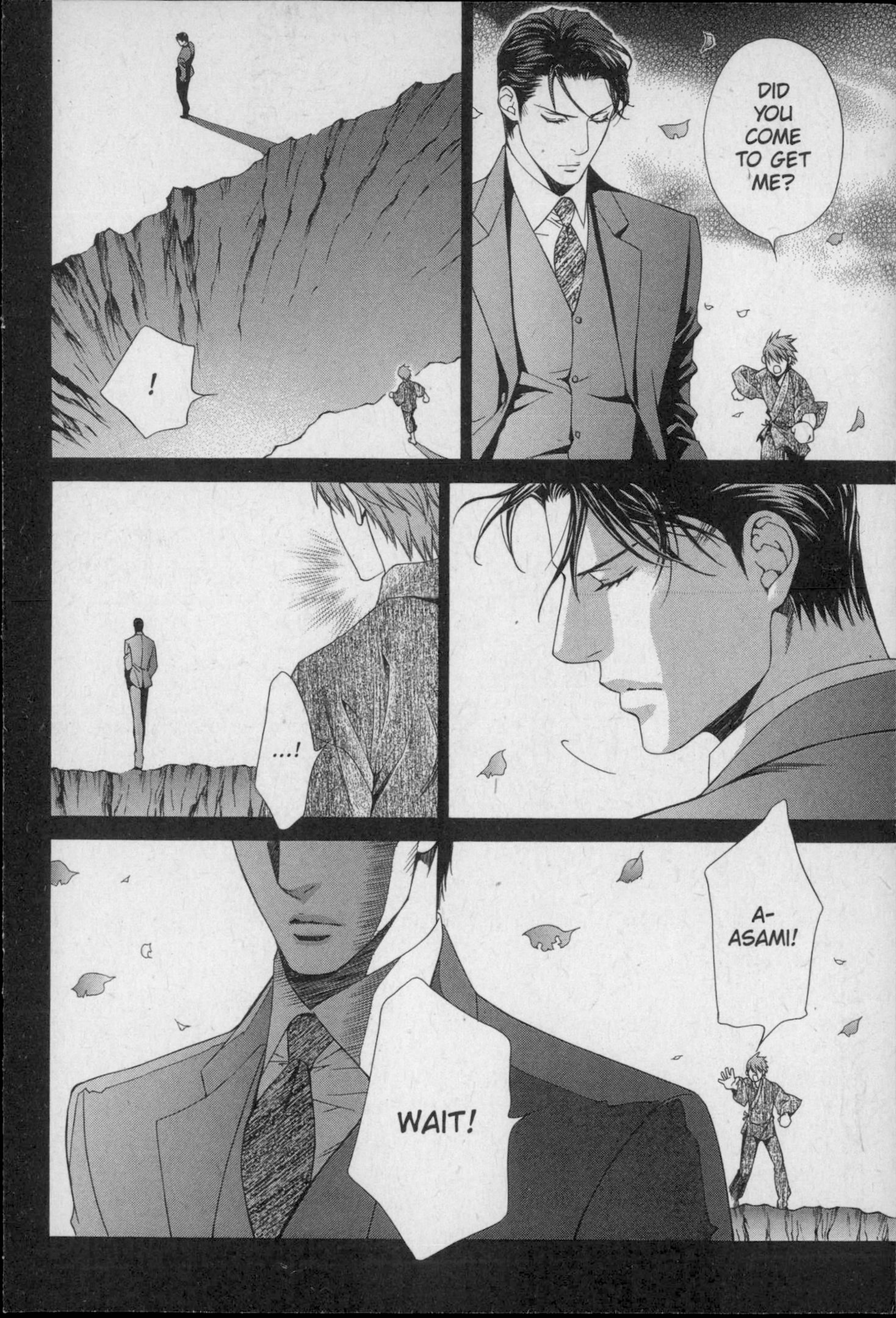
DID YOU COME TO GET ME?
!
...!
A-ASAMI!
WAIT!

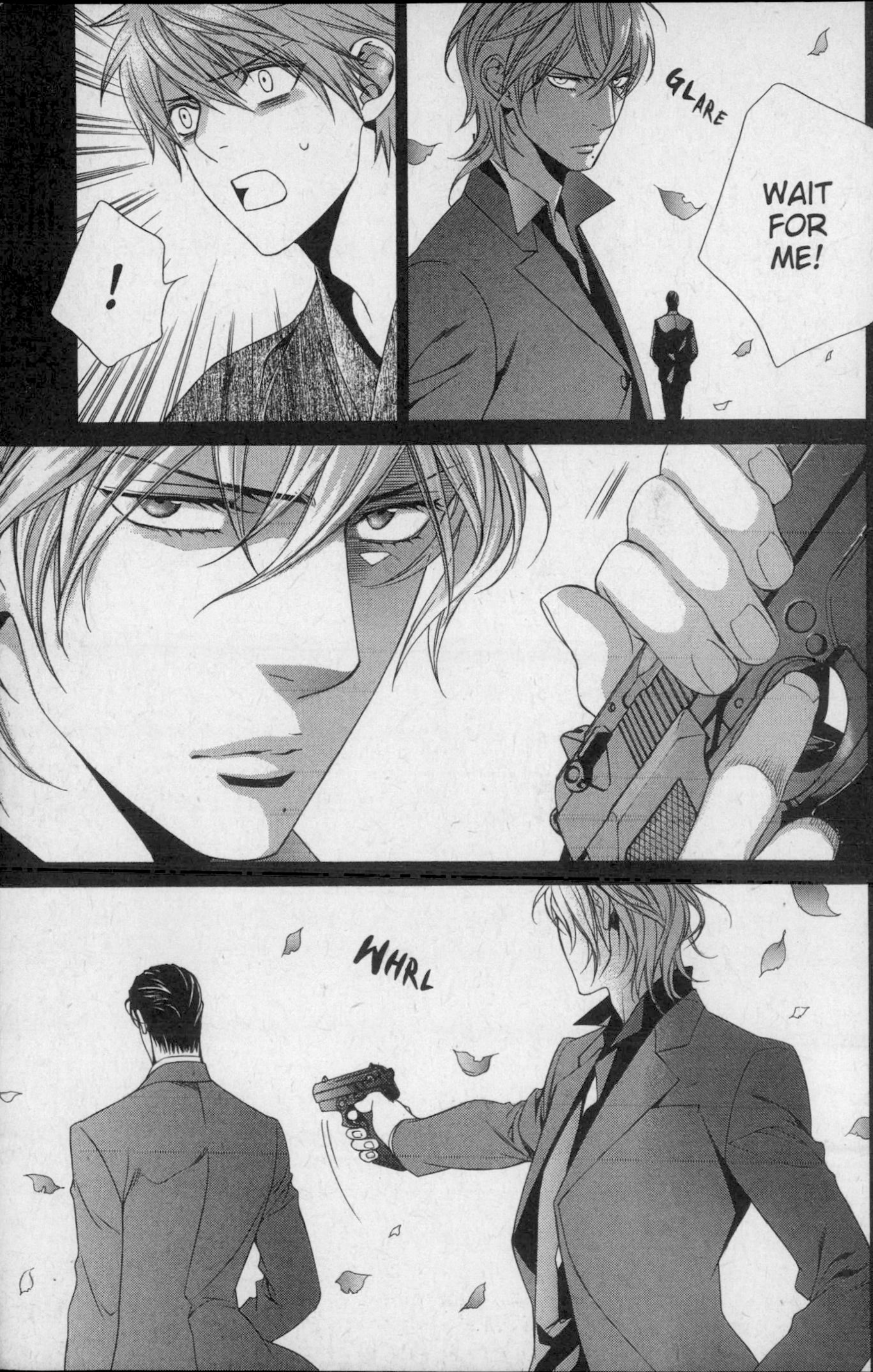
GLARE
WAIT FOR ME!
!
WHRL

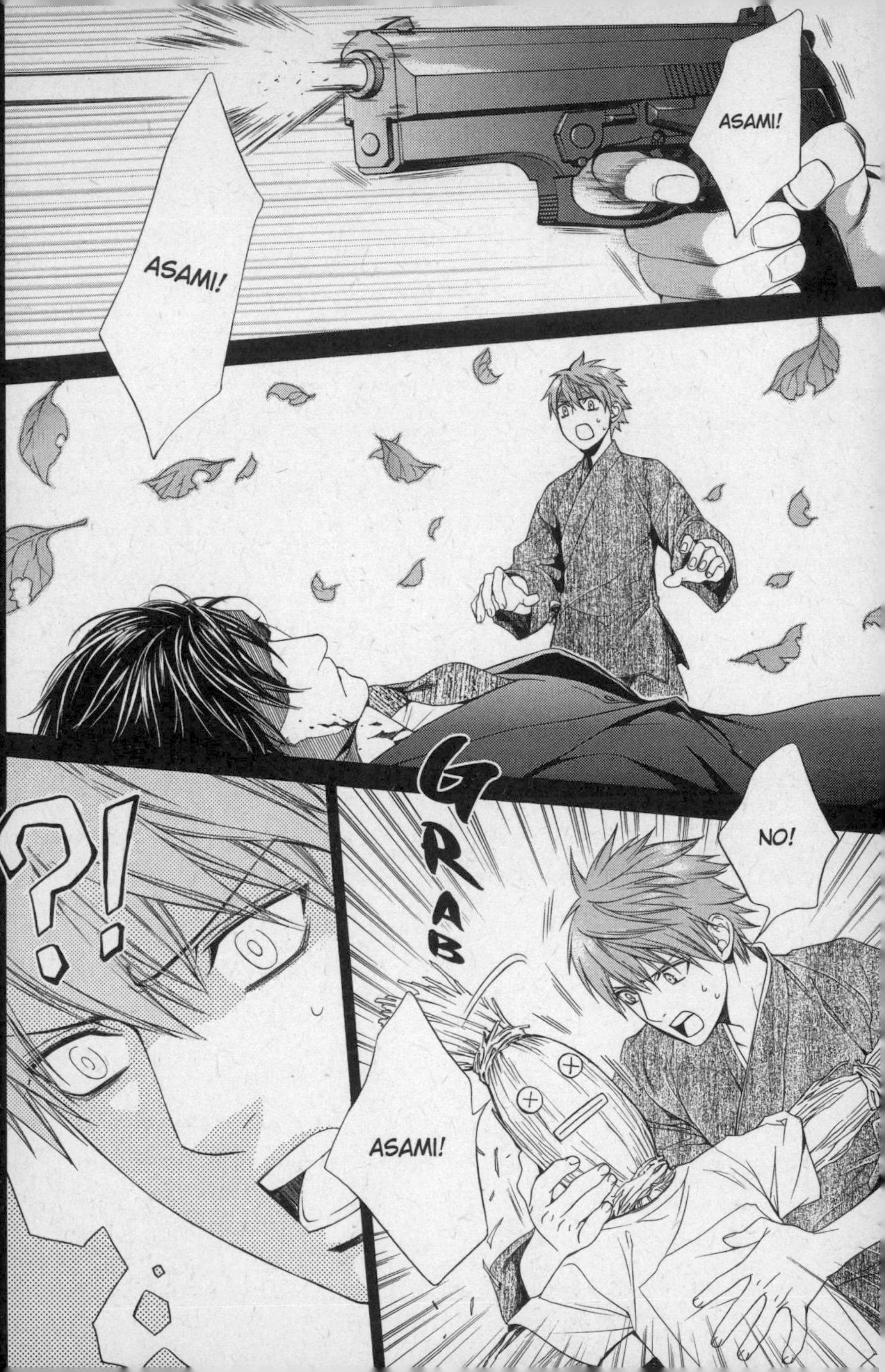
ASAMI!
ASAMI!
NO!
GRAB
ASAMI!
?!

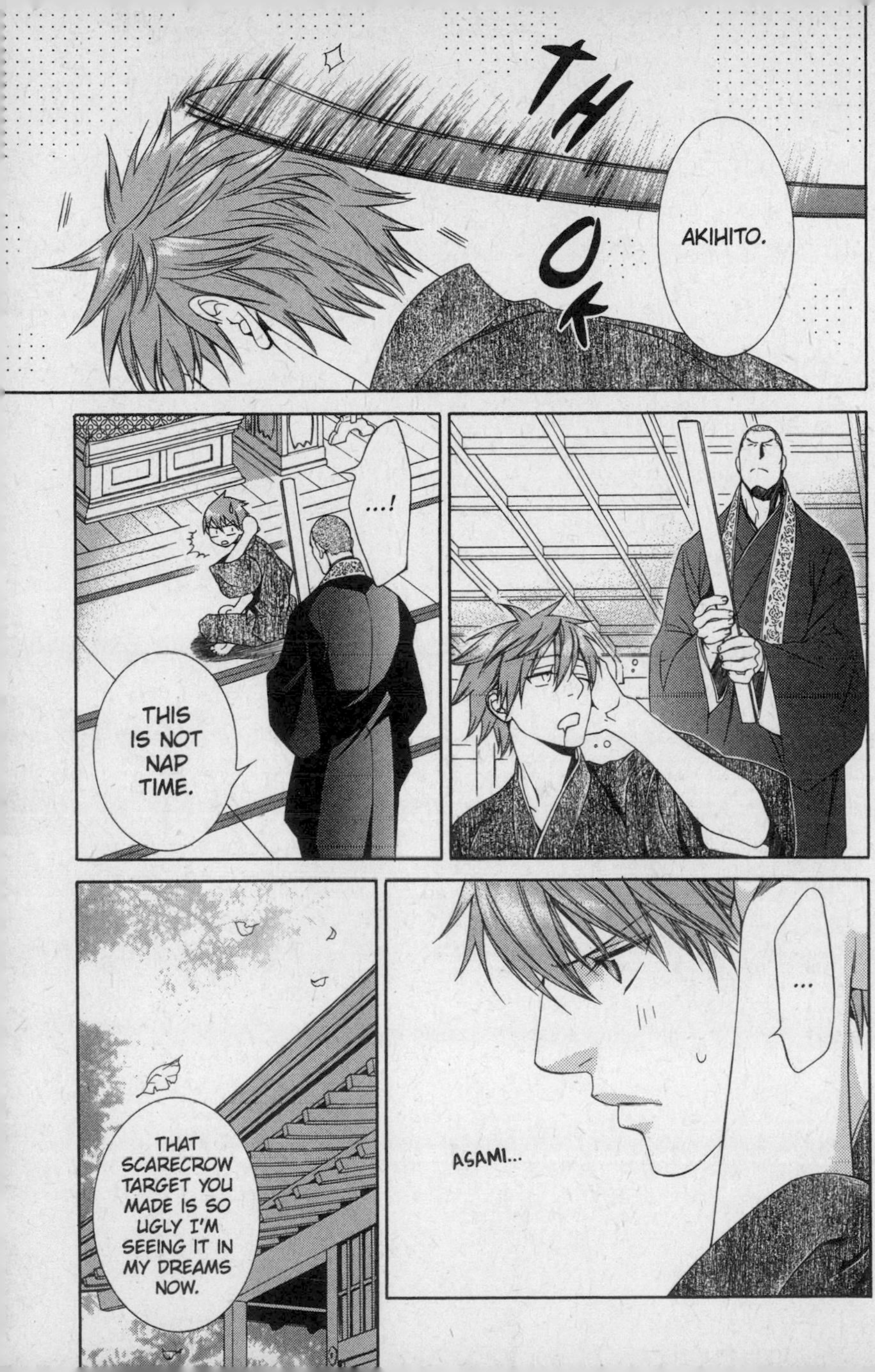
THOK
AKIHITO.
...!
THIS IS NOT NAP TIME.
...
ASAMI...
THAT SCARECROW TARGET YOU MADE IS SO UGLY I'M SEEING IT IN MY DREAMS NOW.

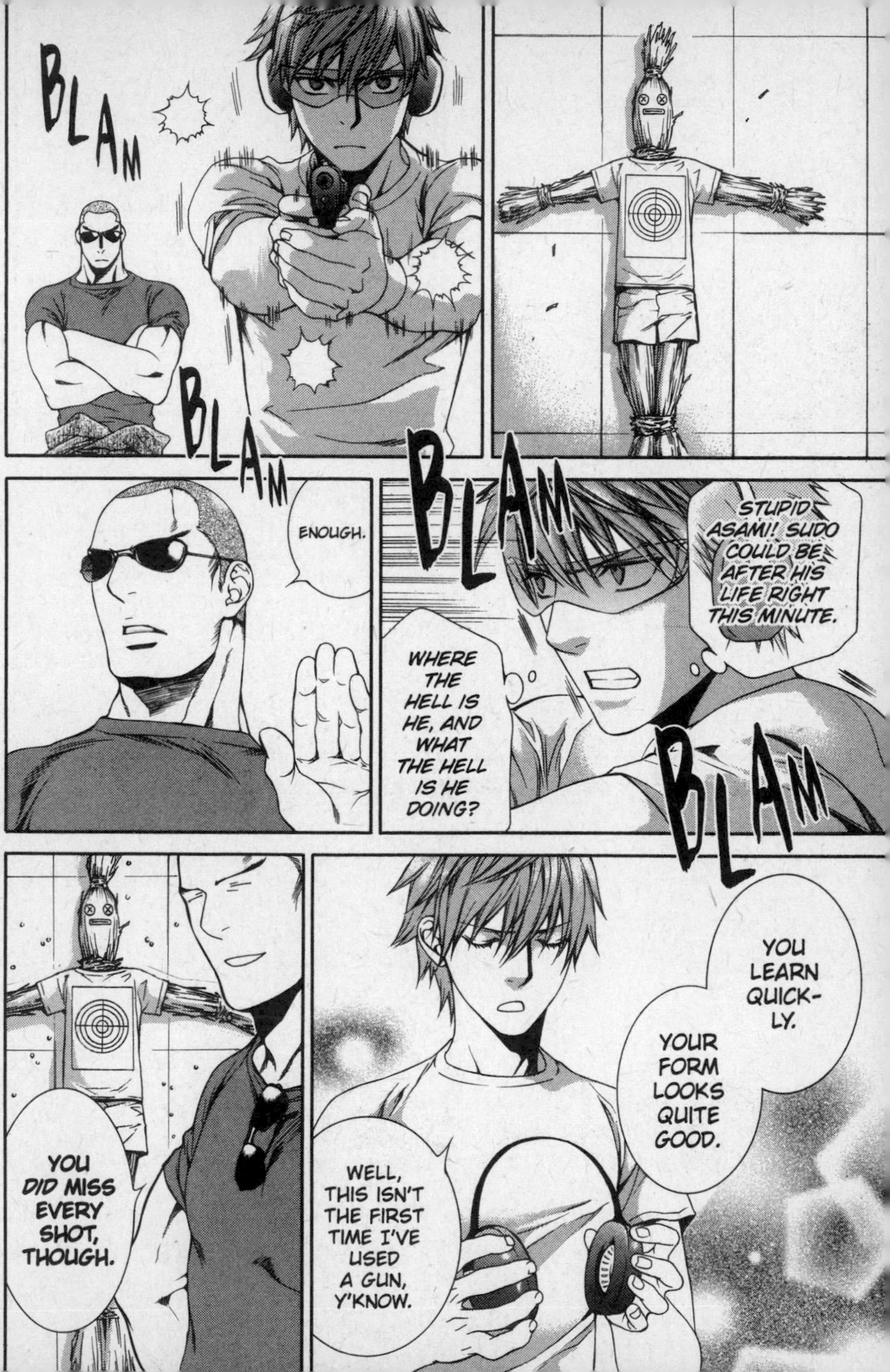
BLAM
BLAM
BLAM
STUPID ASAMI! SUDO COULD BE AFTER HIS LIFE RIGHT THIS MINUTE.
WHERE THE HELL IS HE, AND WHAT THE HELL IS HE DOING?
BLAM
ENOUGH.
YOU LEARN QUICKLY.
YOUR FORM LOOKS QUITE GOOD.
WELL, THIS ISN'T THE FIRST TIME I'VE USED A GUN, Y'KNOW.
YOU DID MISS EVERY SHOT, THOUGH.

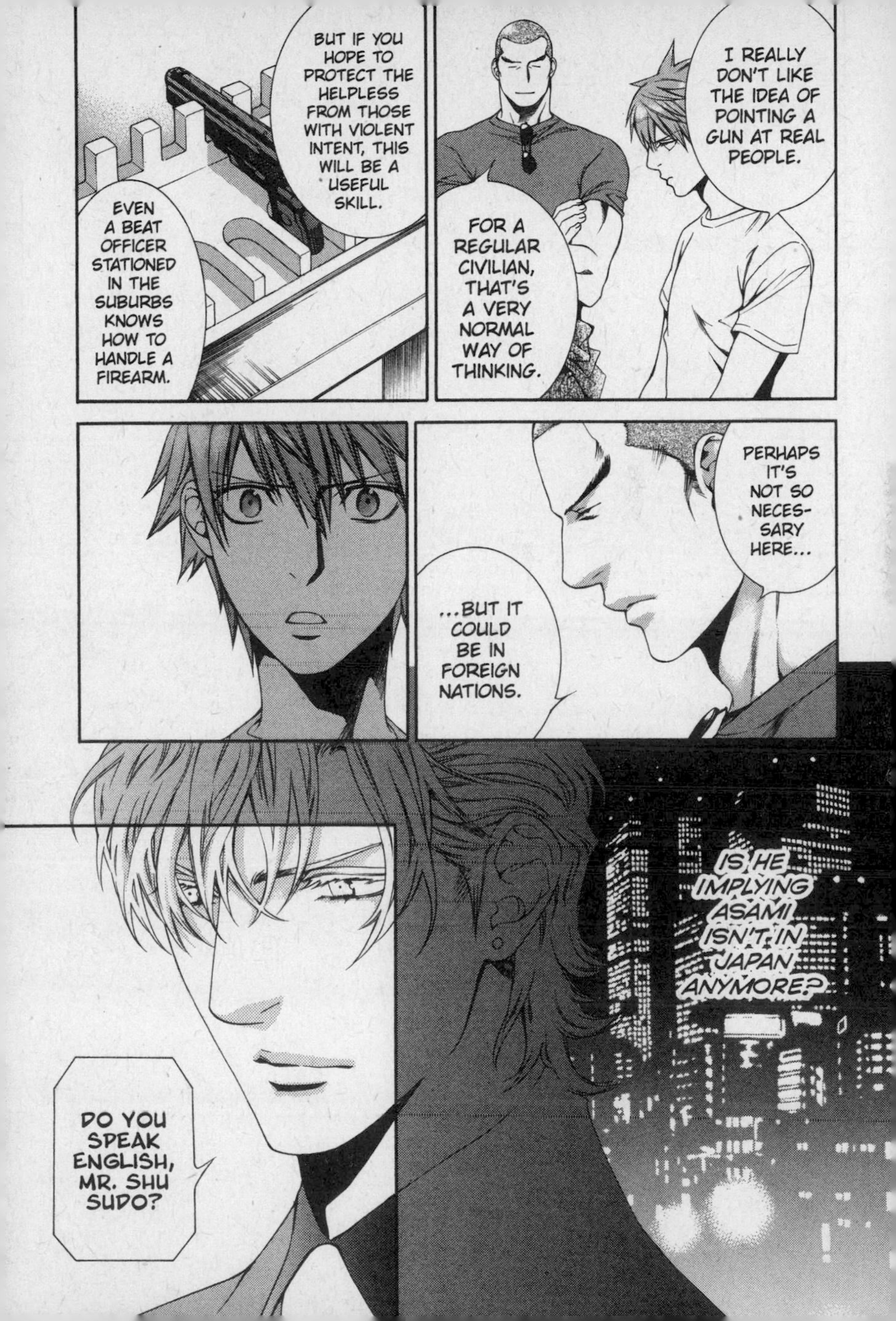
I REALLY DON'T LIKE THE IDEA OF POINTING A GUN AT REAL PEOPLE.
FOR A REGULAR CIVILIAN, THAT'S A VERY NORMAL WAY OF THINKING.
BUT IF YOU HOPE TO PROTECT THE HELPLESS FROM THOSE WITH VIOLENT INTENT, THIS WILL BE A USEFUL SKILL.
EVEN A BEAT OFFICER STATIONED IN THE SUBURBS KNOWS HOW TO HANDLE A FIREARM.
PERHAPS IT'S NOT SO NECES-SARY HERE...
...BUT IT COULD BE IN FOREIGN NATIONS.
IS HE IMPLYING ASAMI ISN'T IN JAPAN ANYMORE?
DO YOU SPEAK ENGLISH, MR. SHU SUDO?

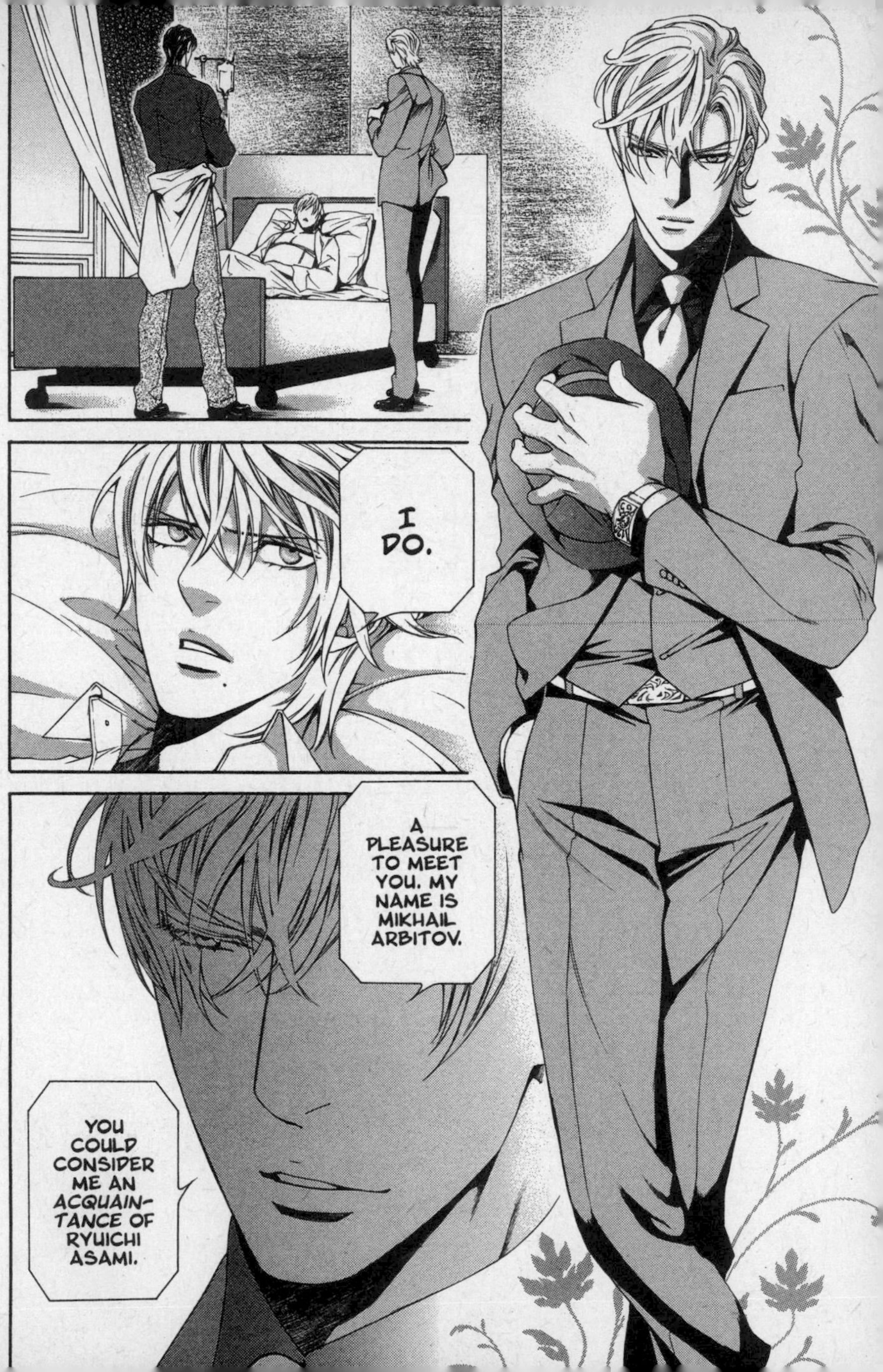
I DO.
A PLEASURE TO MEET YOU. MY NAME IS MIKHAIL ARBITOV.
YOU COULD CONSIDER ME AN ACQUAIN-TANCE OF RYUICHI ASAMI.

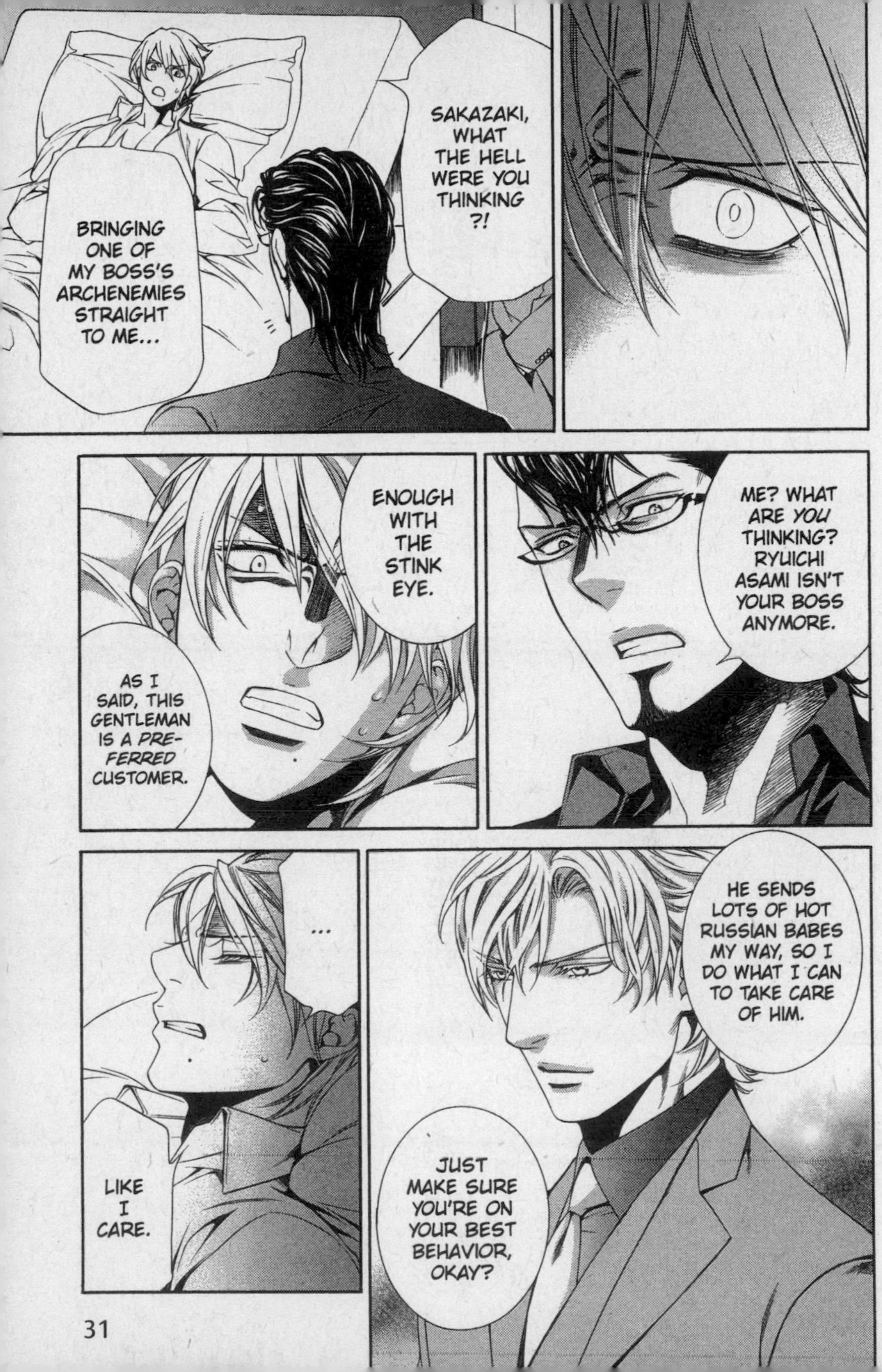
SAKAZAKI, WHAT THE HELL WERE YOU THINKING?!
BRINGING ONE OF MY BOSS'S ARCHENEMIES STRAIGHT TO ME...
ME? WHAT ARE *YOU* THINKING? RYUICHI ASAMI ISN'T YOUR BOSS ANYMORE.
ENOUGH WITH THE STINK EYE.
AS I SAID, THIS GENTLEMAN IS A *PRE-FERRED* CUSTOMER.
HE SENDS LOTS OF HOT RUSSIAN BABES MY WAY, SO I DO WHAT I CAN TO TAKE CARE OF HIM.
JUST MAKE SURE YOU'RE ON YOUR BEST BEHAVIOR, OKAY?
...
LIKE I CARE.

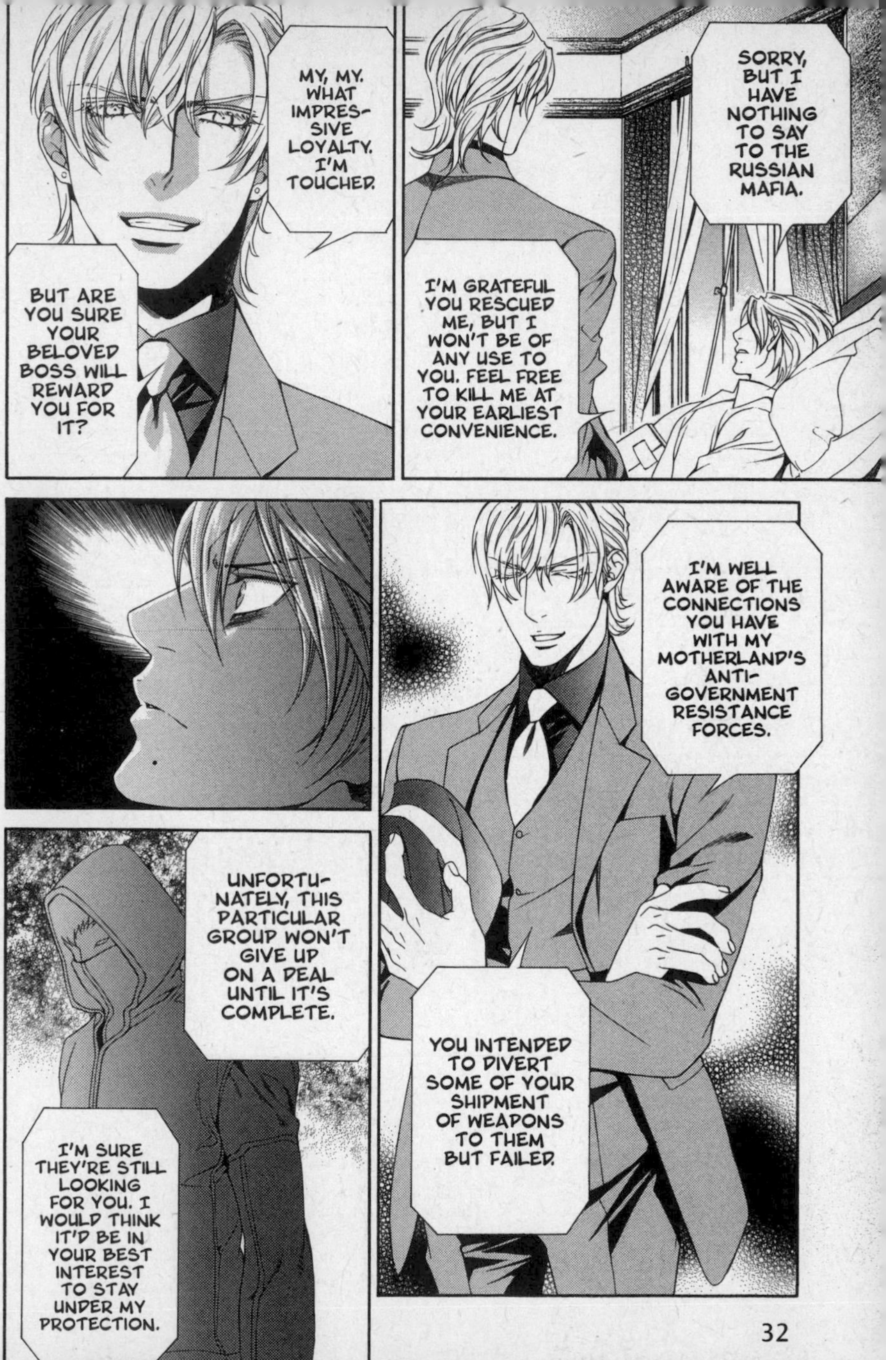
SORRY, BUT I HAVE NOTHING TO SAY TO THE RUSSIAN MAFIA.
I'M GRATEFUL YOU RESCUED ME, BUT I WON'T BE OF ANY USE TO YOU. FEEL FREE TO KILL ME AT YOUR EARLIEST CONVENIENCE.
MY, MY. WHAT IMPRES-SIVE LOYALTY. I'M TOUCHED.
BUT ARE YOU SURE YOUR BELOVED BOSS WILL REWARD YOU FOR IT?
I'M WELL AWARE OF THE CONNECTIONS YOU HAVE WITH MY MOTHERLAND'S ANTI-GOVERNMENT RESISTANCE FORCES.
YOU INTENDED TO DIVERT SOME OF YOUR SHIPMENT OF WEAPONS TO THEM BUT FAILED.
UNFORTU-NATELY, THIS PARTICULAR GROUP WON'T GIVE UP ON A DEAL UNTIL IT'S COMPLETE.
I'M SURE THEY'RE STILL LOOKING FOR YOU. I WOULD THINK IT'D BE IN YOUR BEST INTEREST TO STAY UNDER MY PROTECTION.

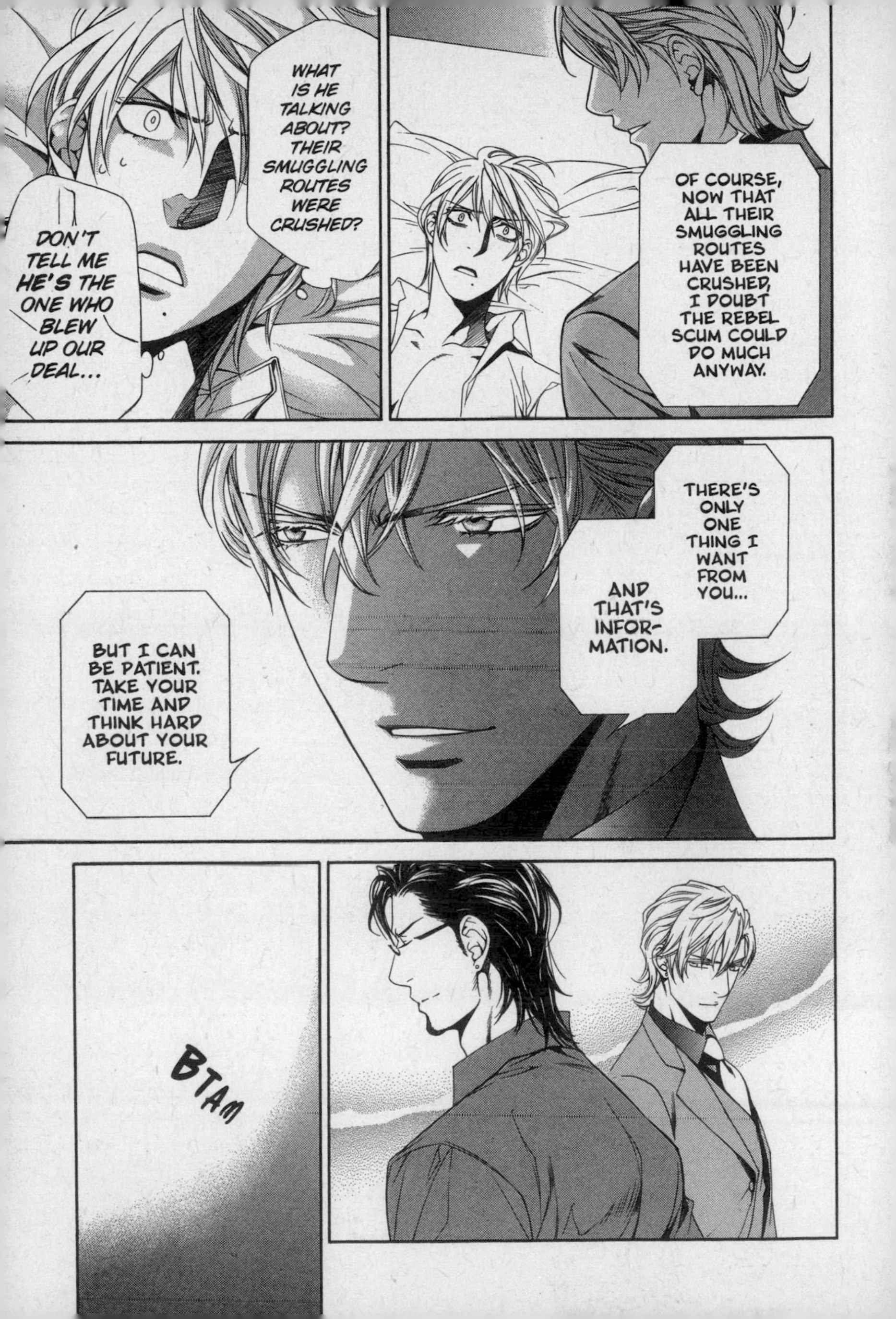
OF COURSE, NOW THAT ALL THEIR SMUGGLING ROUTES HAVE BEEN CRUSHED, I DOUBT THE REBEL SCUM COULD DO MUCH ANYWAY.
WHAT IS HE TALKING ABOUT? THEIR SMUGGLING ROUTES WERE CRUSHED?
DON'T TELL ME HE'S THE ONE WHO BLEW UP OUR DEAL...
THERE'S ONLY ONE THING I WANT FROM YOU...
AND THAT'S INFORMATION.
BUT I CAN BE PATIENT. TAKE YOUR TIME AND THINK HARD ABOUT YOUR FUTURE.
BTAM

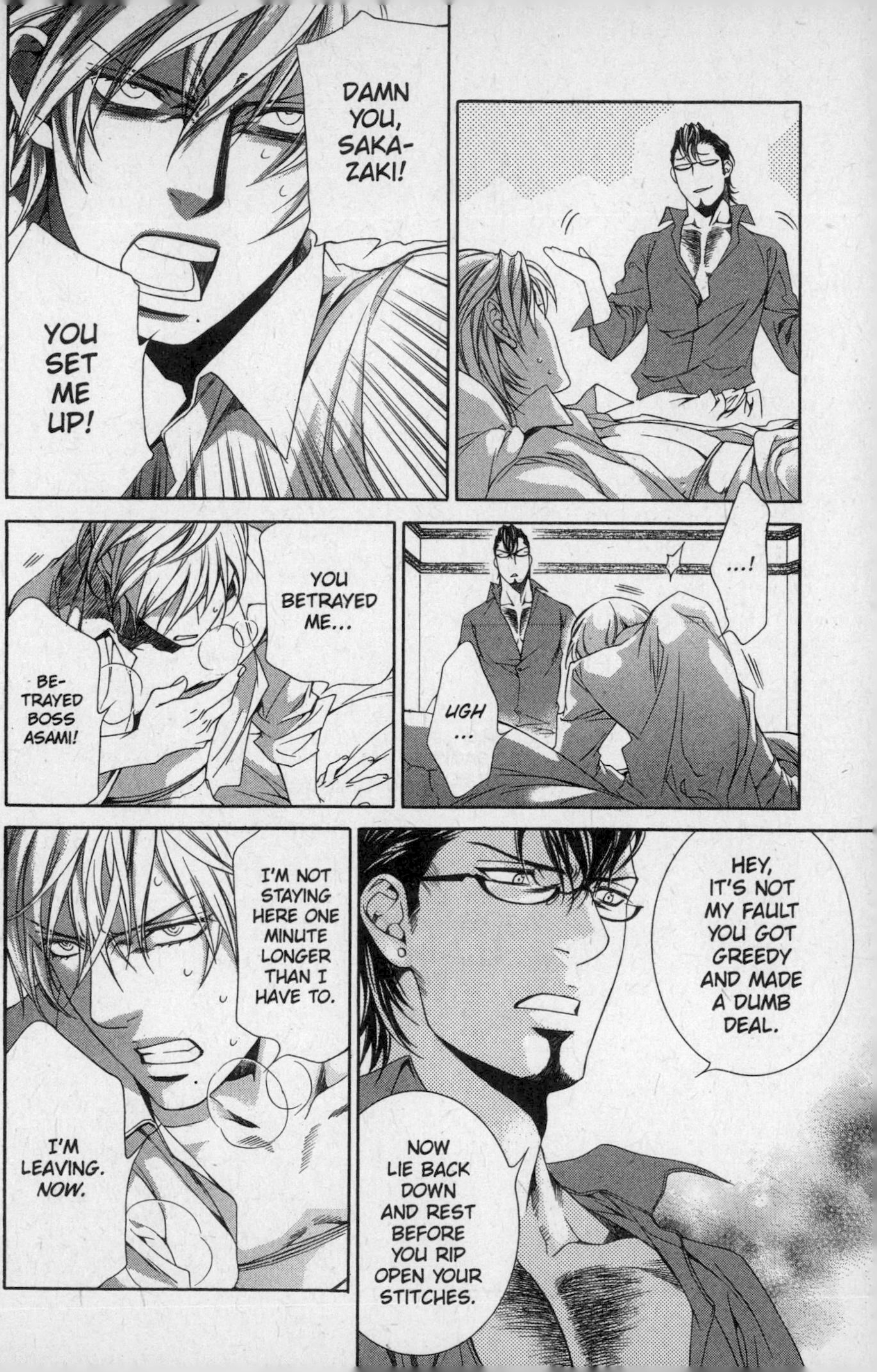
DAMN YOU, SAKA-ZAKI!
YOU SET ME UP!
...!
UGH...
YOU BETRAYED ME...
BE-TRAYED BOSS ASAMI!
HEY, IT'S NOT MY FAULT YOU GOT GREEDY AND MADE A DUMB DEAL.
NOW LIE BACK DOWN AND REST BEFORE YOU RIP OPEN YOUR STITCHES.
I'M NOT STAYING HERE ONE MINUTE LONGER THAN I HAVE TO.
I'M LEAVING. NOW.

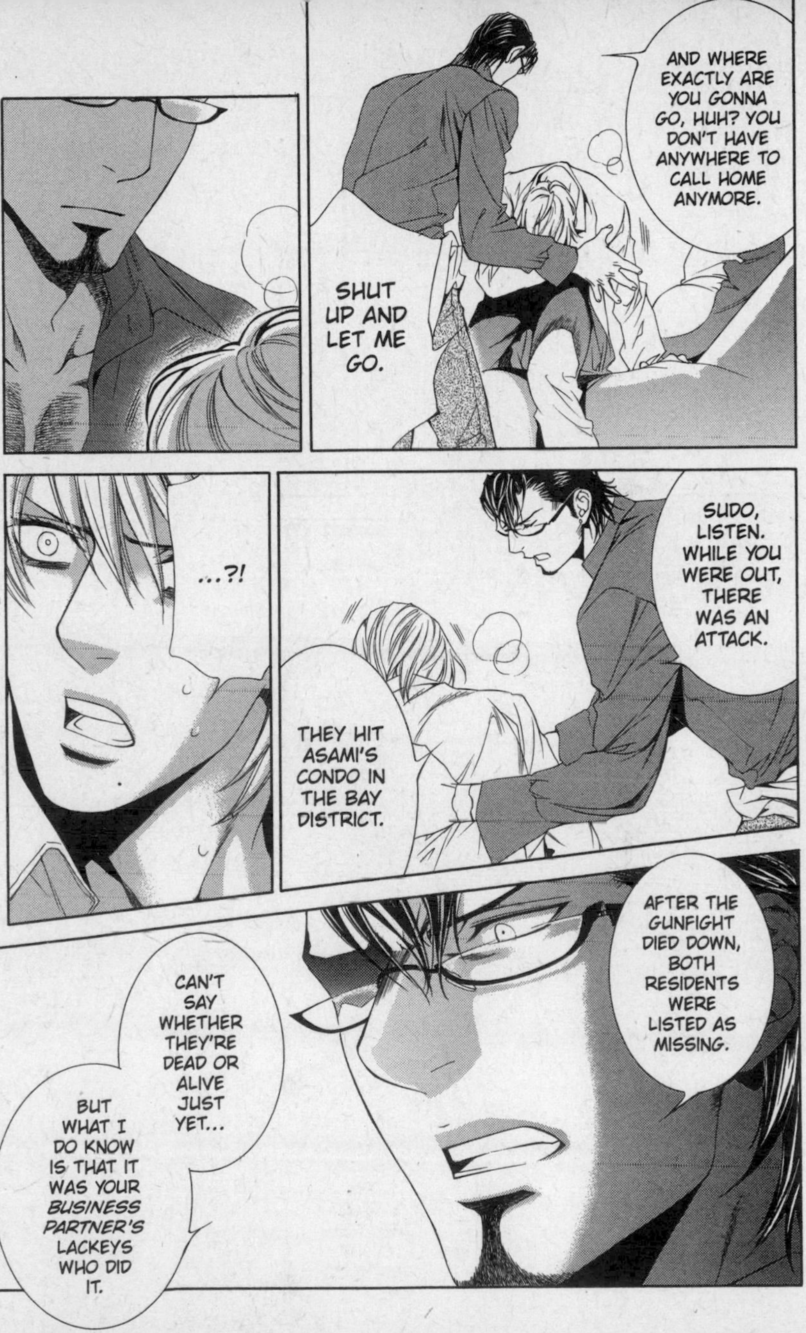
AND WHERE EXACTLY ARE YOU GONNA GO, HUH? YOU DON'T HAVE ANYWHERE TO CALL HOME ANYMORE.
SHUT UP AND LET ME GO.
SUDO, LISTEN. WHILE YOU WERE OUT, THERE WAS AN ATTACK.
THEY HIT ASAMI'S CONDO IN THE BAY DISTRICT.
...?!
AFTER THE GUNFIGHT DIED DOWN, BOTH RESIDENTS WERE LISTED AS MISSING.
CAN'T SAY WHETHER THEY'RE DEAD OR ALIVE JUST YET...
BUT WHAT I DO KNOW IS THAT IT WAS YOUR *BUSINESS PARTNER'S* LACKEYS WHO DID IT.

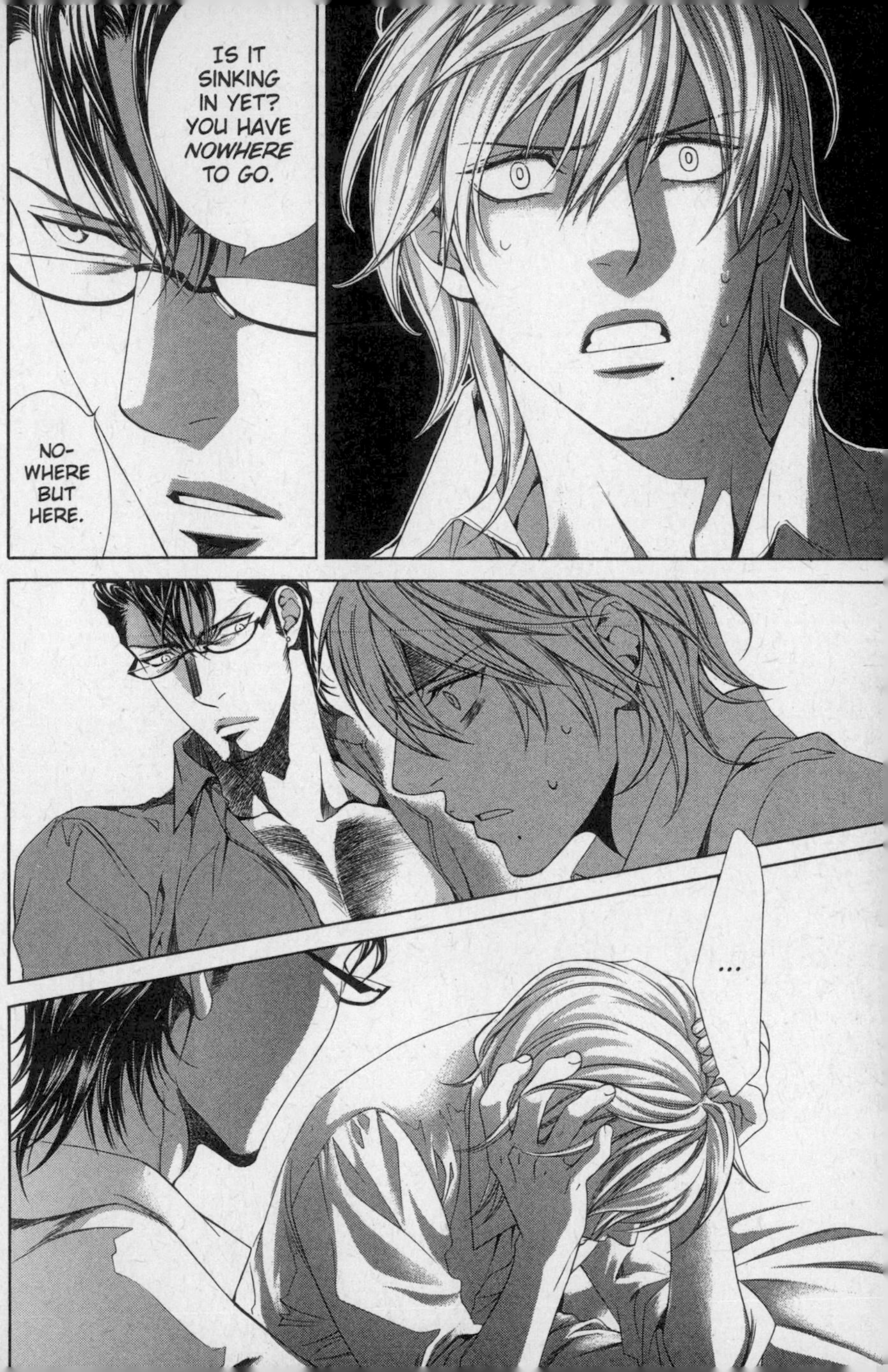
IS IT SINKING IN YET? YOU HAVE NOWHERE TO GO.
NO-WHERE BUT HERE.
...

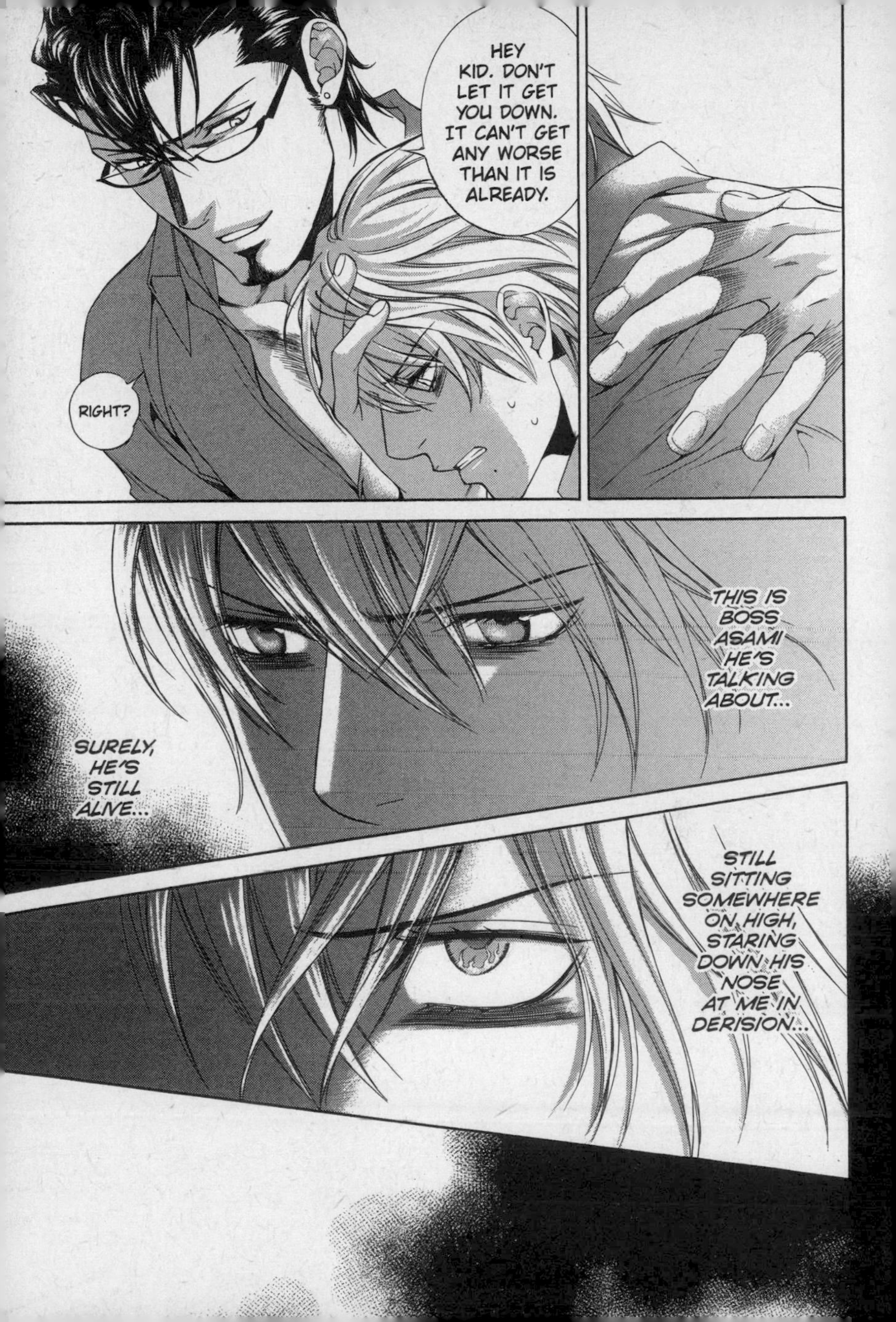
HEY KID. DON'T LET IT GET YOU DOWN. IT CAN'T GET ANY WORSE THAN IT IS ALREADY.
RIGHT?
THIS IS BOSS ASAMI HE'S TALKING ABOUT...
SURELY, HE'S STILL ALIVE...
STILL SITTING SOMEWHERE ON HIGH, STARING DOWN HIS NOSE AT ME IN DERISION...

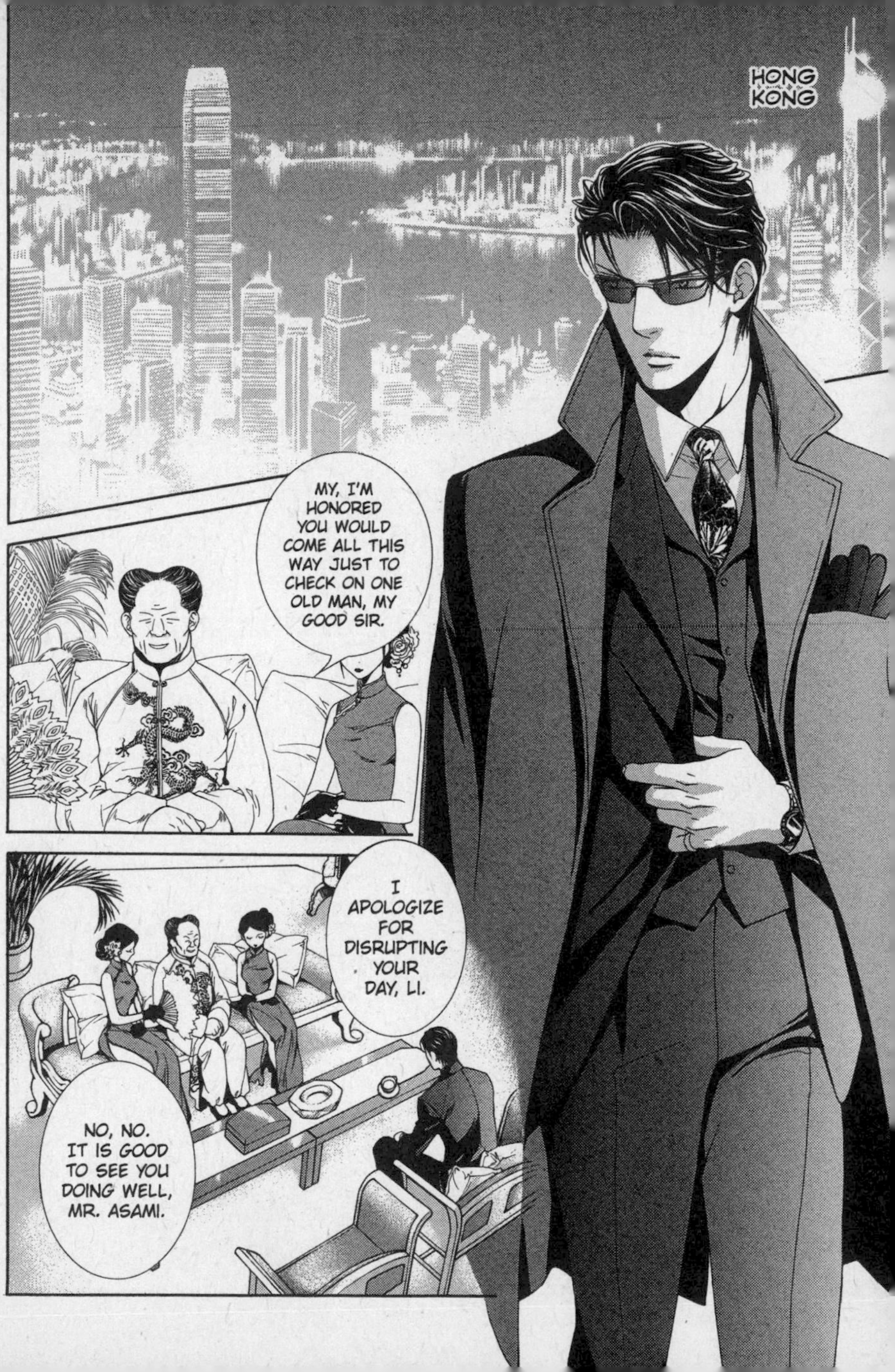

HONG KONG
MY, I'M HONORED YOU WOULD COME ALL THIS WAY JUST TO CHECK ON ONE OLD MAN, MY GOOD SIR.
I APOLOGIZE FOR DISRUPTING YOUR DAY, LI.
NO, NO. IT IS GOOD TO SEE YOU DOING WELL, MR. ASAMI.

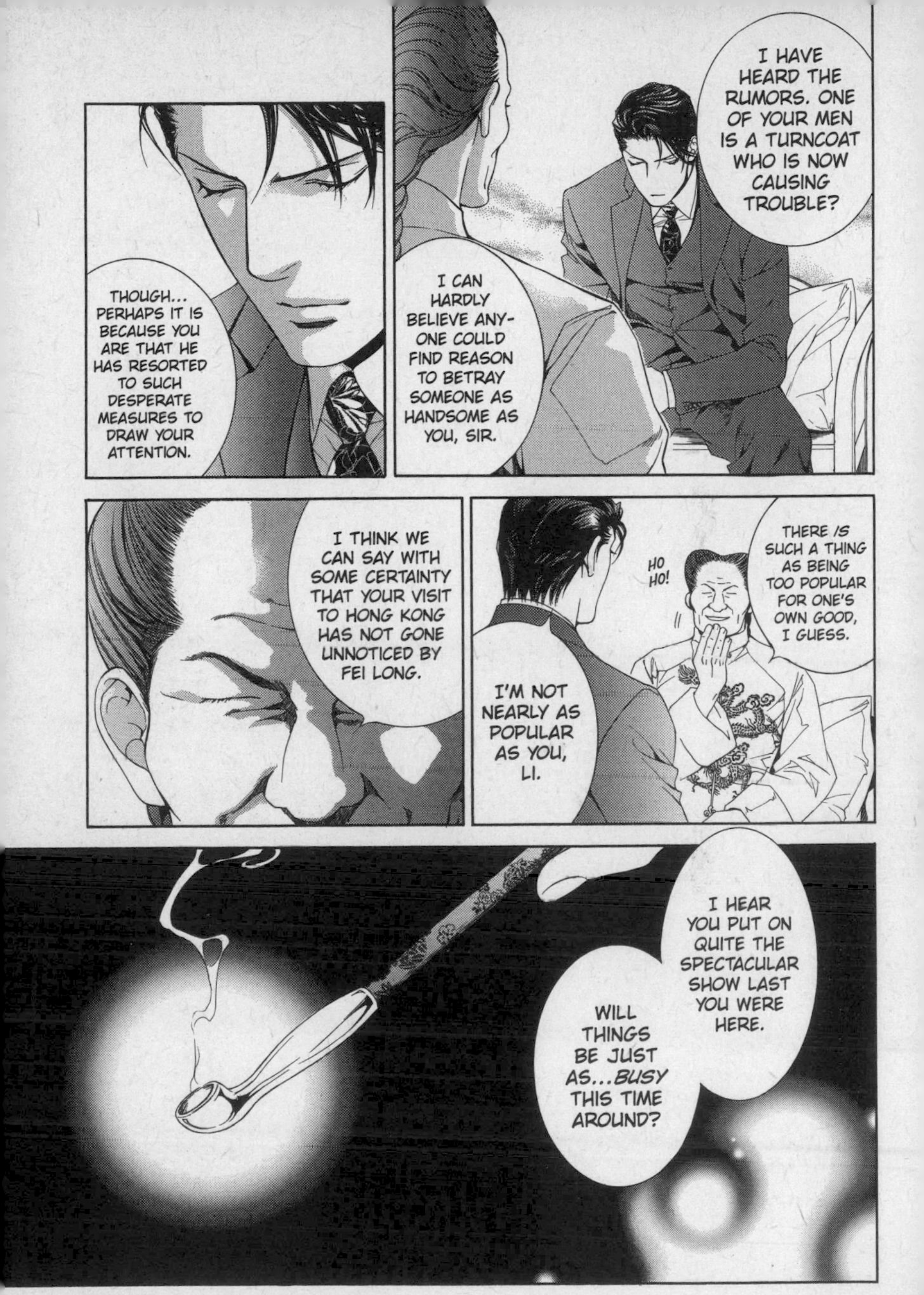
I HAVE HEARD THE RUMORS. ONE OF YOUR MEN IS A TURNCOAT WHO IS NOW CAUSING TROUBLE?
I CAN HARDLY BELIEVE ANYONE COULD FIND REASON TO BETRAY SOMEONE AS HANDSOME AS YOU, SIR.
THOUGH... PERHAPS IT IS BECAUSE YOU ARE THAT HE HAS RESORTED TO SUCH DESPERATE MEASURES TO DRAW YOUR ATTENTION.
THERE *IS* SUCH A THING AS BEING TOO POPULAR FOR ONE'S OWN GOOD, I GUESS.
HO HO!
I'M NOT NEARLY AS POPULAR AS YOU, LI.
I THINK WE CAN SAY WITH SOME CERTAINTY THAT YOUR VISIT TO HONG KONG HAS NOT GONE UNNOTICED BY FEI LONG.
I HEAR YOU PUT ON QUITE THE SPECTACULAR SHOW LAST YOU WERE HERE.
WILL THINGS BE JUST AS...*BUSY* THIS TIME AROUND?

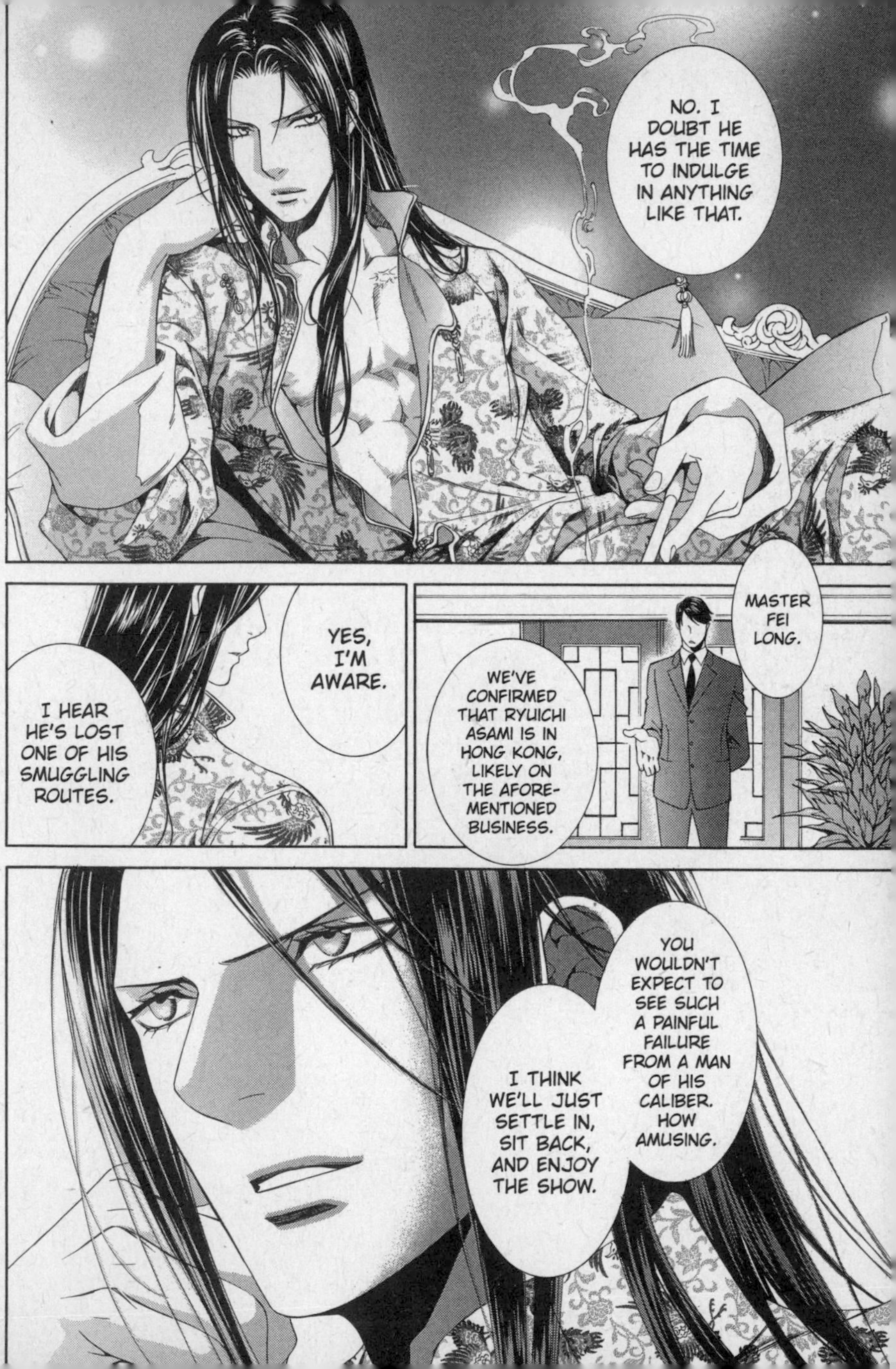
NO. I DOUBT HE HAS THE TIME TO INDULGE IN ANYTHING LIKE THAT.
MASTER FEI LONG.
WE'VE CONFIRMED THAT RYUICHI ASAMI IS IN HONG KONG, LIKELY ON THE AFORE-MENTIONED BUSINESS.
YES, I'M AWARE.
I HEAR HE'S LOST ONE OF HIS SMUGGLING ROUTES.
YOU WOULDN'T EXPECT TO SEE SUCH A PAINFUL FAILURE FROM A MAN OF HIS CALIBER. HOW AMUSING.
I THINK WE'LL JUST SETTLE IN, SIT BACK, AND ENJOY THE SHOW.

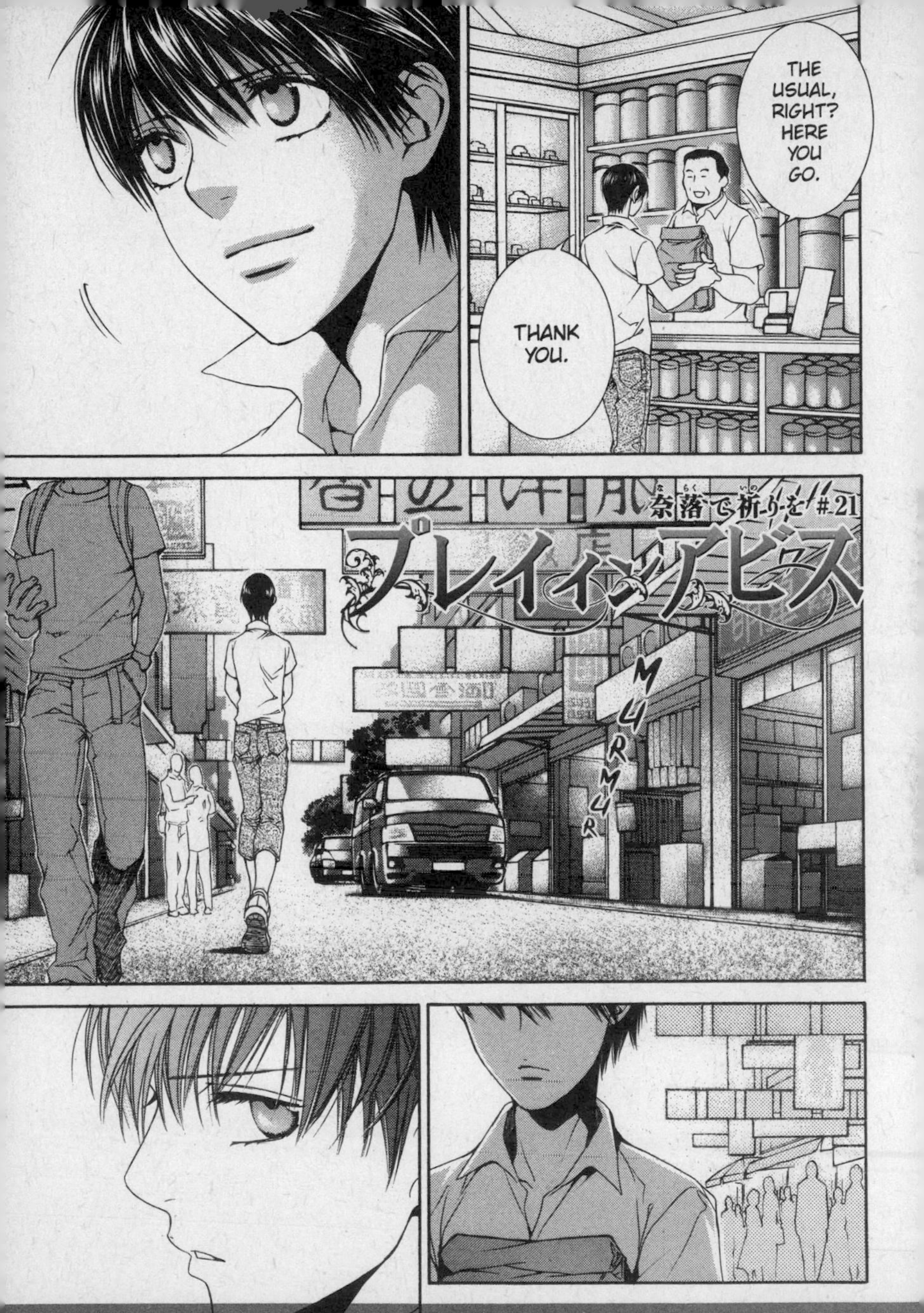
THE USUAL, RIGHT? HERE YOU GO.
THANK YOU.
奈落で祈りを #21
プレイインアビス
MURMURMUR

Pray in the Abyss

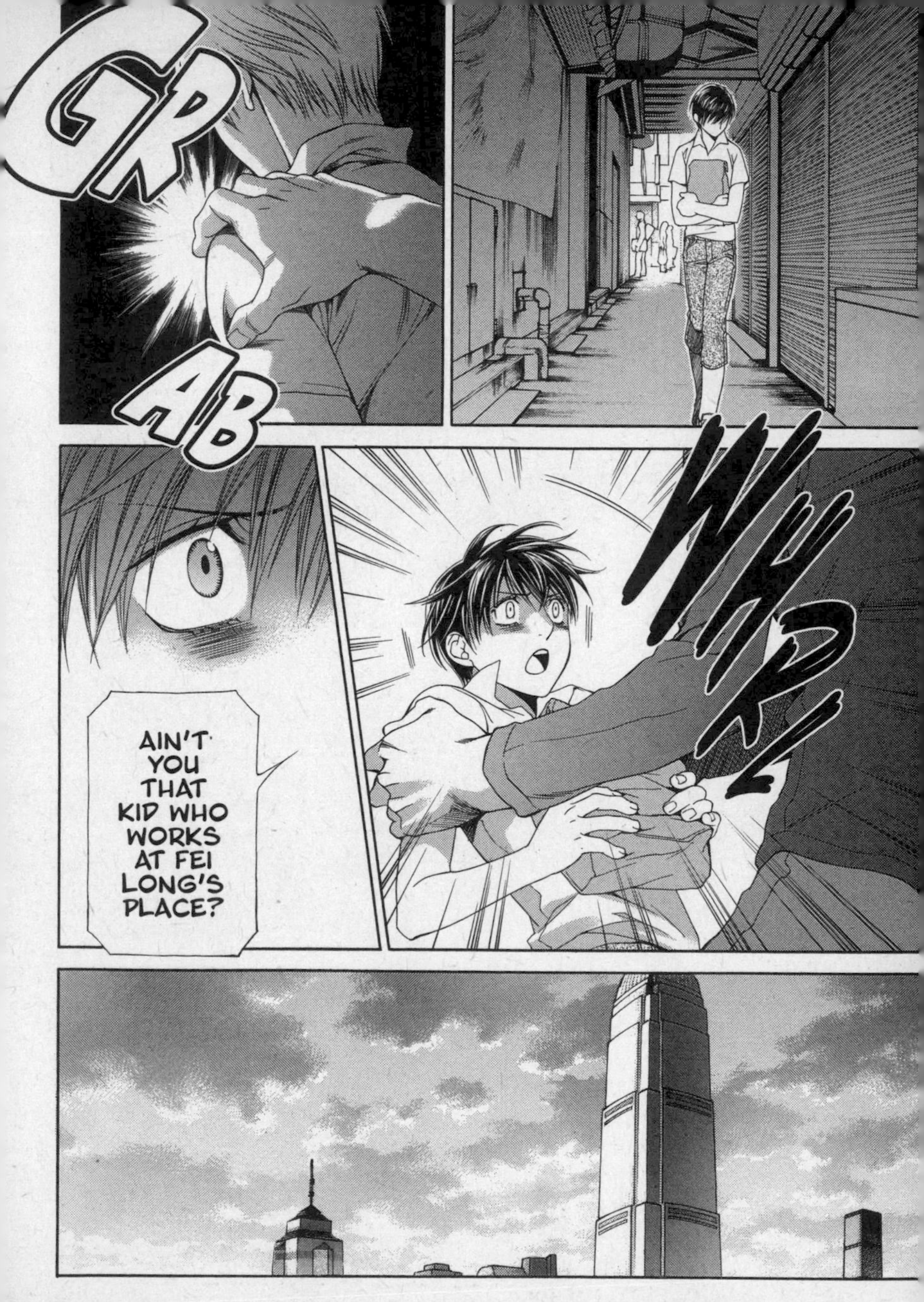
GRAB
AIN'T YOU THAT KID WHO WORKS AT FEI LONG'S PLACE?

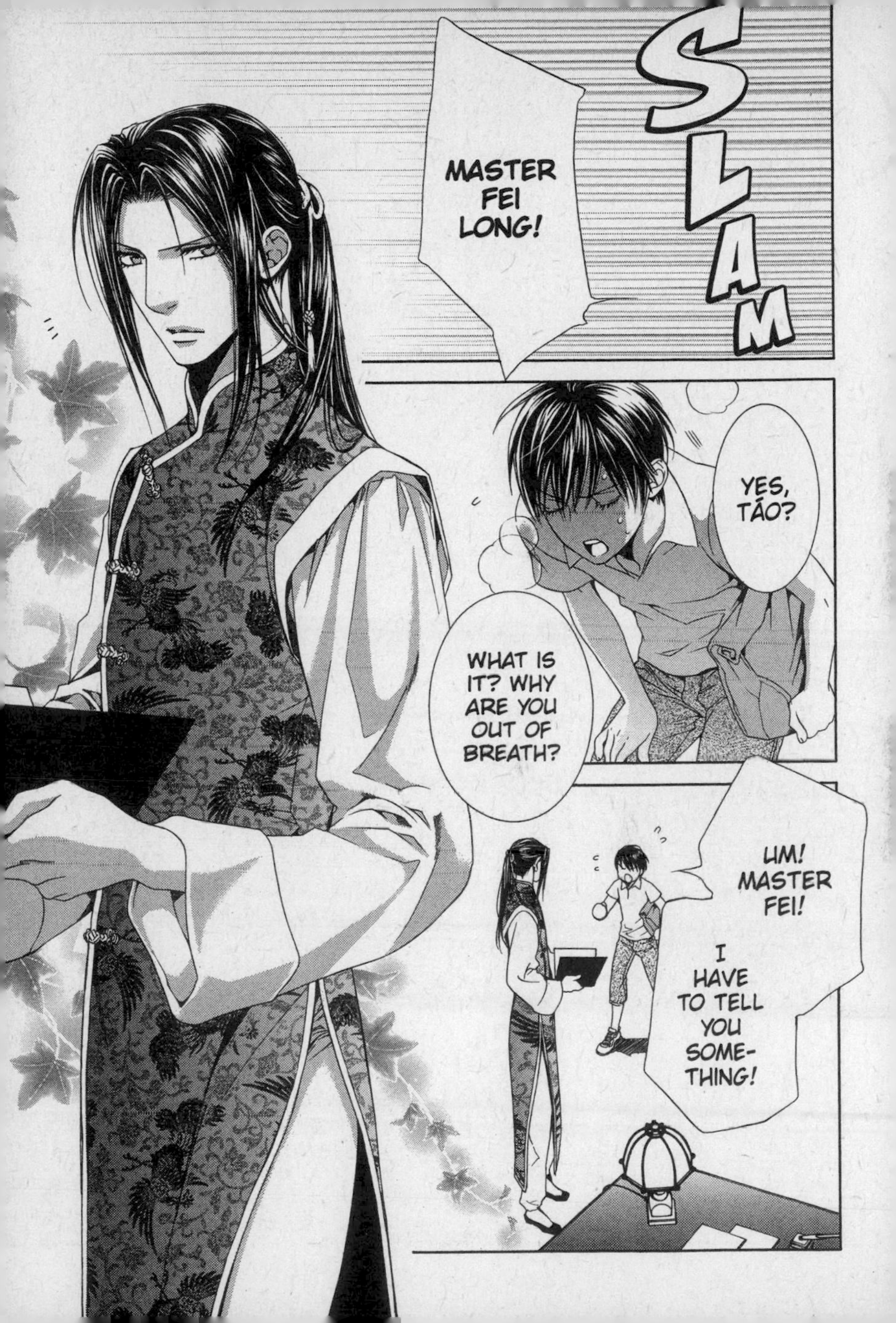
SLAM
MASTER FEI LONG!
YES, TÁO?
WHAT IS IT? WHY ARE YOU OUT OF BREATH?
UM! MASTER FEI!
I HAVE TO TELL YOU SOME-THING!

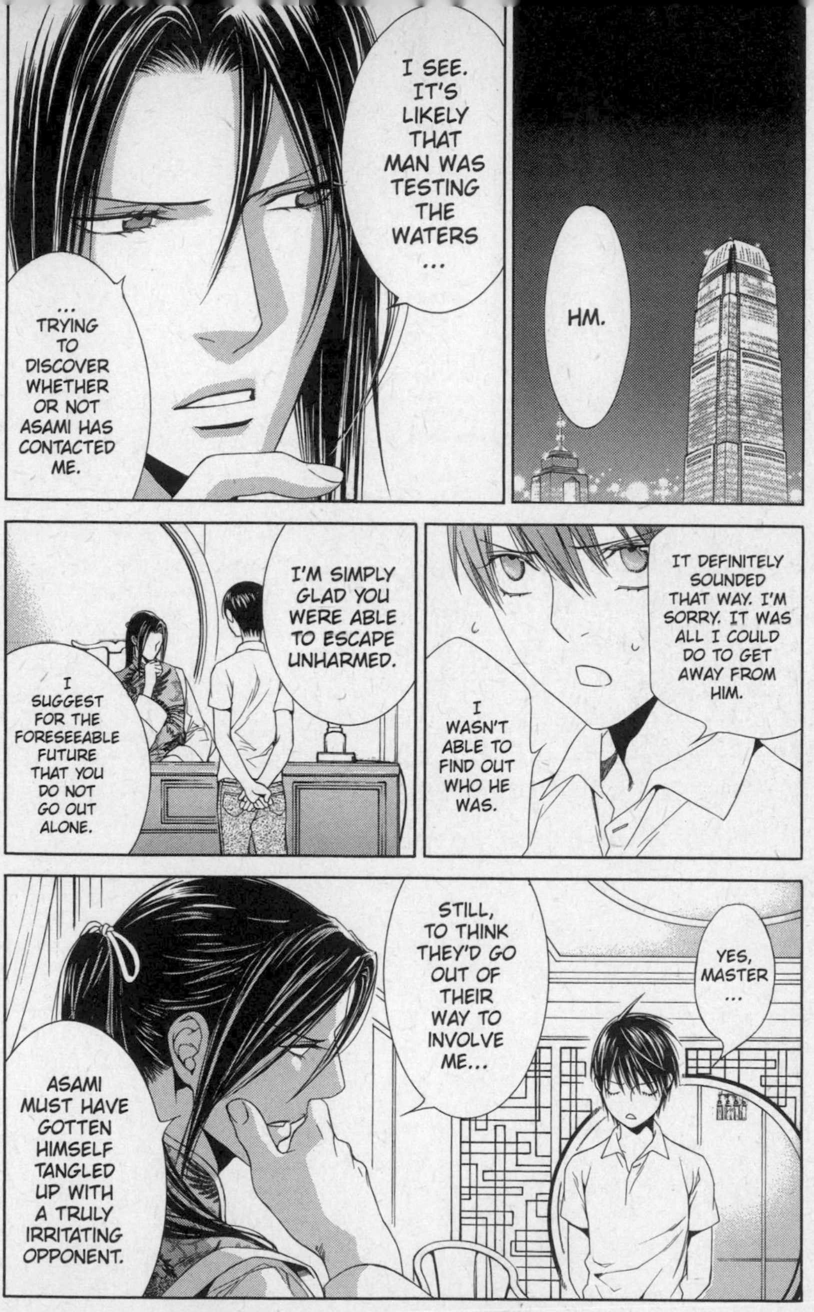
HM.
I SEE. IT'S LIKELY THAT MAN WAS TESTING THE WATERS...
...TRYING TO DISCOVER WHETHER OR NOT ASAMI HAS CONTACTED ME.
IT DEFINITELY SOUNDED THAT WAY. I'M SORRY. IT WAS ALL I COULD DO TO GET AWAY FROM HIM.
I WASN'T ABLE TO FIND OUT WHO HE WAS.
I'M SIMPLY GLAD YOU WERE ABLE TO ESCAPE UNHARMED.
I SUGGEST FOR THE FORESEEABLE FUTURE THAT YOU DO NOT GO OUT ALONE.
YES, MASTER...
STILL, TO THINK THEY'D GO OUT OF THEIR WAY TO INVOLVE ME...
ASAMI MUST HAVE GOTTEN HIMSELF TANGLED UP WITH A TRULY IRRITATING OPPONENT.

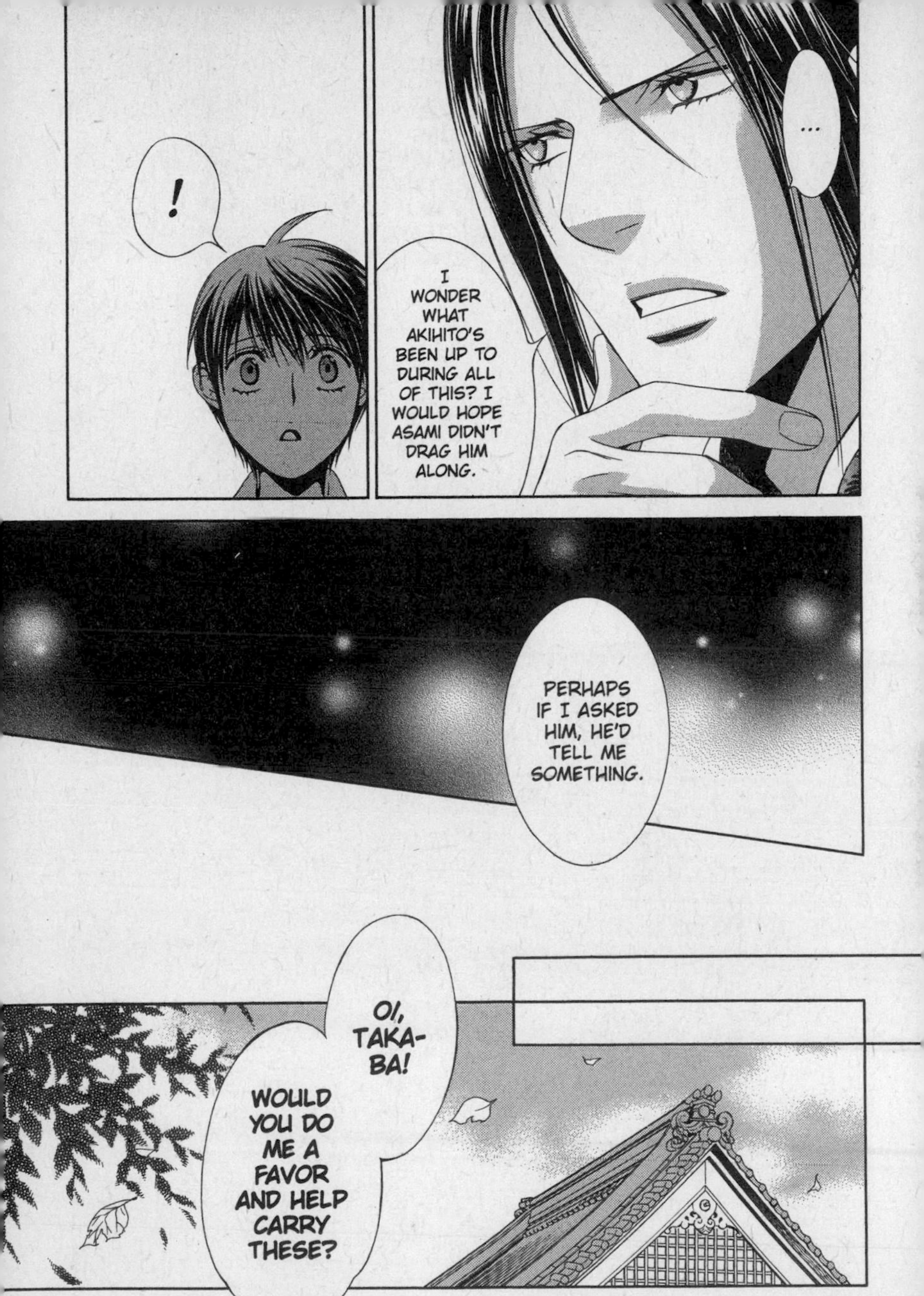
...
I WONDER WHAT AKIHITO'S BEEN UP TO DURING ALL OF THIS? I WOULD HOPE ASAMI DIDN'T DRAG HIM ALONG.
!
PERHAPS IF I ASKED HIM, HE'D TELL ME SOMETHING.
OI, TAKA-BA!
WOULD YOU DO ME A FAVOR AND HELP CARRY THESE?

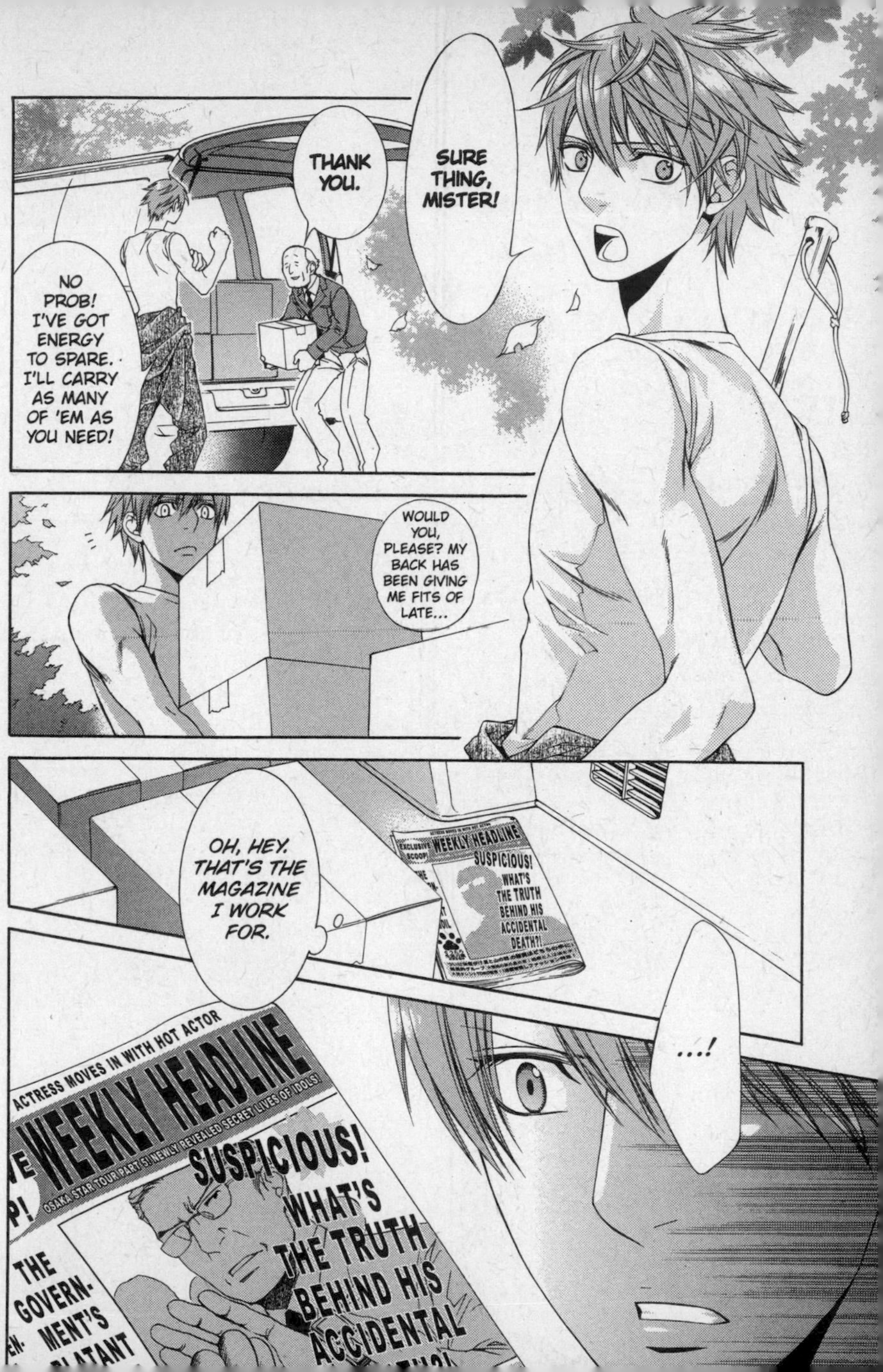
SURE THING, MISTER!
THANK YOU.
NO PROB! I'VE GOT ENERGY TO SPARE. I'LL CARRY AS MANY OF 'EM AS YOU NEED!
WOULD YOU, PLEASE? MY BACK HAS BEEN GIVING ME FITS OF LATE...
EXCLUSIVE SCOOP!
WEEKLY HEADLINE
SUSPICIOUS! WHAT'S THE TRUTH BEHIND HIS ACCIDENTAL DEATH?!
OH, HEY. THAT'S THE MAGAZINE I WORK FOR.
...!
ACTRESS MOVES IN WITH HOT ACTOR
WEEKLY HEADLINE
OSAKA STAR TOUR PART 5! NEWLY REVEALED SECRET LIVES OF IDOLS
SUSPICIOUS!
WHAT'S THE TRUTH BEHIND HIS ACCIDENTAL
THE GOVERN- MENT'S BLATANT

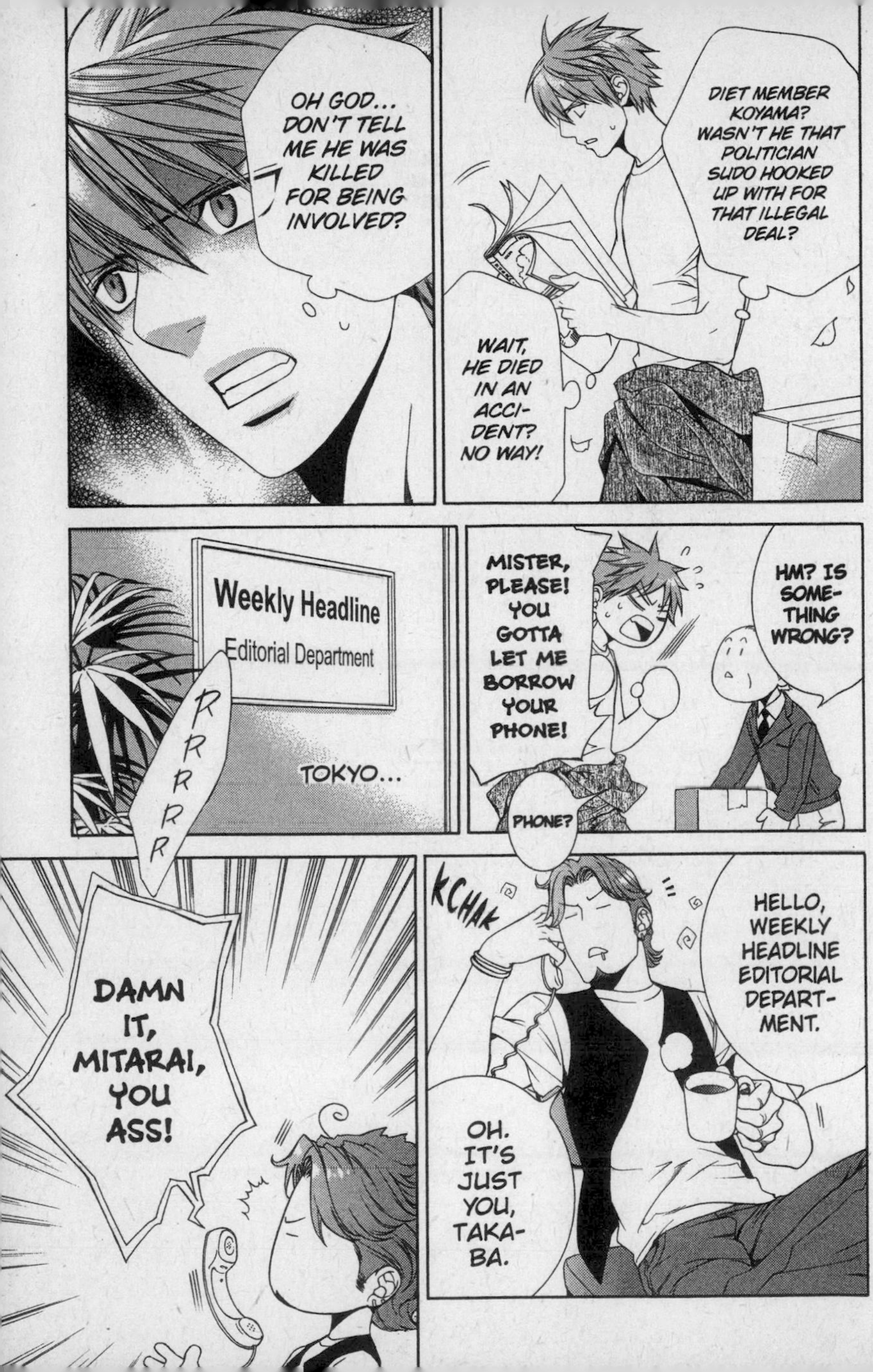
DIET MEMBER KOYAMA? WASN'T HE THAT POLITICIAN SUDO HOOKED UP WITH FOR THAT ILLEGAL DEAL?
WAIT, HE DIED IN AN ACCIDENT? NO WAY!
OH GOD... DON'T TELL ME HE WAS KILLED FOR BEING INVOLVED?
HM? IS SOMETHING WRONG?
MISTER, PLEASE! YOU GOTTA LET ME BORROW YOUR PHONE!
PHONE?
Weekly Headline
Editorial Department
TOKYO...
RRRRR
KCHAK
HELLO, WEEKLY HEADLINE EDITORIAL DEPARTMENT.
OH. IT'S JUST YOU, TAKABA.
DAMN IT, MITARAI, YOU ASS!

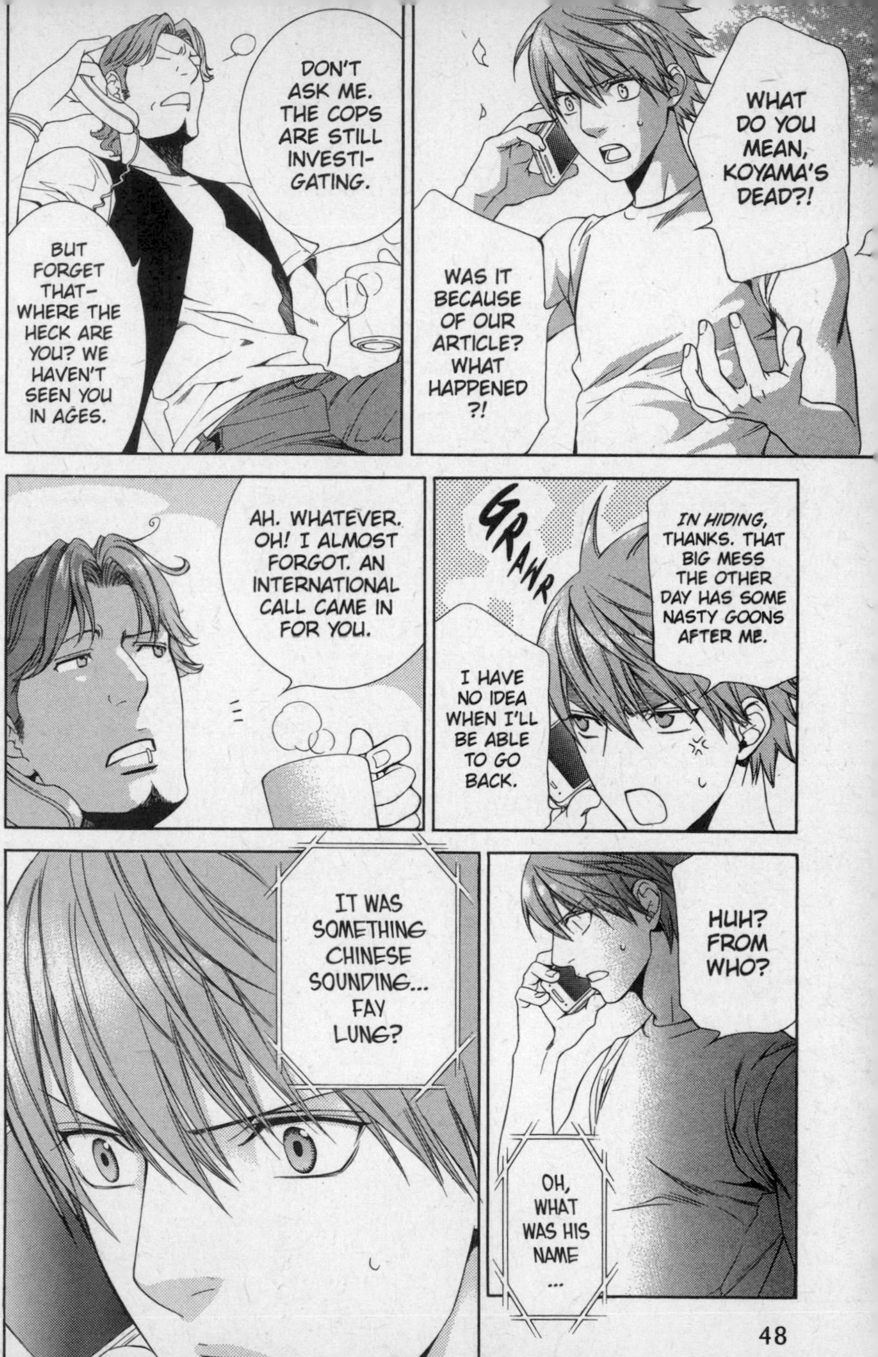
WHAT DO YOU MEAN, KOYAMA'S DEAD?!
WAS IT BECAUSE OF OUR ARTICLE? WHAT HAPPENED?!
DON'T ASK ME. THE COPS ARE STILL INVESTI-GATING.
BUT FORGET THAT—WHERE THE HECK ARE YOU? WE HAVEN'T SEEN YOU IN AGES.
GRAWR
IN HIDING, THANKS. THAT BIG MESS THE OTHER DAY HAS SOME NASTY GOONS AFTER ME.
I HAVE NO IDEA WHEN I'LL BE ABLE TO GO BACK.
AH. WHATEVER. OH! I ALMOST FORGOT. AN INTERNATIONAL CALL CAME IN FOR YOU.
HUH? FROM WHO?
OH, WHAT WAS HIS NAME ...
IT WAS SOMETHING CHINESE SOUNDING... FAY LUNG?

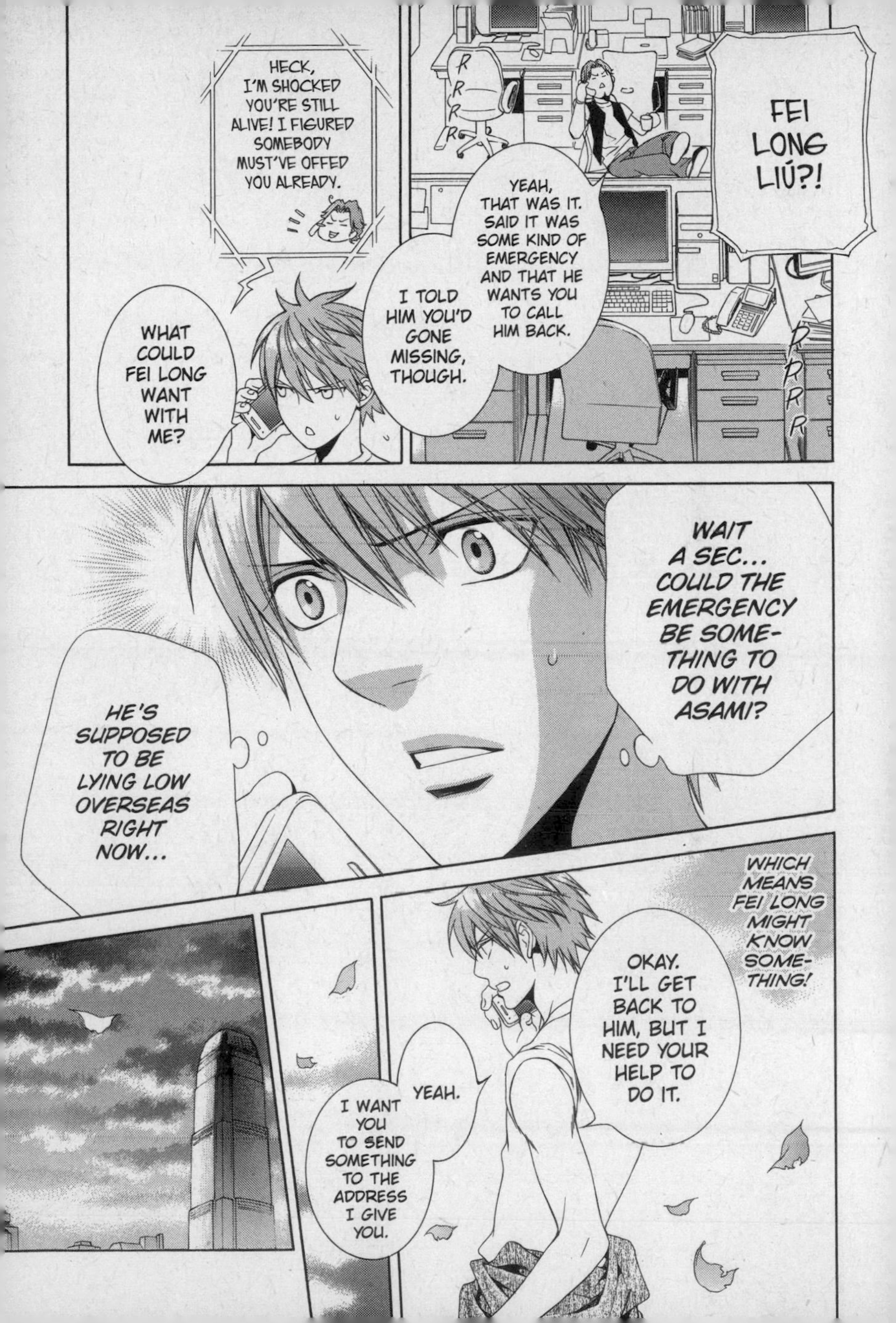
RRRR
FEI LONG LIÚ?!
RRRR
YEAH, THAT WAS IT. SAID IT WAS SOME KIND OF EMERGENCY AND THAT HE WANTS YOU TO CALL HIM BACK.
I TOLD HIM YOU'D GONE MISSING, THOUGH.
HECK, I'M SHOCKED YOU'RE STILL ALIVE! I FIGURED SOMEBODY MUST'VE OFFED YOU ALREADY.
WHAT COULD FEI LONG WANT WITH ME?
WAIT A SEC... COULD THE EMERGENCY BE SOME-THING TO DO WITH ASAMI?
HE'S SUPPOSED TO BE LYING LOW OVERSEAS RIGHT NOW...
WHICH MEANS FEI LONG MIGHT KNOW SOME-THING!
OKAY. I'LL GET BACK TO HIM, BUT I NEED YOUR HELP TO DO IT.
YEAH.
I WANT YOU TO SEND SOMETHING TO THE ADDRESS I GIVE YOU.

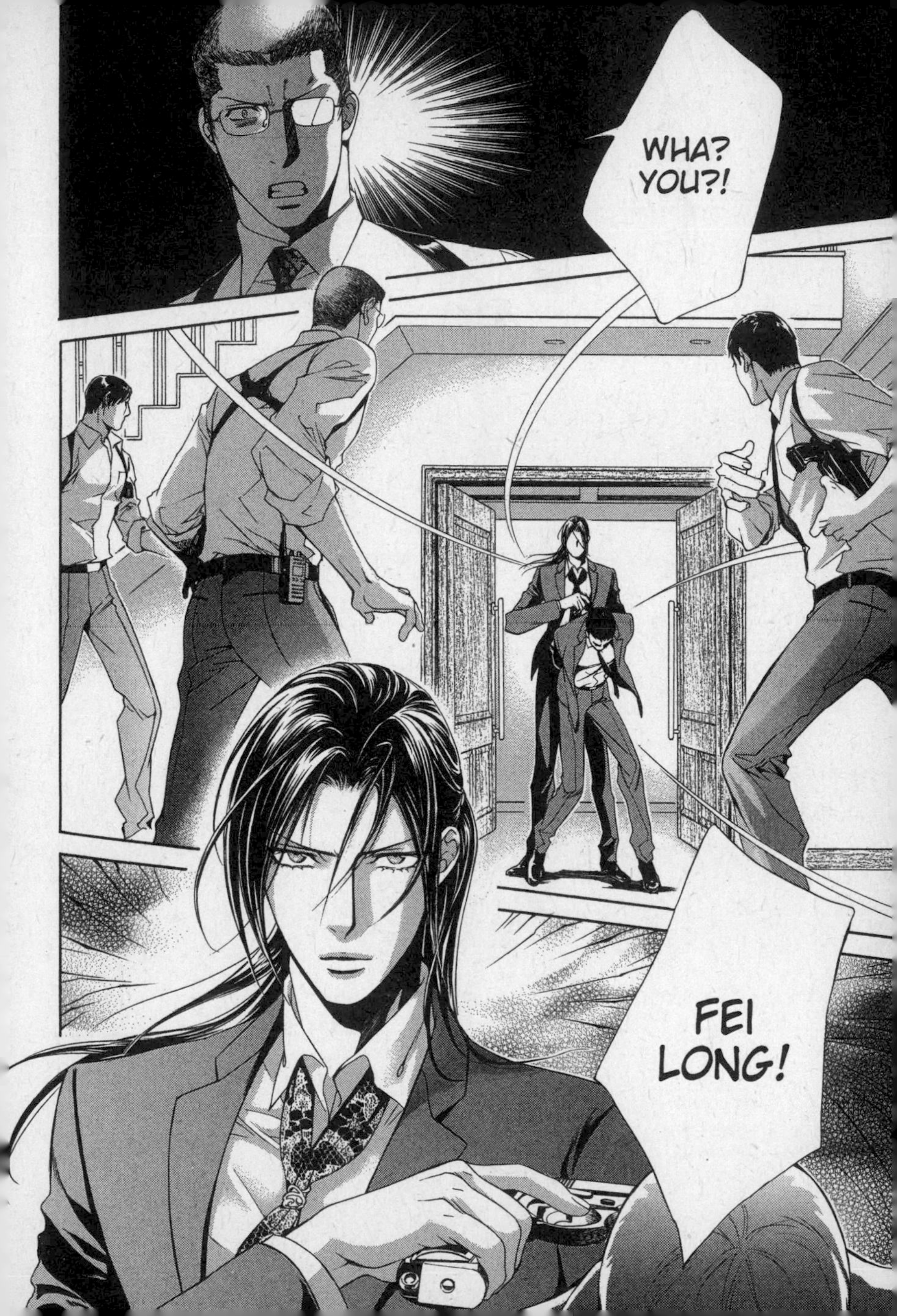
WHA? YOU?!
FEI LONG!

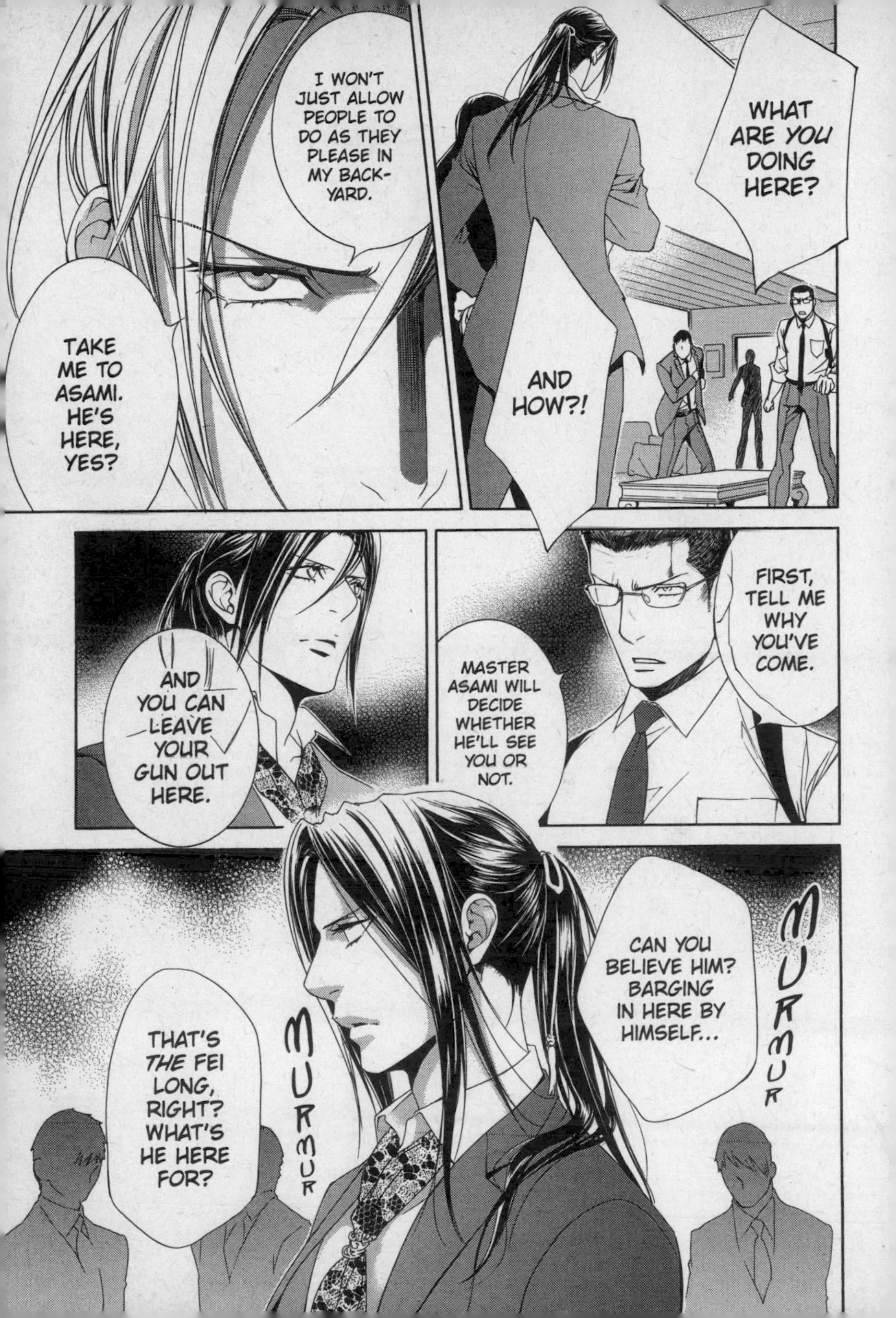
WHAT ARE *YOU* DOING HERE?
AND HOW?!
I WON'T JUST ALLOW PEOPLE TO DO AS THEY PLEASE IN MY BACK-YARD.
TAKE ME TO ASAMI. HE'S HERE, YES?
FIRST, TELL ME WHY YOU'VE COME.
MASTER ASAMI WILL DECIDE WHETHER HE'LL SEE YOU OR NOT.
AND YOU CAN LEAVE YOUR GUN OUT HERE.
MURMUR
CAN YOU BELIEVE HIM? BARGING IN HERE BY HIMSELF...
MURMUR
THAT'S *THE* FEI LONG, RIGHT? WHAT'S HE HERE FOR?

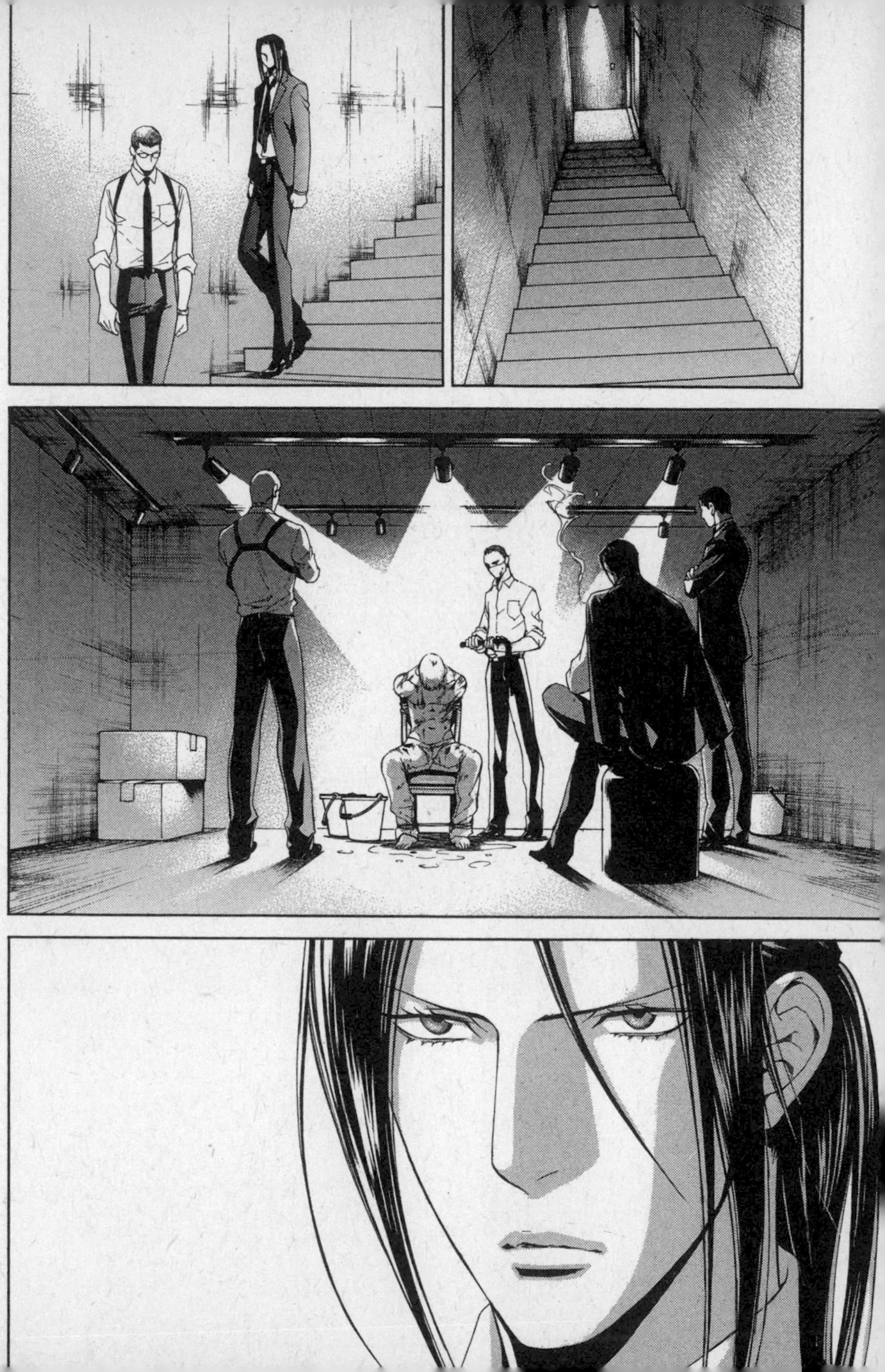

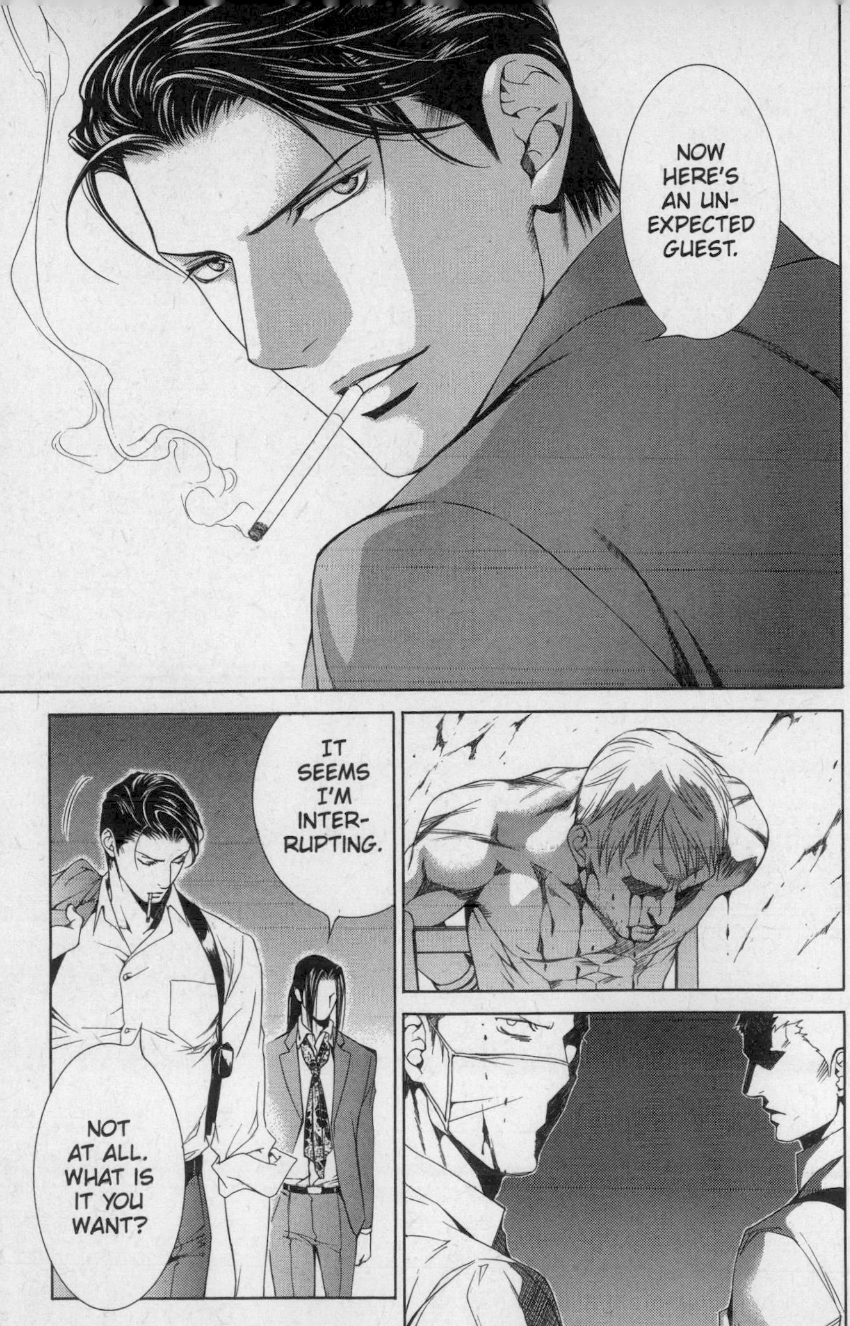
NOW HERE'S AN UN-EXPECTED GUEST.
IT SEEMS I'M INTER-RUPTING.
NOT AT ALL. WHAT IS IT YOU WANT?

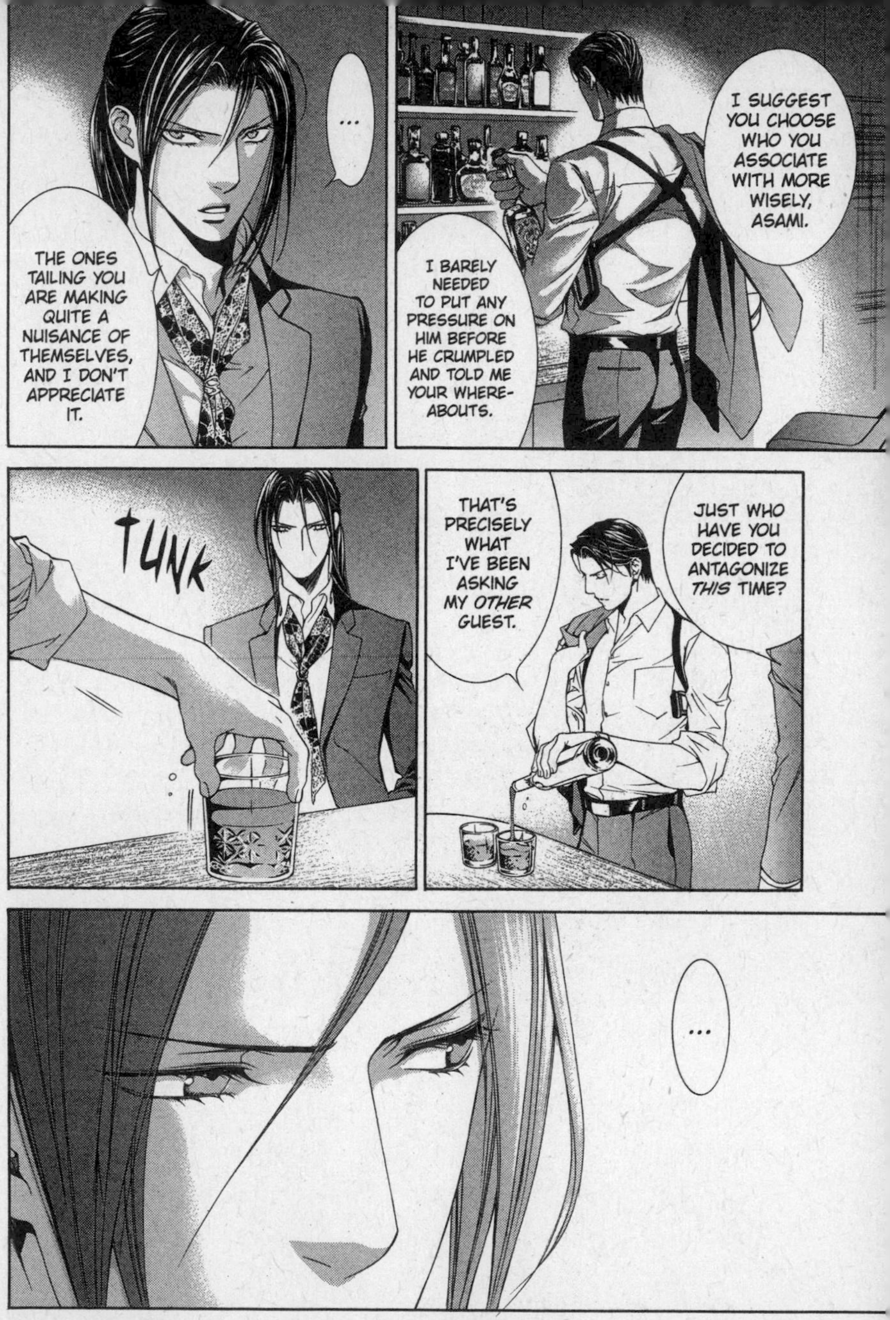
I SUGGEST YOU CHOOSE WHO YOU ASSOCIATE WITH MORE WISELY, ASAMI.
I BARELY NEEDED TO PUT ANY PRESSURE ON HIM BEFORE HE CRUMPLED AND TOLD ME YOUR WHERE-ABOUTS.
...
THE ONES TAILING YOU ARE MAKING QUITE A NUISANCE OF THEMSELVES, AND I DON'T APPRECIATE IT.
JUST WHO HAVE YOU DECIDED TO ANTAGONIZE *THIS* TIME?
THAT'S PRECISELY WHAT I'VE BEEN ASKING MY *OTHER* GUEST.
TUNK
...

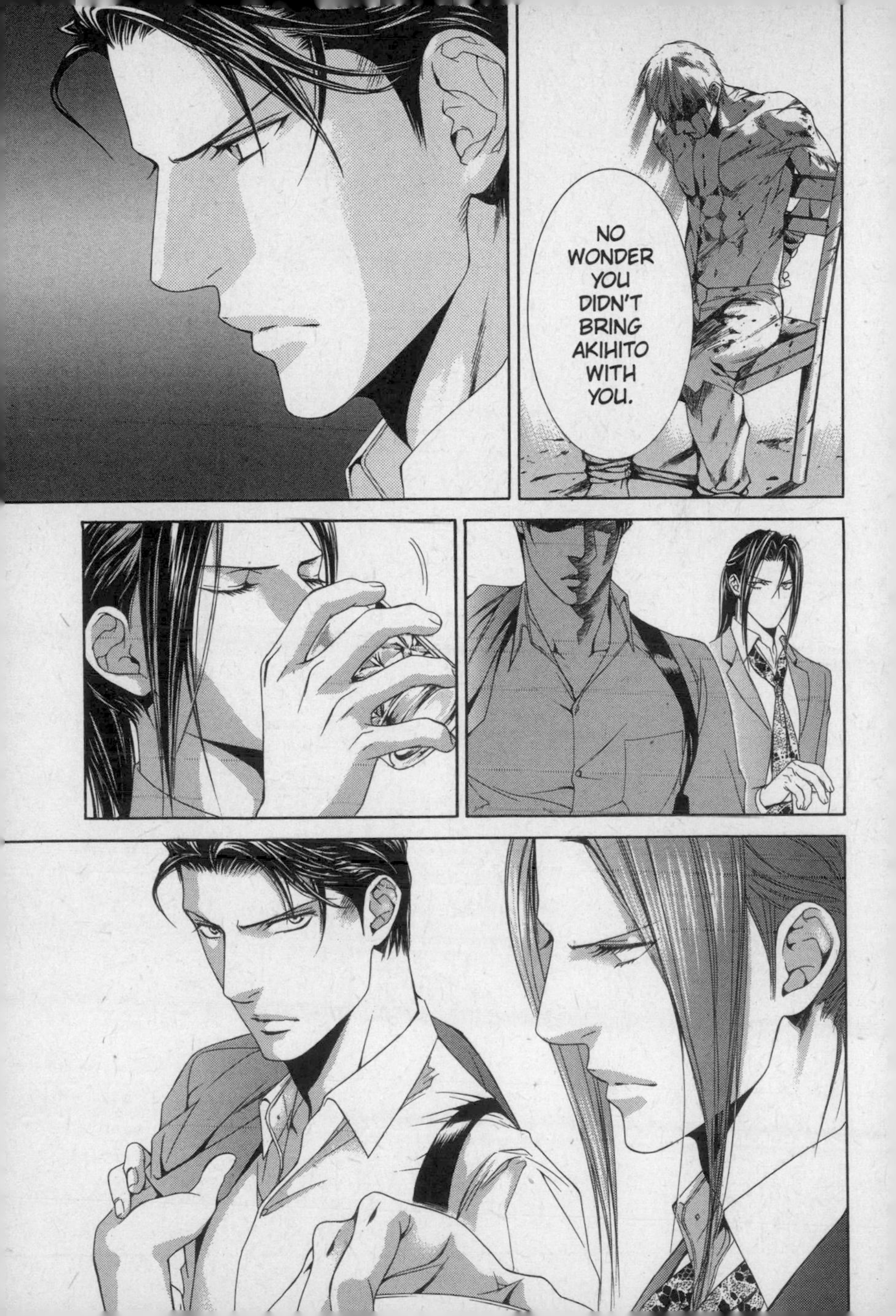
NO WONDER YOU DIDN'T BRING AKIHITO WITH YOU.

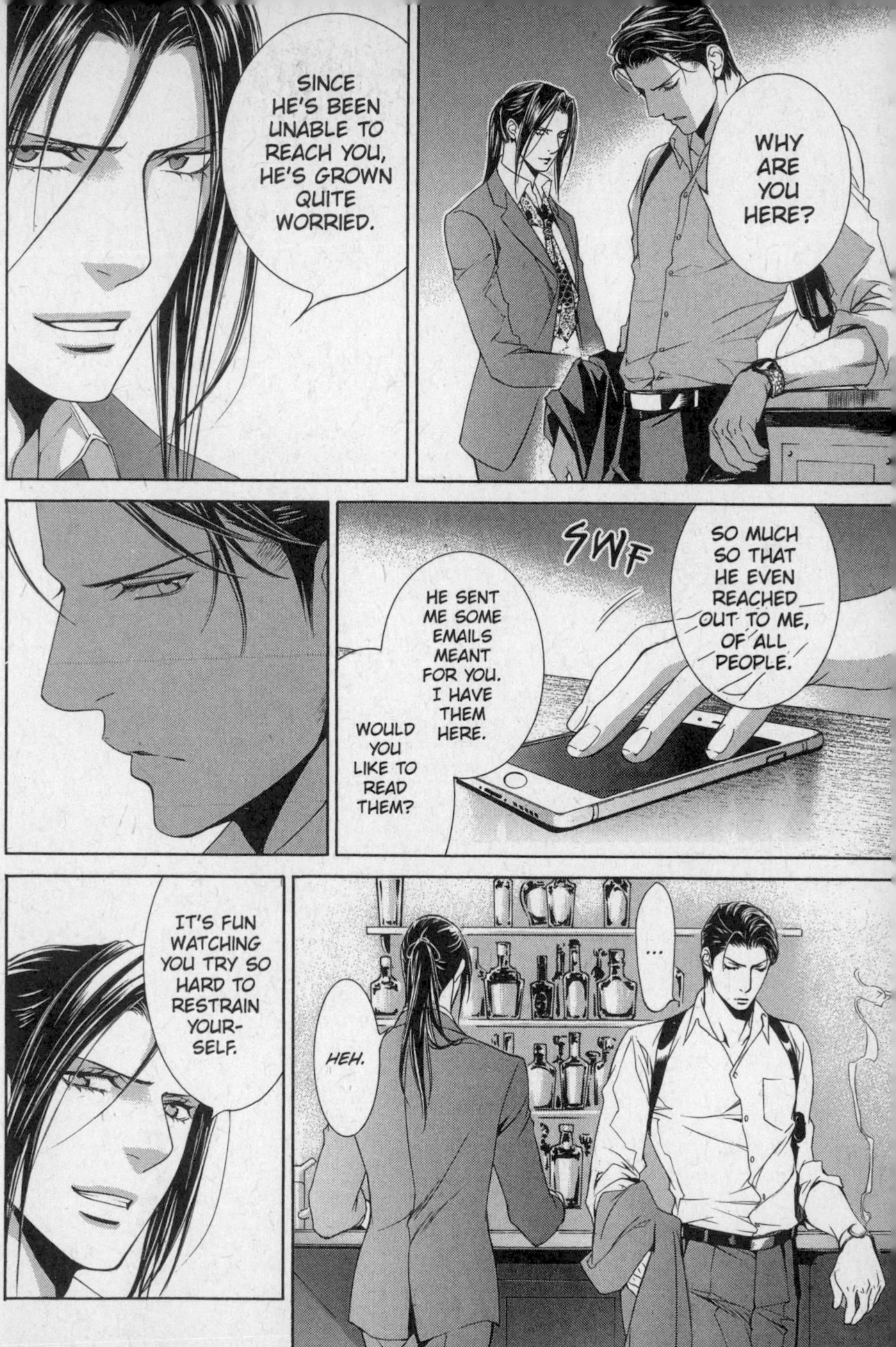
WHY ARE YOU HERE?
SINCE HE'S BEEN UNABLE TO REACH YOU, HE'S GROWN QUITE WORRIED.
SO MUCH SO THAT HE EVEN REACHED OUT TO ME, OF ALL PEOPLE.
SWF
HE SENT ME SOME EMAILS MEANT FOR YOU. I HAVE THEM HERE.
WOULD YOU LIKE TO READ THEM?
...
HEH.
IT'S FUN WATCHING YOU TRY SO HARD TO RESTRAIN YOUR-SELF.

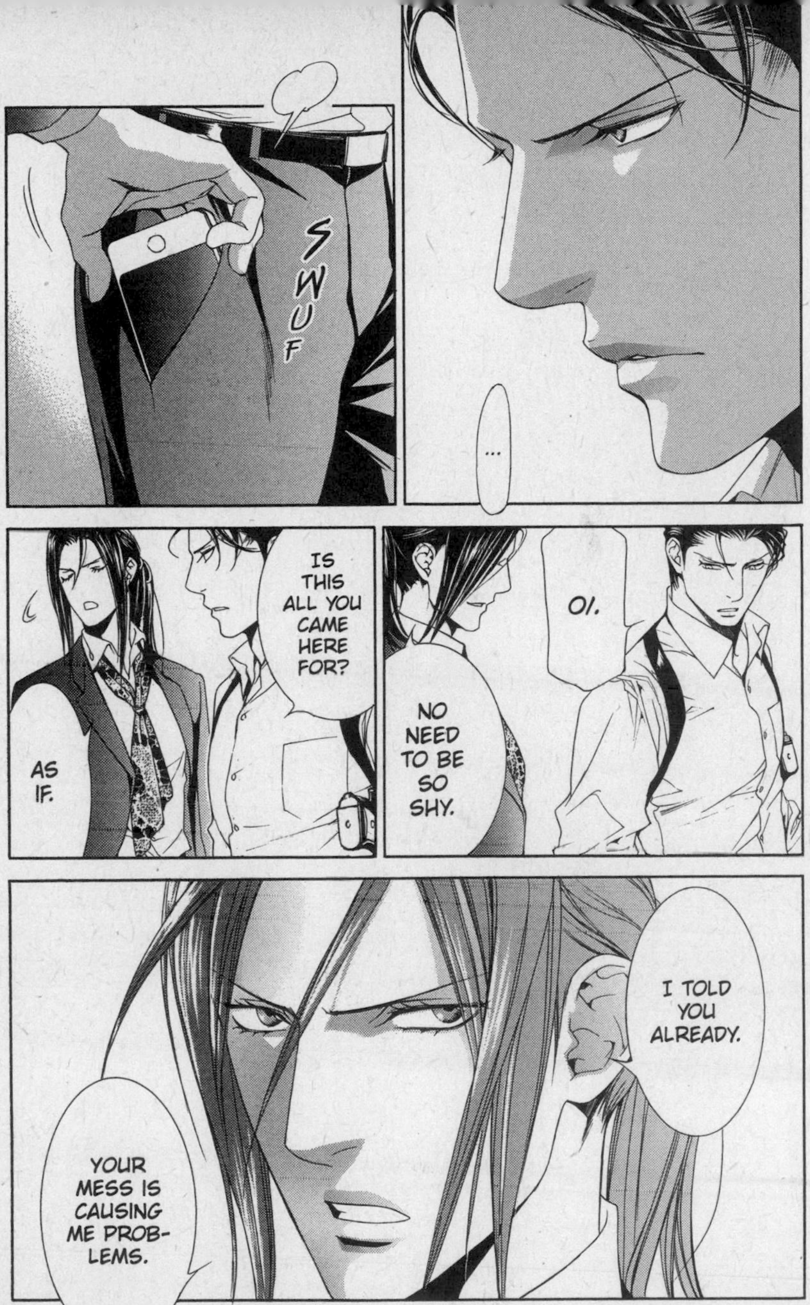
...
SWUF
OI.
NO NEED TO BE SO SHY.
IS THIS ALL YOU CAME HERE FOR?
AS IF.
I TOLD YOU ALREADY.
YOUR MESS IS CAUSING ME PROB-LEMS.

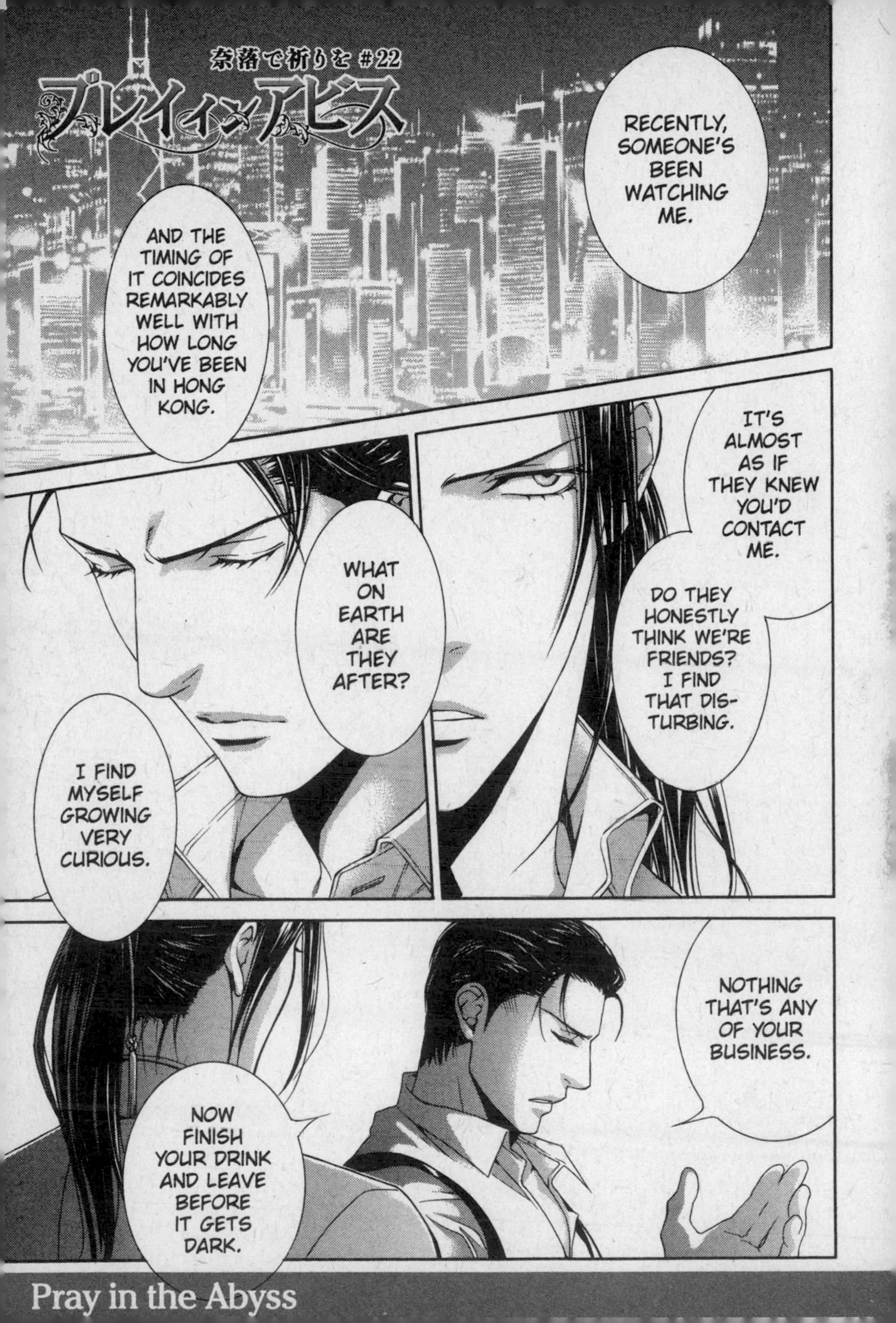
奈落で祈りを #22
プレイ イン アビス
RECENTLY, SOMEONE'S BEEN WATCHING ME.
AND THE TIMING OF IT COINCIDES REMARKABLY WELL WITH HOW LONG YOU'VE BEEN IN HONG KONG.
IT'S ALMOST AS IF THEY KNEW YOU'D CONTACT ME.
DO THEY HONESTLY THINK WE'RE FRIENDS? I FIND THAT DIS-TURBING.
WHAT ON EARTH ARE THEY AFTER?
I FIND MYSELF GROWING VERY CURIOUS.
NOTHING THAT'S ANY OF YOUR BUSINESS.
NOW FINISH YOUR DRINK AND LEAVE BEFORE IT GETS DARK.
Pray in the Abyss

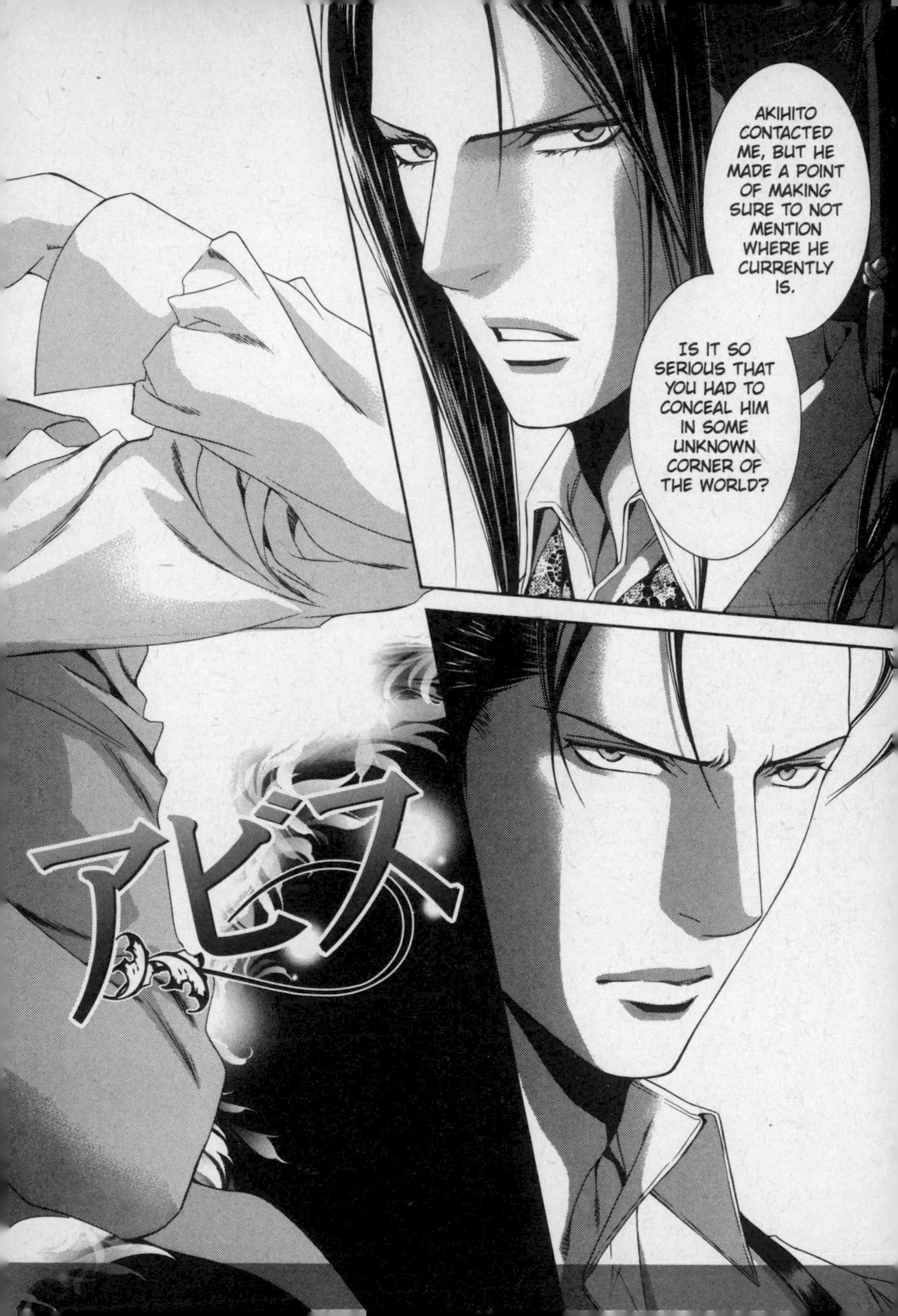
AKIHITO CONTACTED ME, BUT HE MADE A POINT OF MAKING SURE TO NOT MENTION WHERE HE CURRENTLY IS.
IS IT SO SERIOUS THAT YOU HAD TO CONCEAL HIM IN SOME UNKNOWN CORNER OF THE WORLD?
アビス

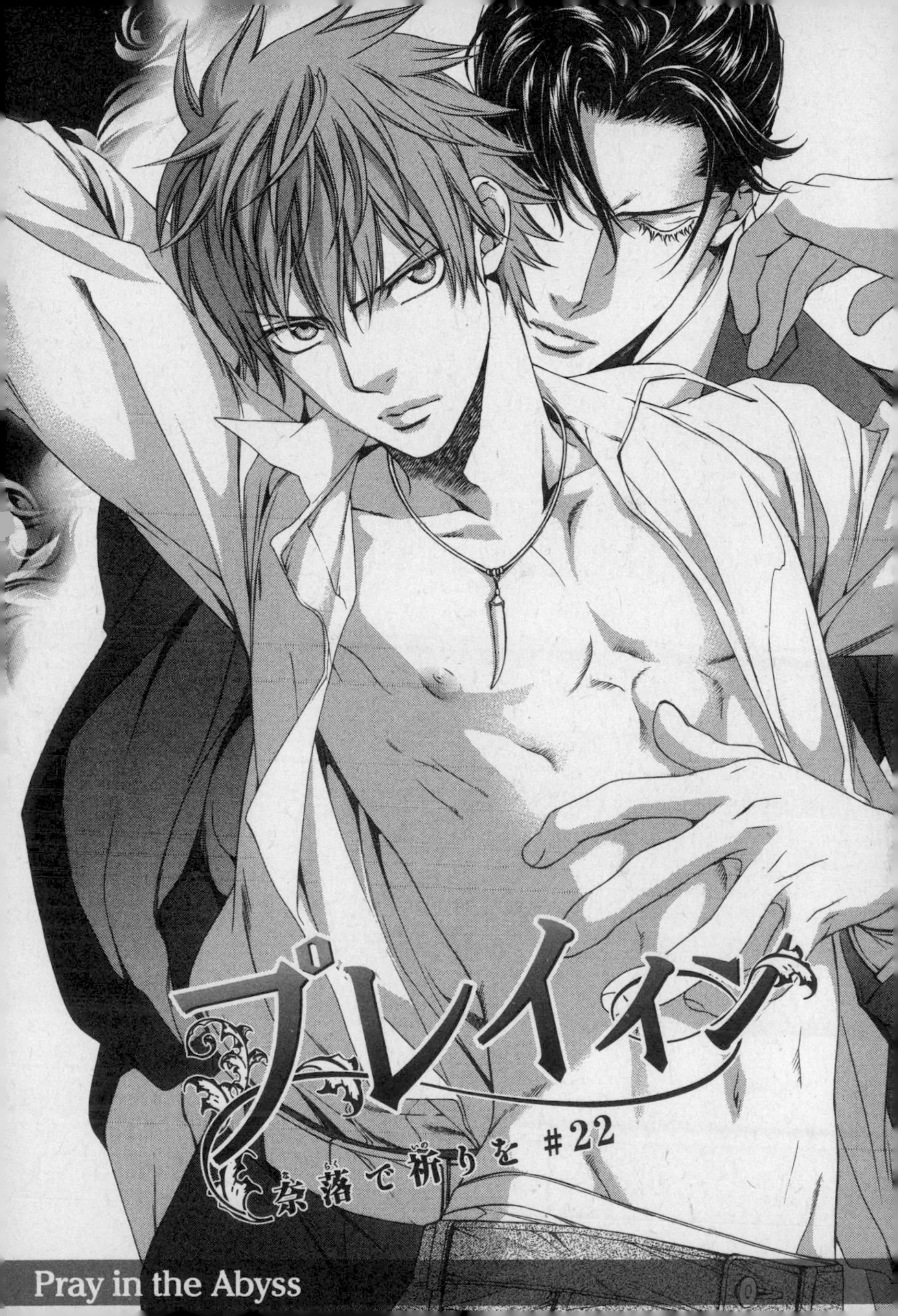
プレイン
奈落で祈りを #22
Pray in the Abyss

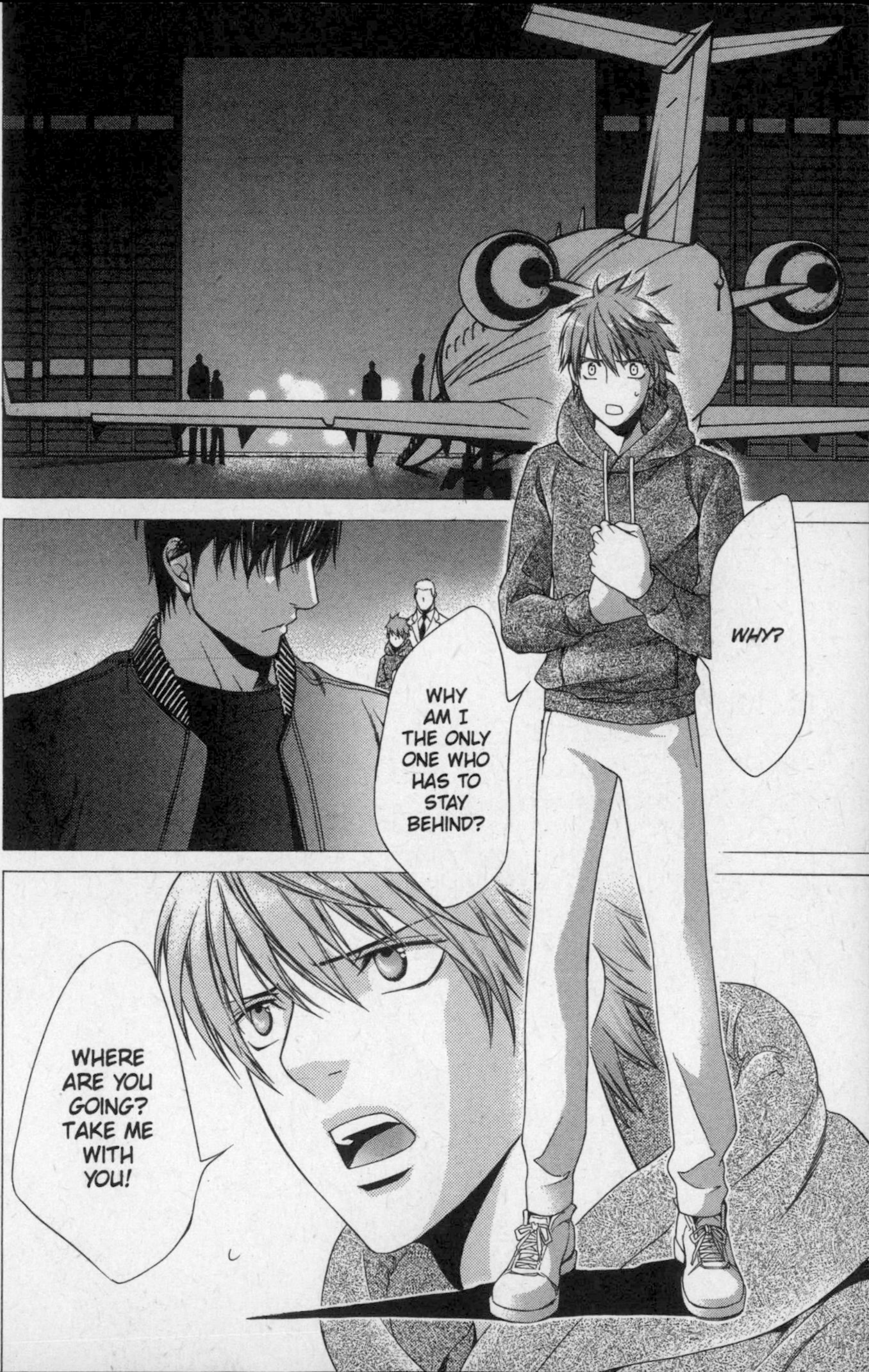
WHY?
WHY AM I THE ONLY ONE WHO HAS TO STAY BEHIND?
WHERE ARE YOU GOING? TAKE ME WITH YOU!

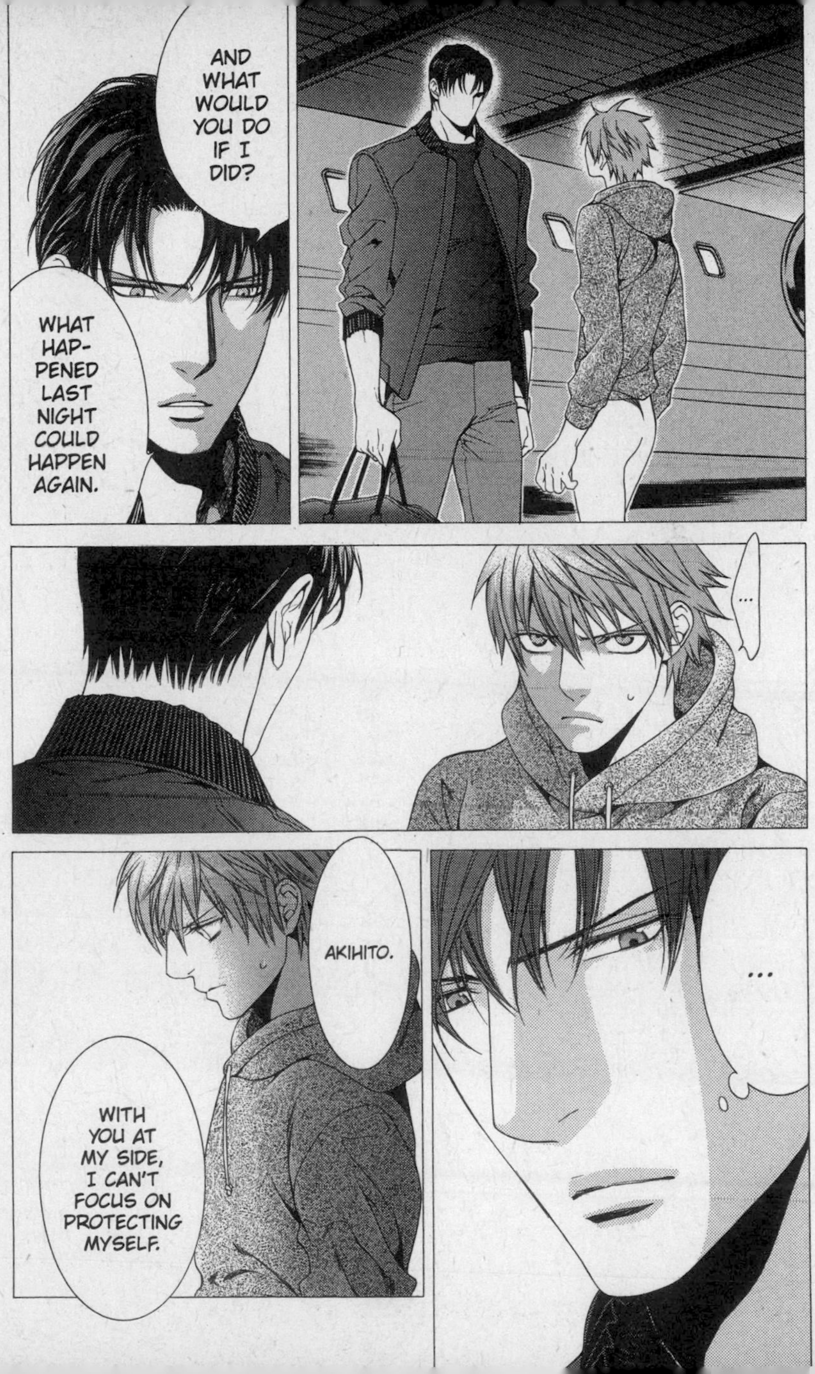
AND WHAT WOULD YOU DO IF I DID?
WHAT HAPPENED LAST NIGHT COULD HAPPEN AGAIN.
...
...
AKIHITO.
WITH YOU AT MY SIDE, I CAN'T FOCUS ON PROTECTING MYSELF.

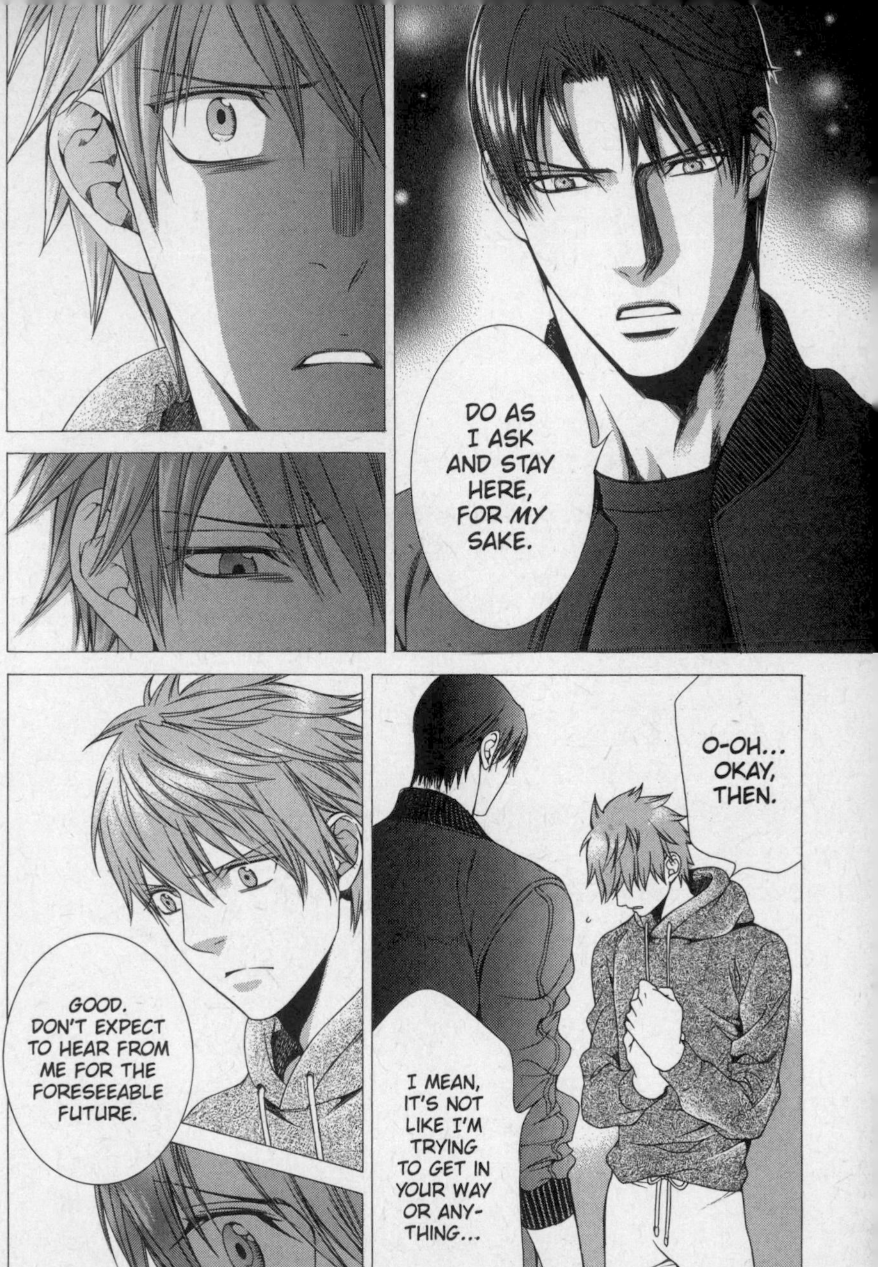
DO AS I ASK AND STAY HERE, FOR *MY* SAKE.
O-OH... OKAY, THEN.
I MEAN, IT'S NOT LIKE I'M TRYING TO GET IN YOUR WAY OR ANY-THING...
GOOD. DON'T EXPECT TO HEAR FROM ME FOR THE FORESEEABLE FUTURE.

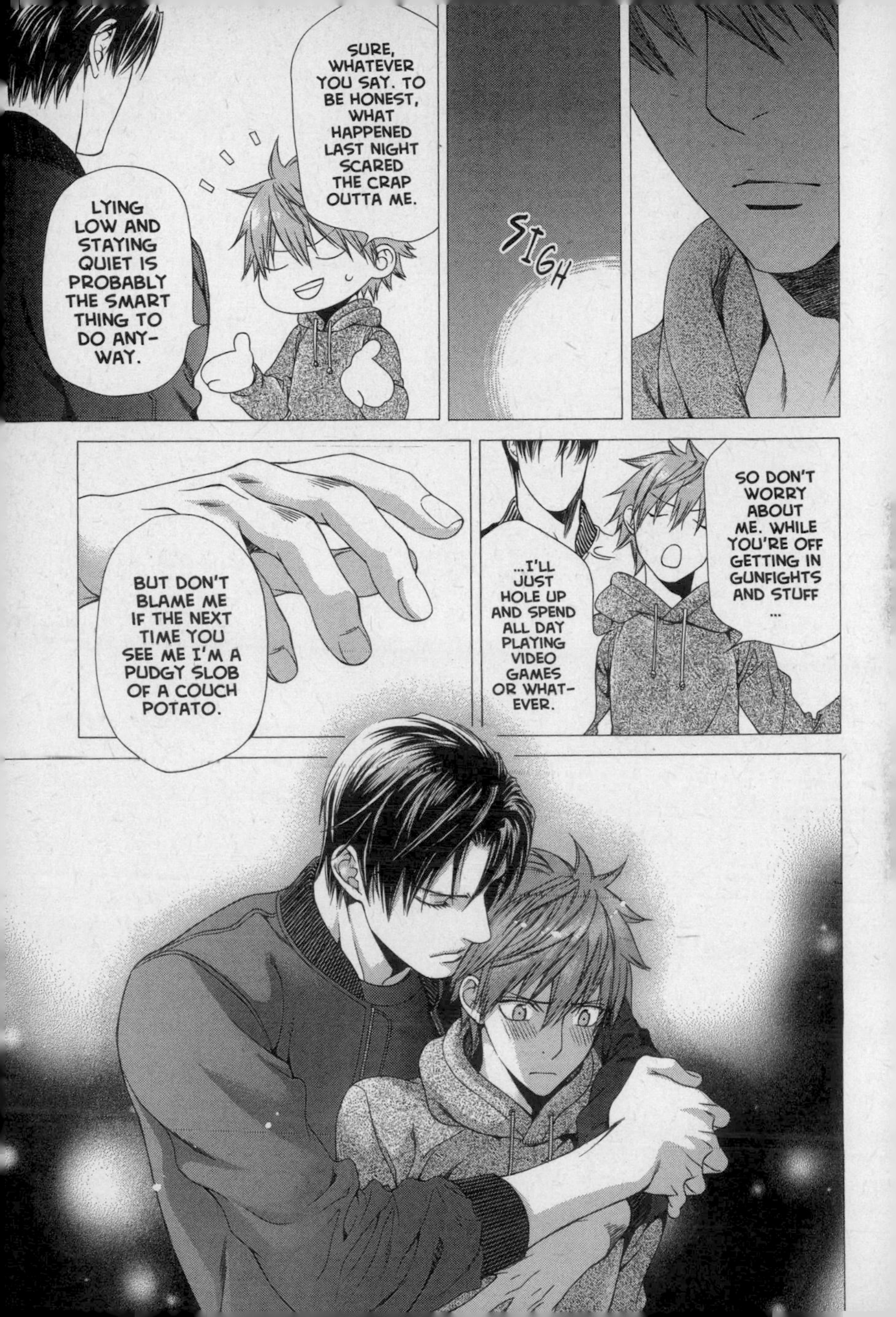
SIGH
SURE, WHATEVER YOU SAY. TO BE HONEST, WHAT HAPPENED LAST NIGHT SCARED THE CRAP OUTTA ME.
LYING LOW AND STAYING QUIET IS PROBABLY THE SMART THING TO DO ANY-WAY.
SO DON'T WORRY ABOUT ME. WHILE YOU'RE OFF GETTING IN GUNFIGHTS AND STUFF ...
...I'LL JUST HOLE UP AND SPEND ALL DAY PLAYING VIDEO GAMES OR WHAT-EVER.
BUT DON'T BLAME ME IF THE NEXT TIME YOU SEE ME I'M A PUDGY SLOB OF A COUCH POTATO.

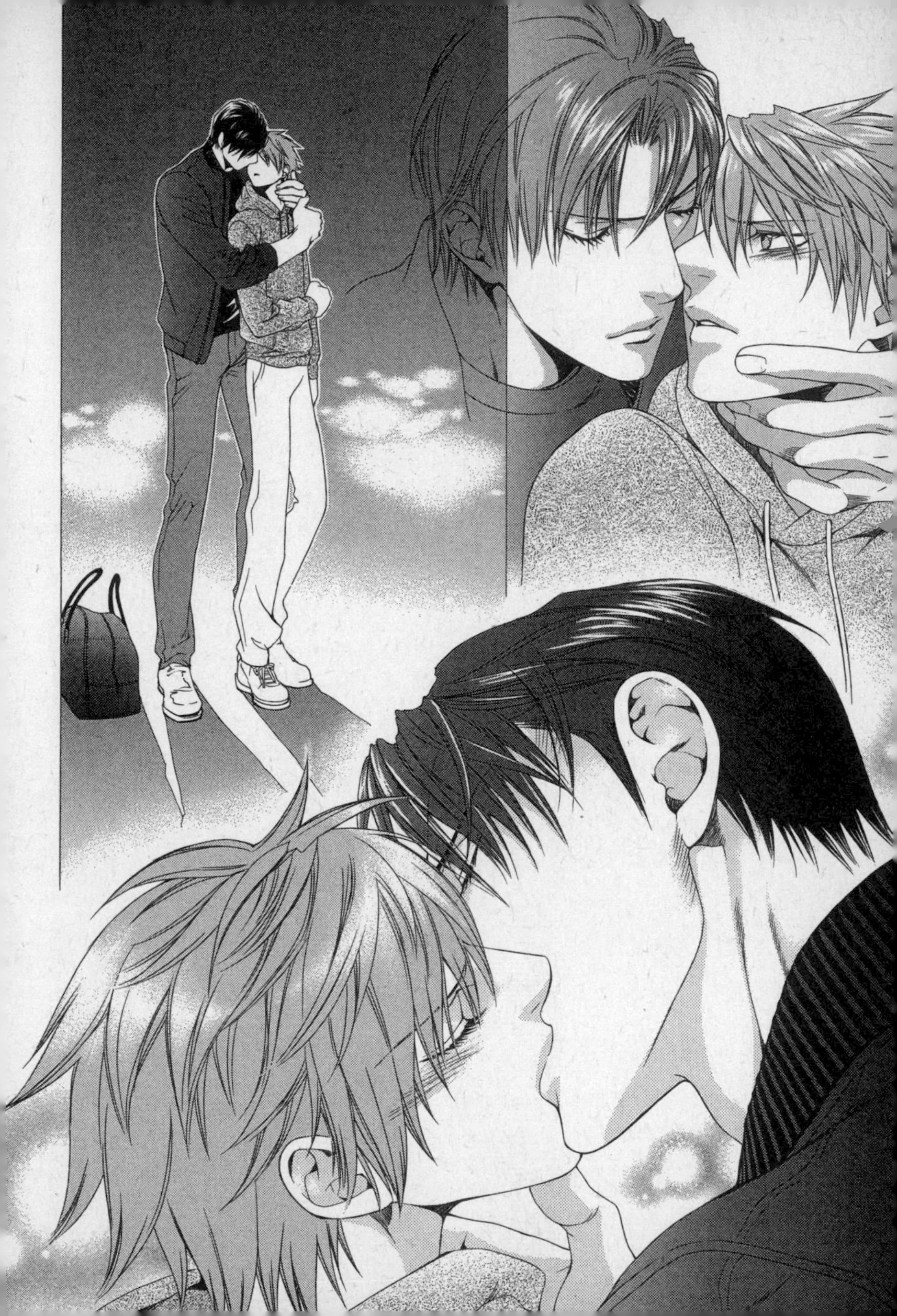

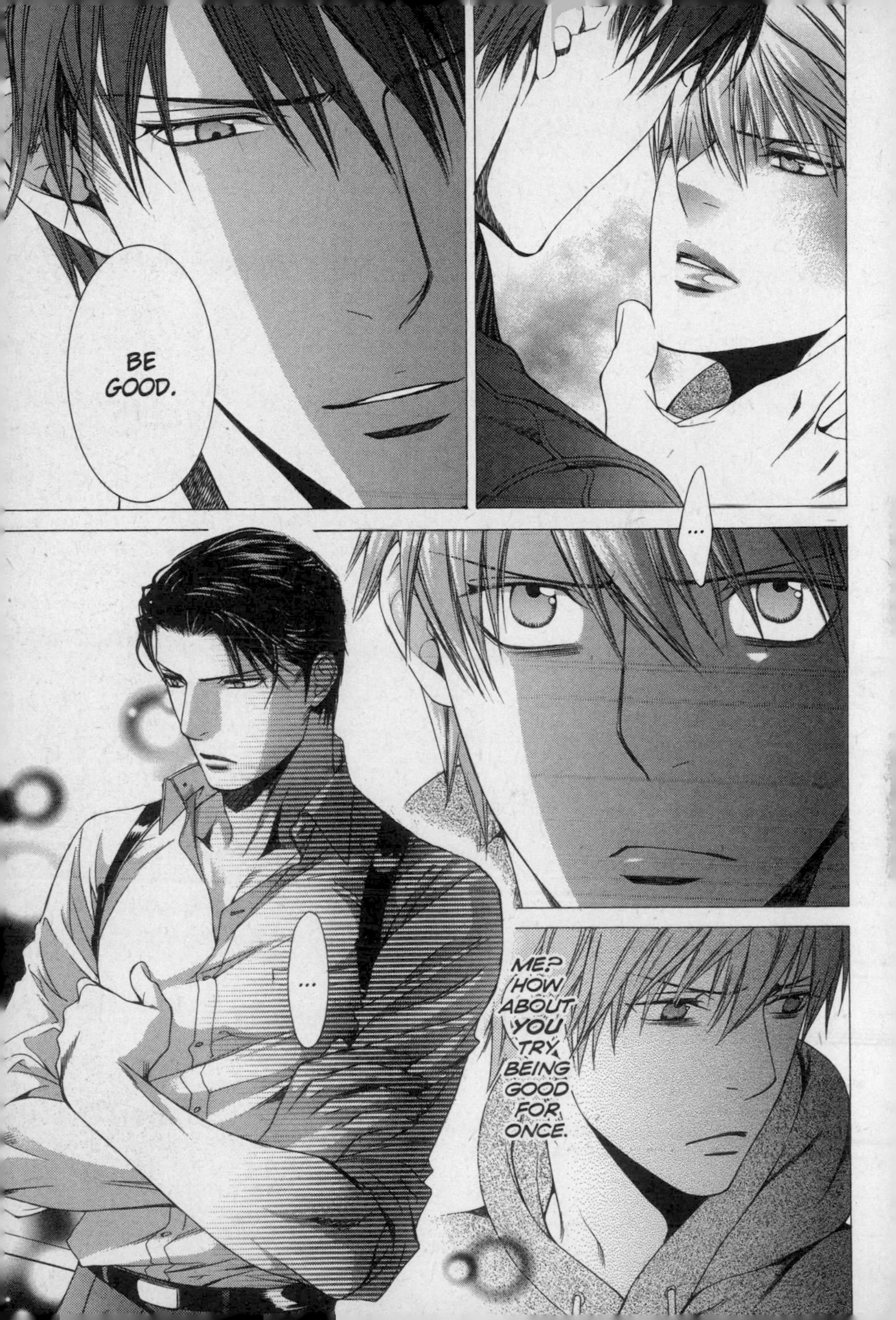
BE GOOD.
...
ME? HOW ABOUT YOU TRY BEING GOOD FOR ONCE.
...

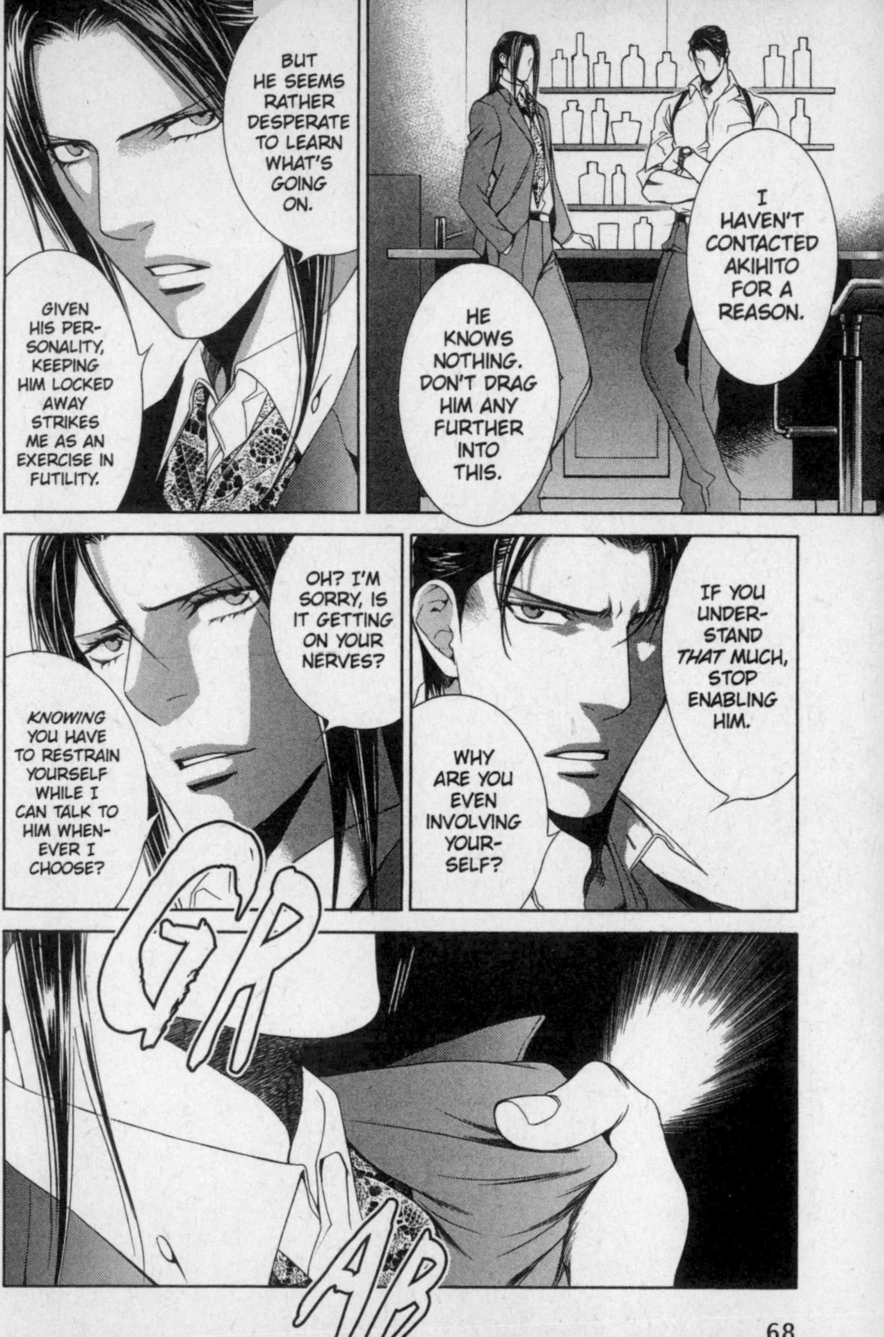

I HAVEN'T CONTACTED AKIHITO FOR A REASON.
HE KNOWS NOTHING. DON'T DRAG HIM ANY FURTHER INTO THIS.
BUT HE SEEMS RATHER DESPERATE TO LEARN WHAT'S GOING ON.
GIVEN HIS PER-SONALITY, KEEPING HIM LOCKED AWAY STRIKES ME AS AN EXERCISE IN FUTILITY.
IF YOU UNDER-STAND *THAT* MUCH, STOP ENABLING HIM.
WHY ARE YOU EVEN INVOLVING YOUR-SELF?
OH? I'M SORRY, IS IT GETTING ON YOUR NERVES?
KNOWING YOU HAVE TO RESTRAIN YOURSELF WHILE I CAN TALK TO HIM WHEN-EVER I CHOOSE?
GRAB

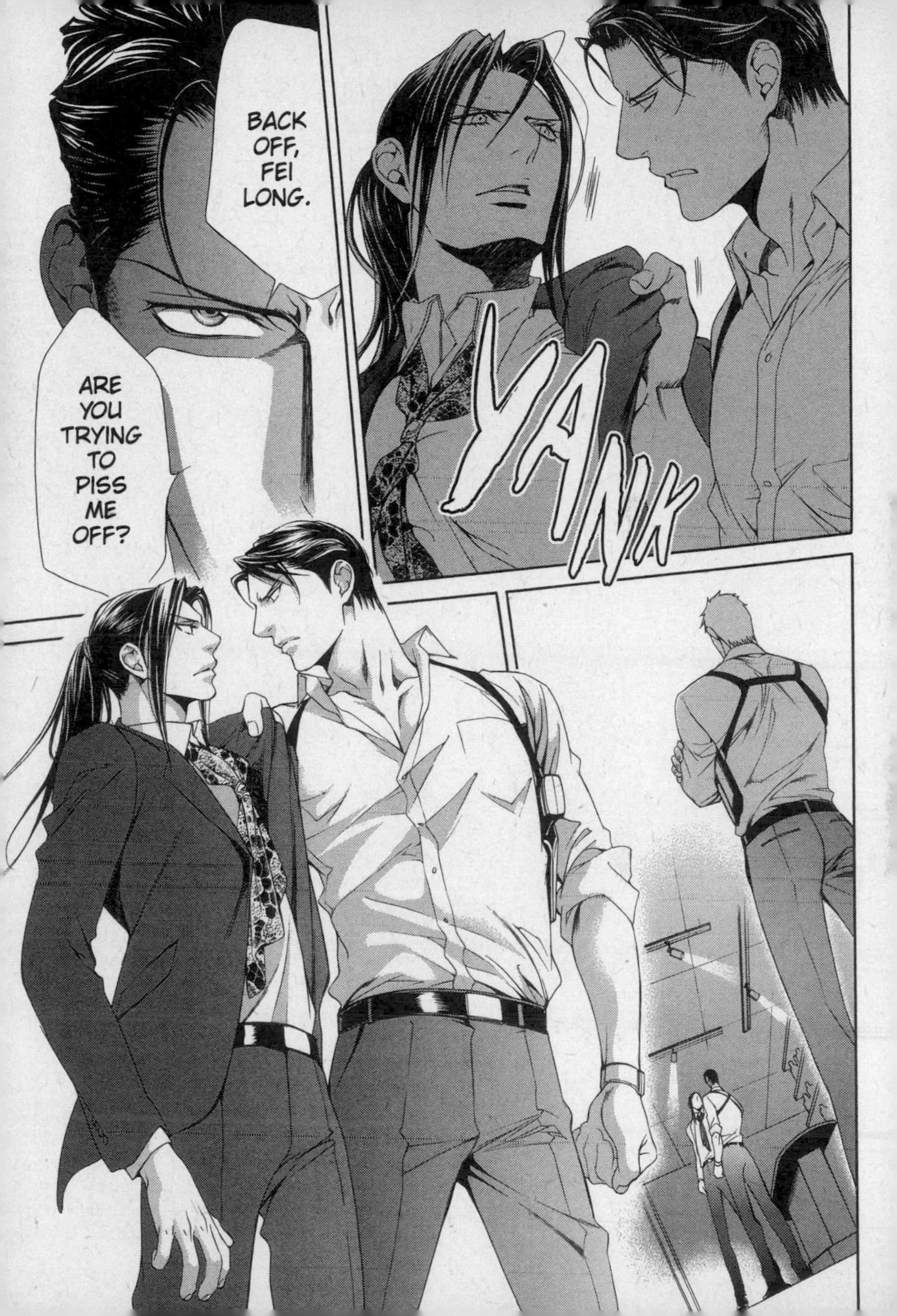
YANK
BACK OFF, FEI LONG.
ARE YOU TRYING TO PISS ME OFF?

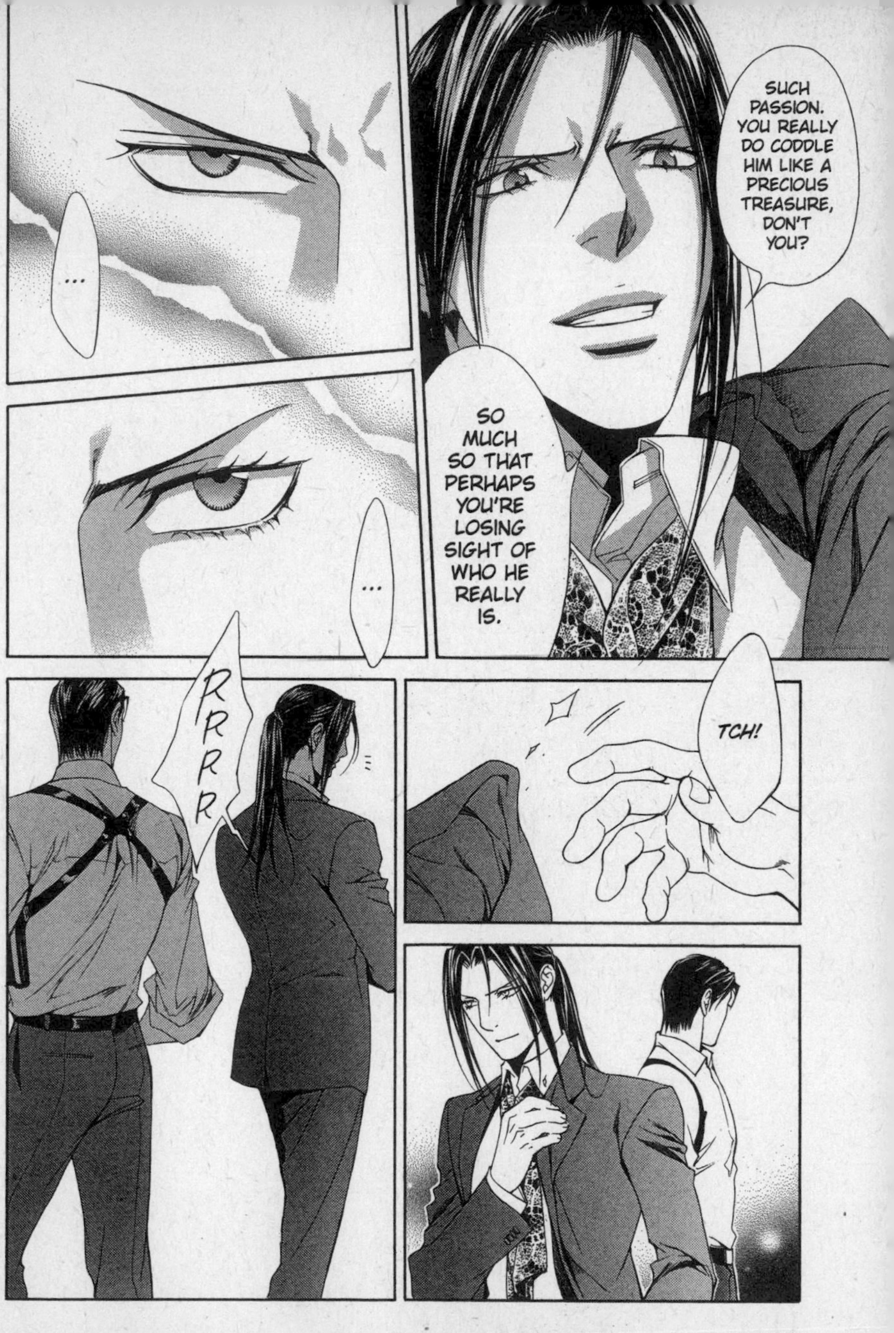
SUCH PASSION. YOU REALLY DO CODDLE HIM LIKE A PRECIOUS TREASURE, DON'T YOU?
SO MUCH SO THAT PERHAPS YOU'RE LOSING SIGHT OF WHO HE REALLY IS.
...
...
TCH!
RRRR

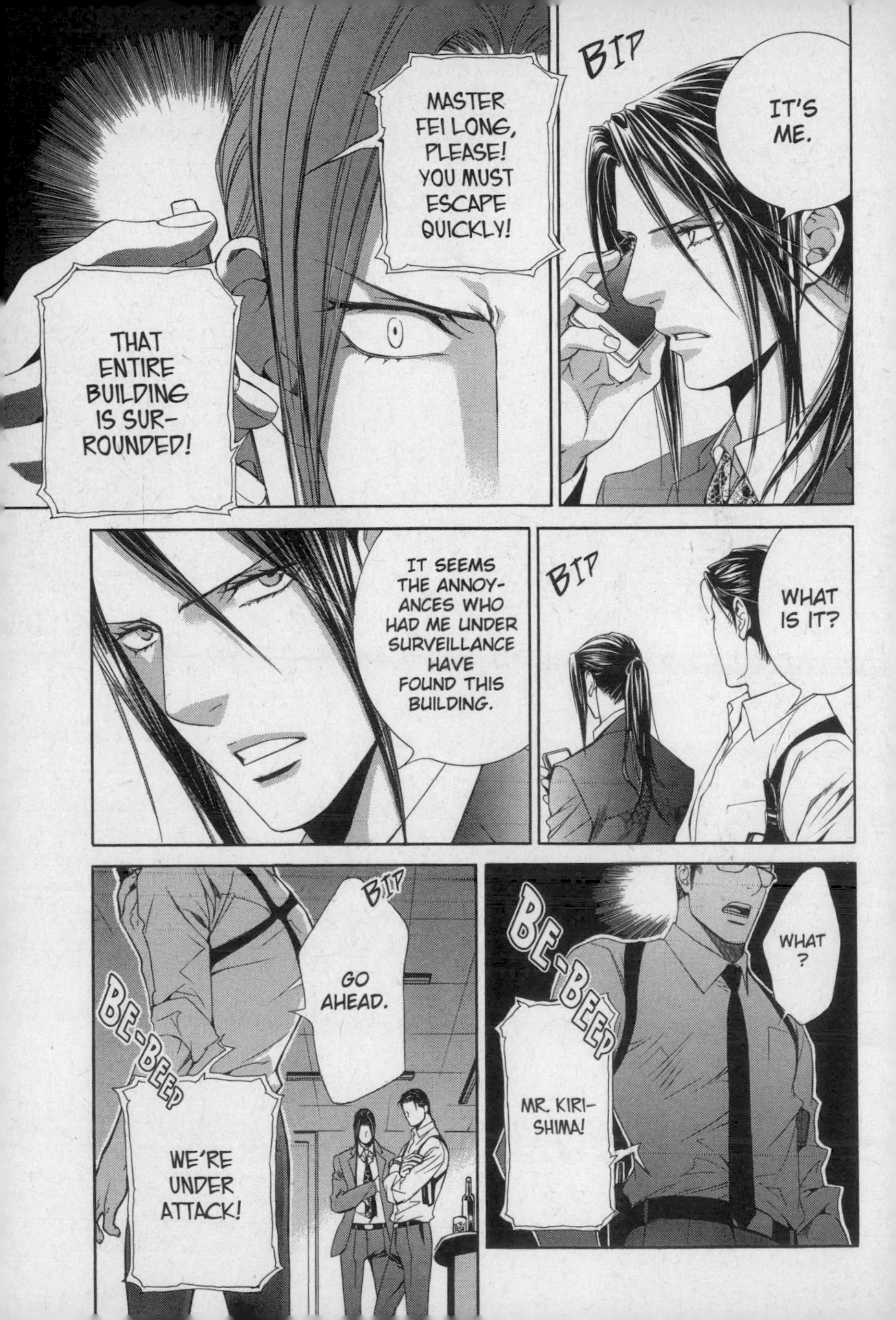
BIP
IT'S ME.
MASTER FEI LONG, PLEASE! YOU MUST ESCAPE QUICKLY!
THAT ENTIRE BUILDING IS SUR-ROUNDED!
BIP
WHAT IS IT?
IT SEEMS THE ANNOY-ANCES WHO HAD ME UNDER SURVEILLANCE HAVE FOUND THIS BUILDING.
BE-BEEP
WHAT?
MR. KIRI-SHIMA!
BIP
GO AHEAD.
BE-BEEP
WE'RE UNDER ATTACK!

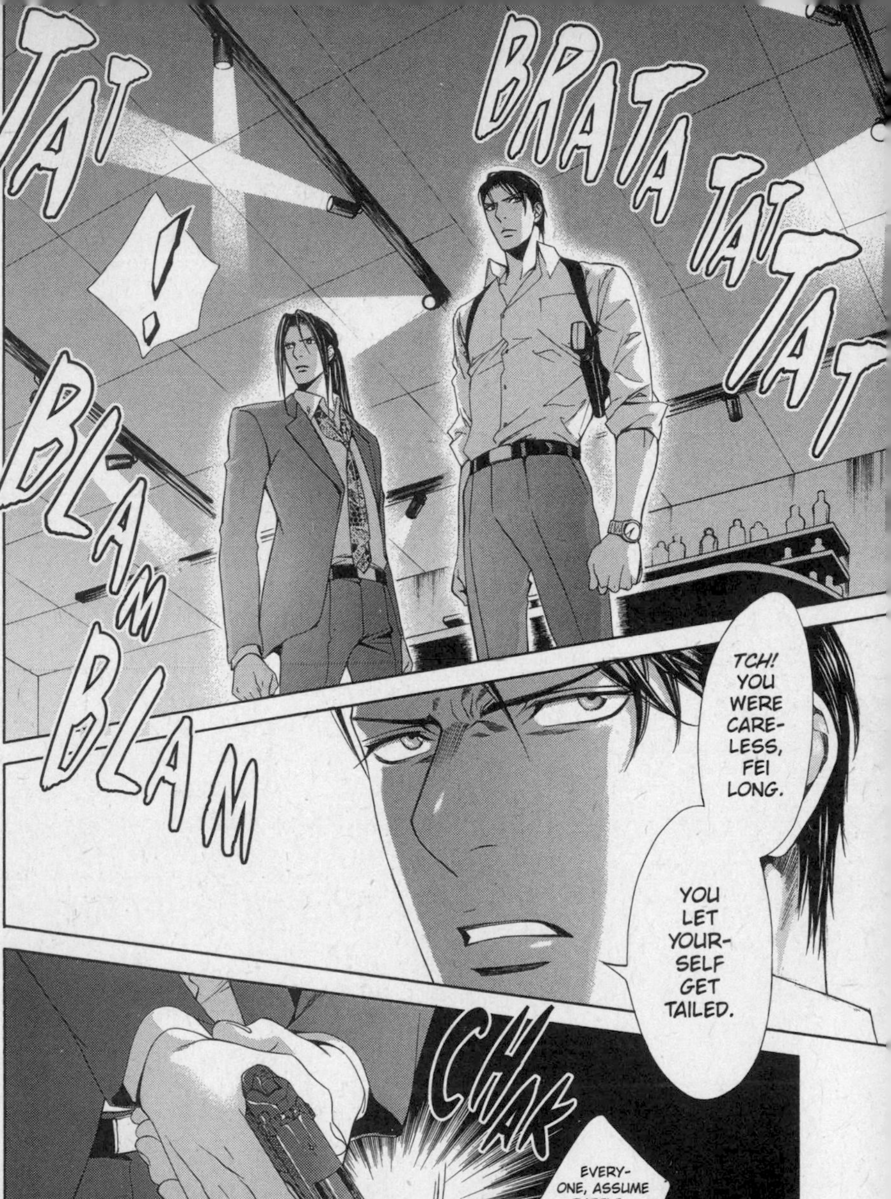
BRATA TATATAT
!
TAT
BLAM BLAM BLAM
TCH! YOU WERE CARE-LESS, FEI LONG.
YOU LET YOUR-SELF GET TAILED.
CHAK
EVERY-ONE, ASSUME BATTLE POSITIONS! PROTECT MASTER ASAMI AT ALL COSTS!

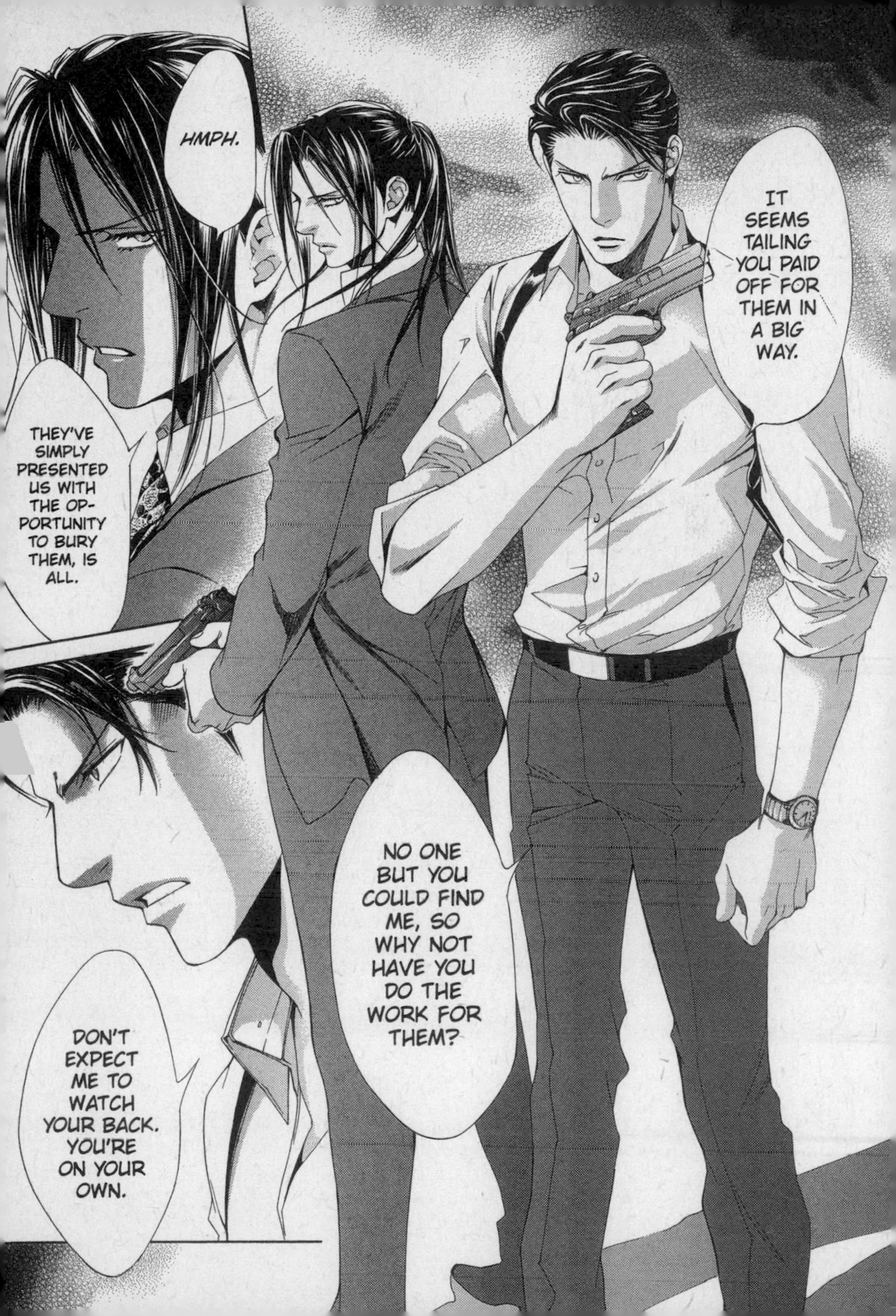
IT SEEMS TAILING YOU PAID OFF FOR THEM IN A BIG WAY.
NO ONE BUT YOU COULD FIND ME, SO WHY NOT HAVE YOU DO THE WORK FOR THEM?
HMPH.
THEY'VE SIMPLY PRESENTED US WITH THE OP-PORTUNITY TO BURY THEM, IS ALL.
DON'T EXPECT ME TO WATCH YOUR BACK. YOU'RE ON YOUR OWN.

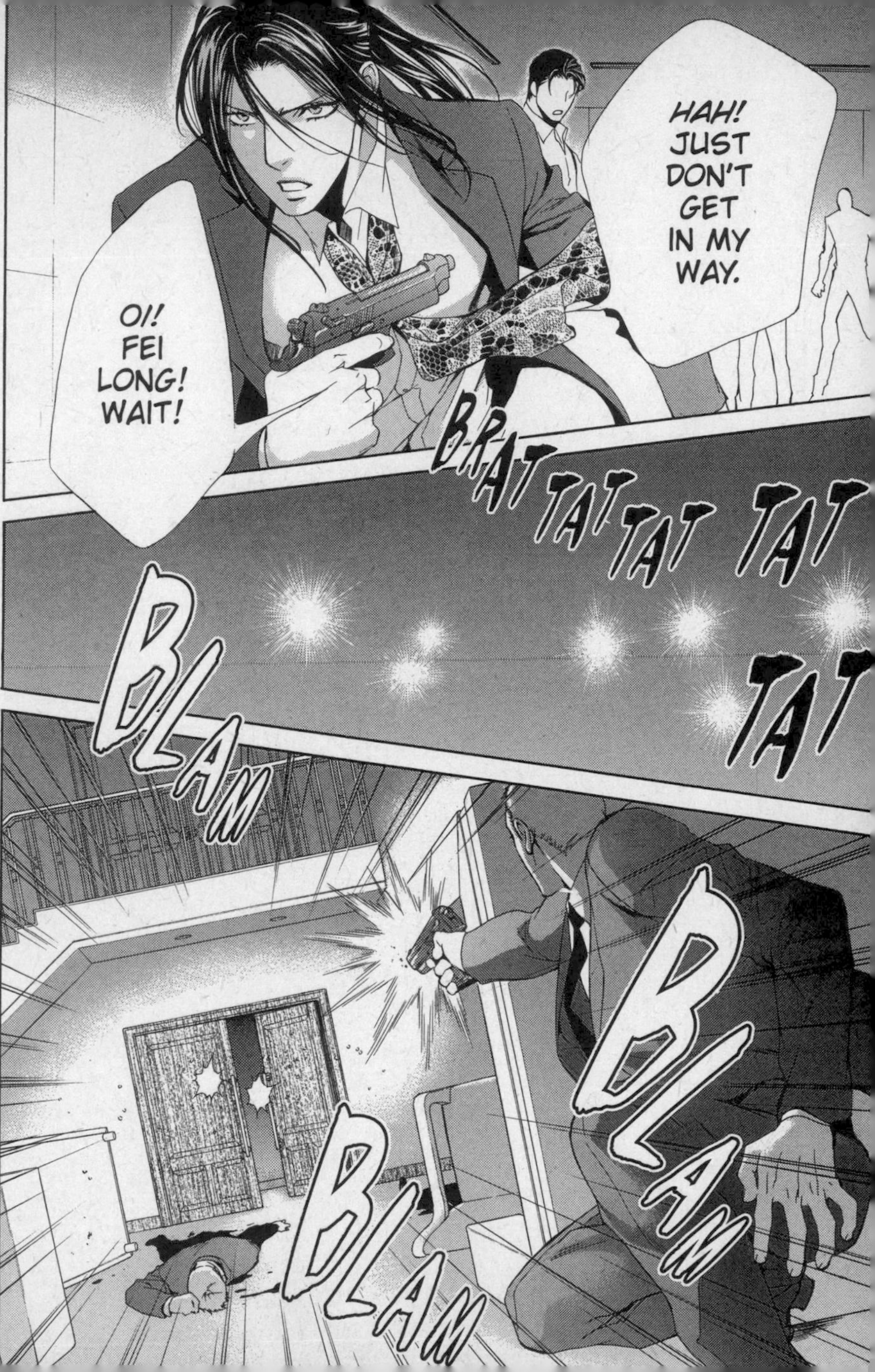
HAH! JUST DON'T GET IN MY WAY.
OI! FEI LONG! WAIT!
BRAT TAT TAT TAT
TAT TAT
BLAM
BLAM
BLAM
BLAM

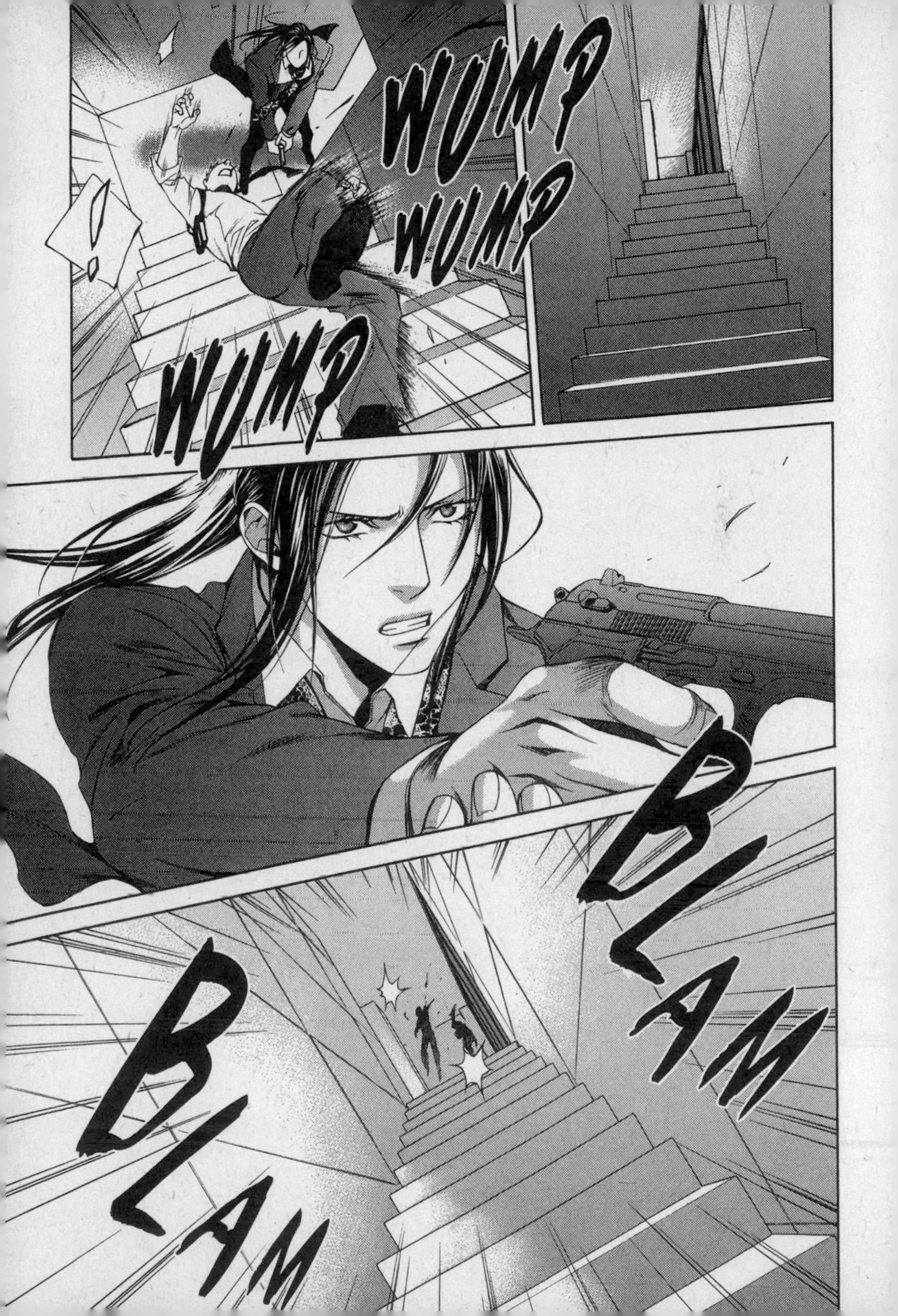
WUMP
WUMP
!
WUMP
BLAM
BLAM

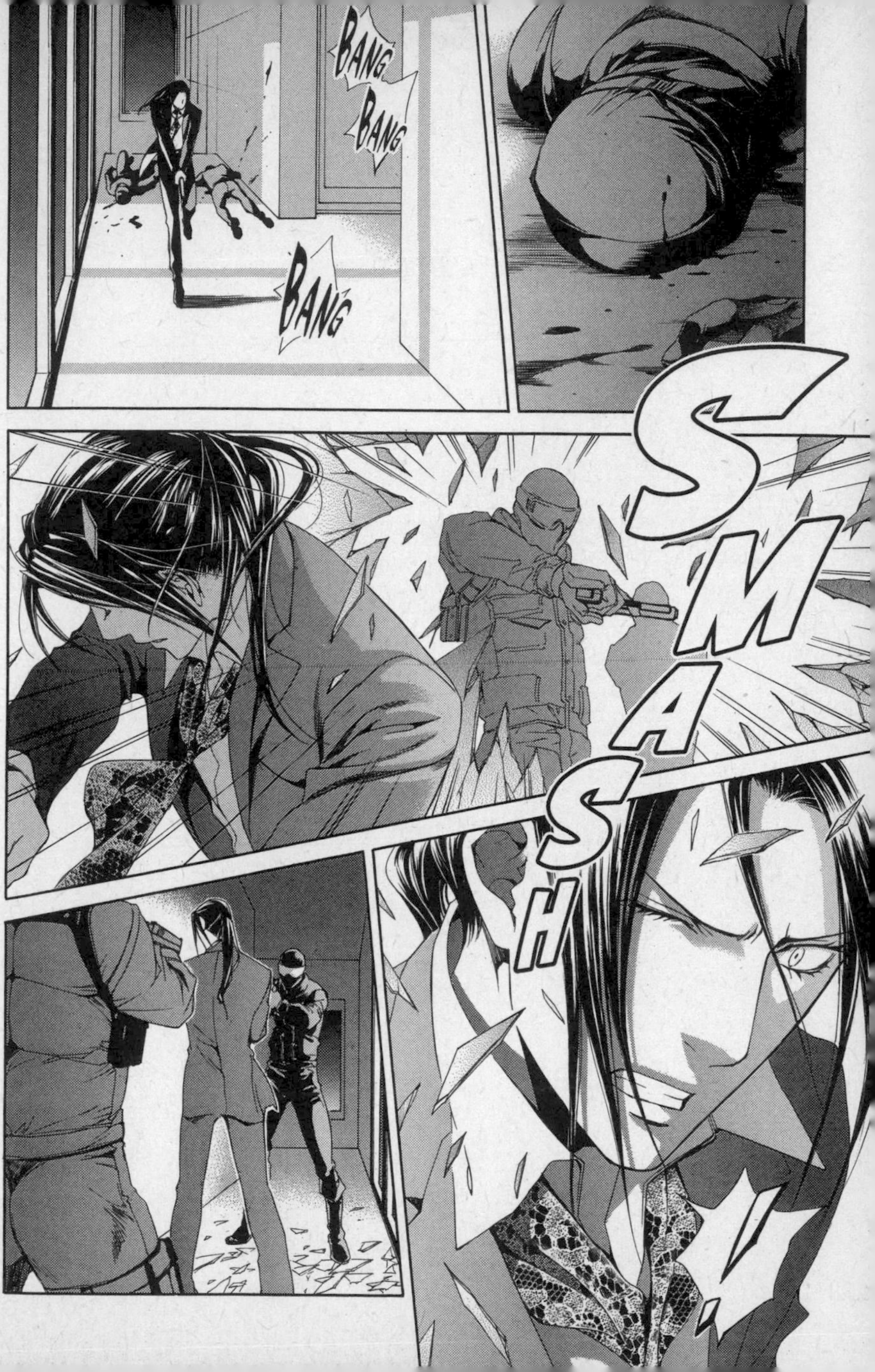
BANG BANG
BANG
SMASH

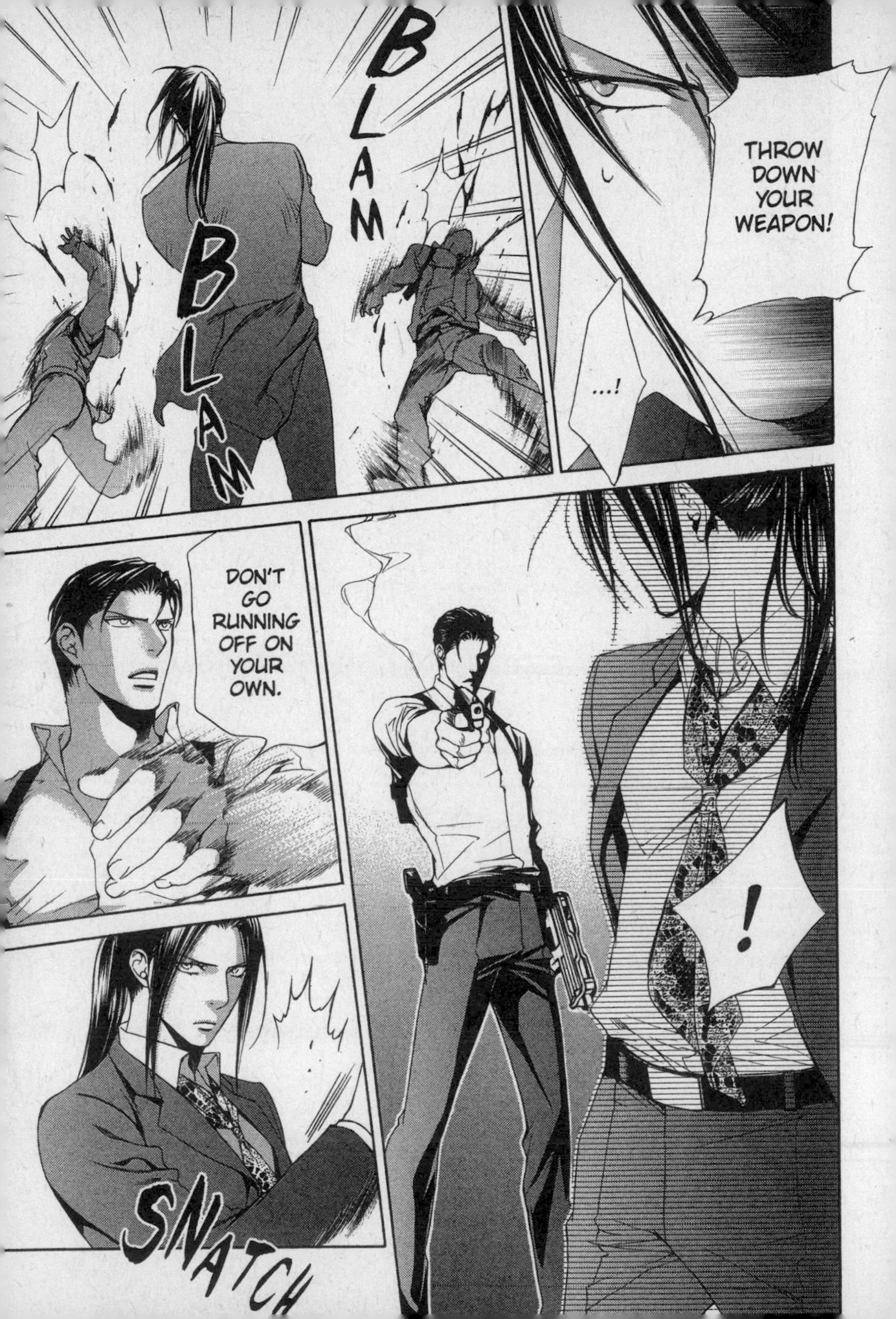
THROW DOWN YOUR WEAPON!
...!
BLAM
BLAM
!
DON'T GO RUNNING OFF ON YOUR OWN.
SNATCH

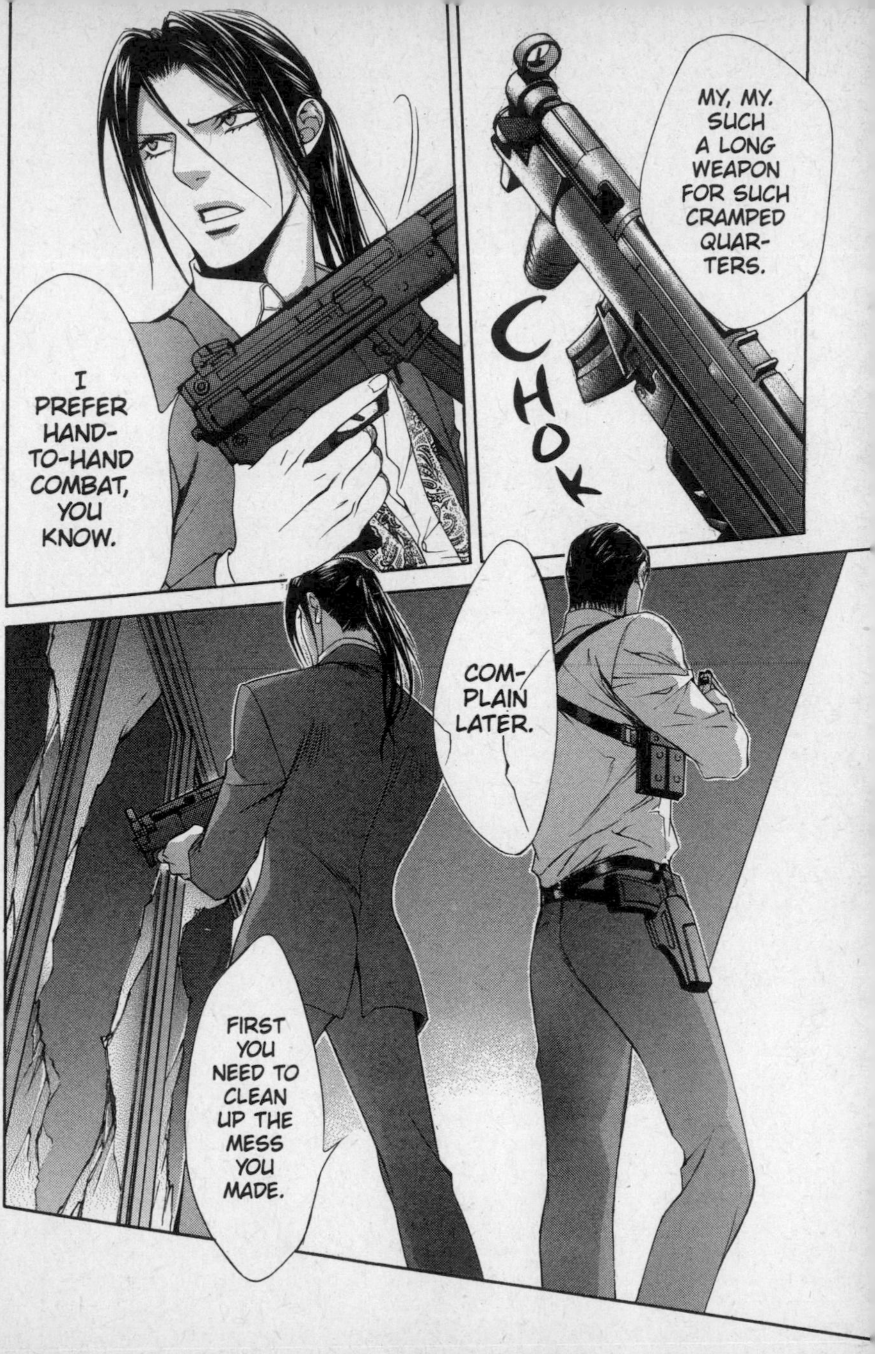
MY, MY. SUCH A LONG WEAPON FOR SUCH CRAMPED QUAR-TERS.
CHOK
I PREFER HAND-TO-HAND COMBAT, YOU KNOW.
COM-PLAIN LATER.
FIRST YOU NEED TO CLEAN UP THE MESS YOU MADE.

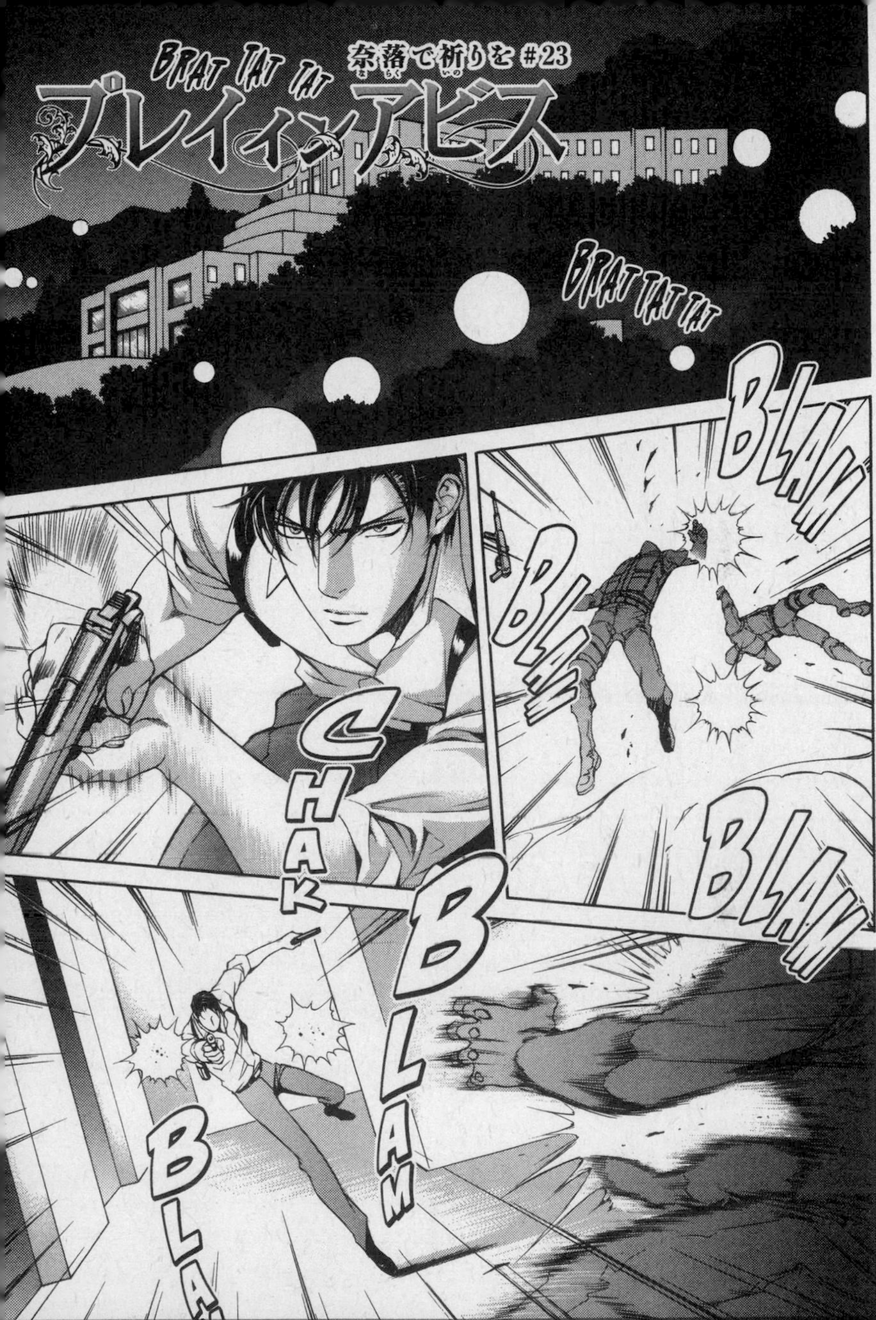
奈落で祈りを #23
プレイインアビス
BRAT TAT TAT
BRAT TAT TAT
BLAM
BLAM
BLAM
CHAK
BLAM
BLAM

Pray in the Abyss

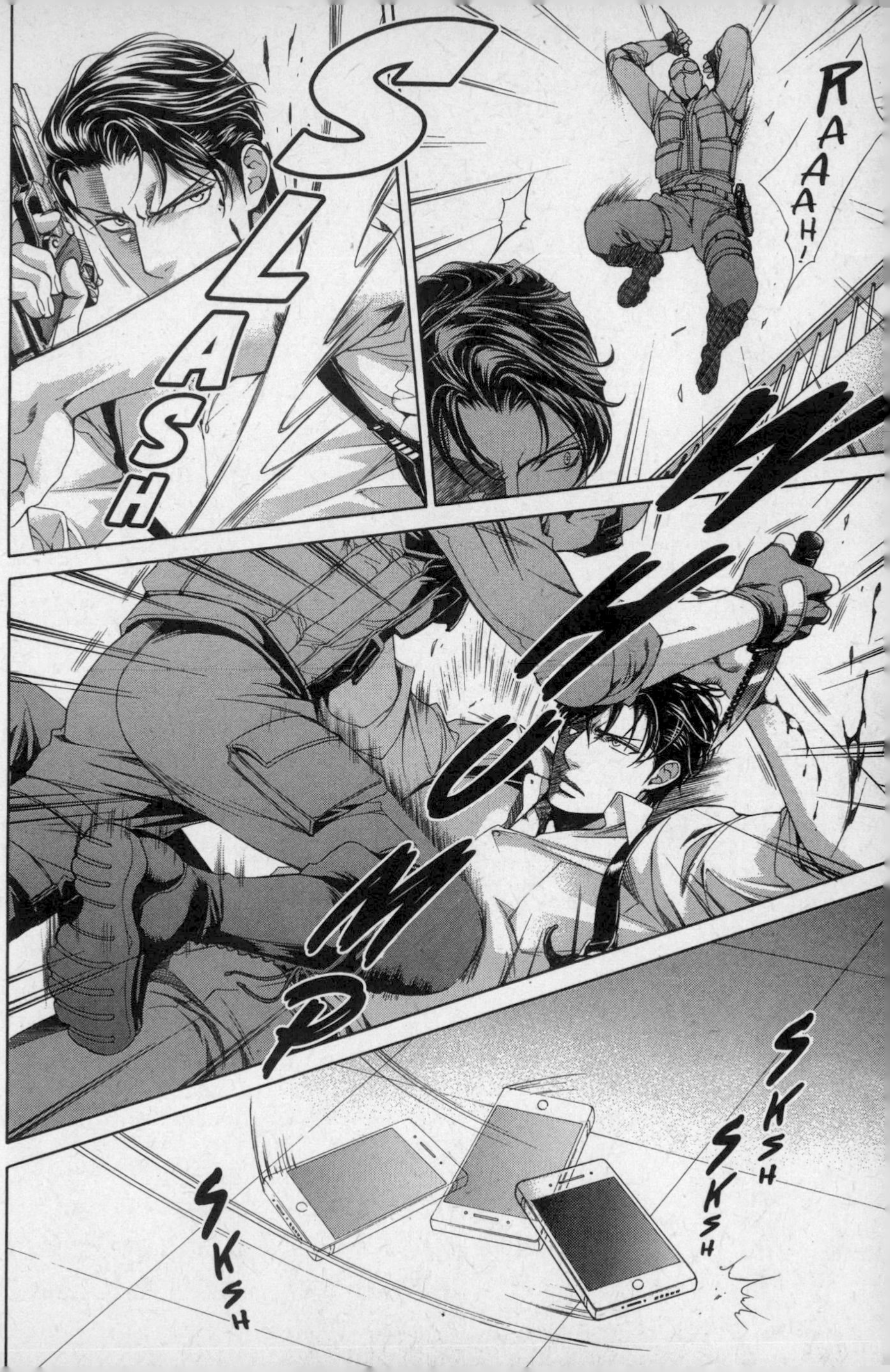
RAAAAH!
SLASH
WHUMP
SKSH
SKSH
SKSH

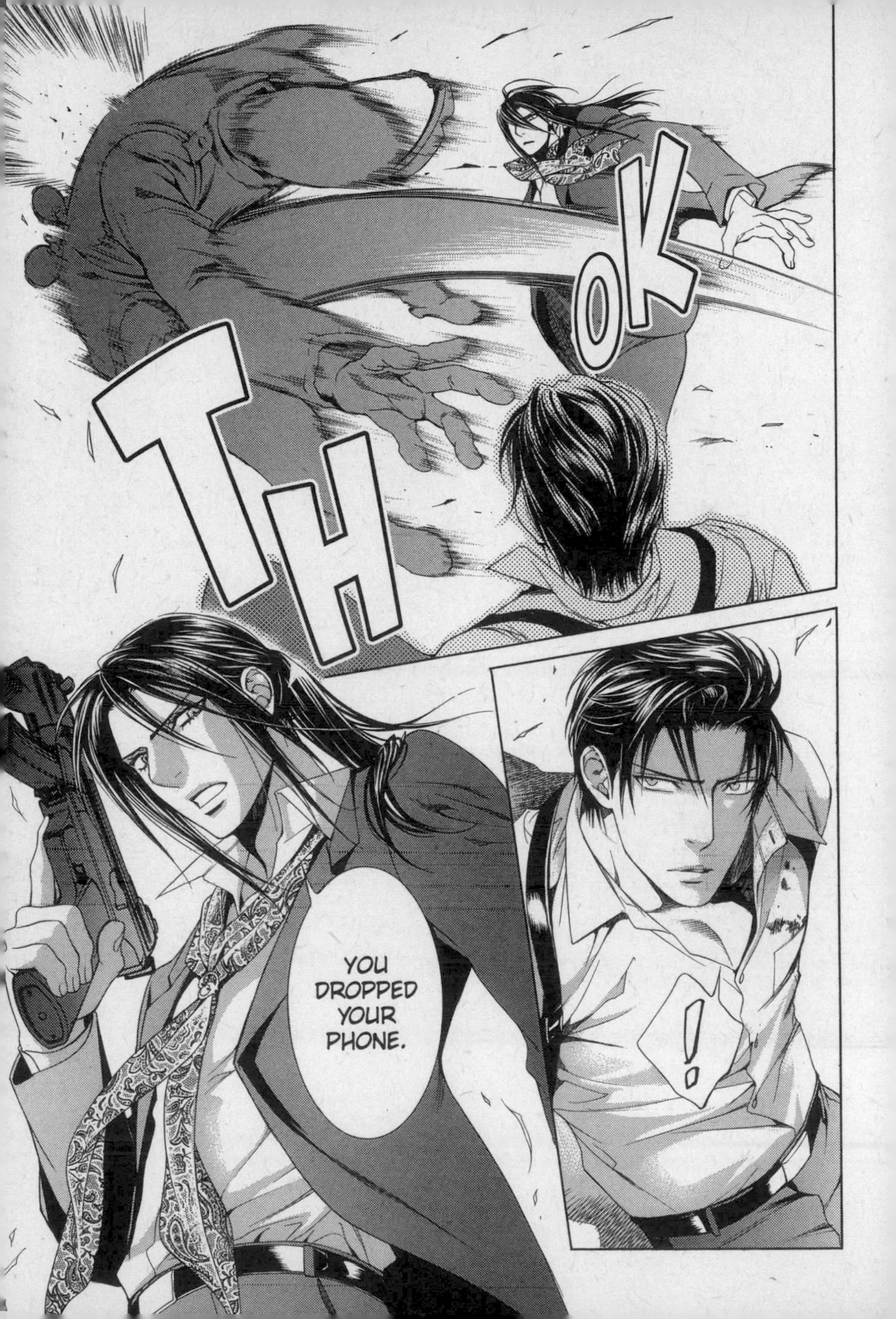
THOK
!
YOU DROPPED YOUR PHONE.

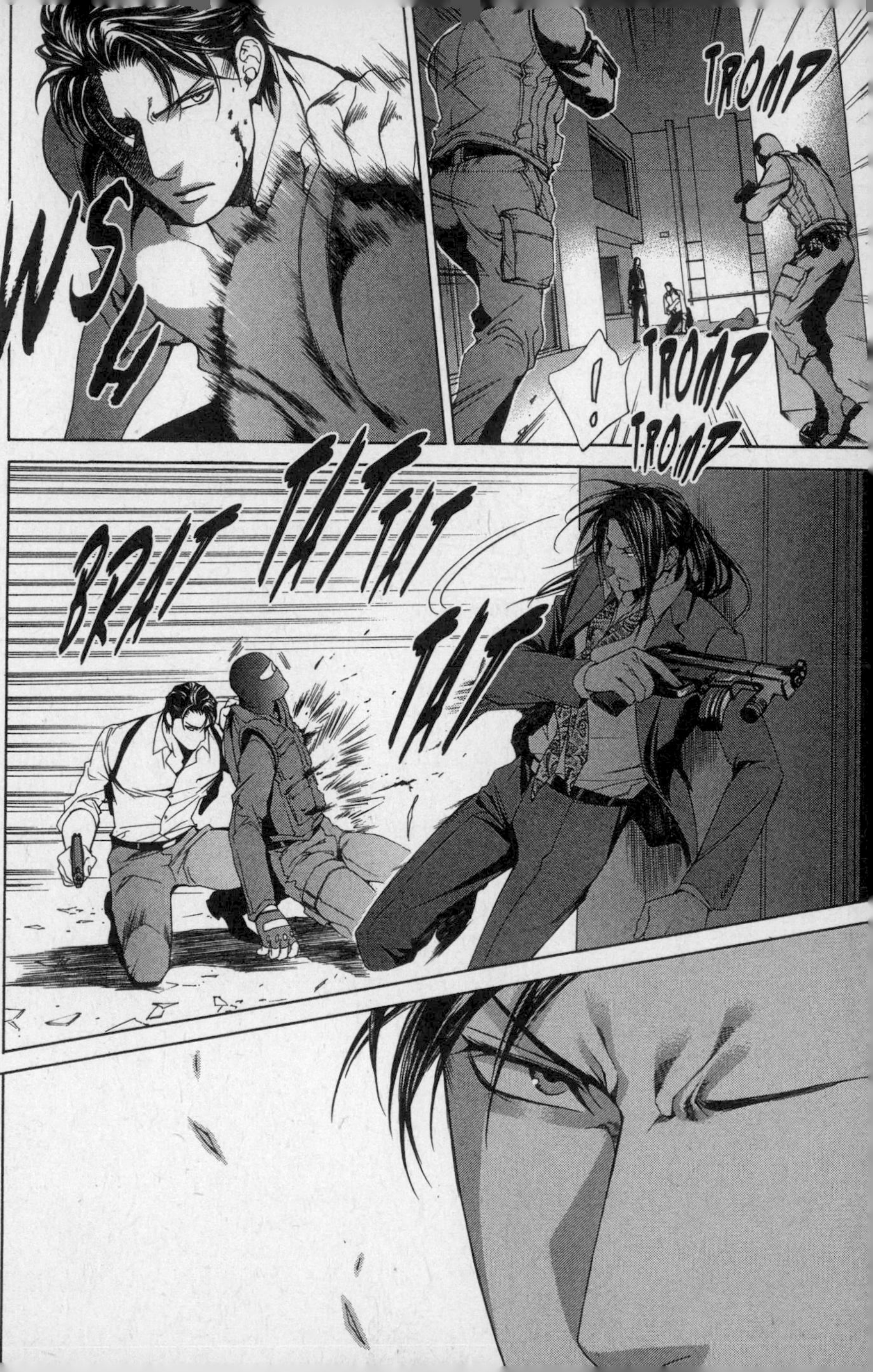
TROMP
!
TROMP
TROMP
WSH
BRAT
TATATAT
TAT

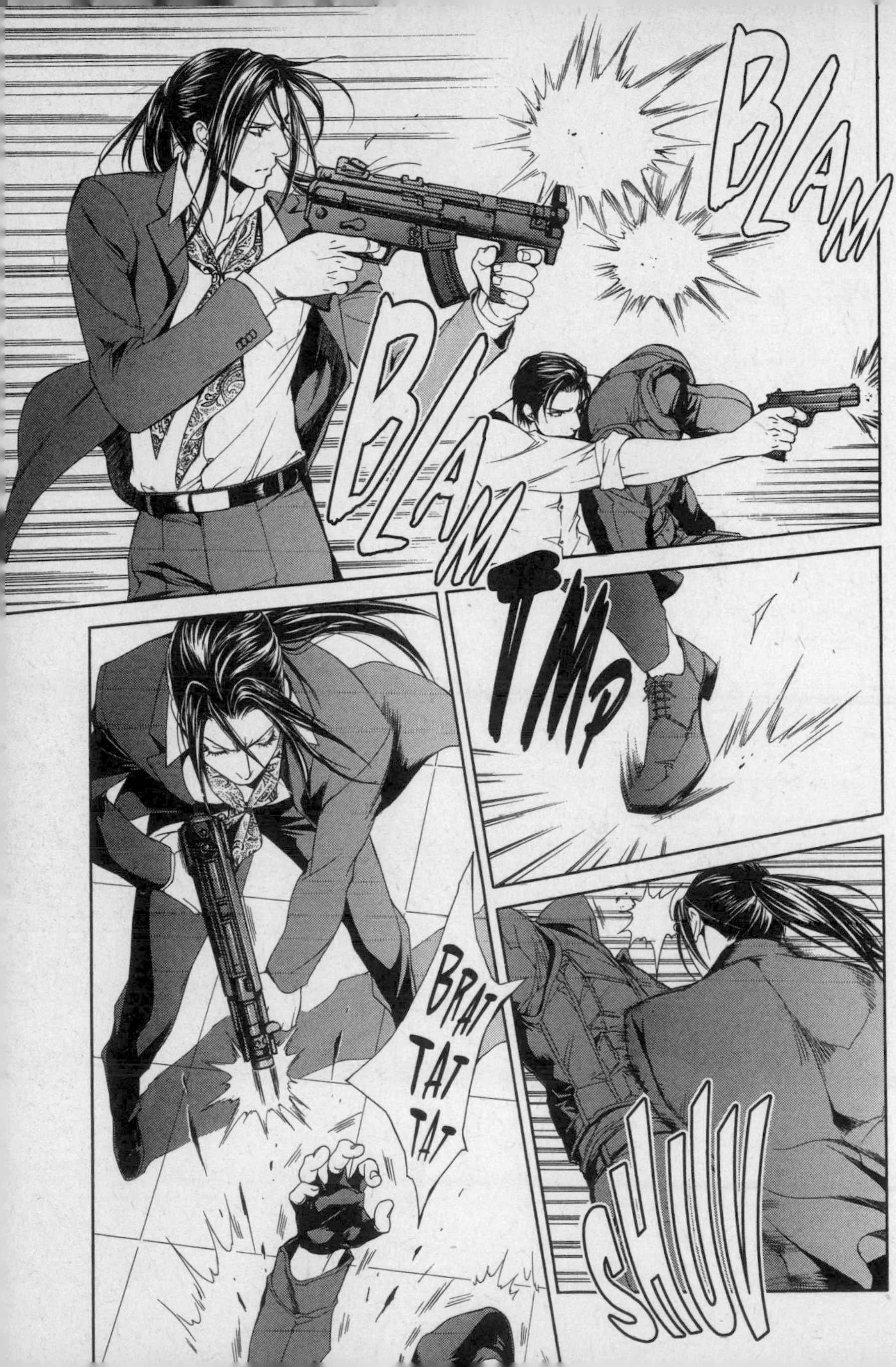
BLAM
BLAM
TMP
SHUUU
BRAT
TAT
TAT

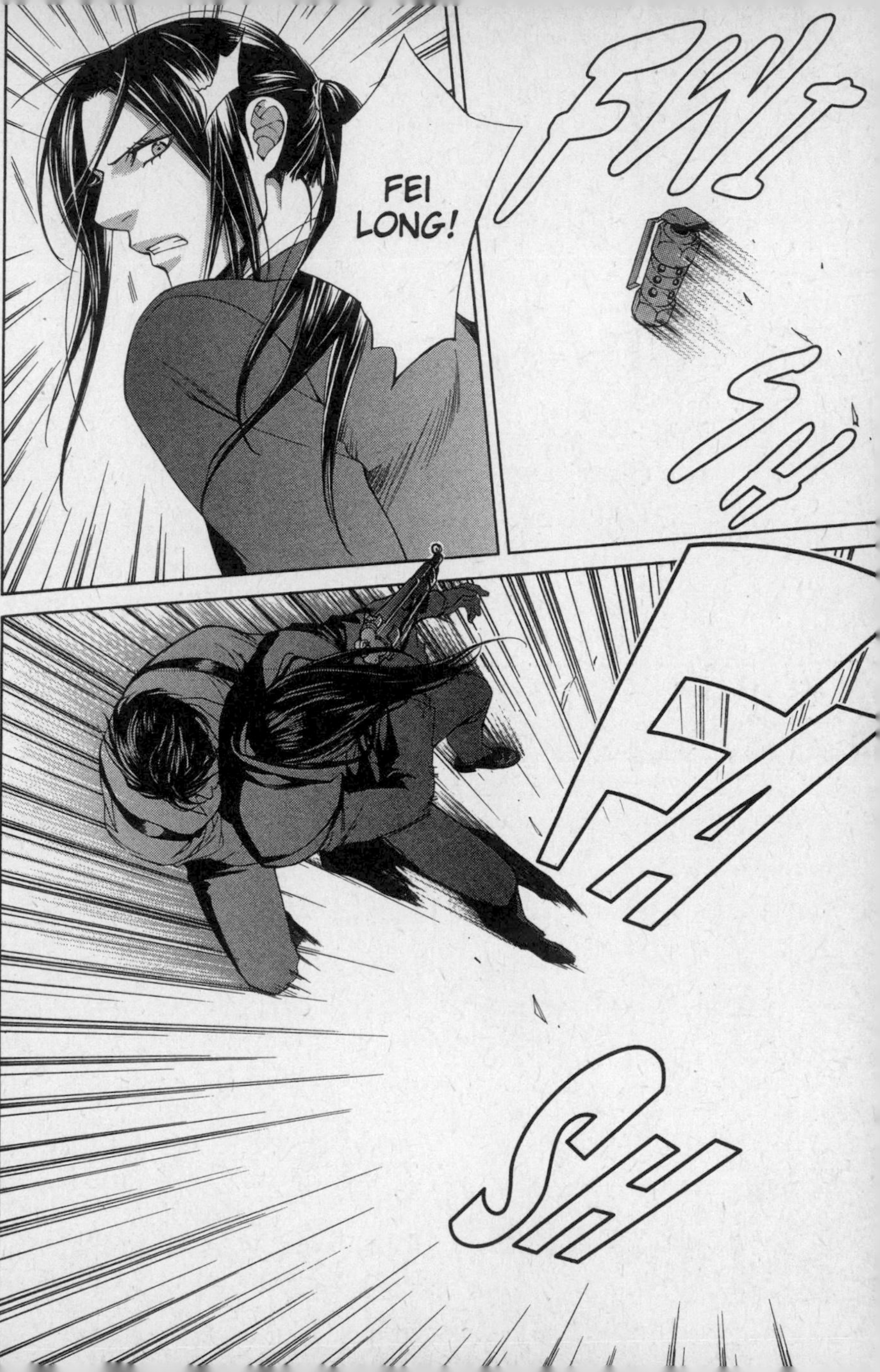
FEI LONG!
SH

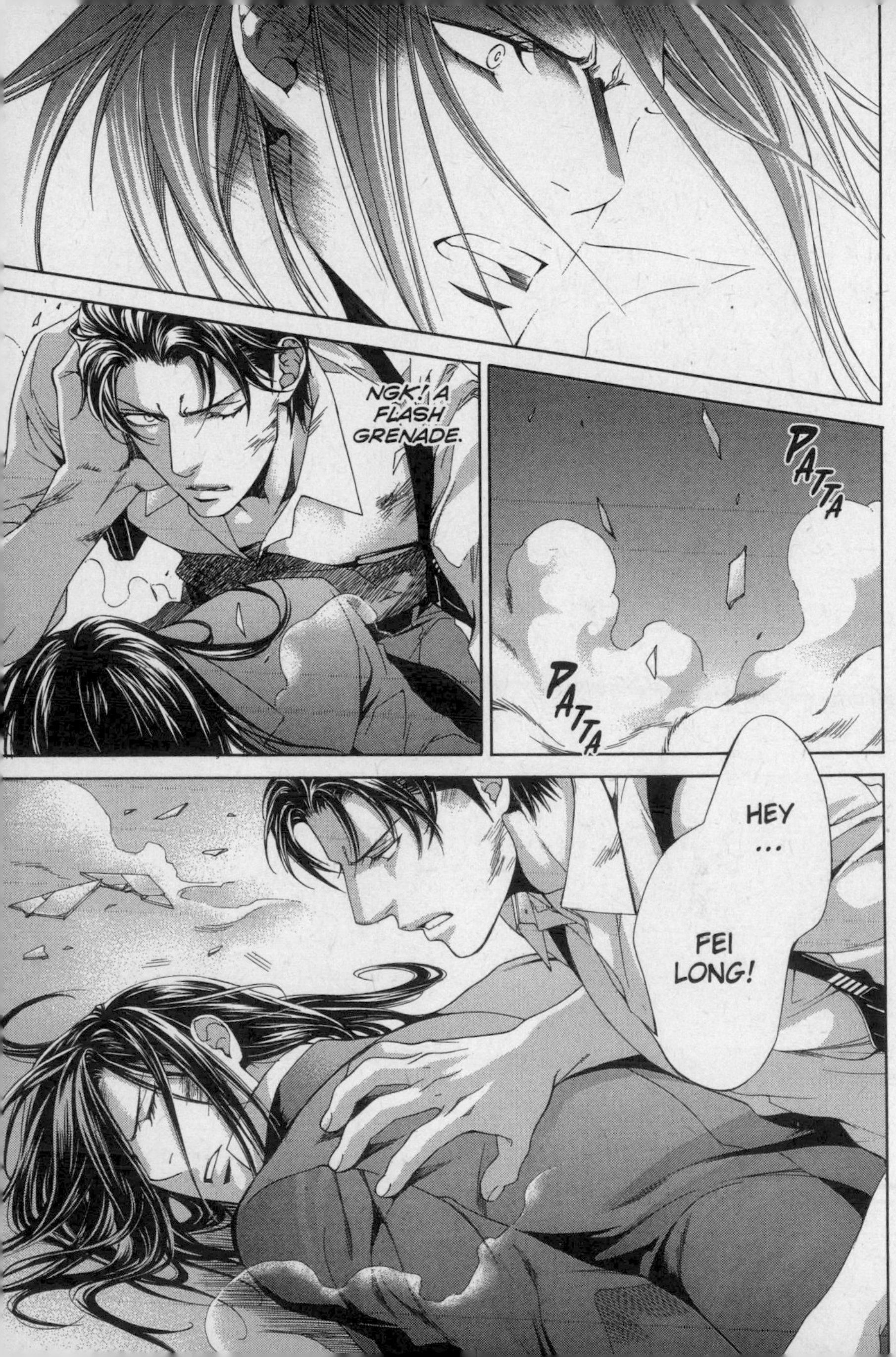
PATTA
PATTA
NGK! A FLASH GRENADE.
HEY ...
FEI LONG!

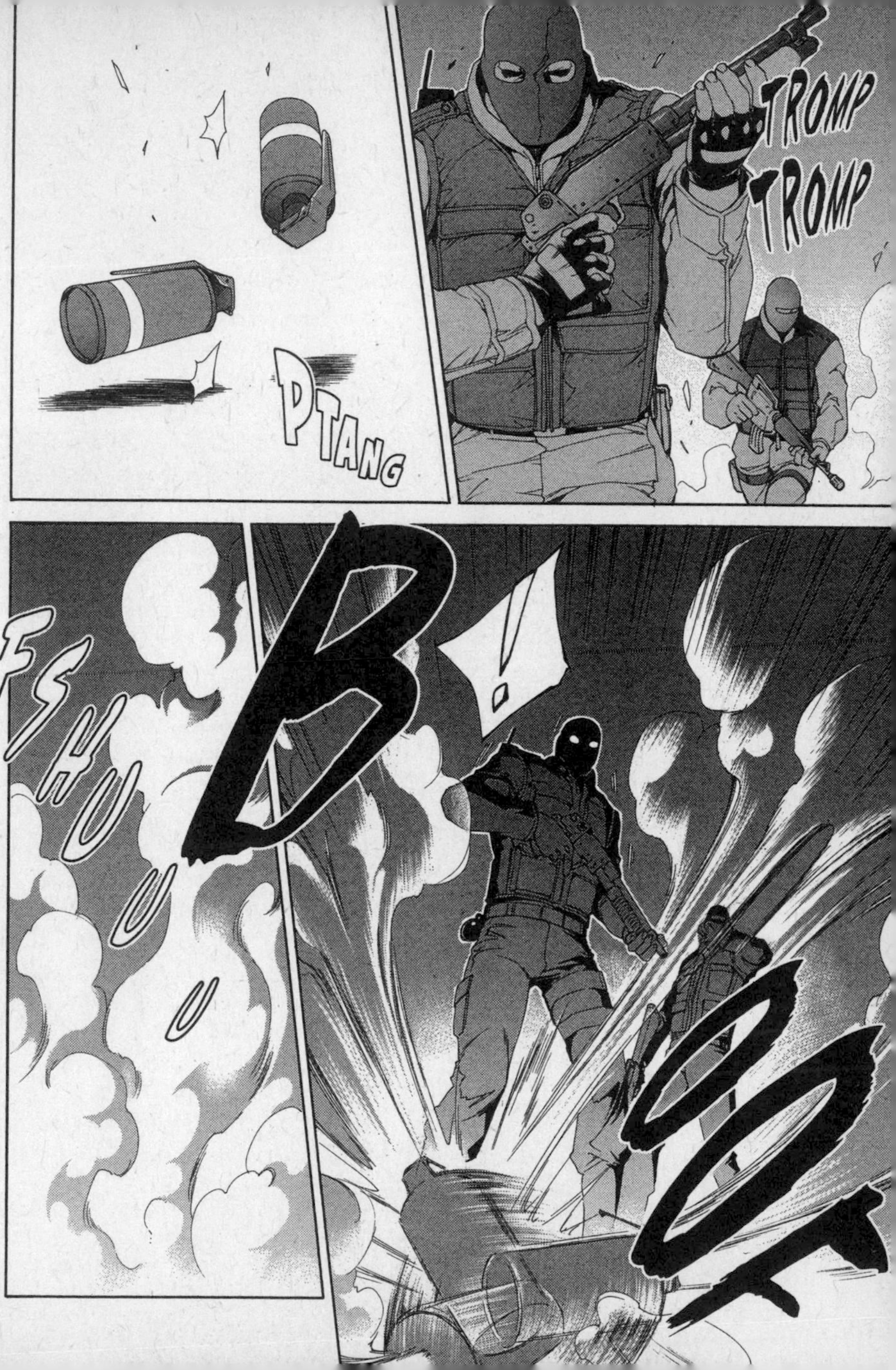
TROMP
TROMP
PTANG
B
!
OOT
FSHUUUU

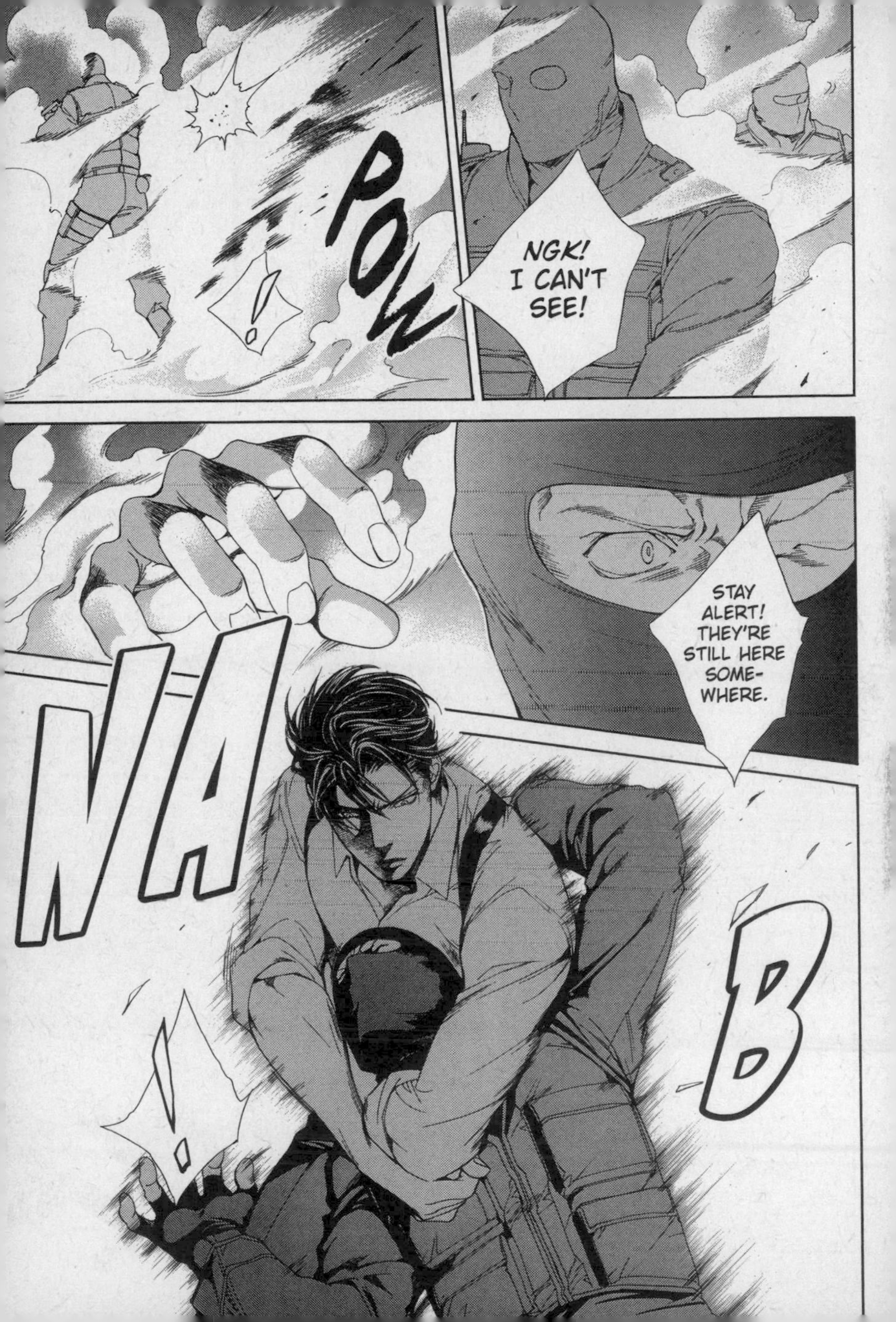
NGK! I CAN'T SEE!
POW
!
STAY ALERT! THEY'RE STILL HERE SOME-WHERE.
NAB
!

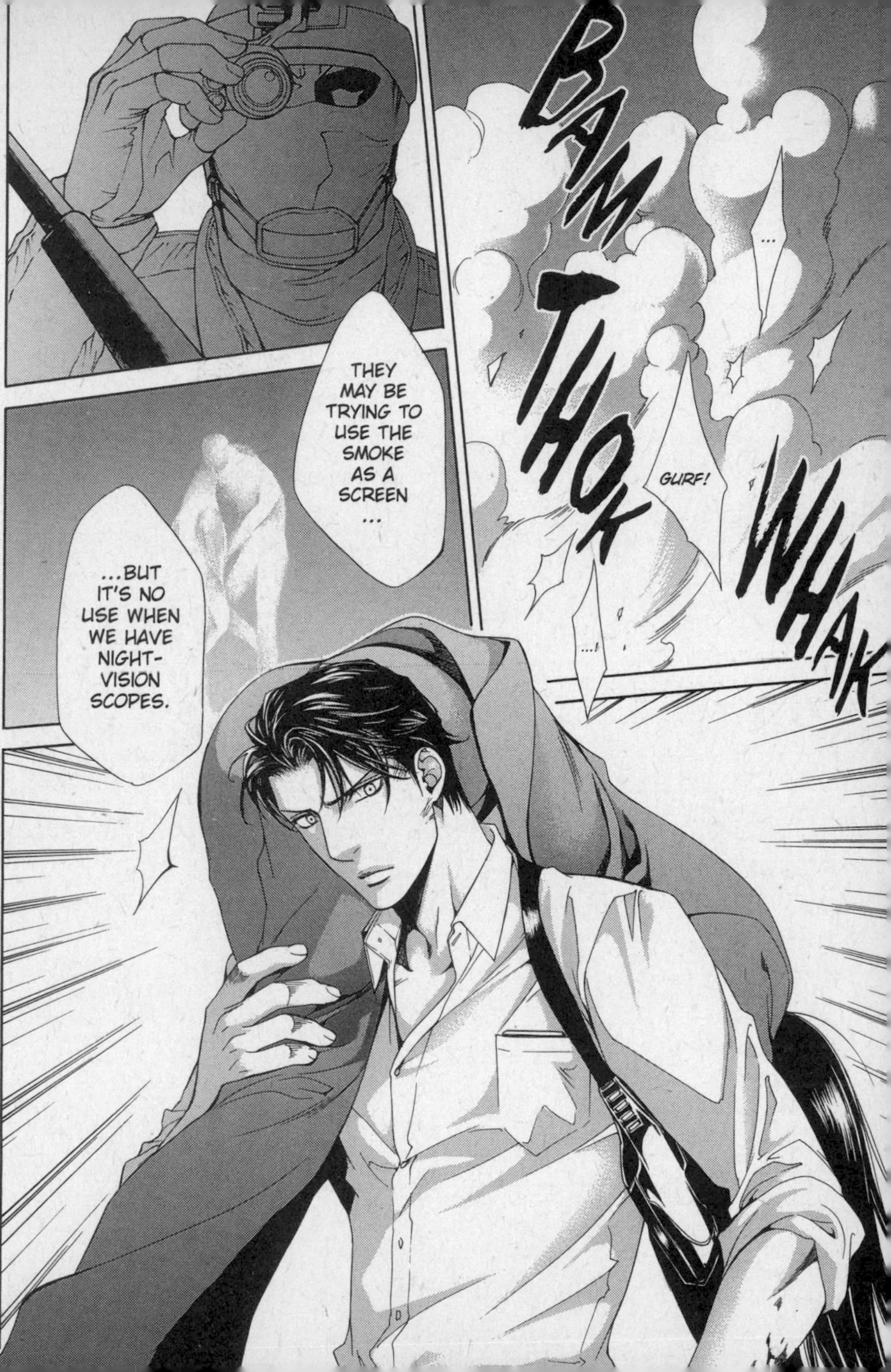
BAM
...
THOK
GURF!
WHAK
...!
THEY MAY BE TRYING TO USE THE SMOKE AS A SCREEN...
...BUT IT'S NO USE WHEN WE HAVE NIGHT-VISION SCOPES.

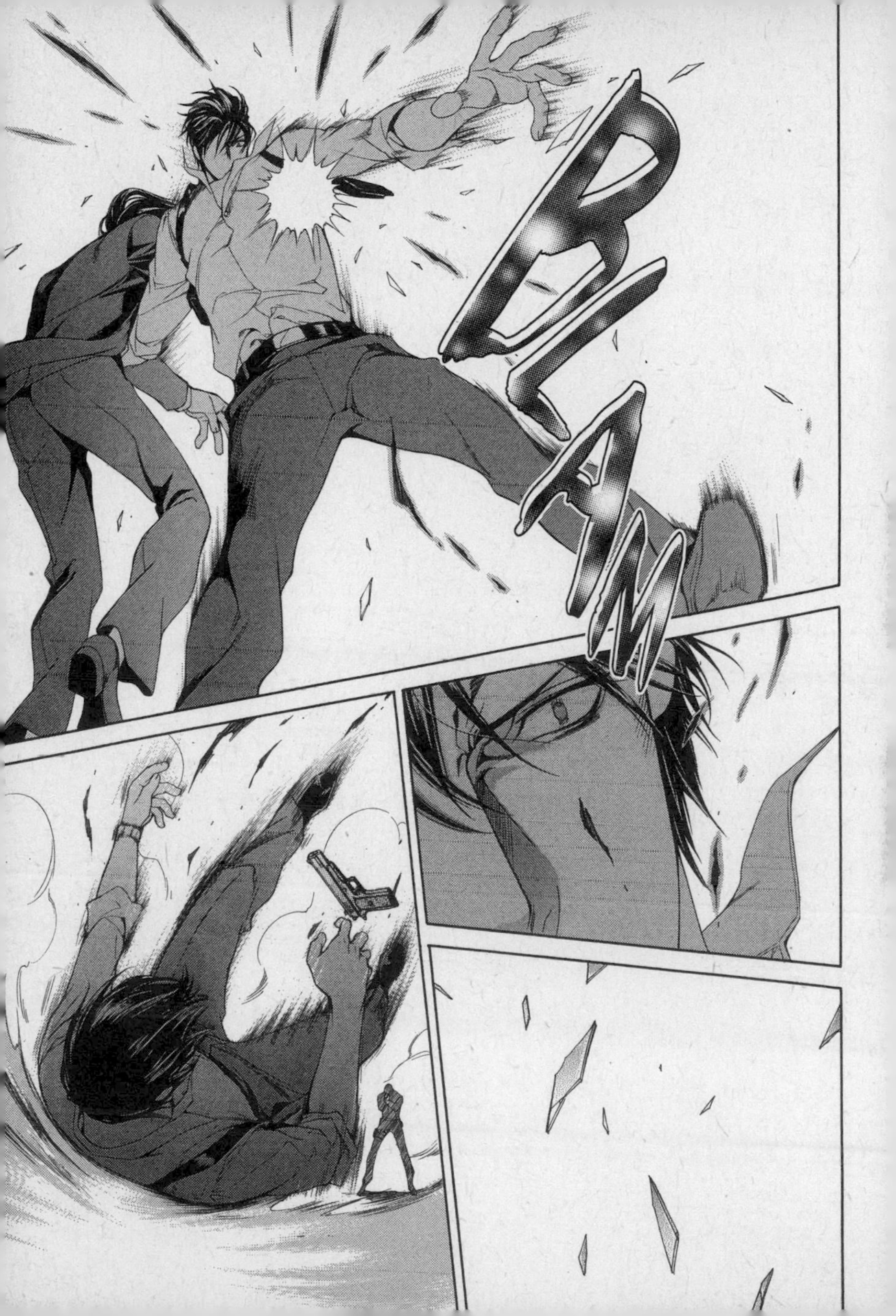
BLAM

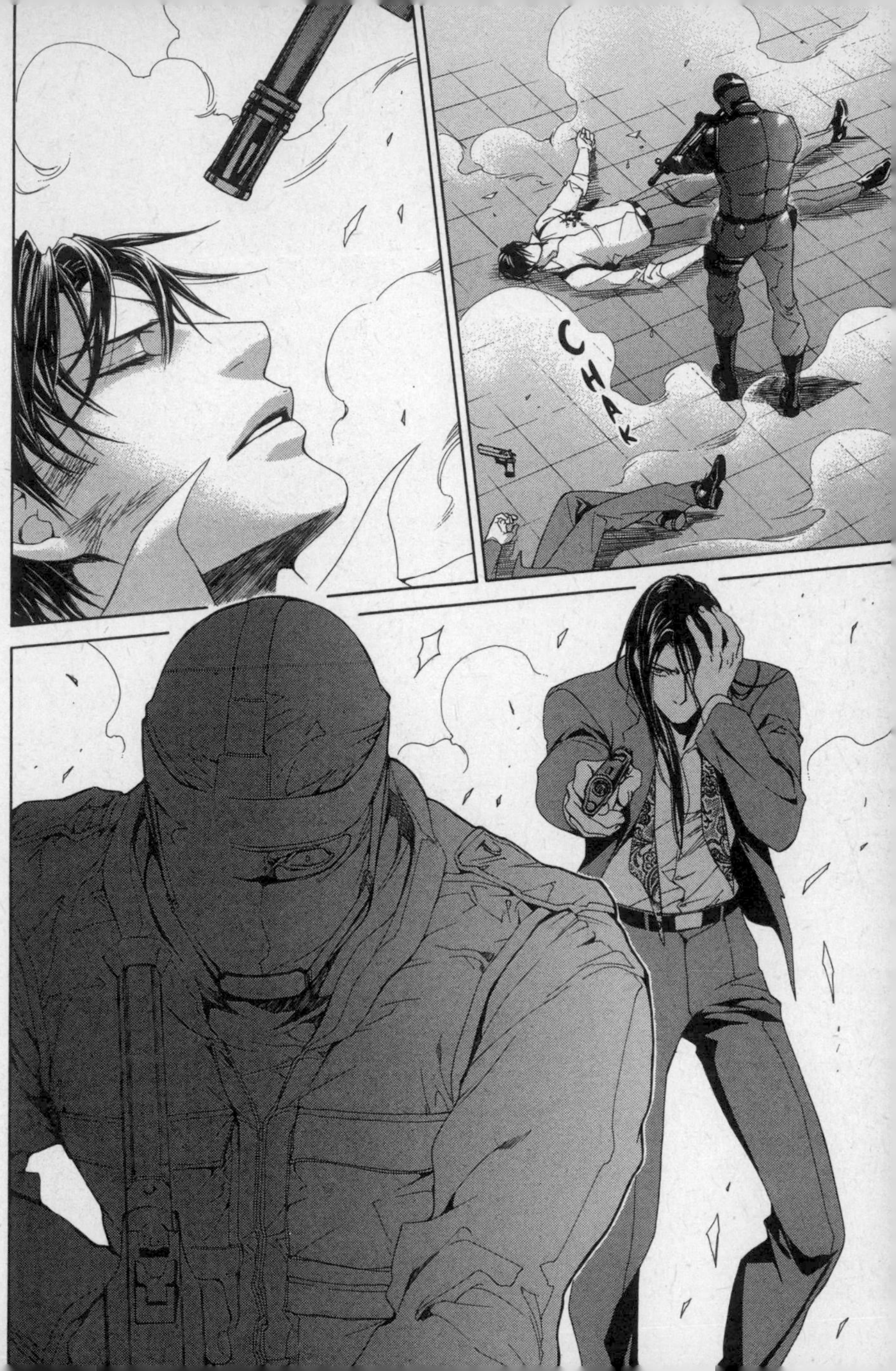
CHAK

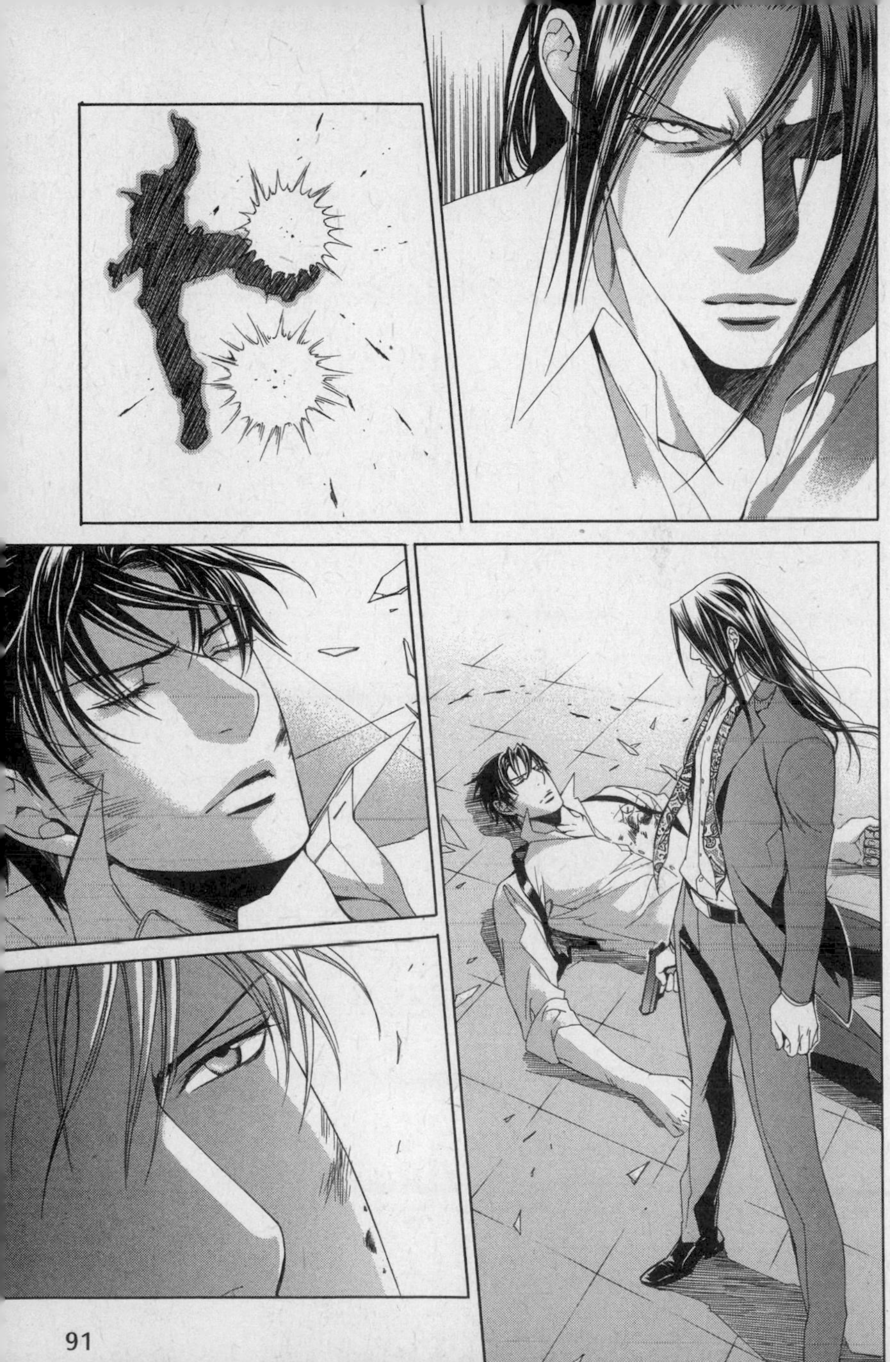

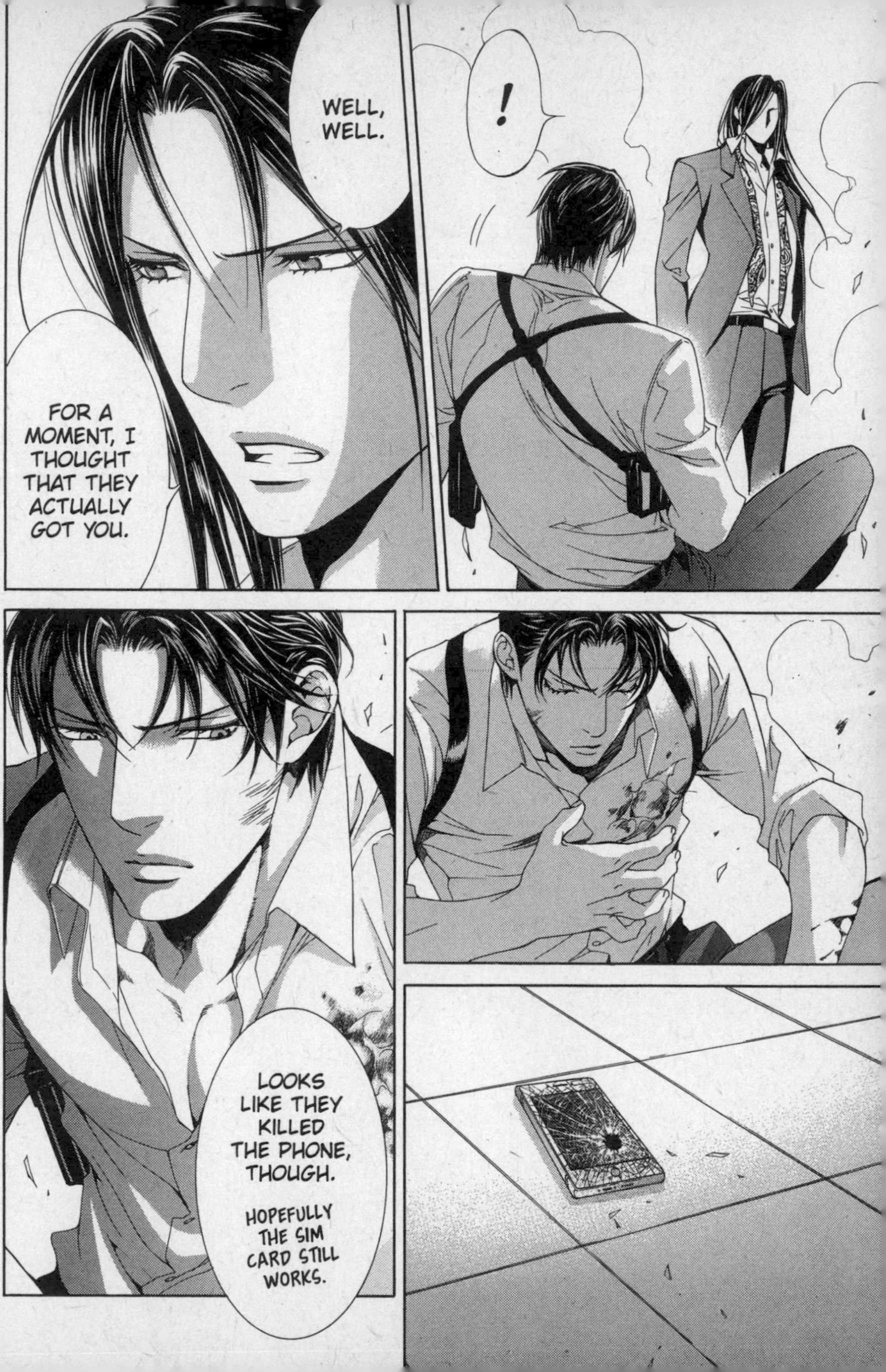
!
WELL, WELL.
FOR A MOMENT, I THOUGHT THAT THEY ACTUALLY GOT YOU.
LOOKS LIKE THEY KILLED THE PHONE, THOUGH.
HOPEFULLY THE SIM CARD STILL WORKS.

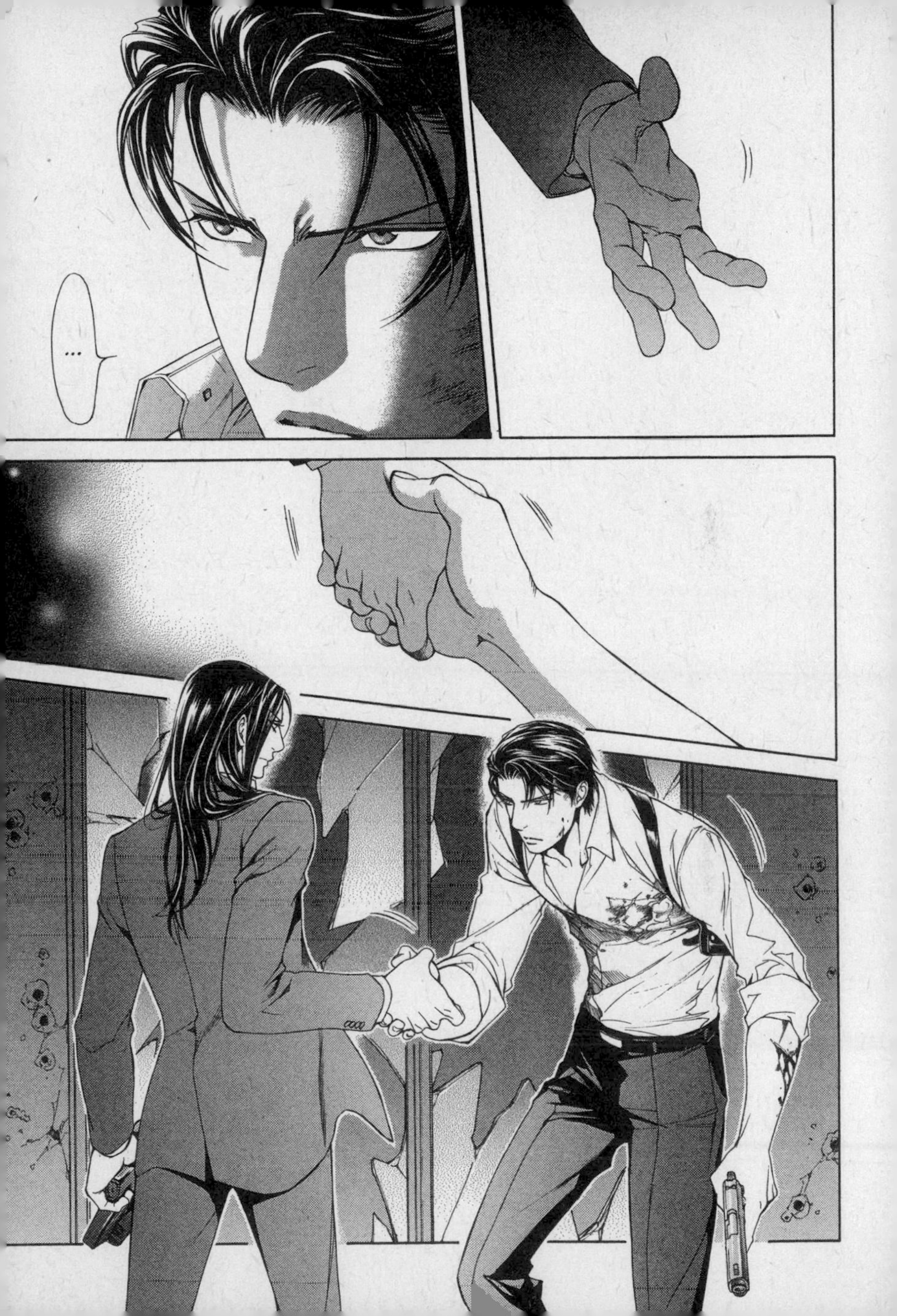
...

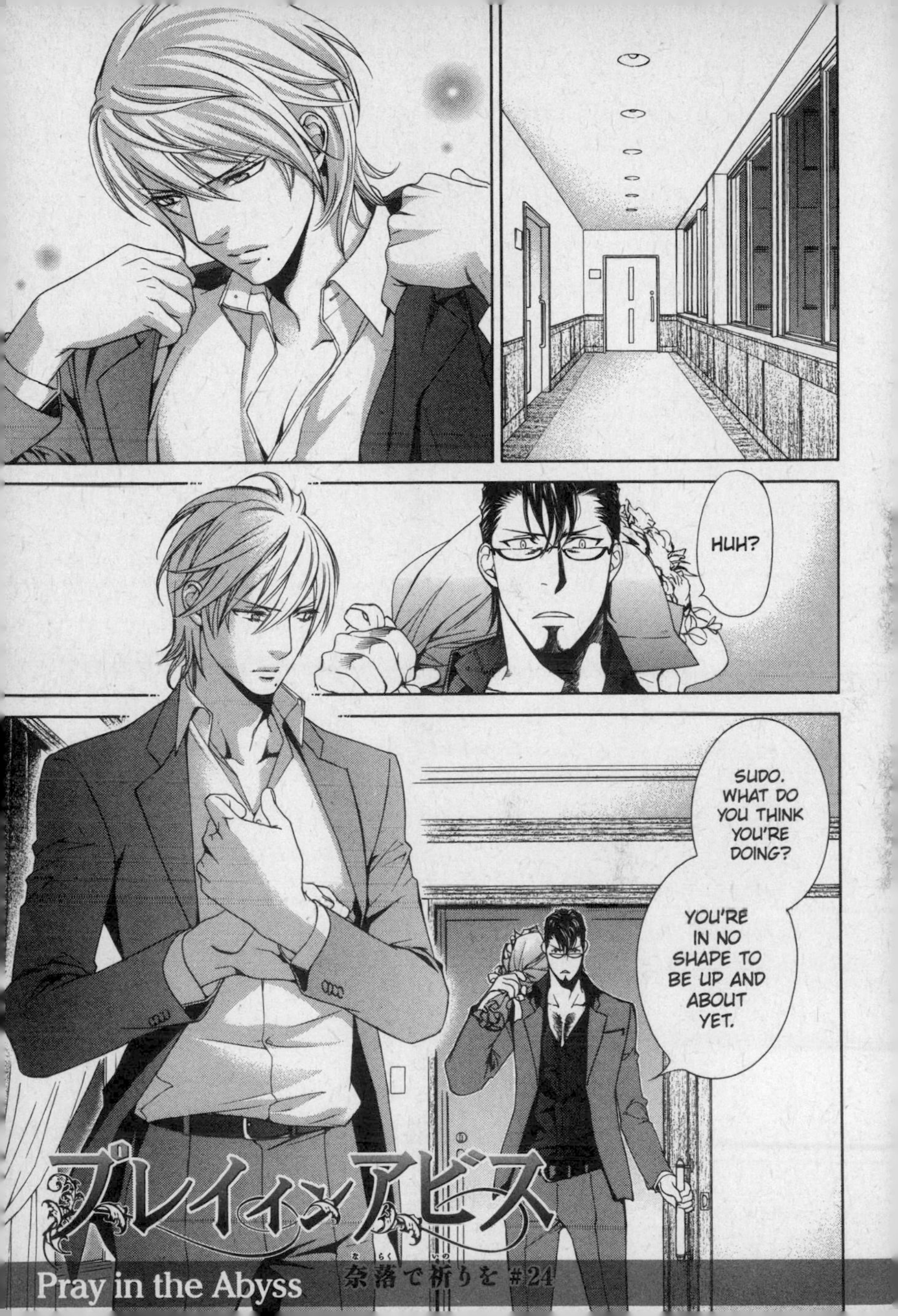
HUH?
SUDO. WHAT DO YOU THINK YOU'RE DOING?
YOU'RE IN NO SHAPE TO BE UP AND ABOUT YET.
プレイインアビス
Pray in the Abyss
奈落で祈りを #24

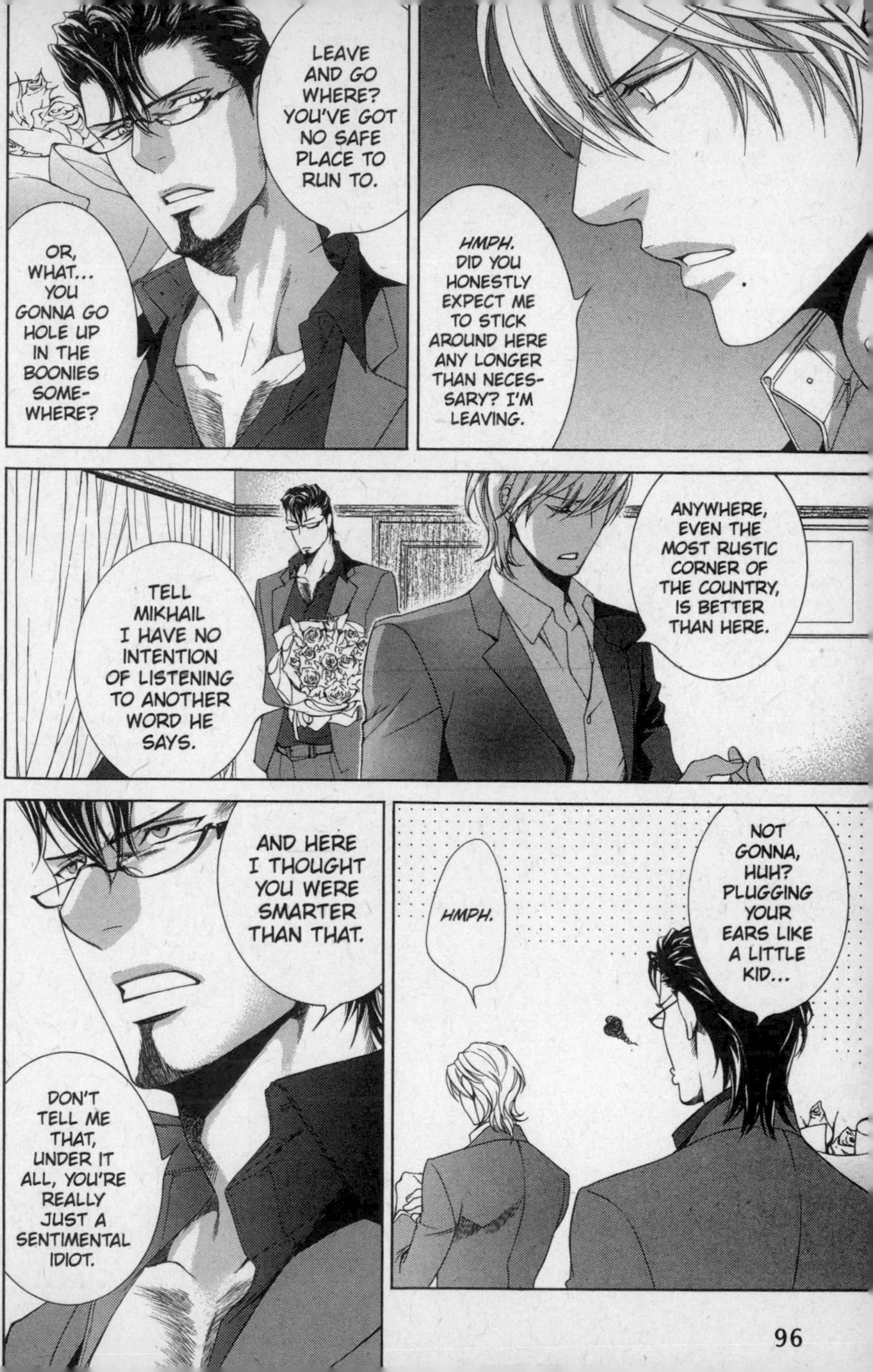
HMPH. DID YOU HONESTLY EXPECT ME TO STICK AROUND HERE ANY LONGER THAN NECES-SARY? I'M LEAVING.
LEAVE AND GO WHERE? YOU'VE GOT NO SAFE PLACE TO RUN TO.
OR, WHAT... YOU GONNA GO HOLE UP IN THE BOONIES SOME-WHERE?
ANYWHERE, EVEN THE MOST RUSTIC CORNER OF THE COUNTRY, IS BETTER THAN HERE.
TELL MIKHAIL I HAVE NO INTENTION OF LISTENING TO ANOTHER WORD HE SAYS.
NOT GONNA, HUH? PLUGGING YOUR EARS LIKE A LITTLE KID...
HMPH.
AND HERE I THOUGHT YOU WERE SMARTER THAN THAT.
DON'T TELL ME THAT, UNDER IT ALL, YOU'RE REALLY JUST A SENTIMENTAL IDIOT.

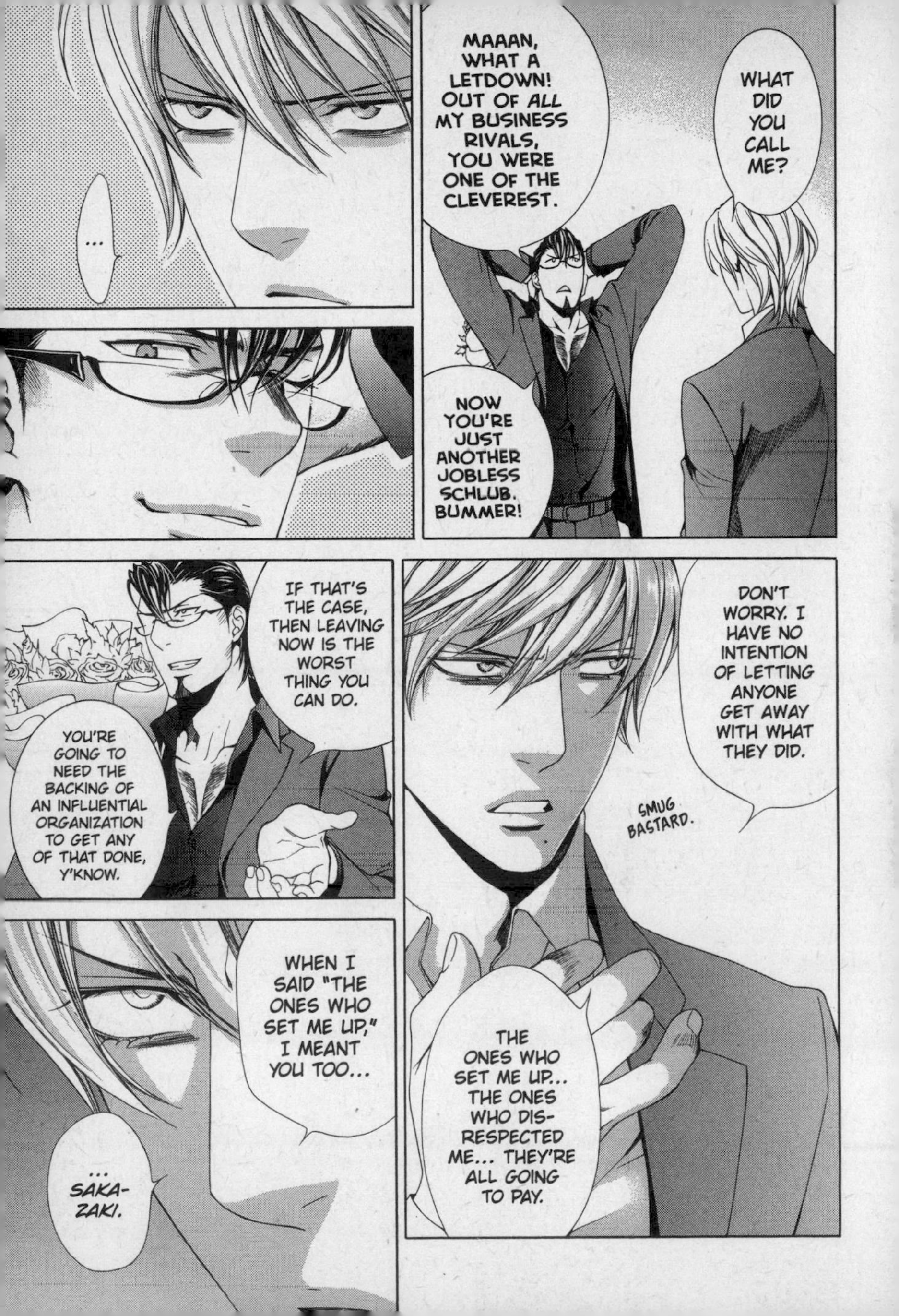
WHAT DID YOU CALL ME?
MAAAN, WHAT A LETDOWN! OUT OF ALL MY BUSINESS RIVALS, YOU WERE ONE OF THE CLEVEREST.
NOW YOU'RE JUST ANOTHER JOBLESS SCHLUB. BUMMER!
...
DON'T WORRY. I HAVE NO INTENTION OF LETTING ANYONE GET AWAY WITH WHAT THEY DID.
SMUG BASTARD.
THE ONES WHO SET ME UP... THE ONES WHO DIS-RESPECTED ME... THEY'RE ALL GOING TO PAY.
IF THAT'S THE CASE, THEN LEAVING NOW IS THE WORST THING YOU CAN DO.
YOU'RE GOING TO NEED THE BACKING OF AN INFLUENTIAL ORGANIZATION TO GET ANY OF THAT DONE, Y'KNOW.
WHEN I SAID "THE ONES WHO SET ME UP," I MEANT YOU TOO...
... SAKA-ZAKI.

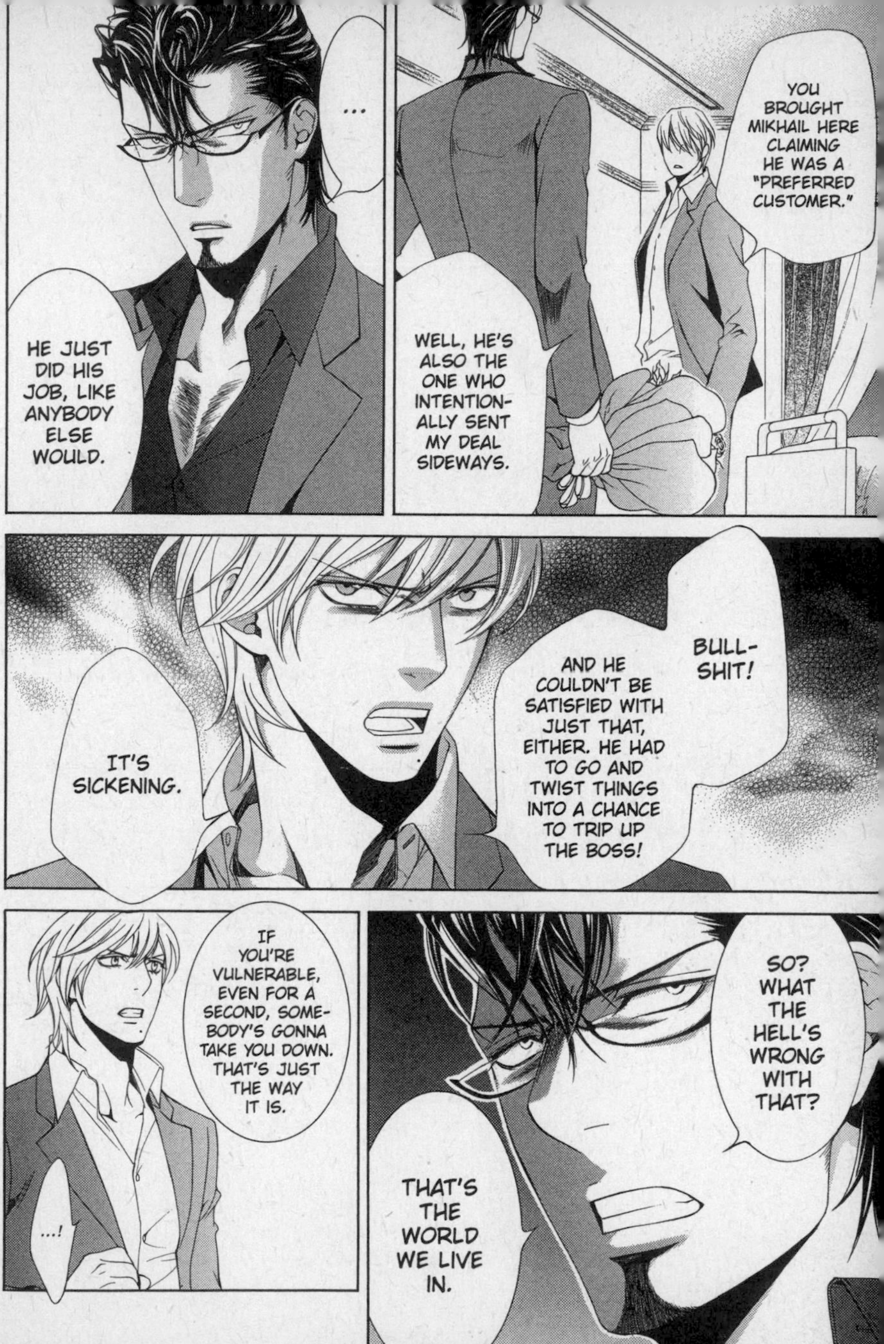
YOU BROUGHT MIKHAIL HERE CLAIMING HE WAS A "PREFERRED CUSTOMER."
WELL, HE'S ALSO THE ONE WHO INTENTION-ALLY SENT MY DEAL SIDEWAYS.
...
HE JUST DID HIS JOB, LIKE ANYBODY ELSE WOULD.
BULL-SHIT!
AND HE COULDN'T BE SATISFIED WITH JUST THAT, EITHER. HE HAD TO GO AND TWIST THINGS INTO A CHANCE TO TRIP UP THE BOSS!
IT'S SICKENING.
SO? WHAT THE HELL'S WRONG WITH THAT?
THAT'S THE WORLD WE LIVE IN.
IF YOU'RE VULNERABLE, EVEN FOR A SECOND, SOME-BODY'S GONNA TAKE YOU DOWN. THAT'S JUST THE WAY IT IS.
...!

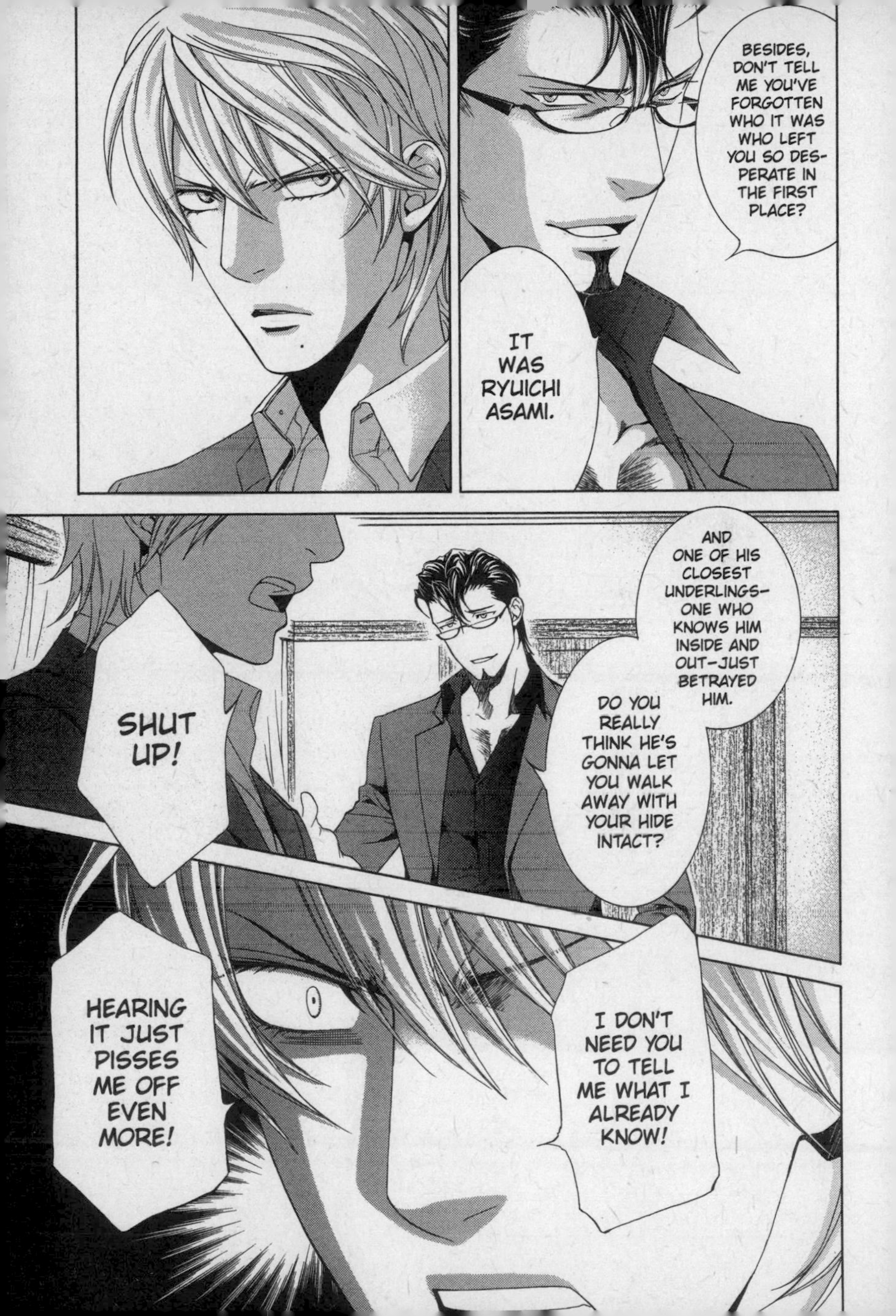
BESIDES, DON'T TELL ME YOU'VE FORGOTTEN WHO IT WAS WHO LEFT YOU SO DES-PERATE IN THE FIRST PLACE?
IT WAS RYUICHI ASAMI.
AND ONE OF HIS CLOSEST UNDERLINGS—ONE WHO KNOWS HIM INSIDE AND OUT—JUST BETRAYED HIM.
DO YOU REALLY THINK HE'S GONNA LET YOU WALK AWAY WITH YOUR HIDE INTACT?
SHUT UP!
I DON'T NEED YOU TO TELL ME WHAT I ALREADY KNOW!
HEARING IT JUST PISSES ME OFF EVEN MORE!

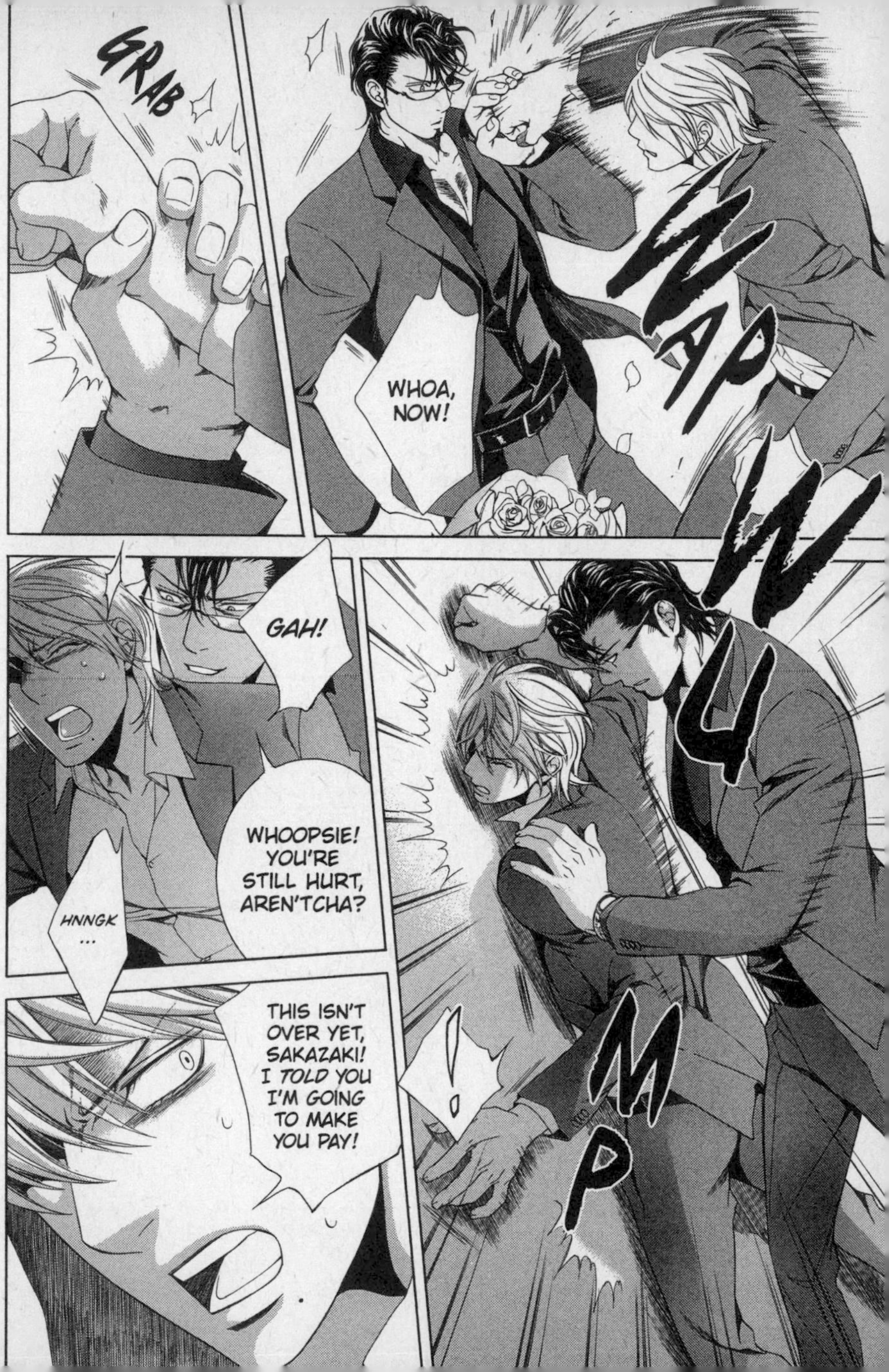
WHAP
WHOA, NOW!
GRAB
WUMP
!
GAH!
WHOOPSIE! YOU'RE STILL HURT, AREN'TCHA?
HNNGK ...
THIS ISN'T OVER YET, SAKAZAKI! I *TOLD* YOU I'M GOING TO MAKE YOU PAY!

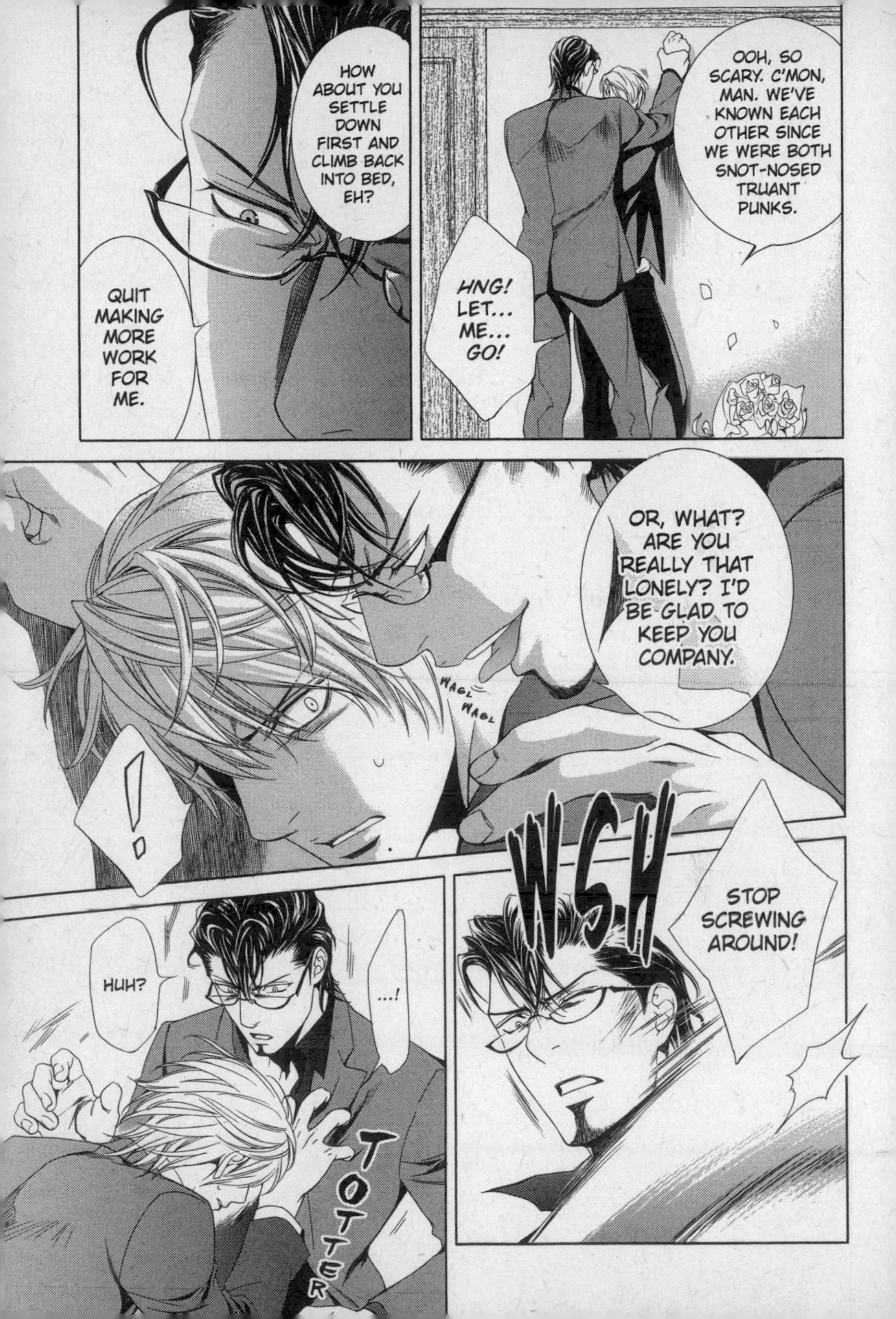
OOH, SO SCARY. C'MON, MAN. WE'VE KNOWN EACH OTHER SINCE WE WERE BOTH SNOT-NOSED TRUANT PUNKS.
HNG! LET... ME... GO!
HOW ABOUT YOU SETTLE DOWN FIRST AND CLIMB BACK INTO BED, EH?
QUIT MAKING MORE WORK FOR ME.
OR, WHAT? ARE YOU REALLY THAT LONELY? I'D BE GLAD TO KEEP YOU COMPANY.
WAGL WAGL
!
WSH
STOP SCREWING AROUND!
...!
HUH?
TOTTER

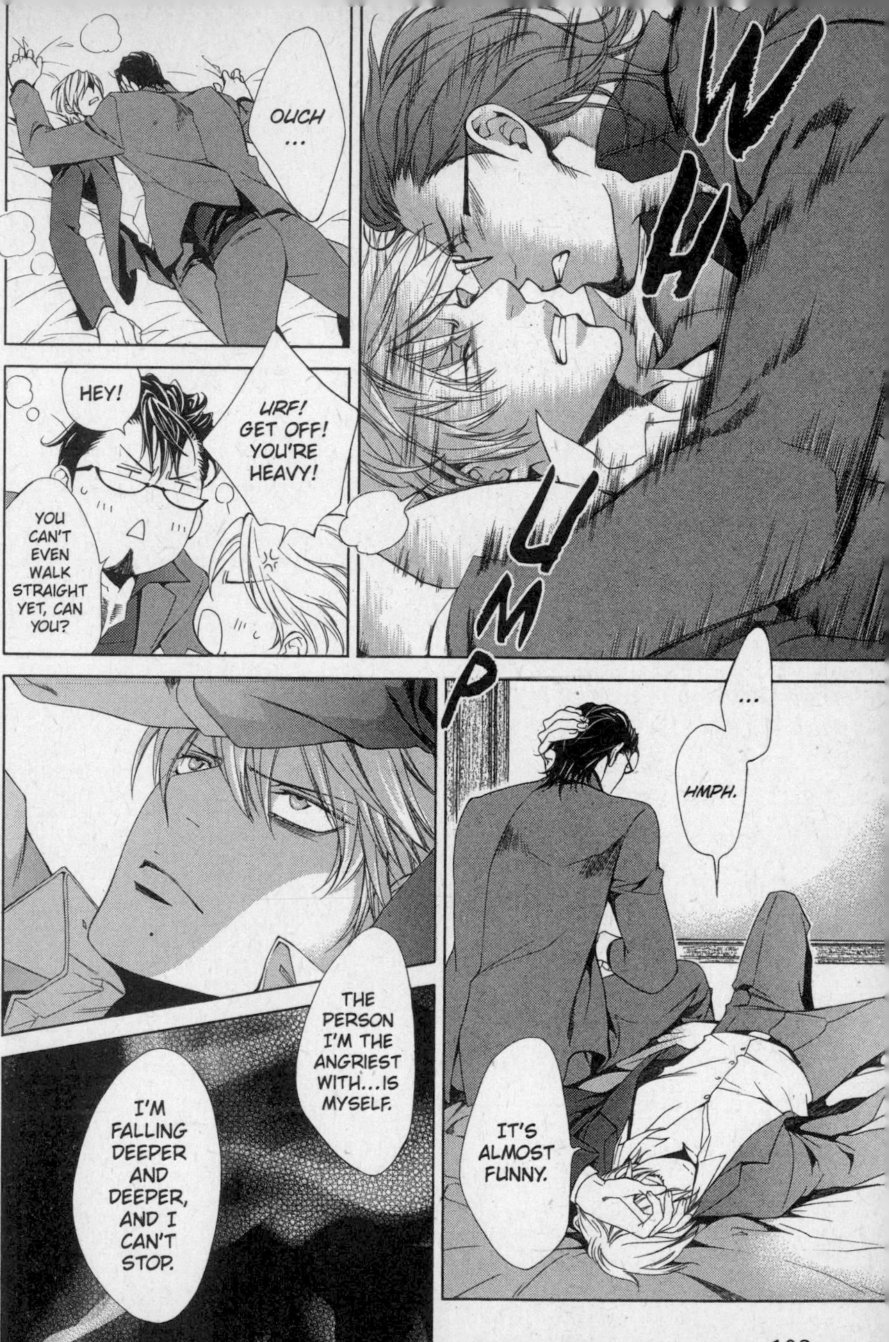
WHUMP
OUCH ...
URF! GET OFF! YOU'RE HEAVY!
HEY!
YOU CAN'T EVEN WALK STRAIGHT YET, CAN YOU?
...
HMPH.
IT'S ALMOST FUNNY.
THE PERSON I'M THE ANGRIEST WITH...IS MYSELF.
I'M FALLING DEEPER AND DEEPER, AND I CAN'T STOP.

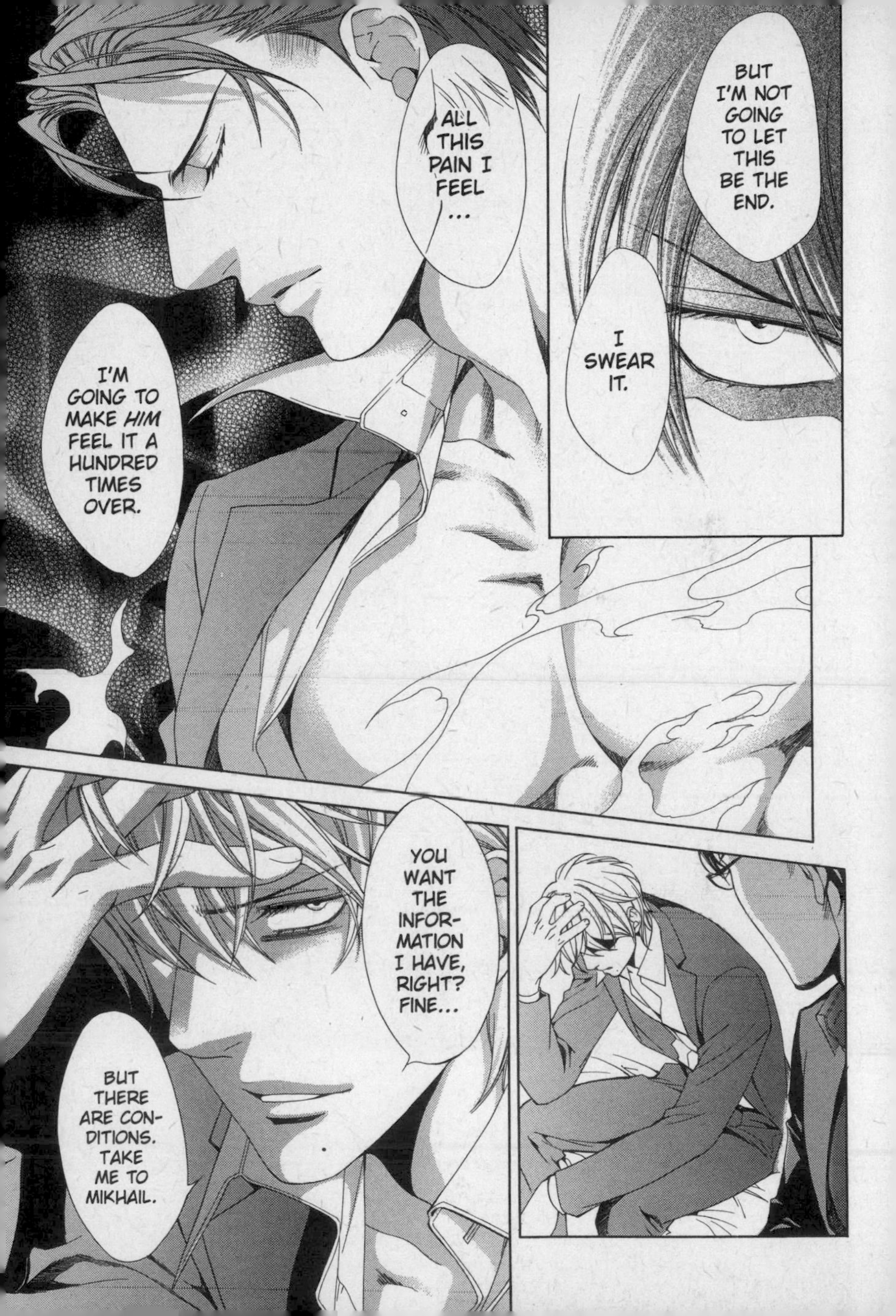
BUT I'M NOT GOING TO LET THIS BE THE END.
I SWEAR IT.
ALL THIS PAIN I FEEL...
I'M GOING TO MAKE *HIM* FEEL IT A HUNDRED TIMES OVER.
YOU WANT THE INFORMATION I HAVE, RIGHT? FINE...
BUT THERE ARE CONDITIONS. TAKE ME TO MIKHAIL.

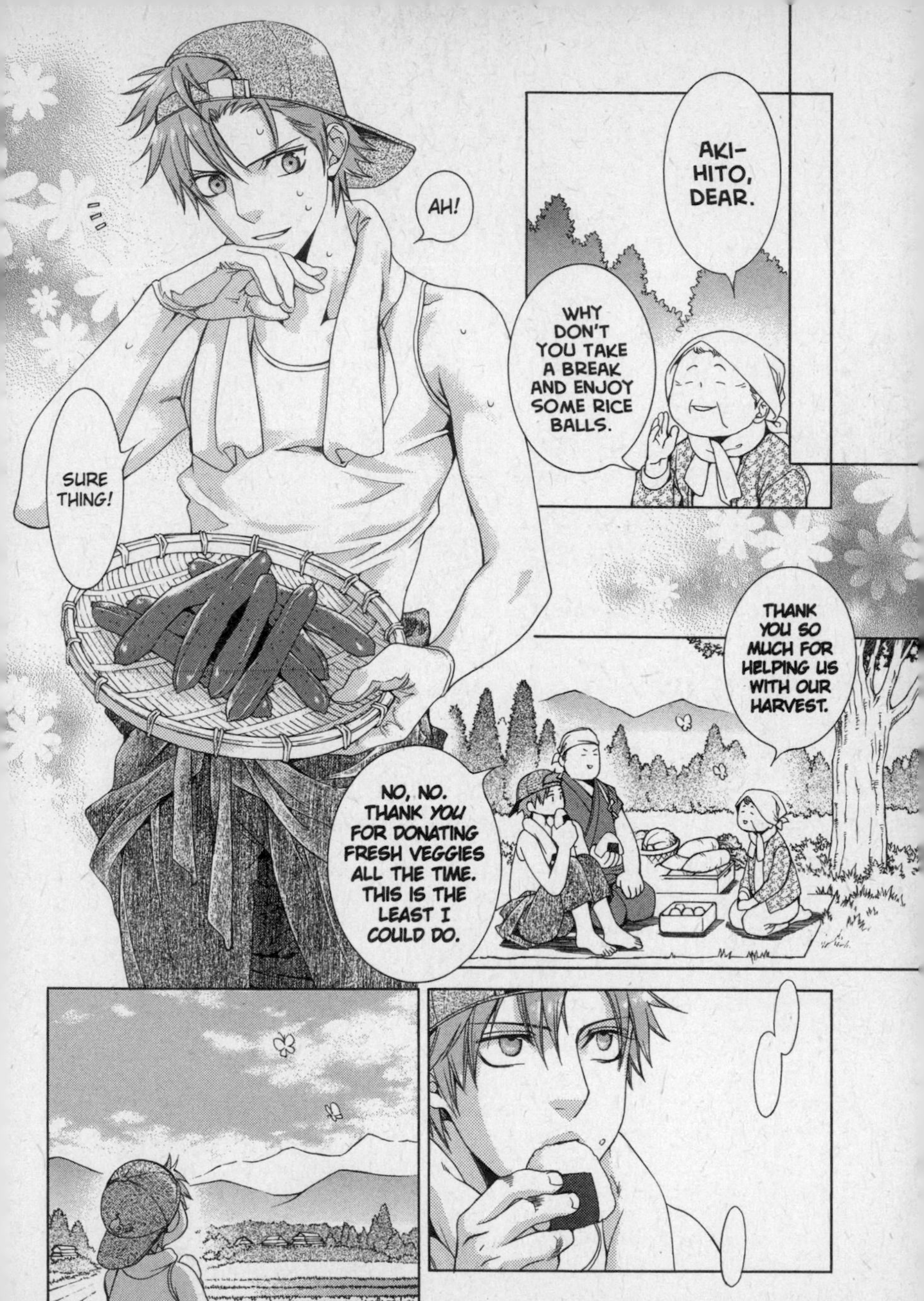
AKI-HITO, DEAR.
WHY DON'T YOU TAKE A BREAK AND ENJOY SOME RICE BALLS.
AH!
SURE THING!
THANK YOU SO MUCH FOR HELPING US WITH OUR HARVEST.
NO, NO. THANK *YOU* FOR DONATING FRESH VEGGIES ALL THE TIME. THIS IS THE LEAST I COULD DO.

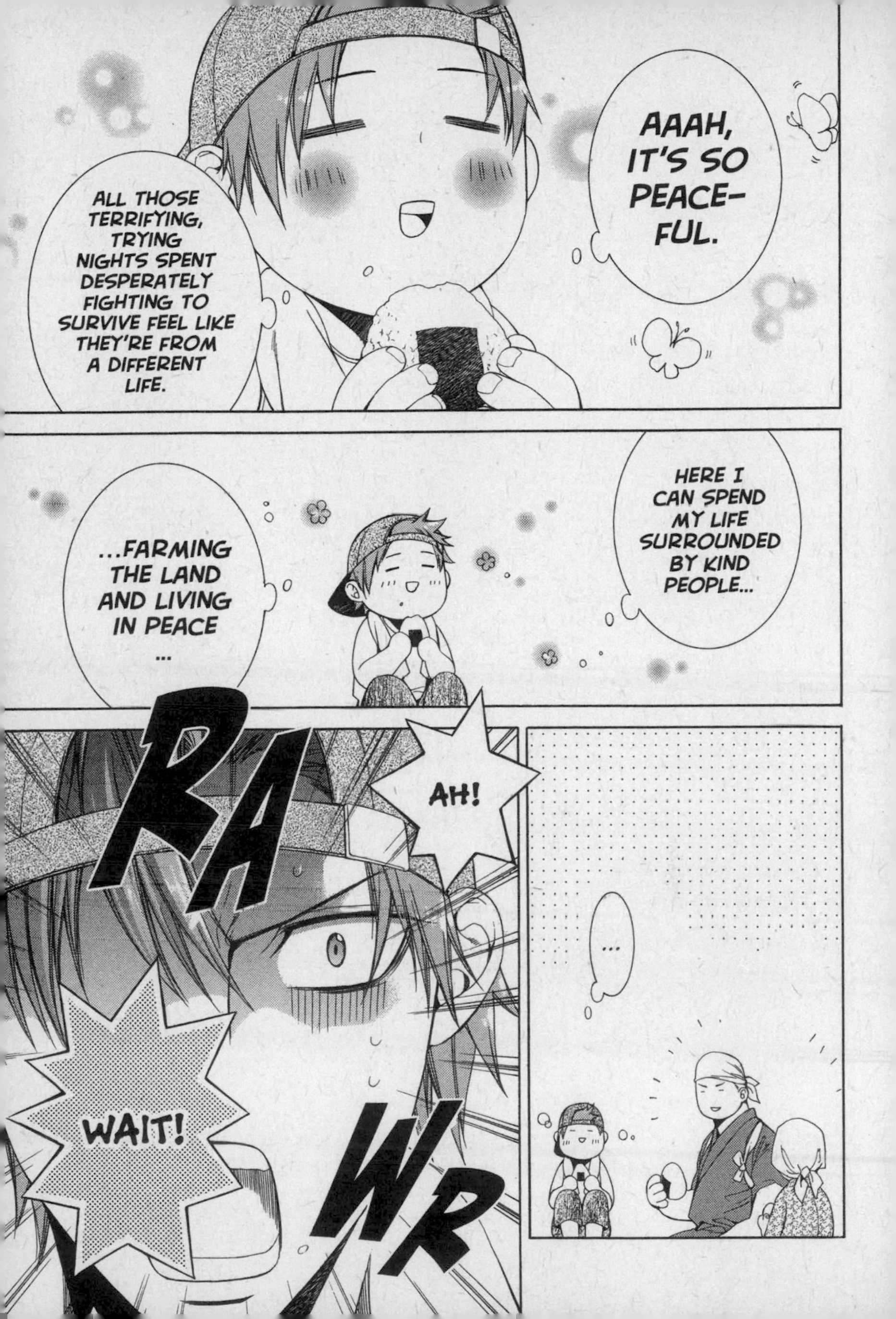
AAAH, IT'S SO PEACE-FUL.
ALL THOSE TERRIFYING, TRYING NIGHTS SPENT DESPERATELY FIGHTING TO SURVIVE FEEL LIKE THEY'RE FROM A DIFFERENT LIFE.
HERE I CAN SPEND MY LIFE SURROUNDED BY KIND PEOPLE...
...FARMING THE LAND AND LIVING IN PEACE ...
...
AH!
RA
WAIT!
WR

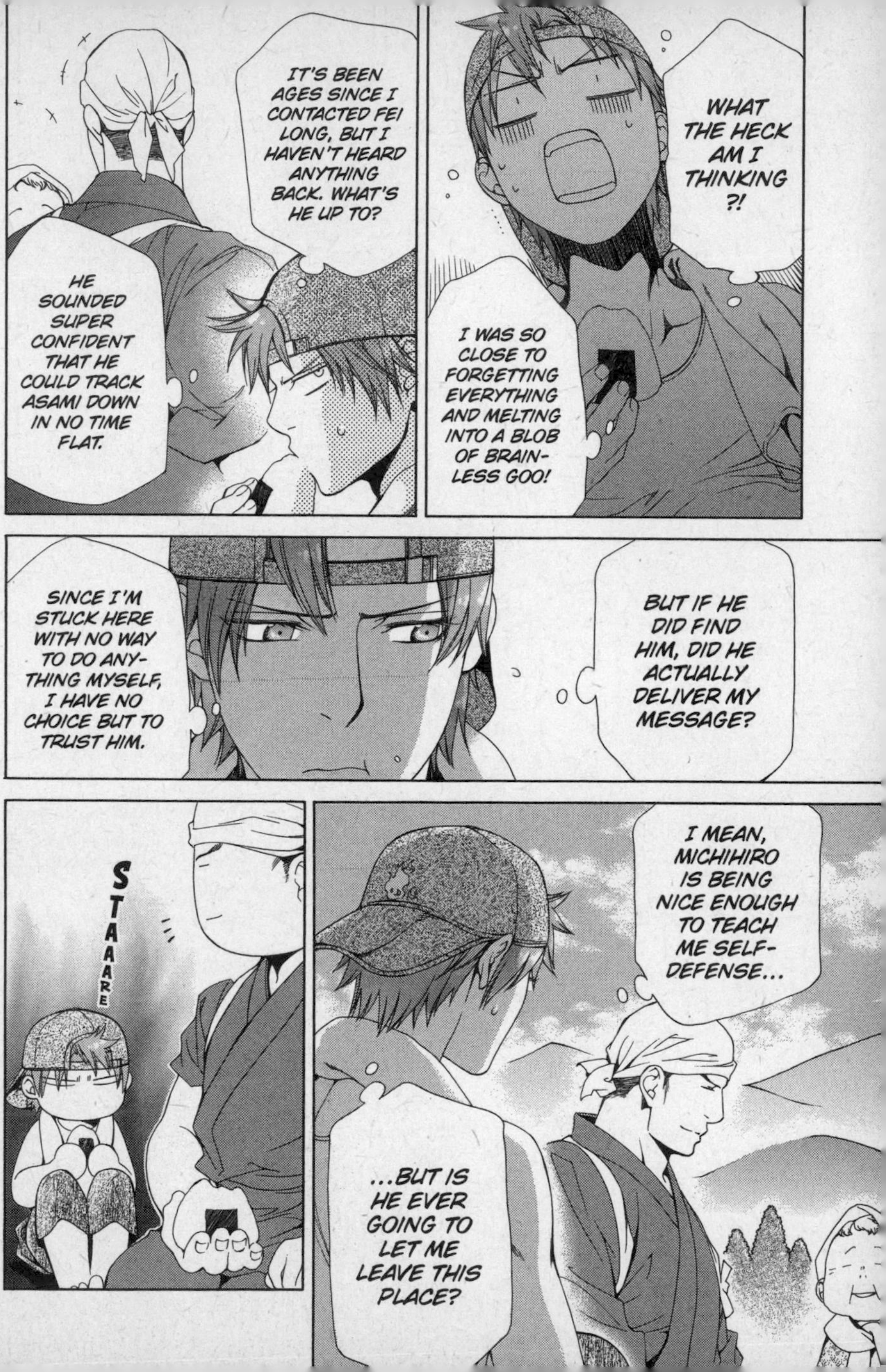
WHAT THE HECK AM I THINKING?!
I WAS SO CLOSE TO FORGETTING EVERYTHING AND MELTING INTO A BLOB OF BRAIN-LESS GOO!
IT'S BEEN AGES SINCE I CONTACTED FEI LONG, BUT I HAVEN'T HEARD ANYTHING BACK. WHAT'S HE UP TO?
HE SOUNDED SUPER CONFIDENT THAT HE COULD TRACK ASAMI DOWN IN NO TIME FLAT.
BUT IF HE DID FIND HIM, DID HE ACTUALLY DELIVER MY MESSAGE?
SINCE I'M STUCK HERE WITH NO WAY TO DO ANY-THING MYSELF, I HAVE NO CHOICE BUT TO TRUST HIM.
I MEAN, MICHIHIRO IS BEING NICE ENOUGH TO TEACH ME SELF-DEFENSE...
...BUT IS HE EVER GOING TO LET ME LEAVE THIS PLACE?
STAAAARE

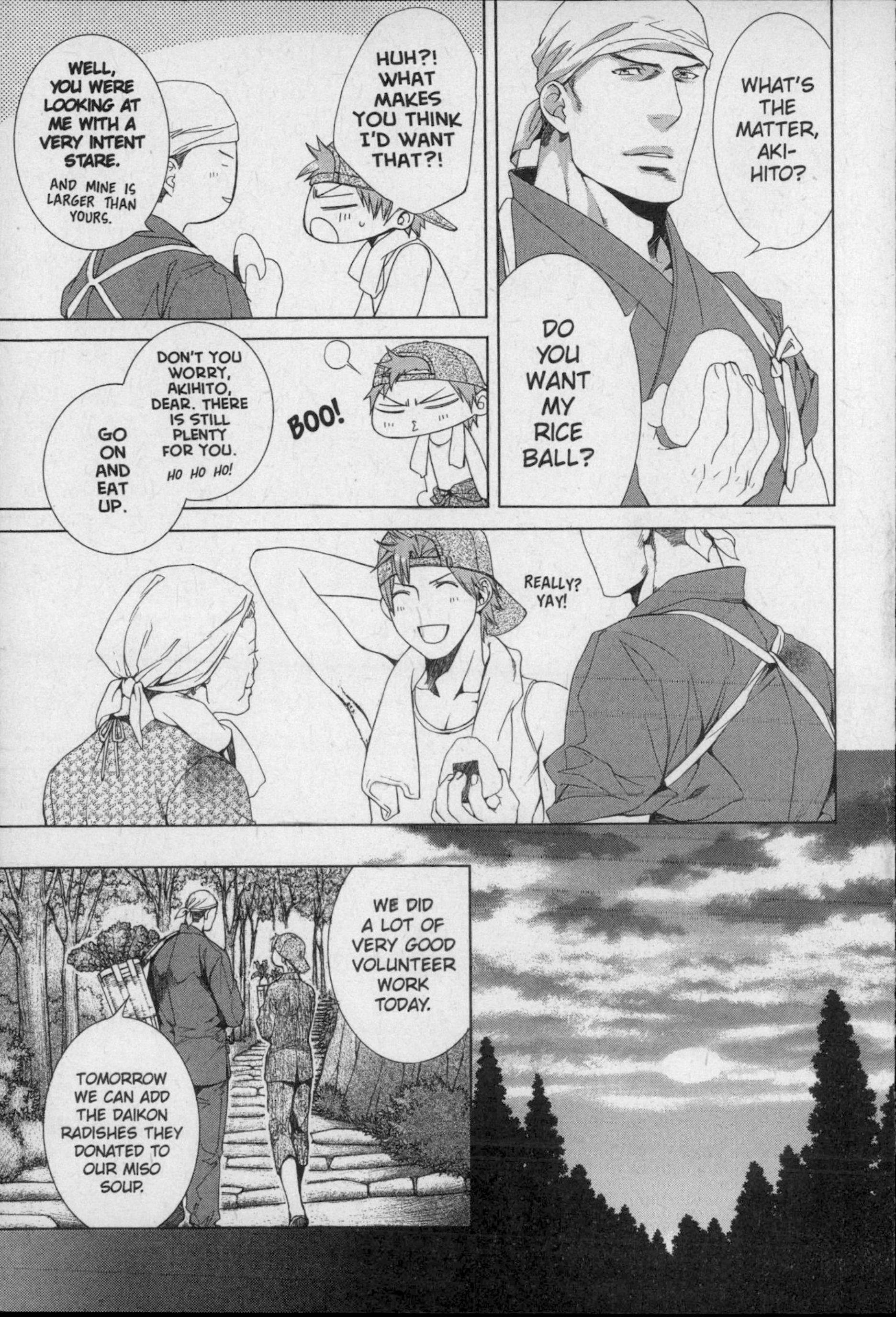
WHAT'S THE MATTER, AKI-HITO?
DO YOU WANT MY RICE BALL?
HUH?! WHAT MAKES YOU THINK I'D WANT THAT?!
WELL, YOU WERE LOOKING AT ME WITH A VERY INTENT STARE.
AND MINE IS LARGER THAN YOURS.
BOO!
DON'T YOU WORRY, AKIHITO, DEAR. THERE IS STILL PLENTY FOR YOU.
HO HO HO!
GO ON AND EAT UP.
REALLY? YAY!
WE DID A LOT OF VERY GOOD VOLUNTEER WORK TODAY.
TOMORROW WE CAN ADD THE DAIKON RADISHES THEY DONATED TO OUR MISO SOUP.

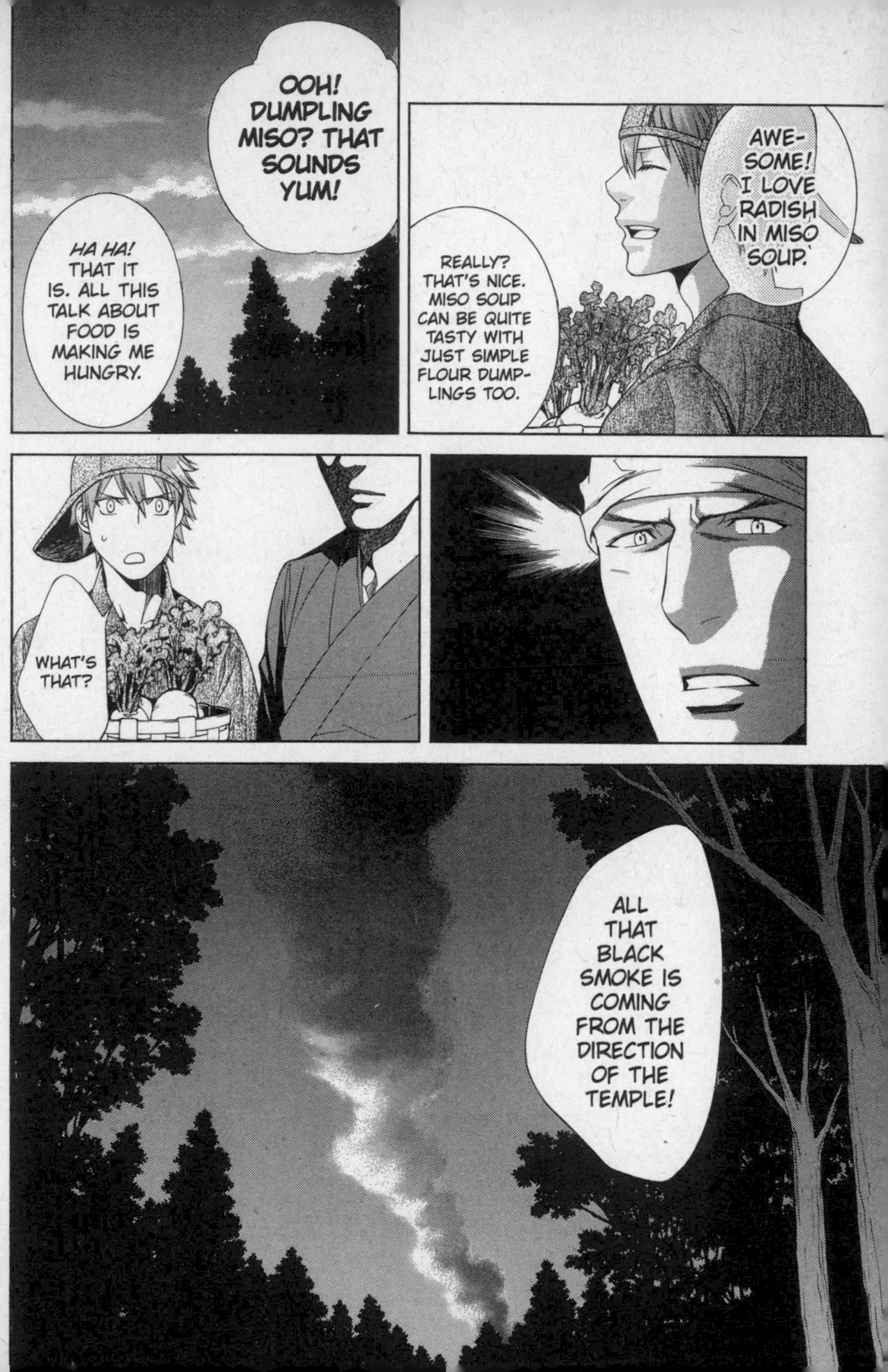
AWE-SOME! I LOVE RADISH IN MISO SOUP.
REALLY? THAT'S NICE. MISO SOUP CAN BE QUITE TASTY WITH JUST SIMPLE FLOUR DUMP-LINGS TOO.
OOH! DUMPLING MISO? THAT SOUNDS YUM!
HA HA! THAT IT IS. ALL THIS TALK ABOUT FOOD IS MAKING ME HUNGRY.
WHAT'S THAT?
ALL THAT BLACK SMOKE IS COMING FROM THE DIRECTION OF THE TEMPLE!

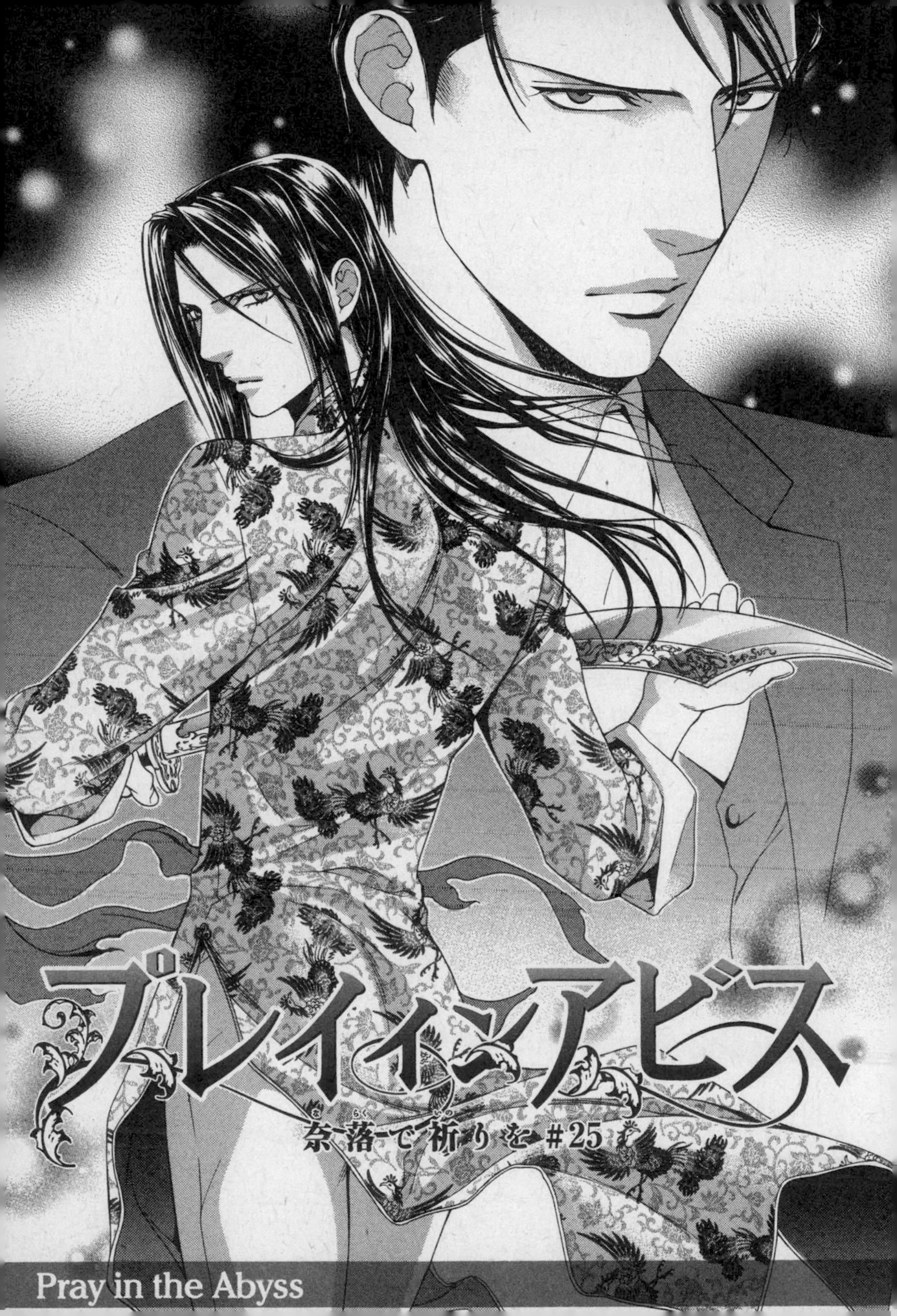
プレイインアビス
奈落で祈りを #25
Pray in the Abyss

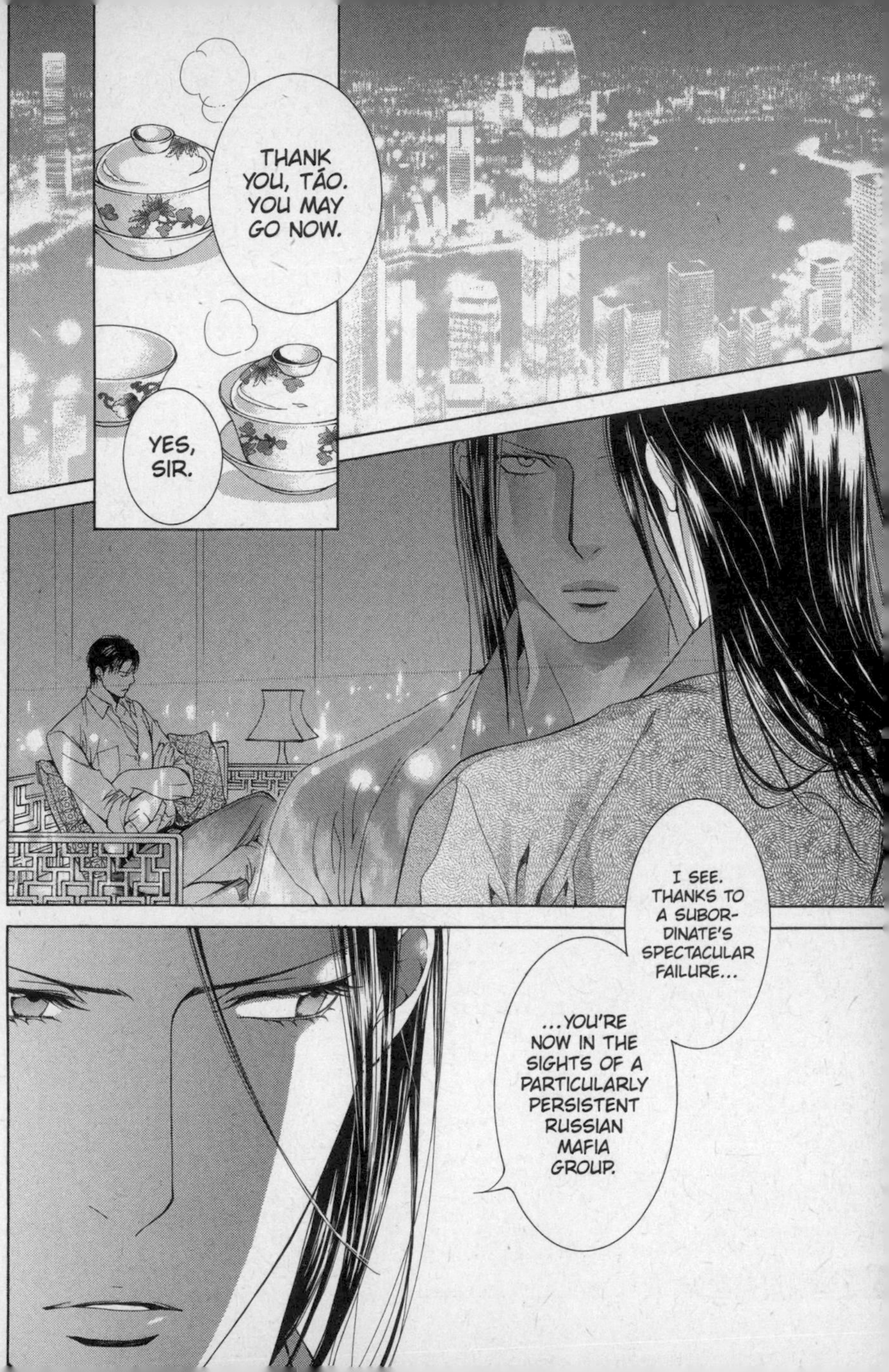
THANK YOU, TÁO. YOU MAY GO NOW.
YES, SIR.
I SEE. THANKS TO A SUBOR-DINATE'S SPECTACULAR FAILURE...
...YOU'RE NOW IN THE SIGHTS OF A PARTICULARLY PERSISTENT RUSSIAN MAFIA GROUP.

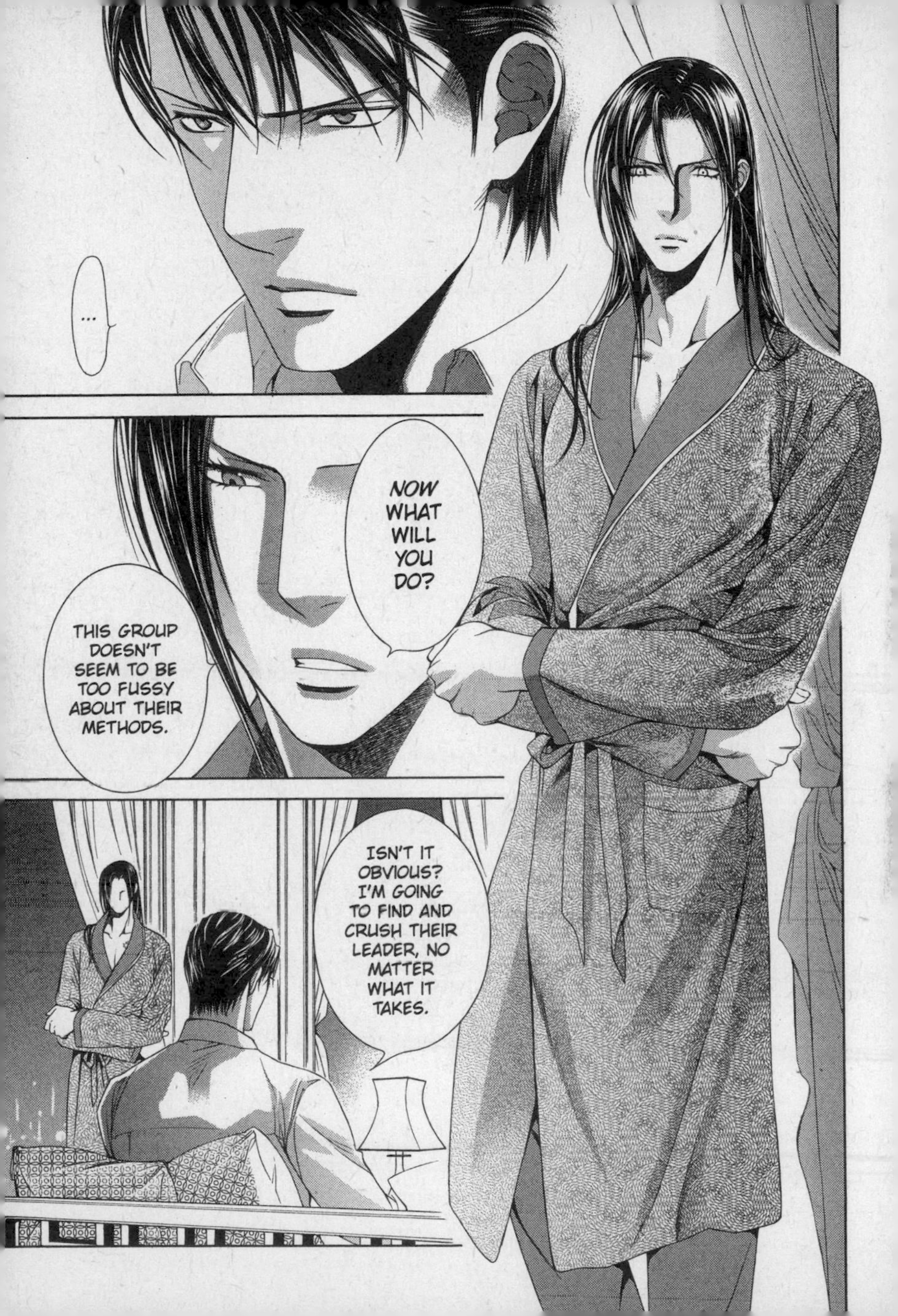
...
NOW WHAT WILL YOU DO?
THIS GROUP DOESN'T SEEM TO BE TOO FUSSY ABOUT THEIR METHODS.
ISN'T IT OBVIOUS? I'M GOING TO FIND AND CRUSH THEIR LEADER, NO MATTER WHAT IT TAKES.

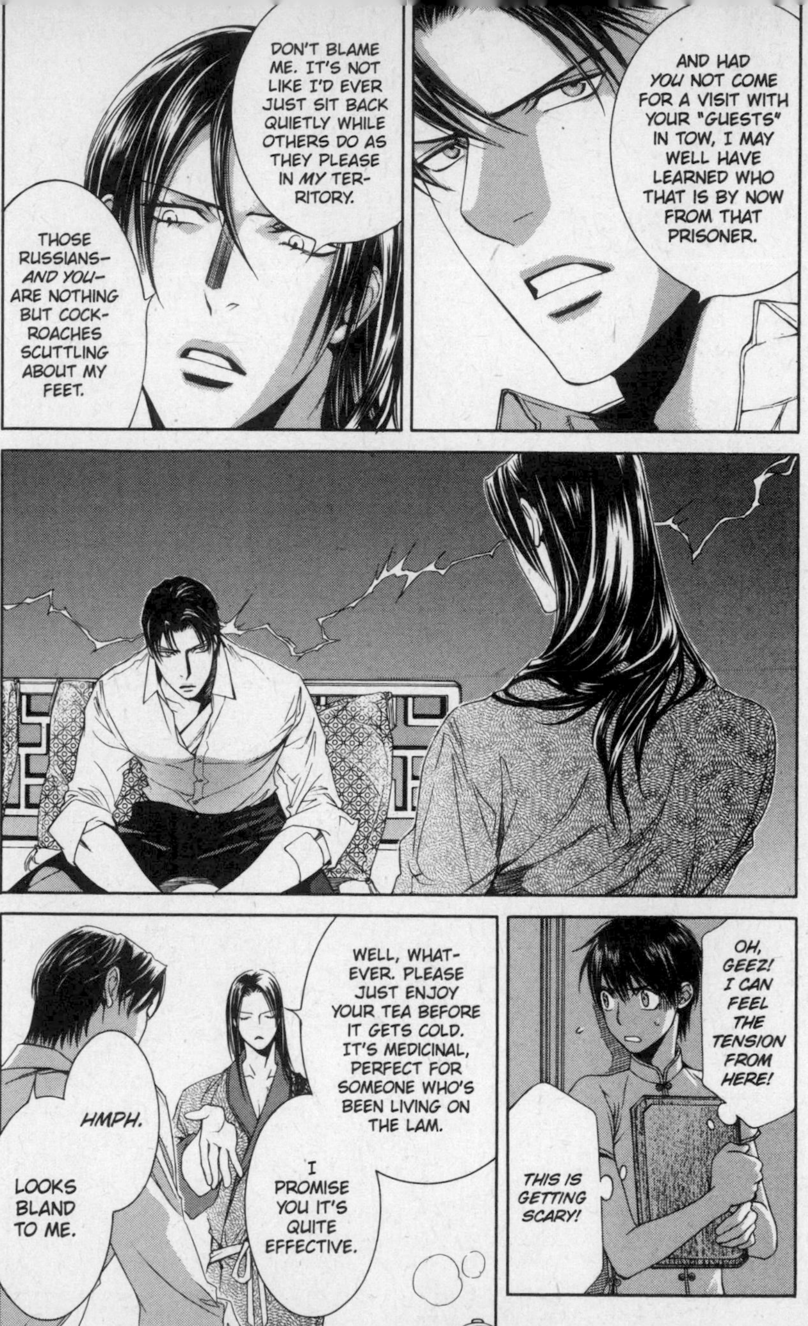
AND HAD *YOU* NOT COME FOR A VISIT WITH YOUR "GUESTS" IN TOW, I MAY WELL HAVE LEARNED WHO THAT IS BY NOW FROM THAT PRISONER.
DON'T BLAME ME. IT'S NOT LIKE I'D EVER JUST SIT BACK QUIETLY WHILE OTHERS DO AS THEY PLEASE IN *MY* TERRITORY.
THOSE RUSSIANS—*AND YOU*—ARE NOTHING BUT COCKROACHES SCUTTLING ABOUT MY FEET.
OH, GEEZ! I CAN FEEL THE TENSION FROM HERE!
THIS IS GETTING SCARY!
WELL, WHATEVER. PLEASE JUST ENJOY YOUR TEA BEFORE IT GETS COLD. IT'S MEDICINAL, PERFECT FOR SOMEONE WHO'S BEEN LIVING ON THE LAM.
HMPH.
LOOKS BLAND TO ME.
I PROMISE YOU IT'S QUITE EFFECTIVE.

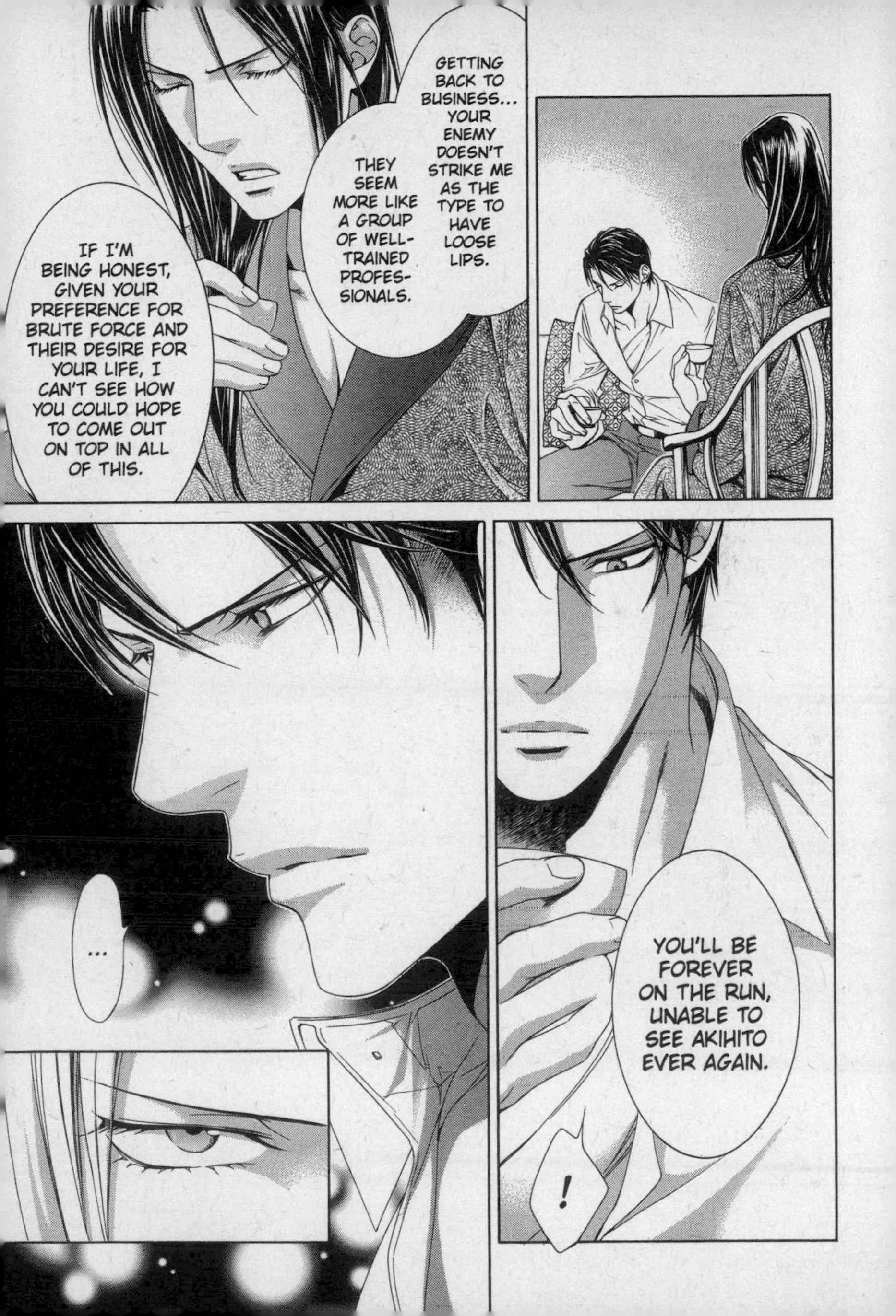
GETTING BACK TO BUSINESS... YOUR ENEMY DOESN'T STRIKE ME AS THE TYPE TO HAVE LOOSE LIPS.
THEY SEEM MORE LIKE A GROUP OF WELL-TRAINED PROFESSIONALS.
IF I'M BEING HONEST, GIVEN YOUR PREFERENCE FOR BRUTE FORCE AND THEIR DESIRE FOR YOUR LIFE, I CAN'T SEE HOW YOU COULD HOPE TO COME OUT ON TOP IN ALL OF THIS.
YOU'LL BE FOREVER ON THE RUN, UNABLE TO SEE AKIHITO EVER AGAIN.
!
...

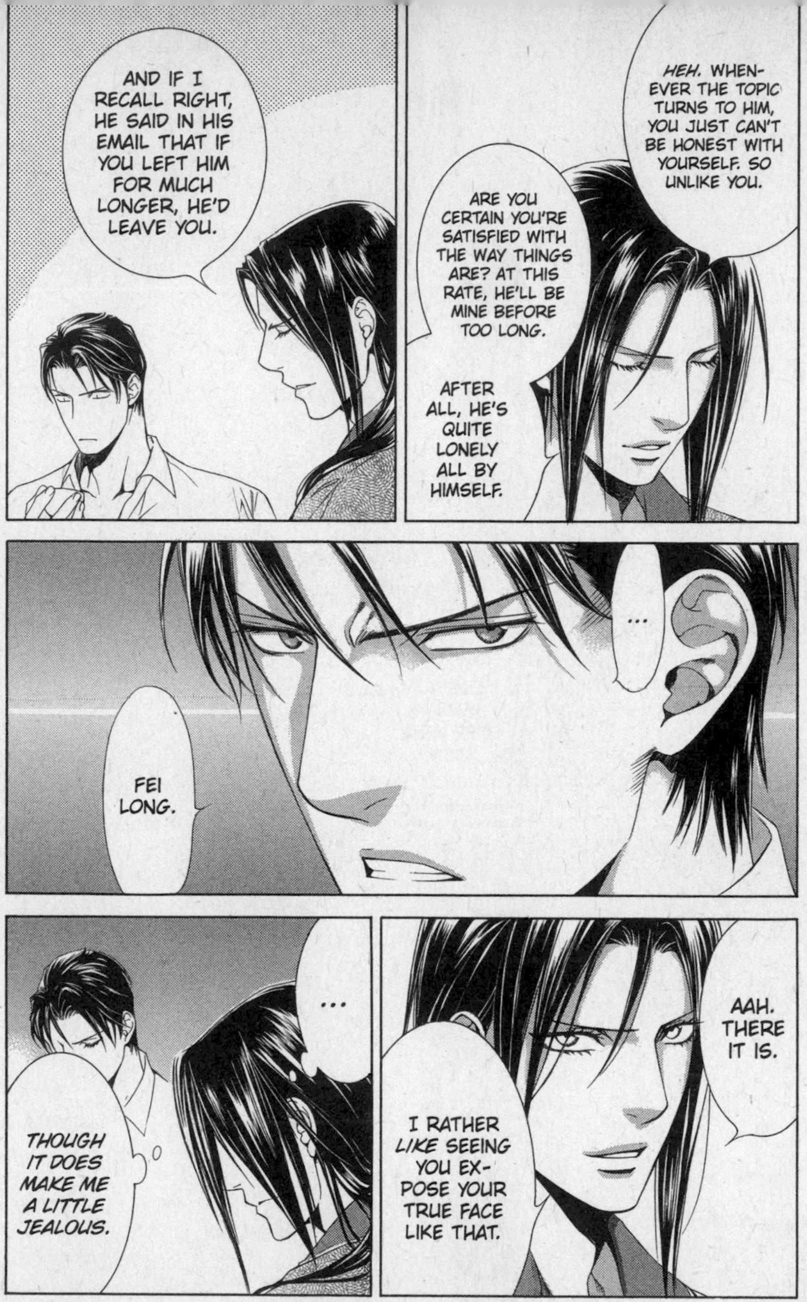
HEH. WHEN-EVER THE TOPIC TURNS TO HIM, YOU JUST CAN'T BE HONEST WITH YOURSELF. SO UNLIKE YOU.
ARE YOU CERTAIN YOU'RE SATISFIED WITH THE WAY THINGS ARE? AT THIS RATE, HE'LL BE MINE BEFORE TOO LONG.
AFTER ALL, HE'S QUITE LONELY ALL BY HIMSELF.
AND IF I RECALL RIGHT, HE SAID IN HIS EMAIL THAT IF YOU LEFT HIM FOR MUCH LONGER, HE'D LEAVE YOU.
...
FEI LONG.
AAH. THERE IT IS.
I RATHER *LIKE* SEEING YOU EX-POSE YOUR TRUE FACE LIKE THAT.
...
THOUGH IT DOES MAKE ME A LITTLE JEALOUS.

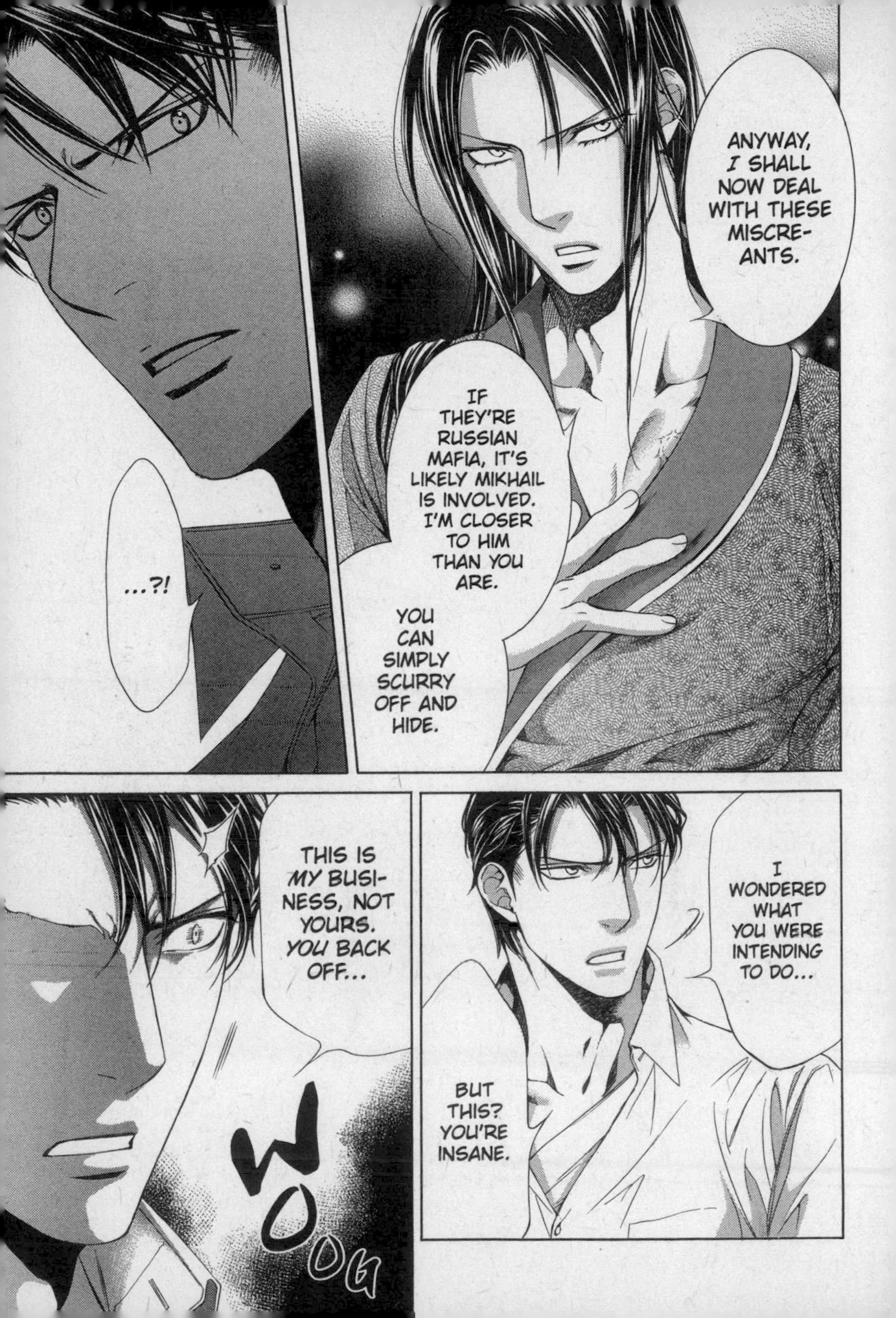
ANYWAY, *I* SHALL NOW DEAL WITH THESE MISCRE- ANTS.
IF THEY'RE RUSSIAN MAFIA, IT'S LIKELY MIKHAIL IS INVOLVED. I'M CLOSER TO HIM THAN YOU ARE.
YOU CAN SIMPLY SCURRY OFF AND HIDE.
...?!
I WONDERED WHAT YOU WERE INTENDING TO DO...
BUT THIS? YOU'RE INSANE.
THIS IS *MY* BUSI- NESS, NOT YOURS. *YOU* BACK OFF...
WOOG

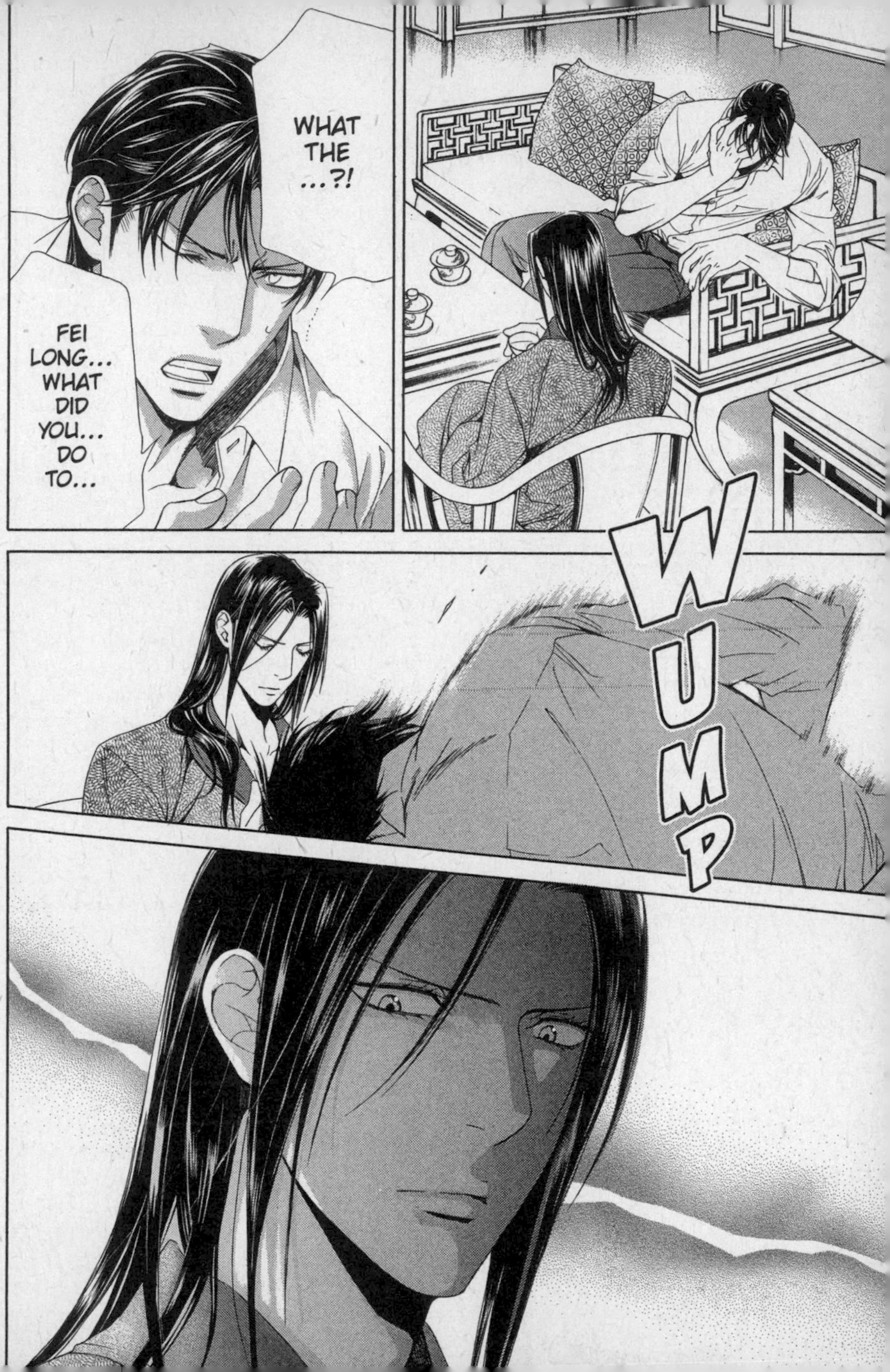
WHAT THE ...?!
FEI LONG... WHAT DID YOU... DO TO...
WUMP

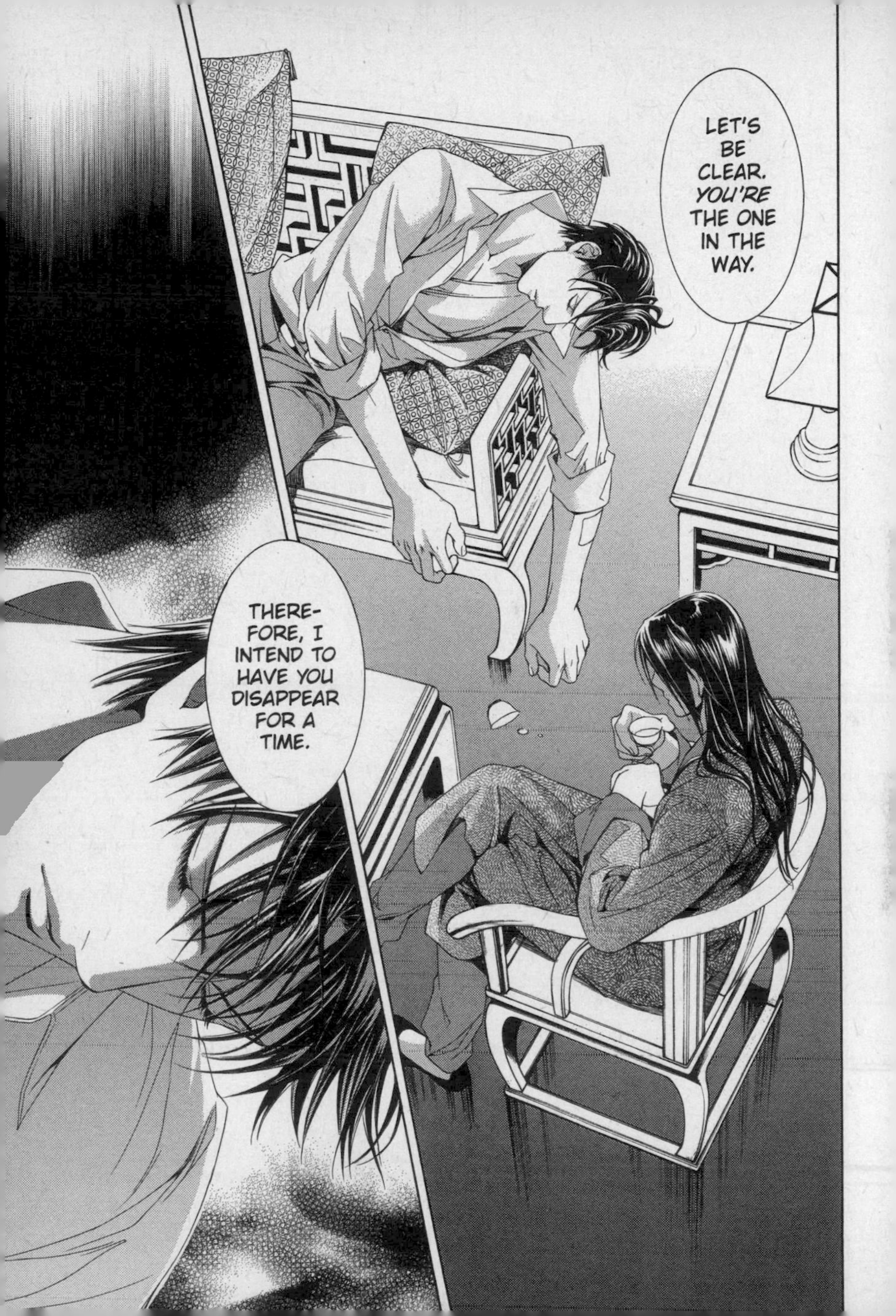
LET'S BE CLEAR. *YOU'RE* THE ONE IN THE WAY.
THERE-FORE, I INTEND TO HAVE YOU DISAPPEAR FOR A TIME.

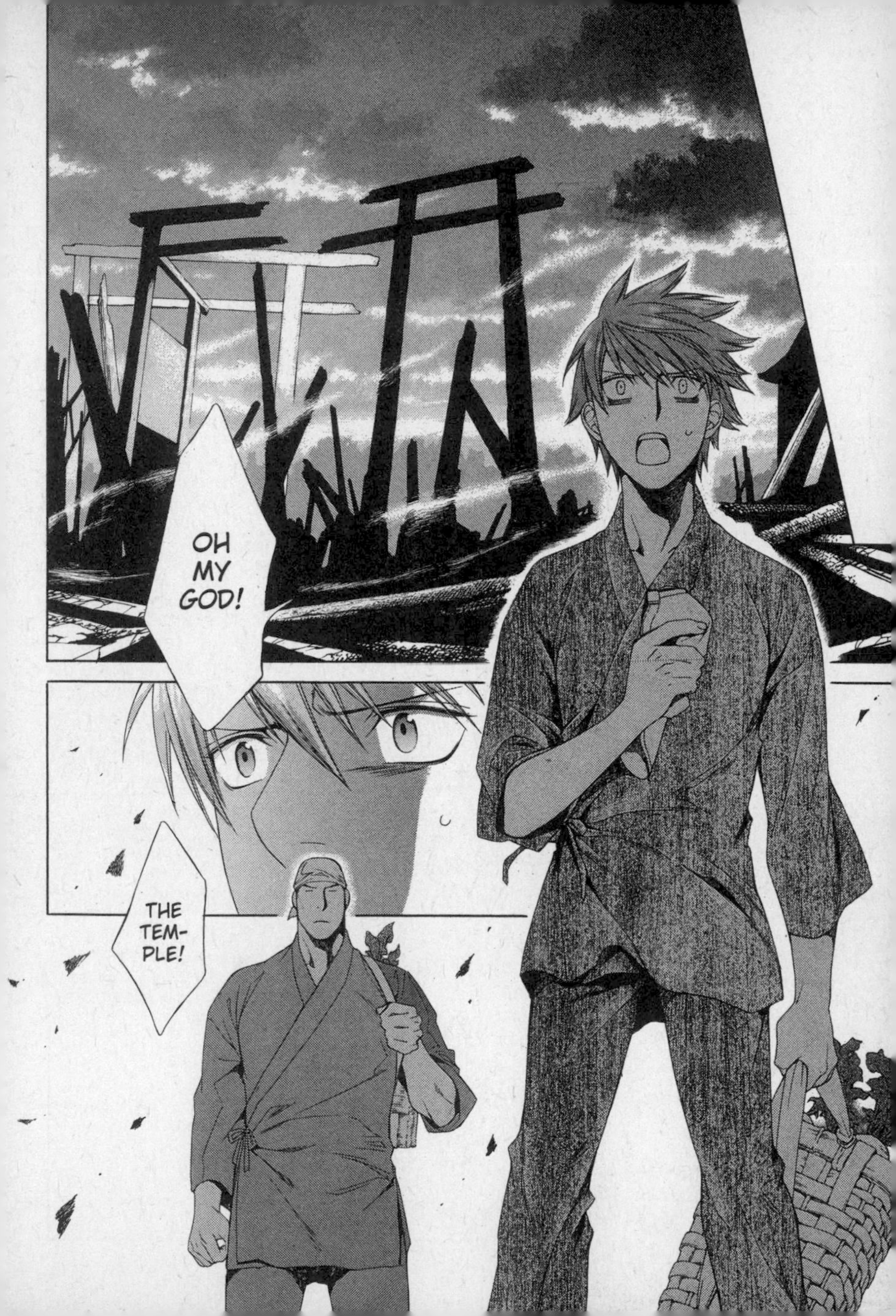
OH MY GOD!
THE TEMPLE!

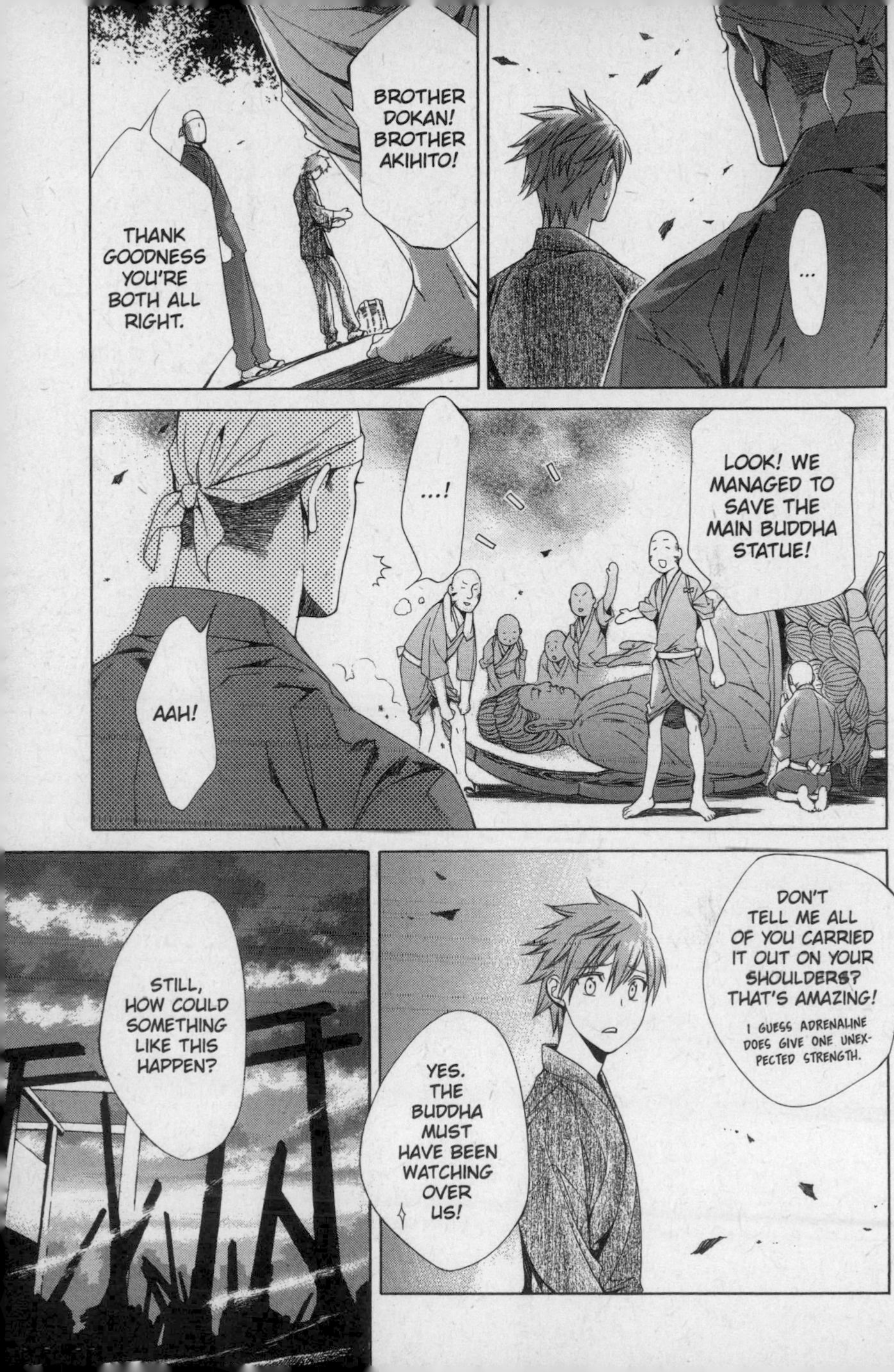
...
BROTHER DOKAN! BROTHER AKIHITO!
THANK GOODNESS YOU'RE BOTH ALL RIGHT.
LOOK! WE MANAGED TO SAVE THE MAIN BUDDHA STATUE!
...!
AAH!
DON'T TELL ME ALL OF YOU CARRIED IT OUT ON YOUR SHOULDERS? THAT'S AMAZING!
I GUESS ADRENALINE DOES GIVE ONE UNEXPECTED STRENGTH.
YES. THE BUDDHA MUST HAVE BEEN WATCHING OVER US!
STILL, HOW COULD SOMETHING LIKE THIS HAPPEN?

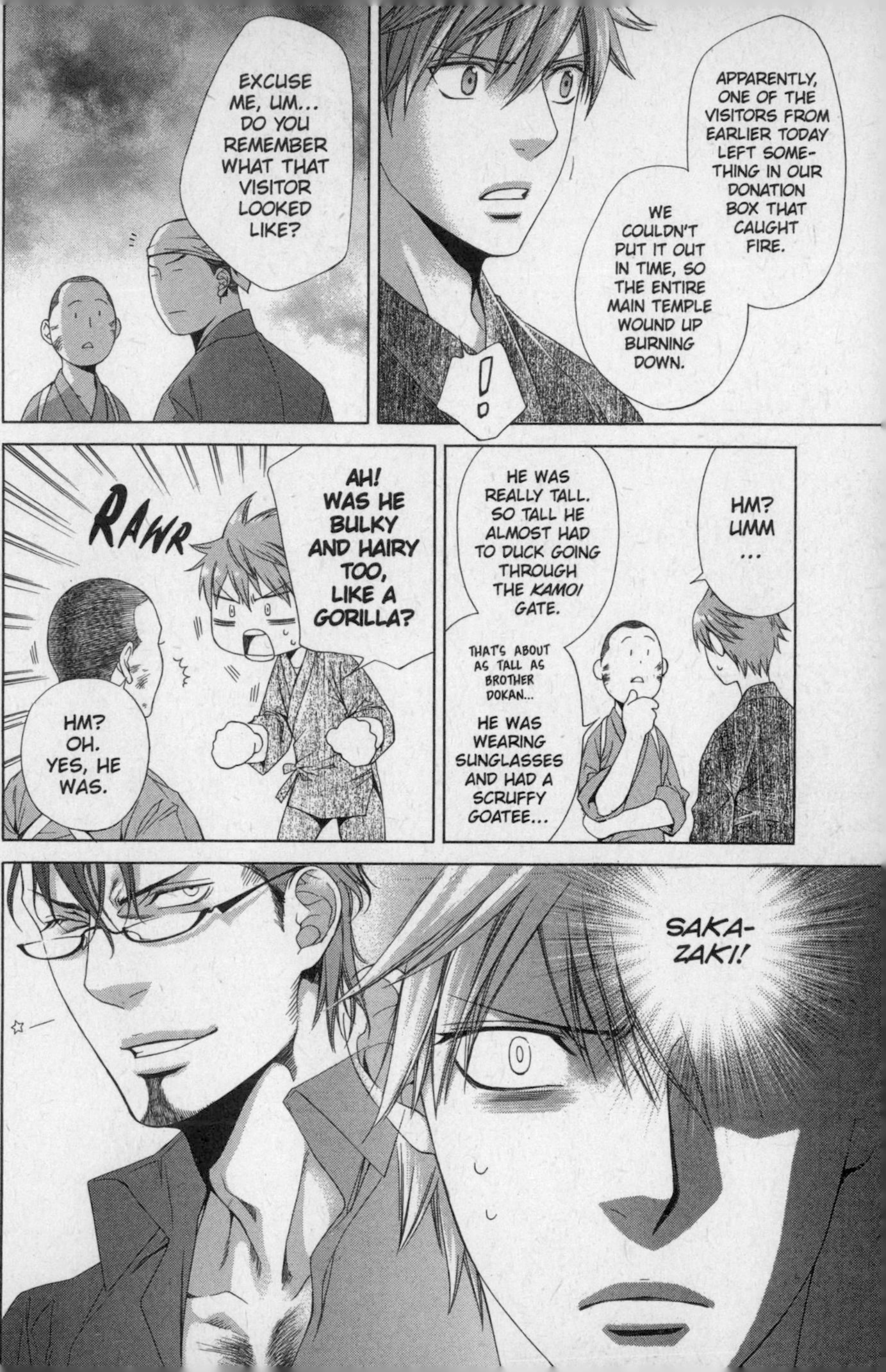
APPARENTLY, ONE OF THE VISITORS FROM EARLIER TODAY LEFT SOME-THING IN OUR DONATION BOX THAT CAUGHT FIRE.
WE COULDN'T PUT IT OUT IN TIME, SO THE ENTIRE MAIN TEMPLE WOUND UP BURNING DOWN.
!
EXCUSE ME, UM... DO YOU REMEMBER WHAT THAT VISITOR LOOKED LIKE?
HM? UMM ...
HE WAS REALLY TALL. SO TALL HE ALMOST HAD TO DUCK GOING THROUGH THE *KAMOI* GATE.
THAT'S ABOUT AS TALL AS BROTHER DOKAN...
HE WAS WEARING SUNGLASSES AND HAD A SCRUFFY GOATEE...
AH! WAS HE BULKY AND HAIRY TOO, LIKE A GORILLA?
RAWR
HM? OH. YES, HE WAS.
SAKA-ZAKI!

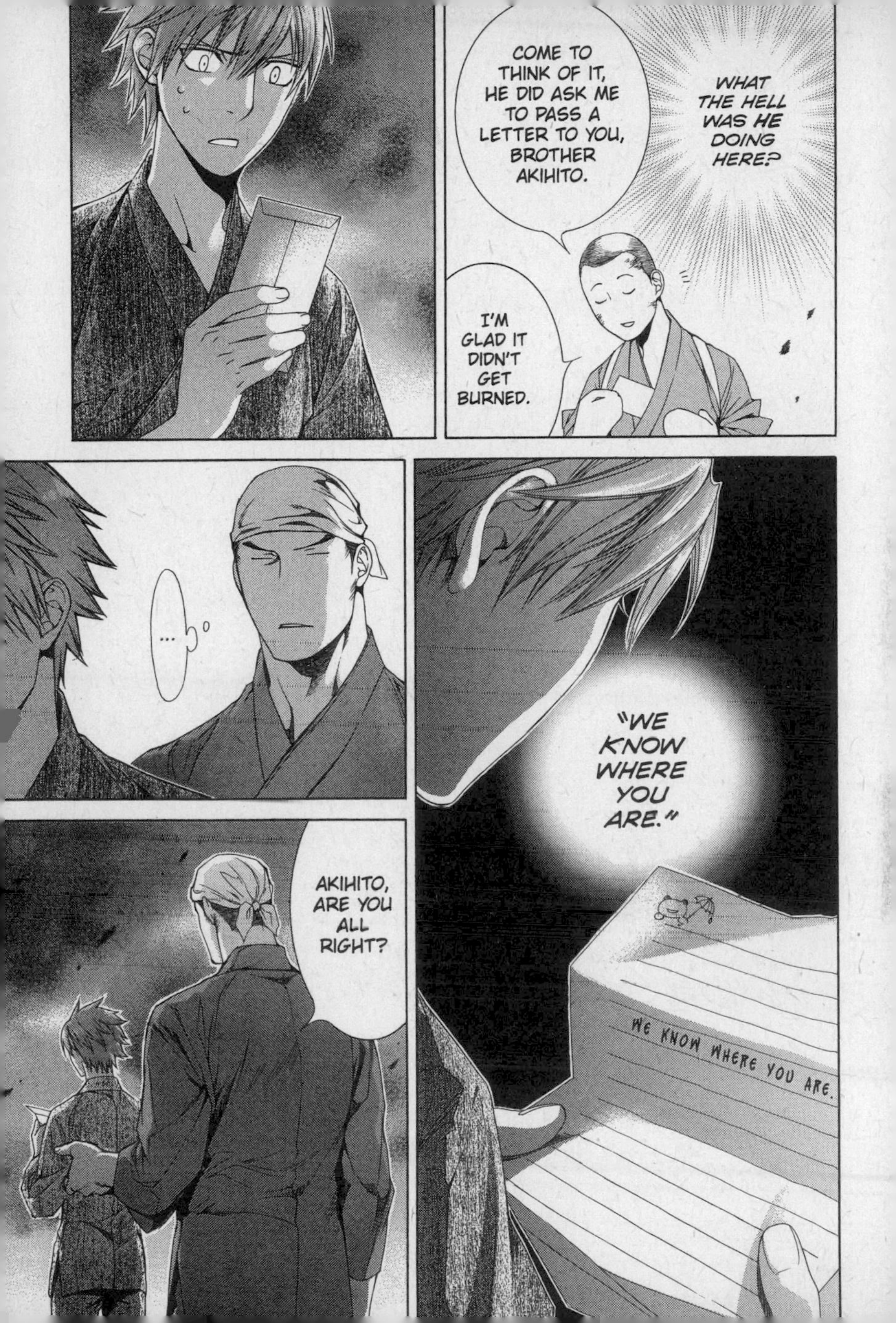
WHAT THE HELL WAS HE DOING HERE?
COME TO THINK OF IT, HE DID ASK ME TO PASS A LETTER TO YOU, BROTHER AKIHITO.
I'M GLAD IT DIDN'T GET BURNED.
"WE KNOW WHERE YOU ARE."
WE KNOW WHERE YOU ARE.
...
AKIHITO, ARE YOU ALL RIGHT?

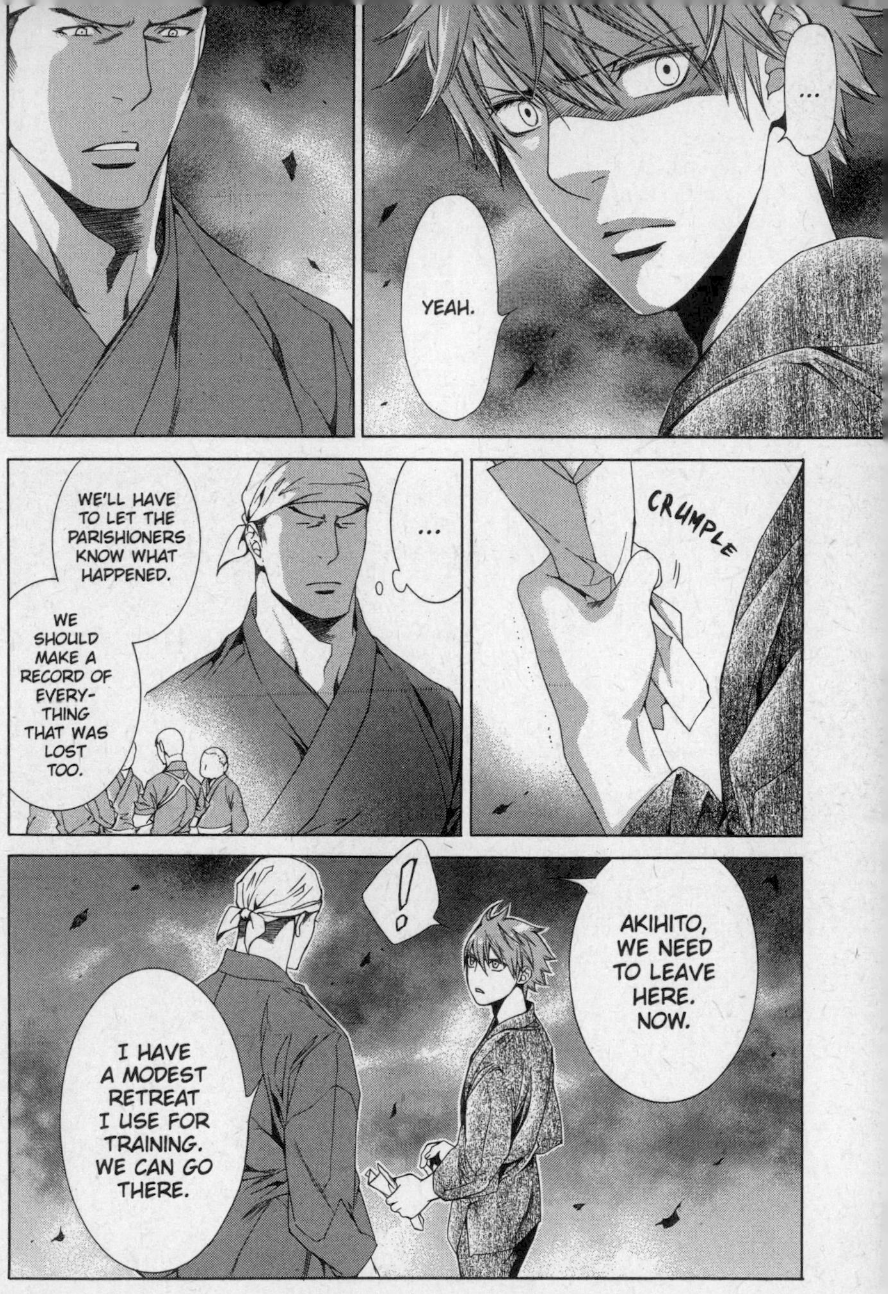
...
YEAH.
CRUMPLE
...
WE'LL HAVE TO LET THE PARISHIONERS KNOW WHAT HAPPENED.
WE SHOULD MAKE A RECORD OF EVERY-THING THAT WAS LOST TOO.
!
AKIHITO, WE NEED TO LEAVE HERE. NOW.
I HAVE A MODEST RETREAT I USE FOR TRAINING. WE CAN GO THERE.

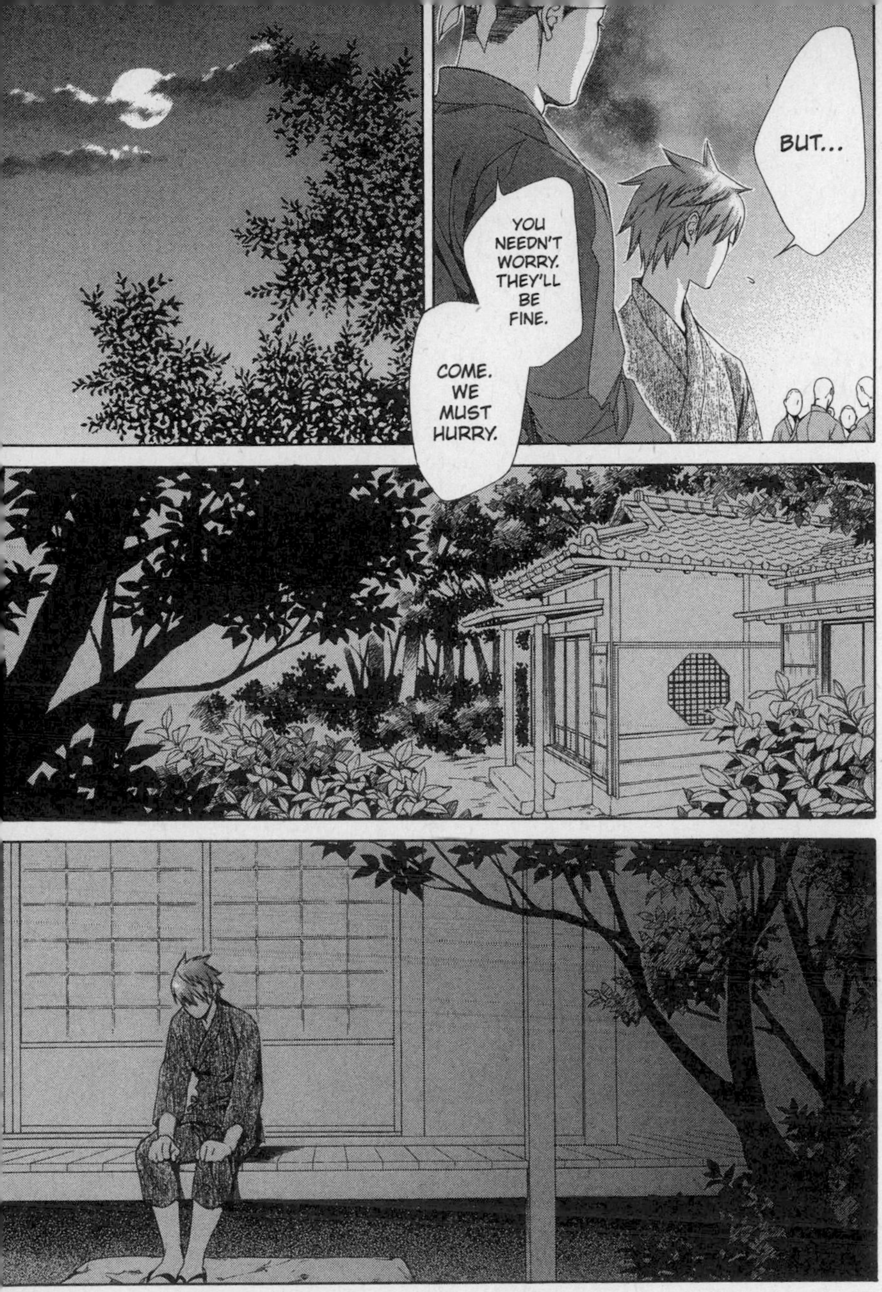
BUT...
YOU NEEDN'T WORRY. THEY'LL BE FINE.
COME. WE MUST HURRY.

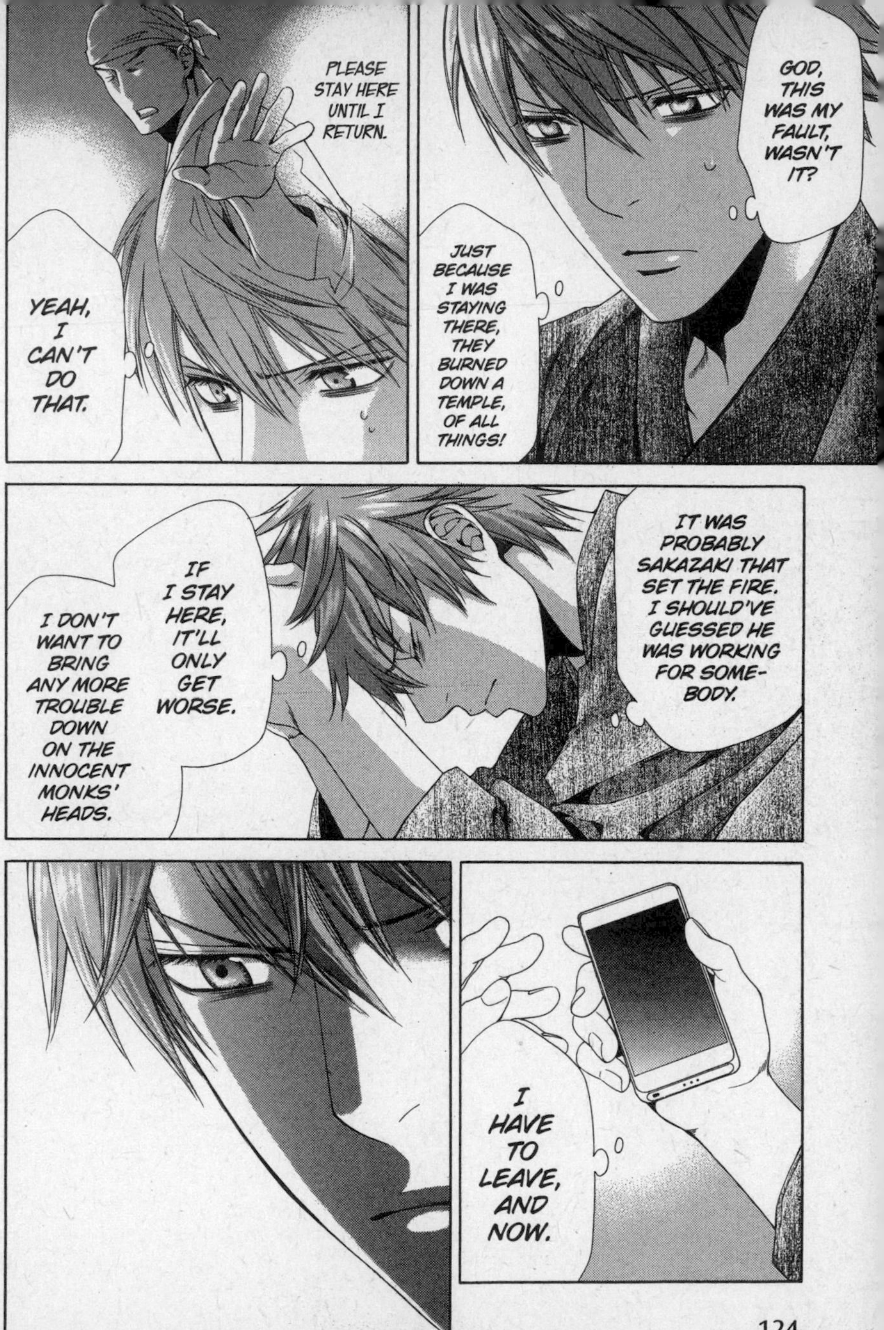
GOD, THIS WAS MY FAULT, WASN'T IT?
JUST BECAUSE I WAS STAYING THERE, THEY BURNED DOWN A TEMPLE, OF ALL THINGS!
PLEASE STAY HERE UNTIL I RETURN.
YEAH, I CAN'T DO THAT.
IT WAS PROBABLY SAKAZAKI THAT SET THE FIRE. I SHOULD'VE GUESSED HE WAS WORKING FOR SOME-BODY.
IF I STAY HERE, IT'LL ONLY GET WORSE.
I DON'T WANT TO BRING ANY MORE TROUBLE DOWN ON THE INNOCENT MONKS' HEADS.
I HAVE TO LEAVE, AND NOW.

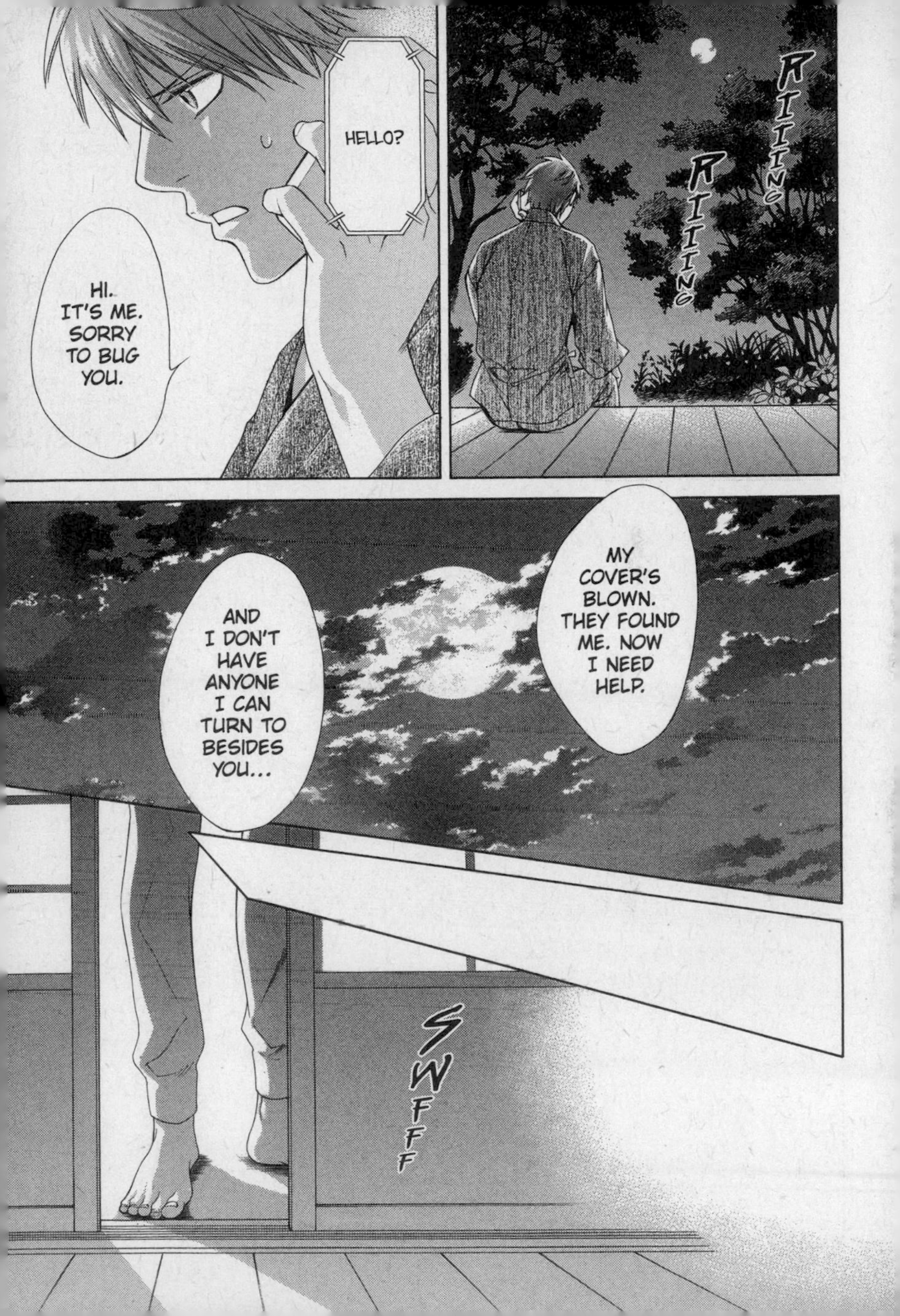
RIIIING
RIIIING
HELLO?
HI. IT'S ME. SORRY TO BUG YOU.
MY COVER'S BLOWN. THEY FOUND ME. NOW I NEED HELP.
AND I DON'T HAVE ANYONE I CAN TURN TO BESIDES YOU...
SWFFF

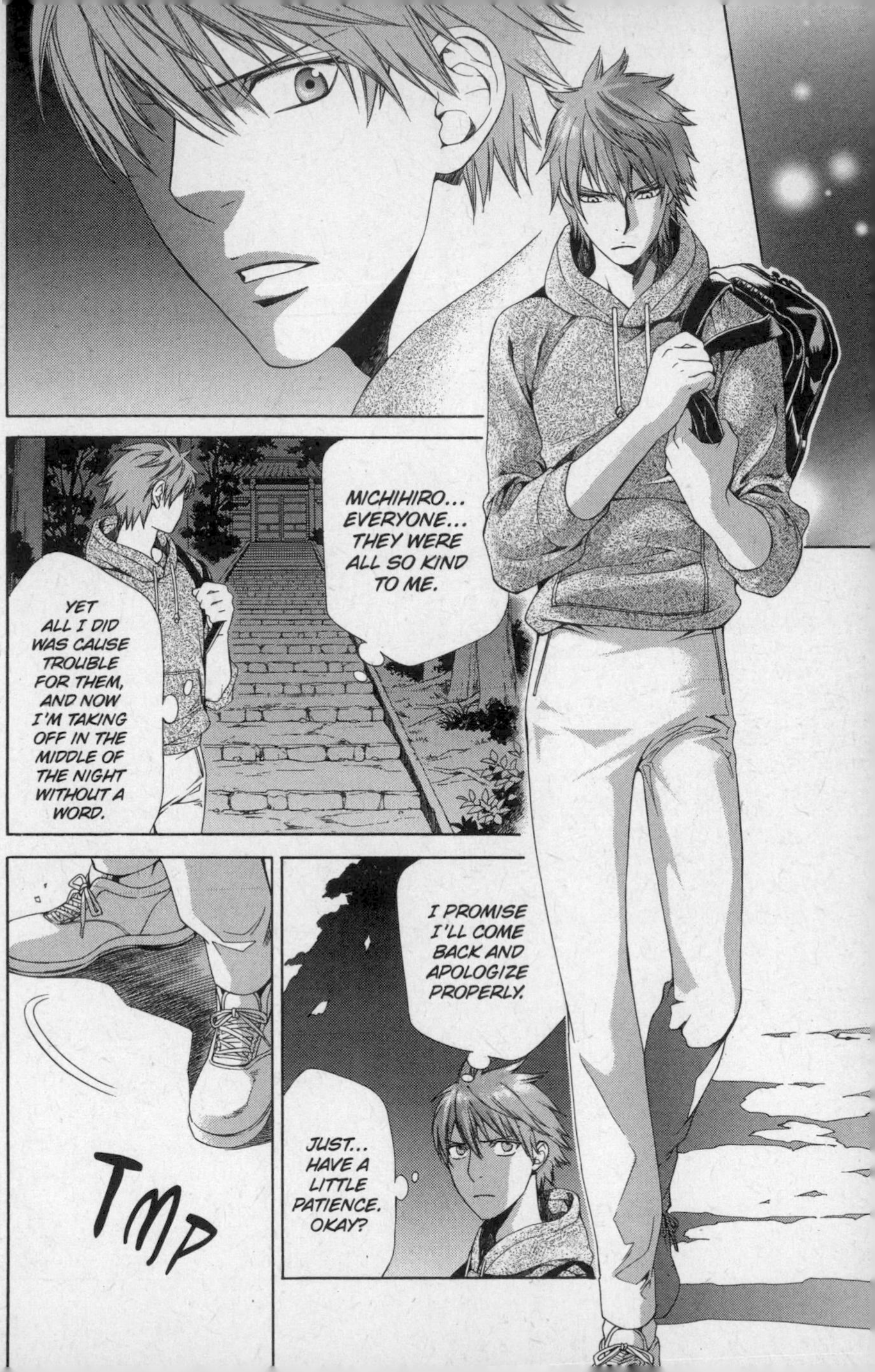
MICHIHIRO... EVERYONE... THEY WERE ALL SO KIND TO ME.
YET ALL I DID WAS CAUSE TROUBLE FOR THEM, AND NOW I'M TAKING OFF IN THE MIDDLE OF THE NIGHT WITHOUT A WORD.
I PROMISE I'LL COME BACK AND APOLOGIZE PROPERLY.
JUST... HAVE A LITTLE PATIENCE. OKAY?
TMP

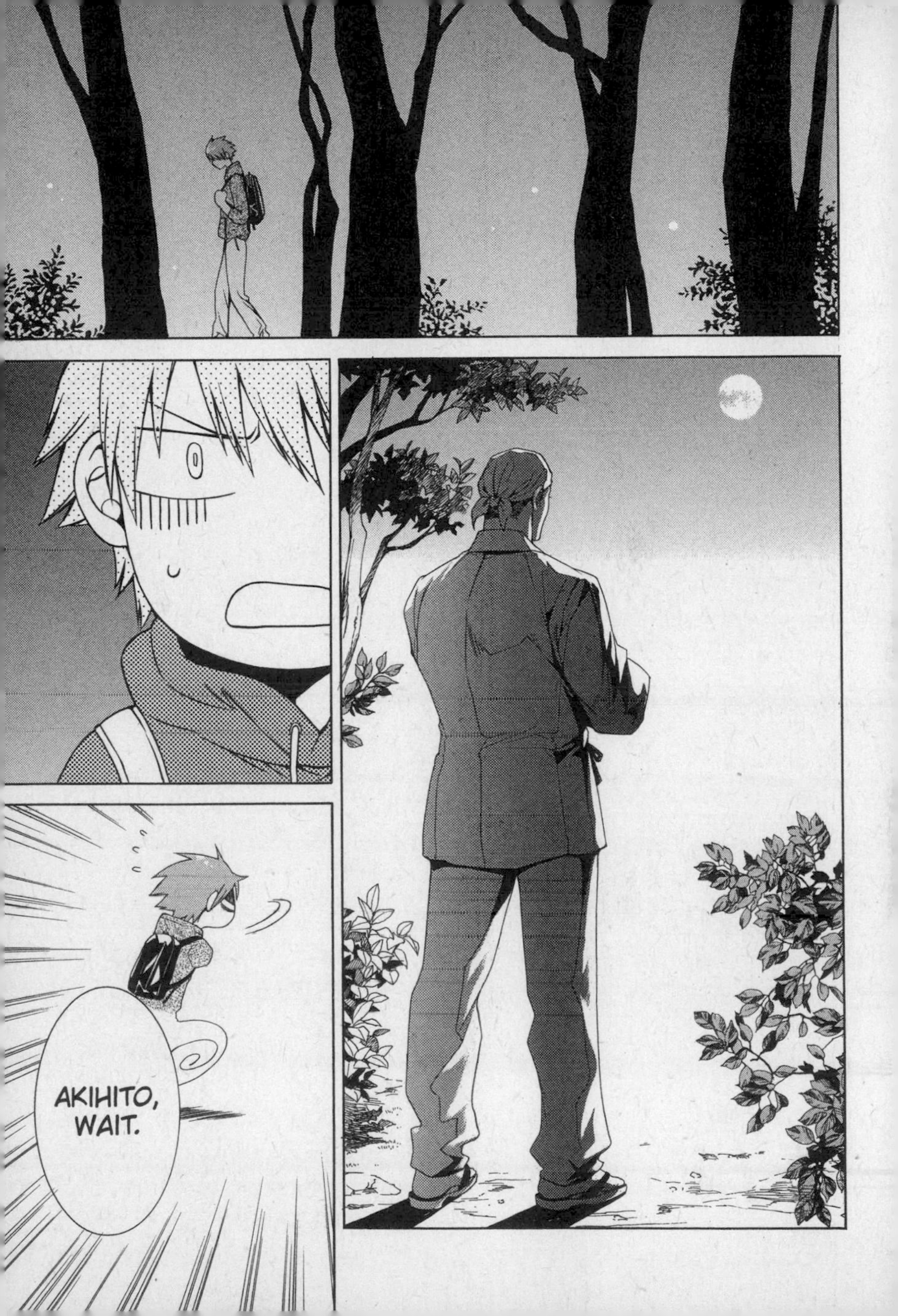
AKIHITO, WAIT.

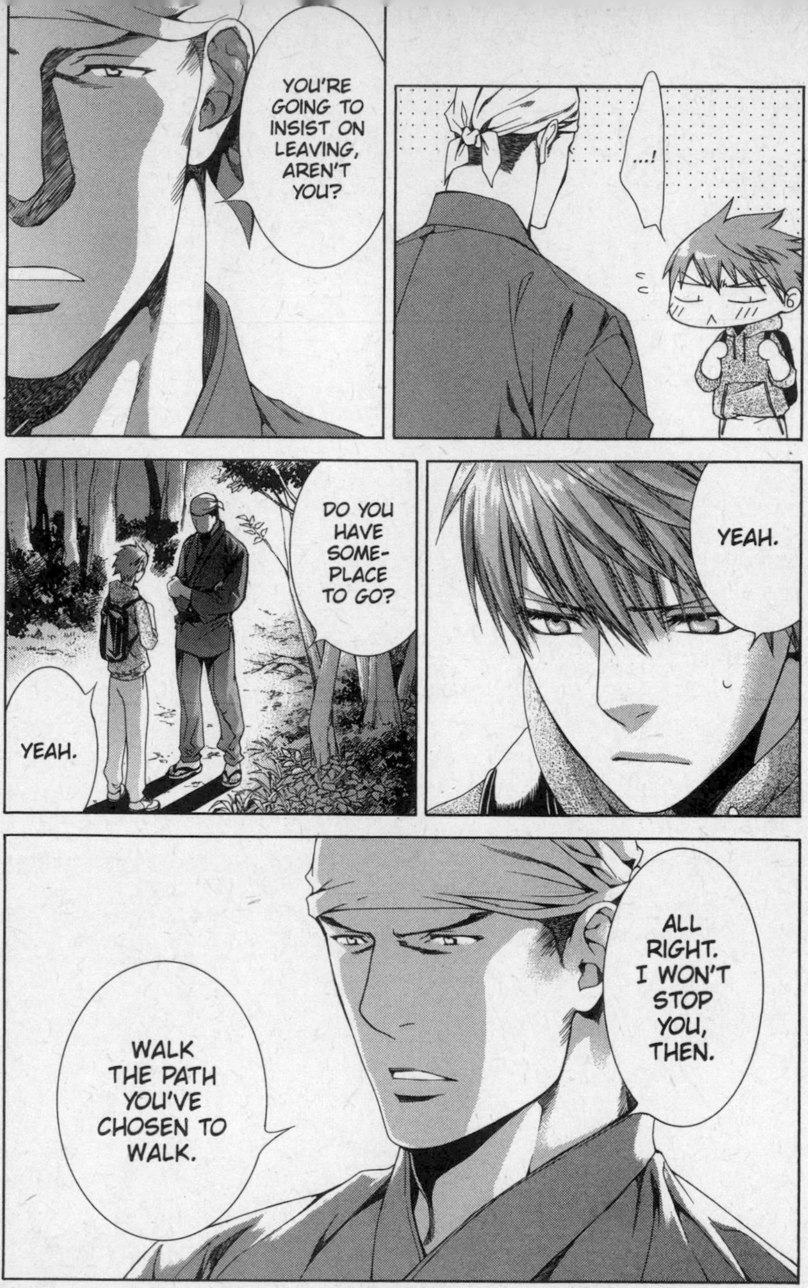
...!
YOU'RE GOING TO INSIST ON LEAVING, AREN'T YOU?
YEAH.
DO YOU HAVE SOME-PLACE TO GO?
YEAH.
ALL RIGHT. I WON'T STOP YOU, THEN.
WALK THE PATH YOU'VE CHOSEN TO WALK.

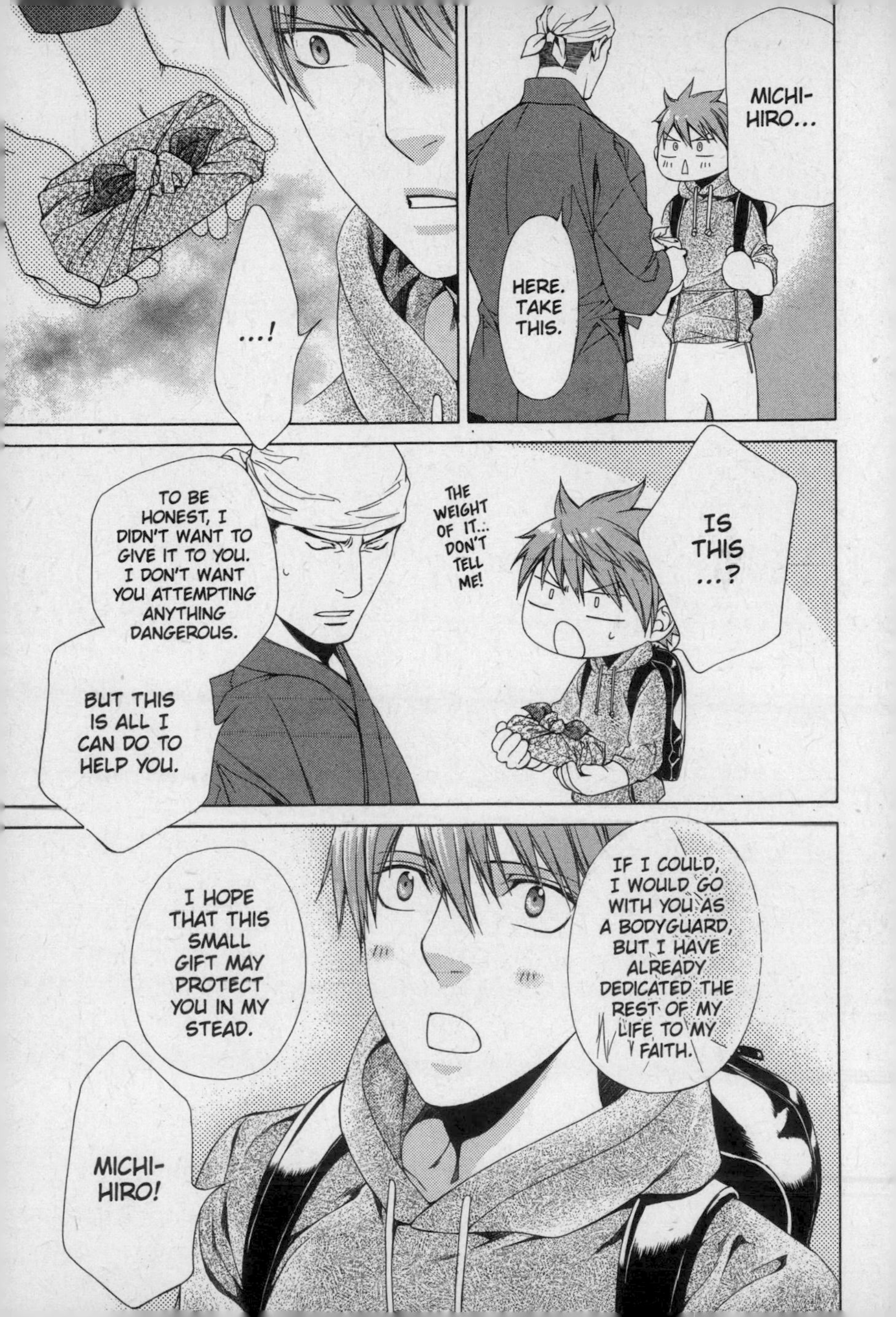
MICHI-HIRO...
HERE. TAKE THIS.
...!
IS THIS ...?
THE WEIGHT OF IT... DON'T TELL ME!
TO BE HONEST, I DIDN'T WANT TO GIVE IT TO YOU. I DON'T WANT YOU ATTEMPTING ANYTHING DANGEROUS.
BUT THIS IS ALL I CAN DO TO HELP YOU.
IF I COULD, I WOULD GO WITH YOU AS A BODYGUARD, BUT I HAVE ALREADY DEDICATED THE REST OF MY LIFE TO MY FAITH.
I HOPE THAT THIS SMALL GIFT MAY PROTECT YOU IN MY STEAD.
MICHI-HIRO!

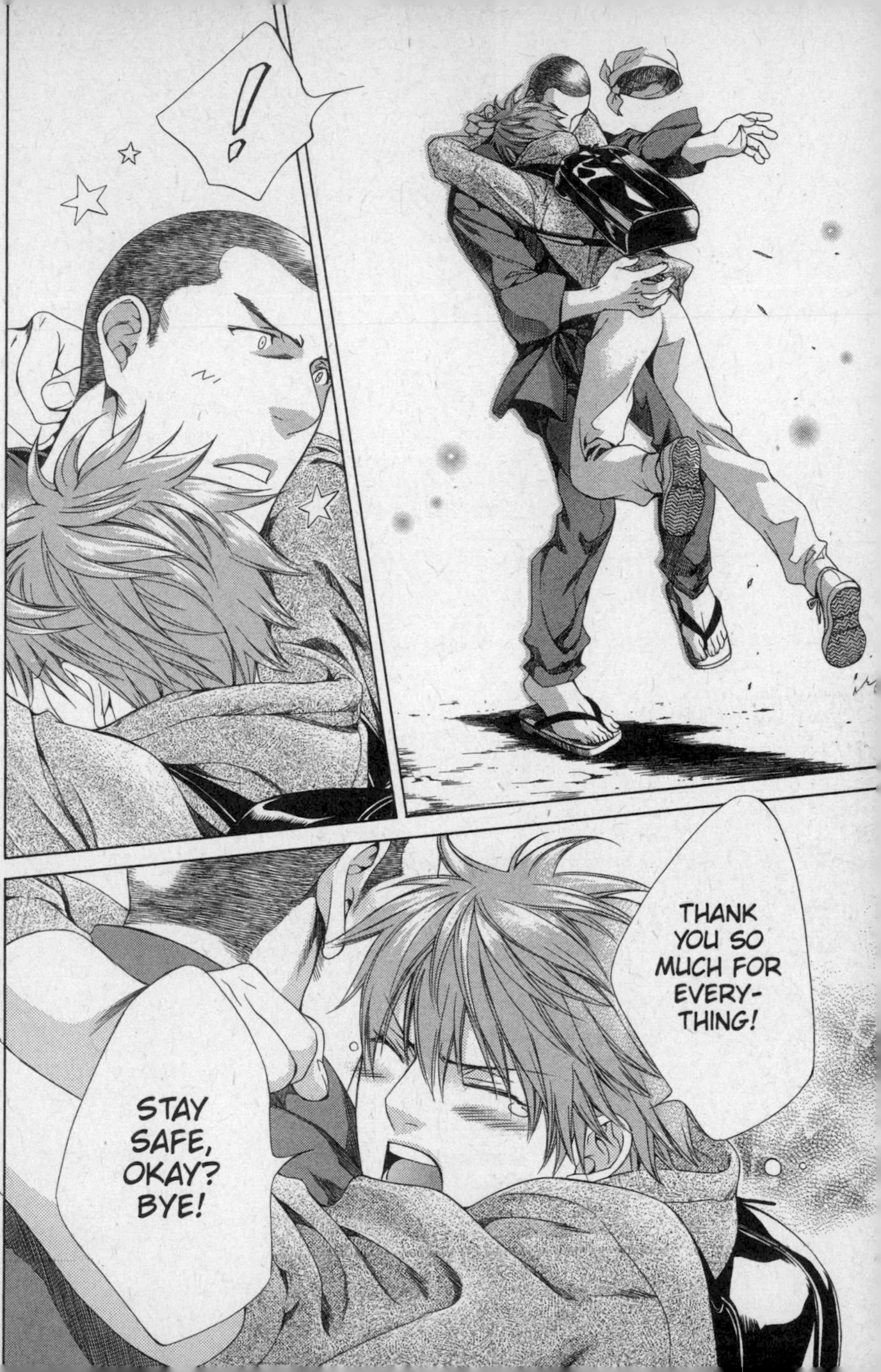
!
THANK YOU SO MUCH FOR EVERY-THING!
STAY SAFE, OKAY? BYE!

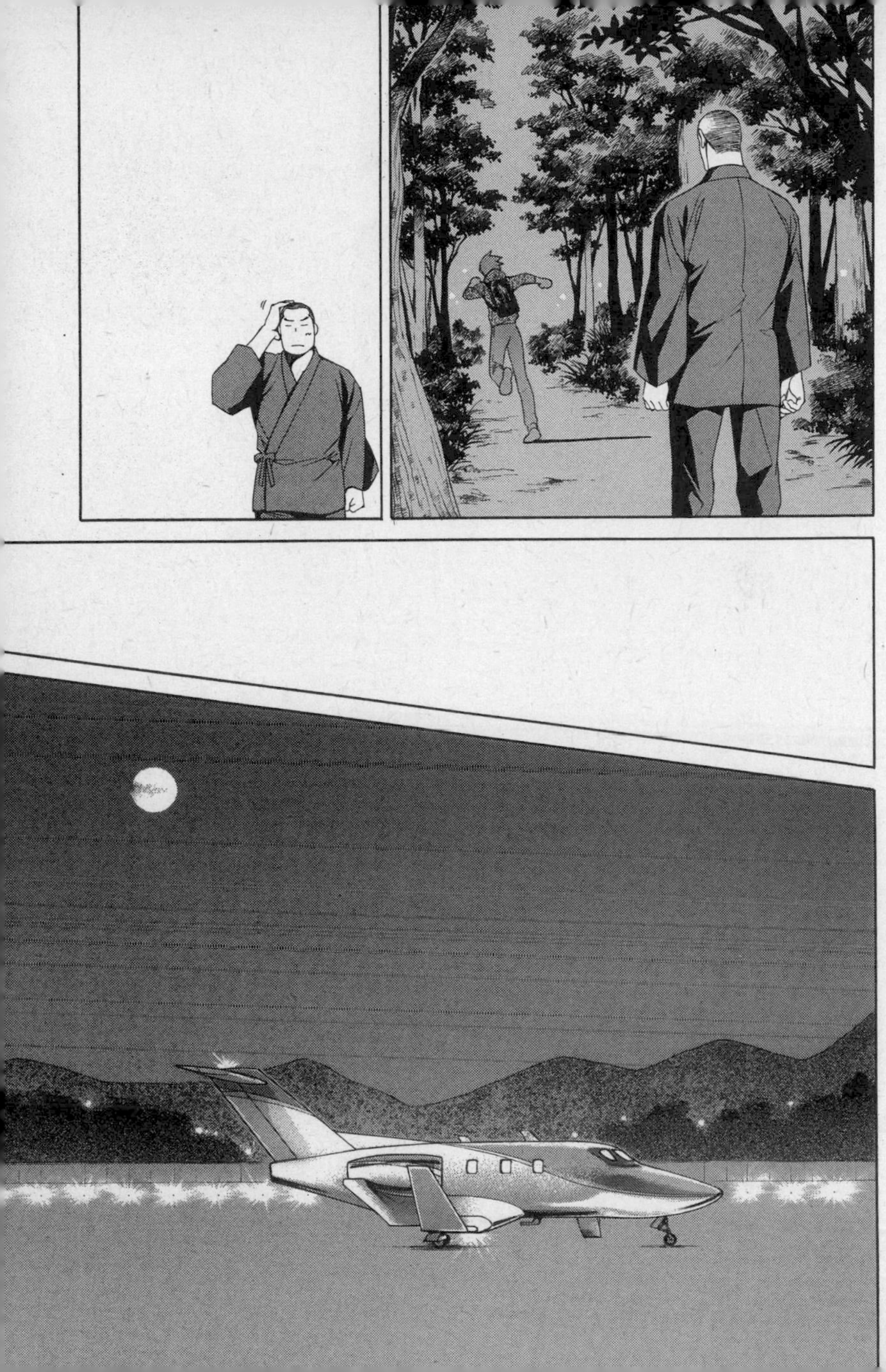

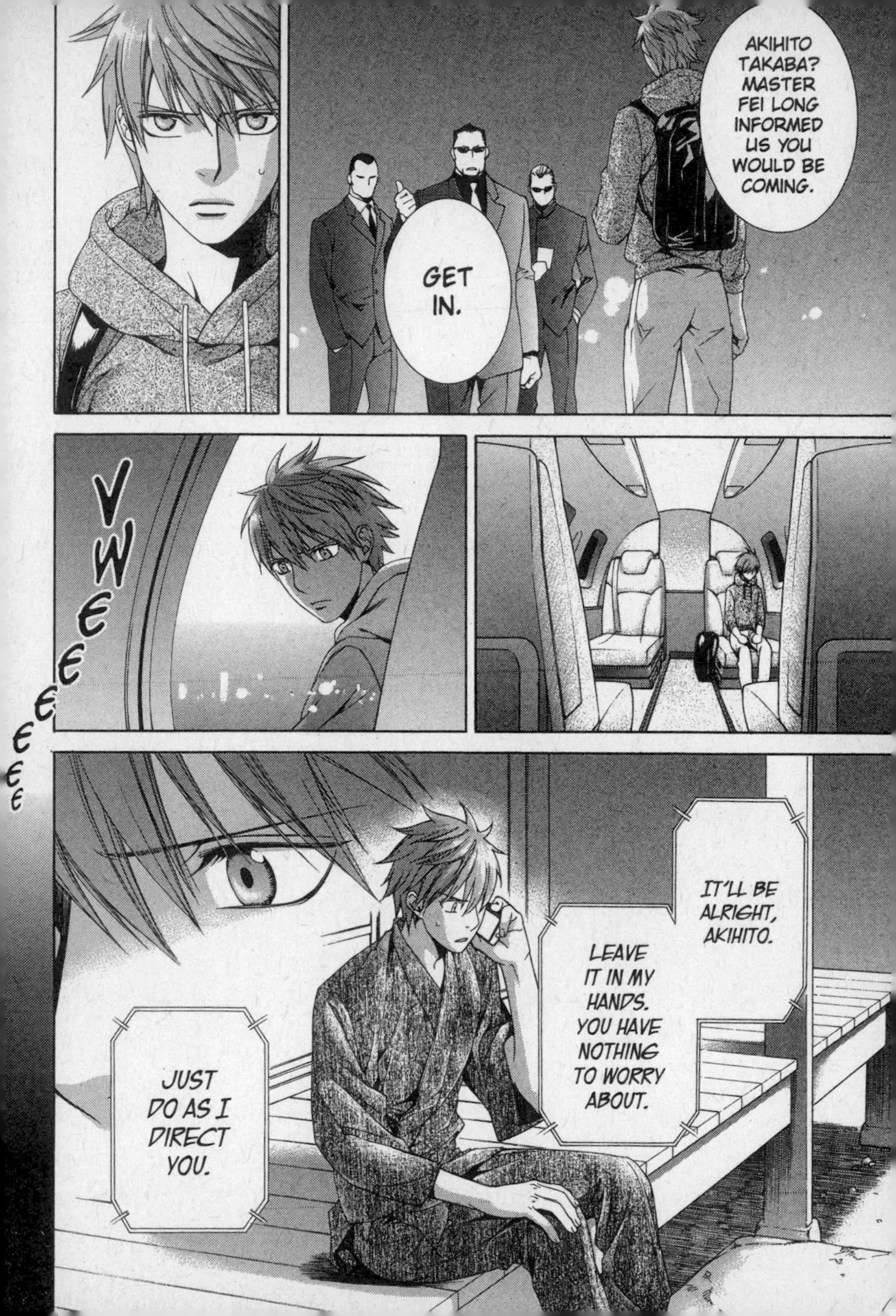
AKIHITO TAKABA? MASTER FEI LONG INFORMED US YOU WOULD BE COMING.
GET IN.
VWEEEEEEE
IT'LL BE ALRIGHT, AKIHITO.
LEAVE IT IN MY HANDS. YOU HAVE NOTHING TO WORRY ABOUT.
JUST DO AS I DIRECT YOU.

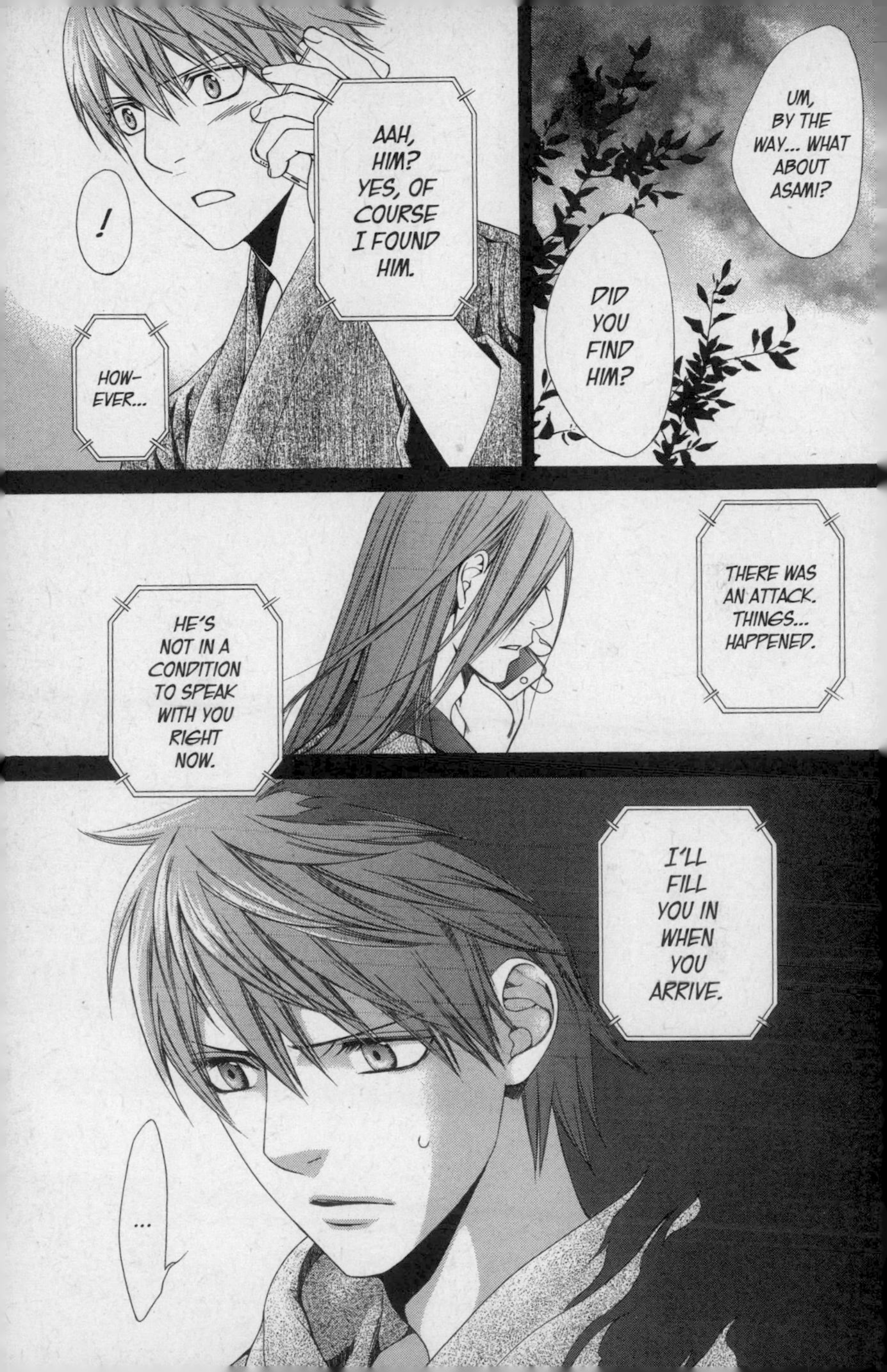
UM, BY THE WAY... WHAT ABOUT ASAMI?
DID YOU FIND HIM?
AAH, HIM? YES, OF COURSE I FOUND HIM.
!
HOW-EVER...
THERE WAS AN ATTACK. THINGS... HAPPENED.
HE'S NOT IN A CONDITION TO SPEAK WITH YOU RIGHT NOW.
I'LL FILL YOU IN WHEN YOU ARRIVE.
...

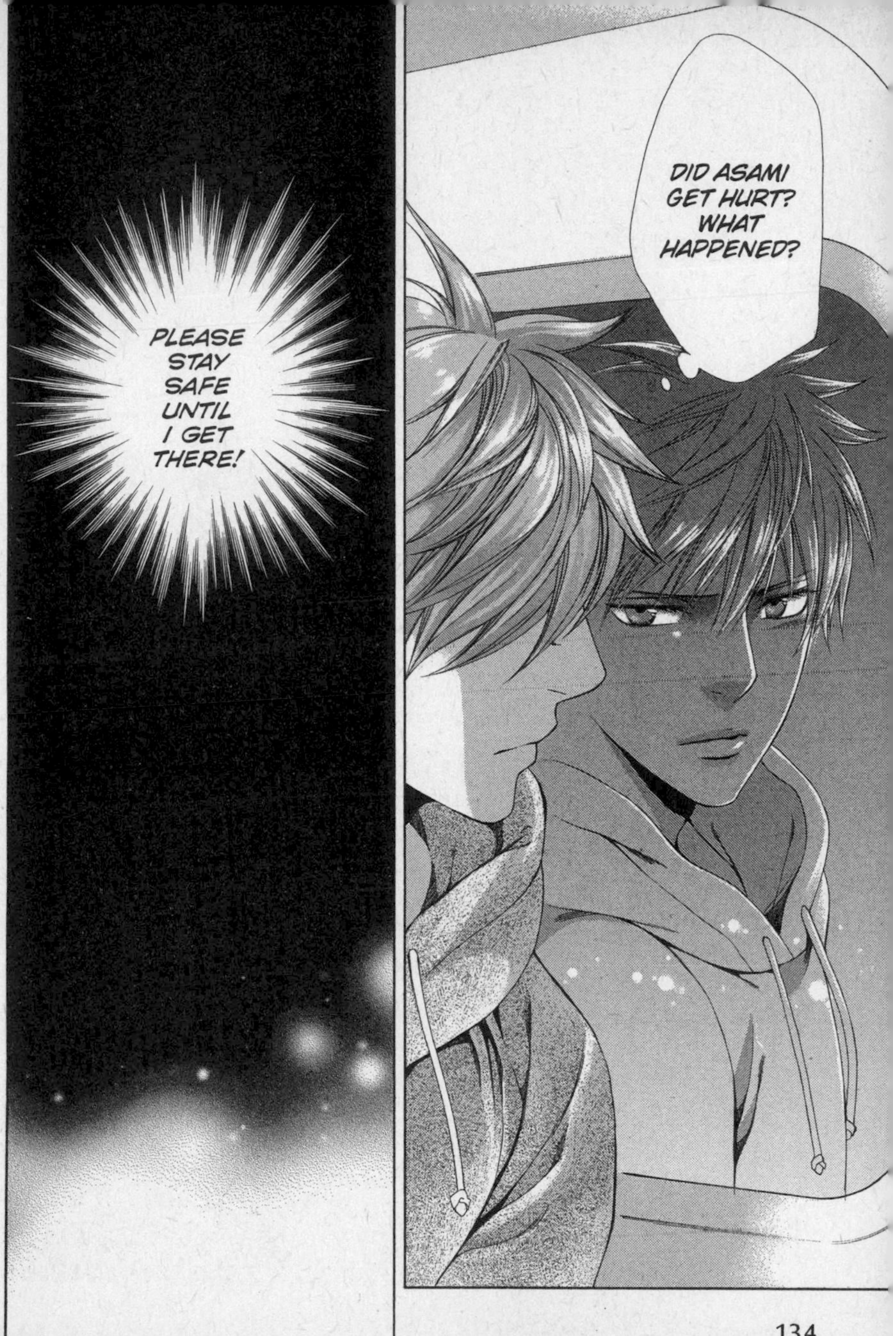
DID ASAMI GET HURT? WHAT HAPPENED?
PLEASE STAY SAFE UNTIL I GET THERE!

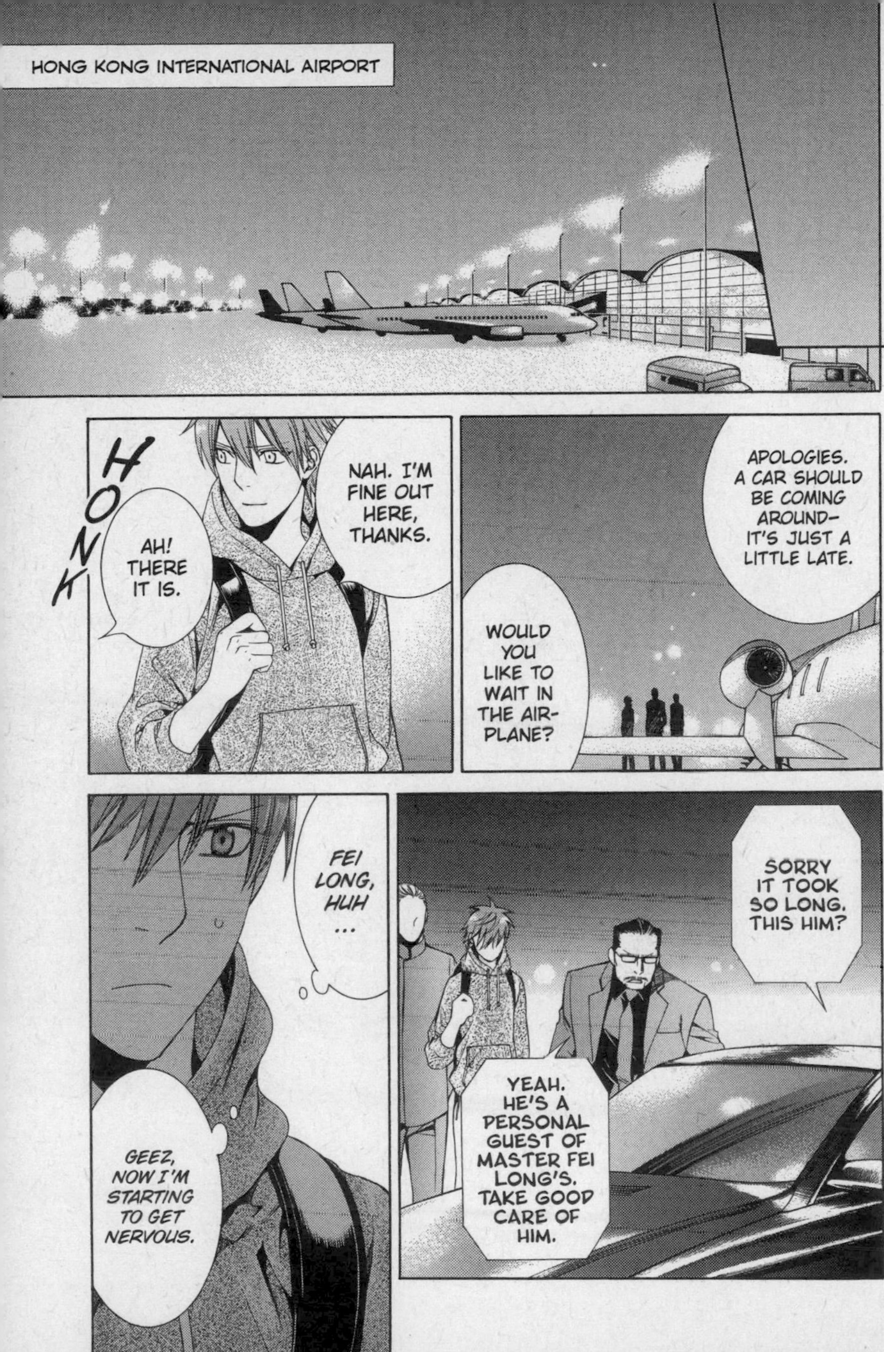
HONG KONG INTERNATIONAL AIRPORT
APOLOGIES. A CAR SHOULD BE COMING AROUND– IT'S JUST A LITTLE LATE.
WOULD YOU LIKE TO WAIT IN THE AIR-PLANE?
NAH. I'M FINE OUT HERE, THANKS.
HONK
AH! THERE IT IS.
SORRY IT TOOK SO LONG. THIS HIM?
YEAH. HE'S A PERSONAL GUEST OF MASTER FEI LONG'S. TAKE GOOD CARE OF HIM.
FEI LONG, HUH ...
GEEZ, NOW I'M STARTING TO GET NERVOUS.

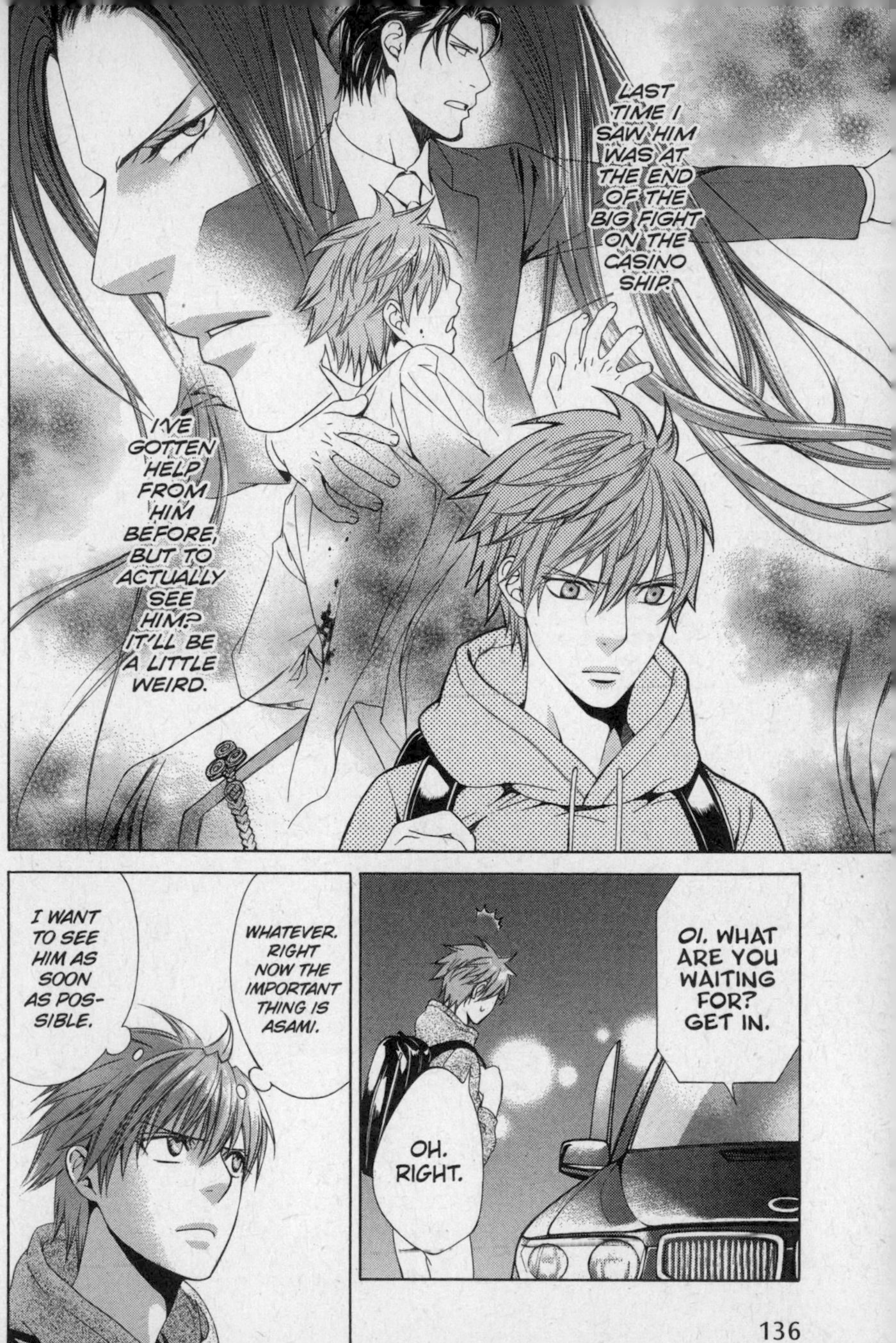
LAST TIME I SAW HIM WAS AT THE END OF THE BIG FIGHT ON THE CASINO SHIP.
I'VE GOTTEN HELP FROM HIM BEFORE, BUT TO ACTUALLY SEE HIM? IT'LL BE A LITTLE WEIRD.
OI. WHAT ARE YOU WAITING FOR? GET IN.
OH. RIGHT.
WHATEVER. RIGHT NOW THE IMPORTANT THING IS ASAMI.
I WANT TO SEE HIM AS SOON AS POS-SIBLE.

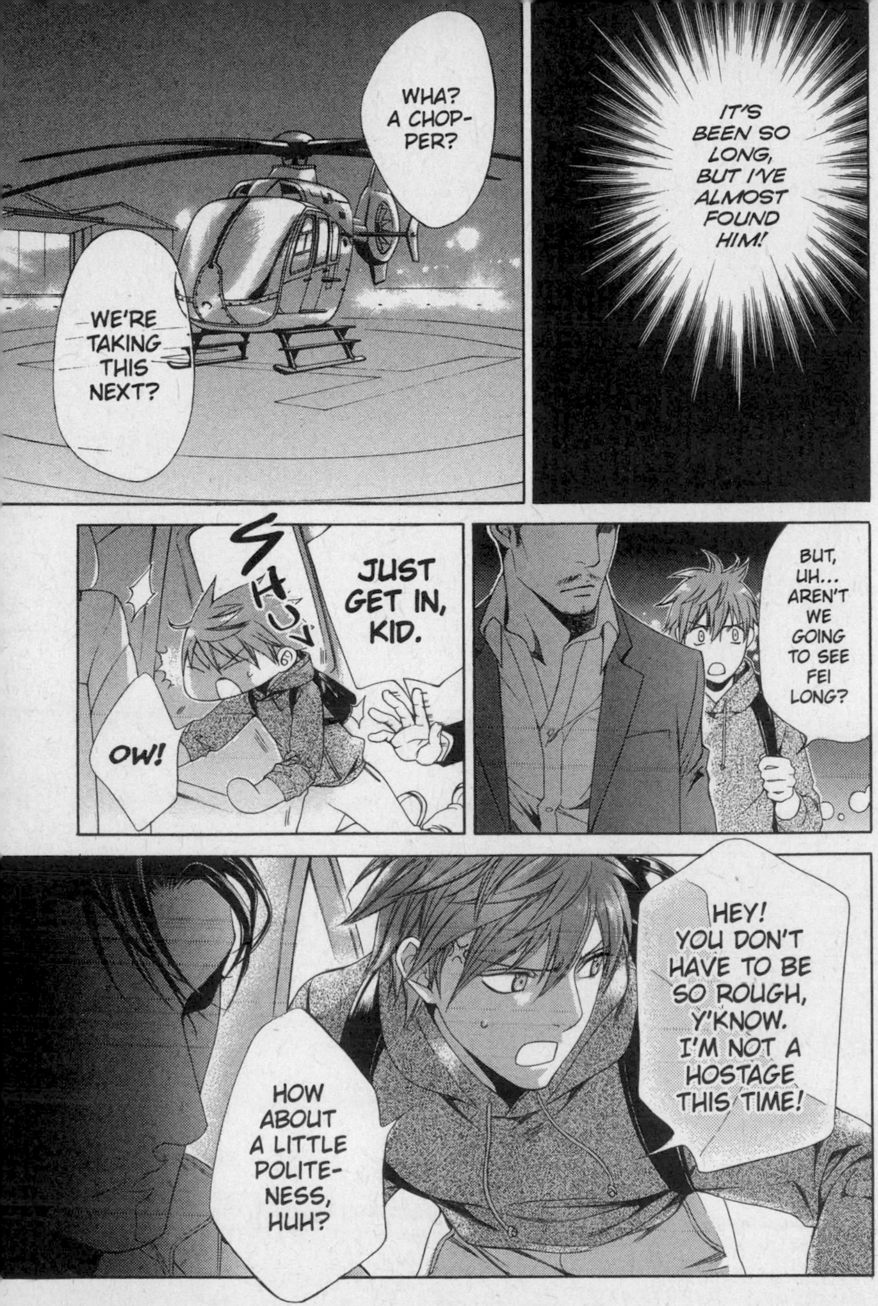
IT'S BEEN SO LONG, BUT I'VE ALMOST FOUND HIM!
WHA? A CHOP-PER?
WE'RE TAKING THIS NEXT?
BUT, UH... AREN'T WE GOING TO SEE FEI LONG?
SHUV
JUST GET IN, KID.
OW!
HEY! YOU DON'T HAVE TO BE SO ROUGH, Y'KNOW. I'M NOT A HOSTAGE THIS TIME!
HOW ABOUT A LITTLE POLITE-NESS, HUH?

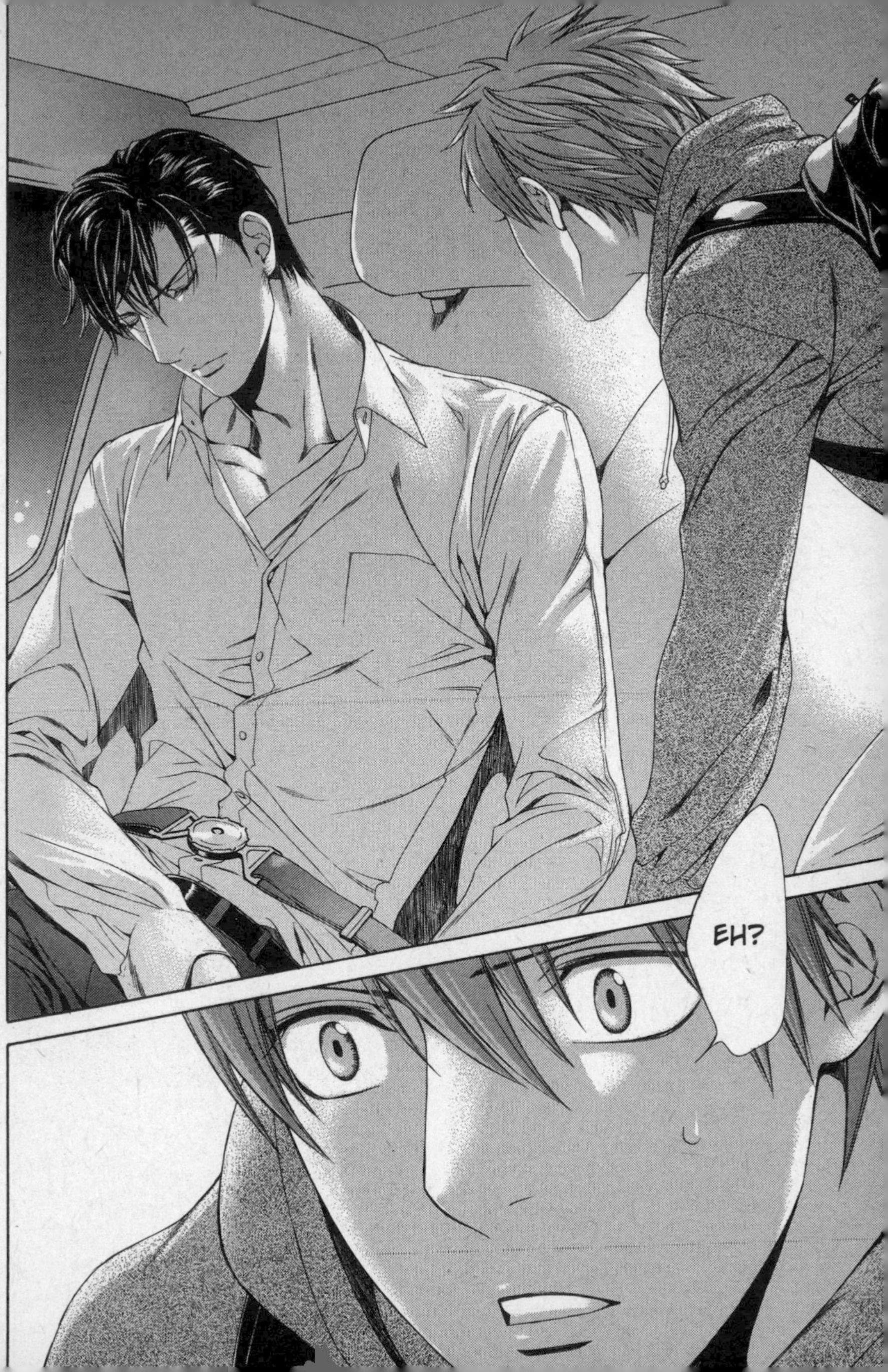
EH?

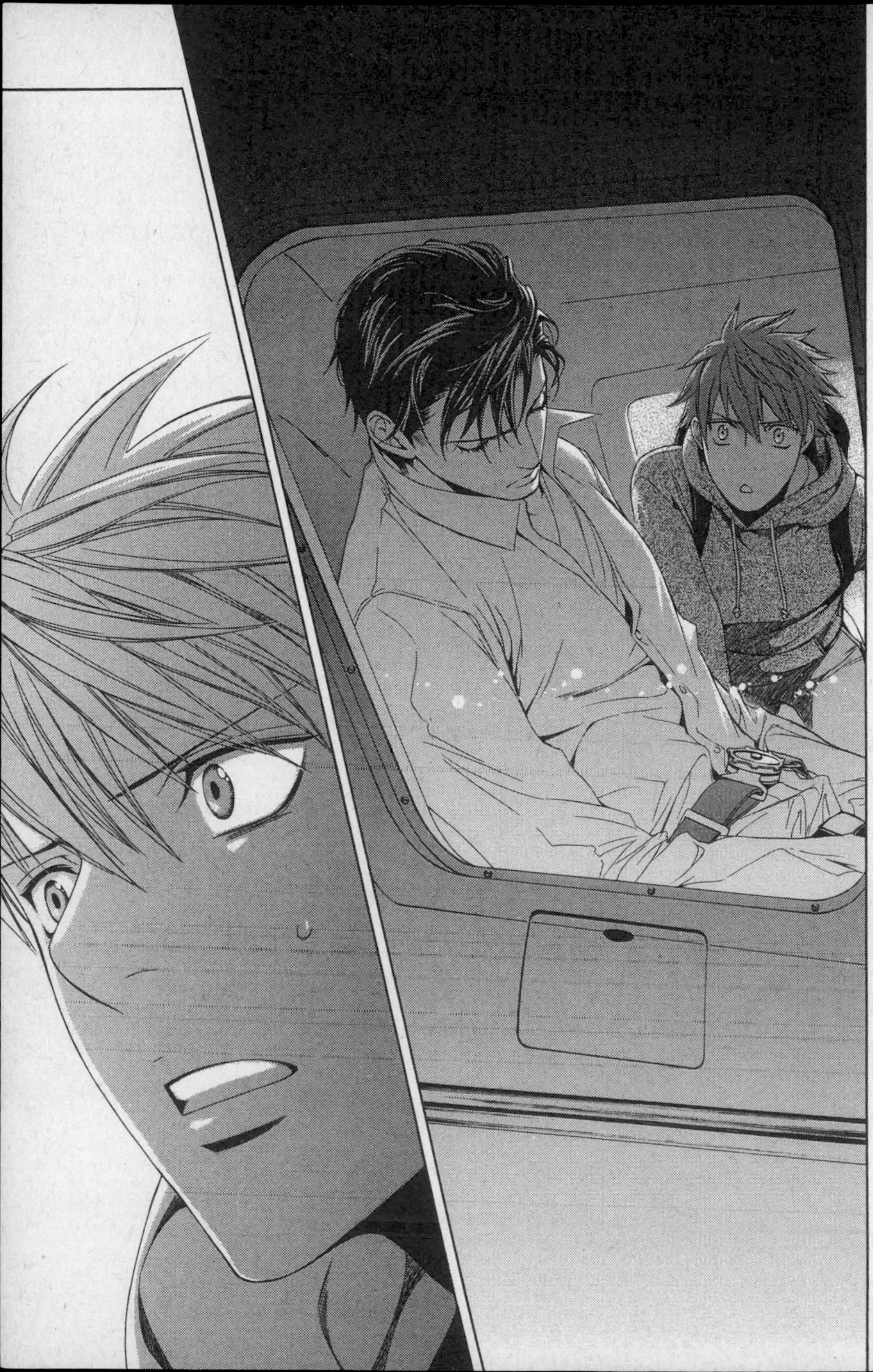

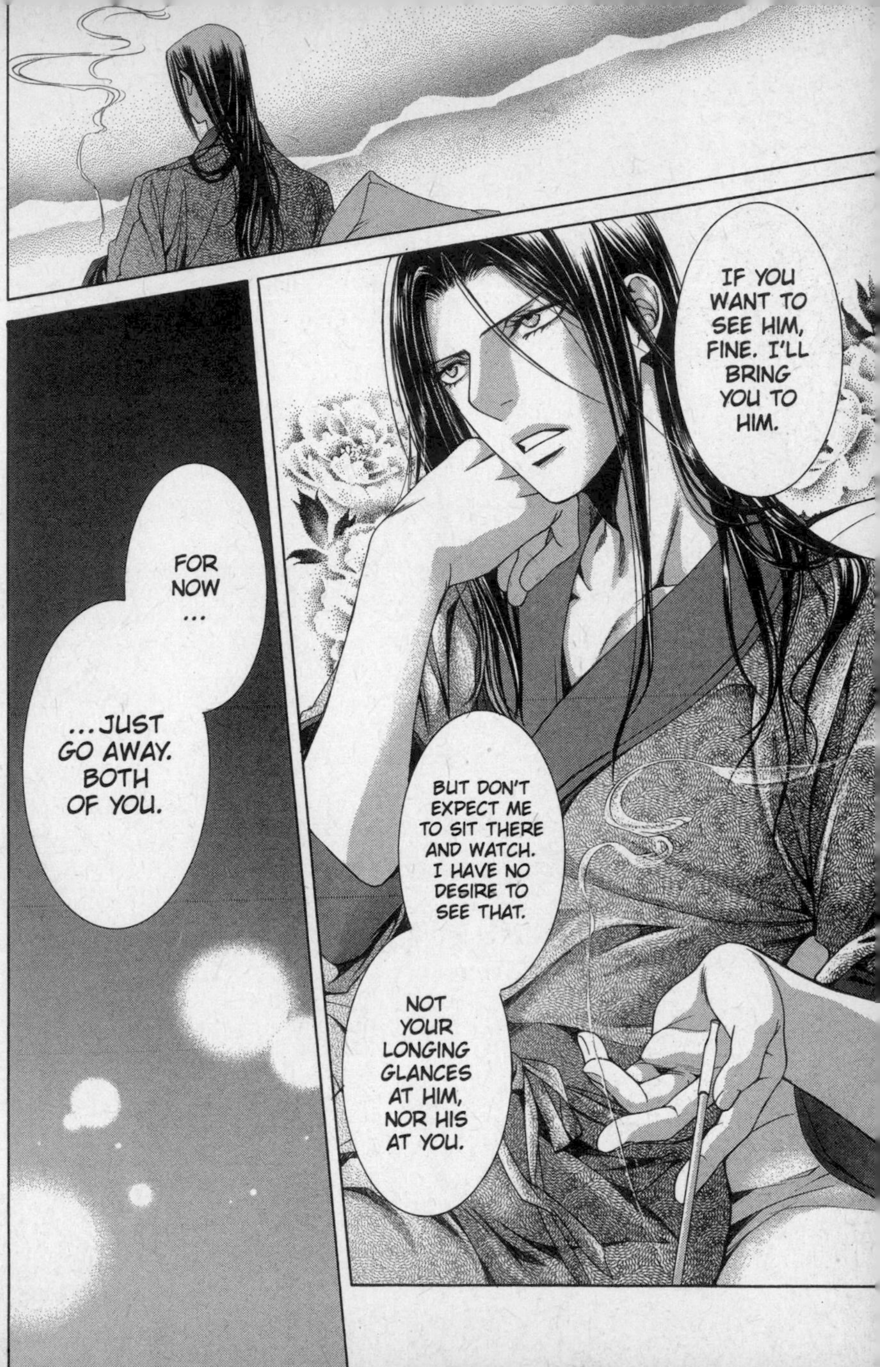
IF YOU WANT TO SEE HIM, FINE. I'LL BRING YOU TO HIM.
BUT DON'T EXPECT ME TO SIT THERE AND WATCH. I HAVE NO DESIRE TO SEE THAT.
NOT YOUR LONGING GLANCES AT HIM, NOR HIS AT YOU.
FOR NOW ...
...JUST GO AWAY. BOTH OF YOU.

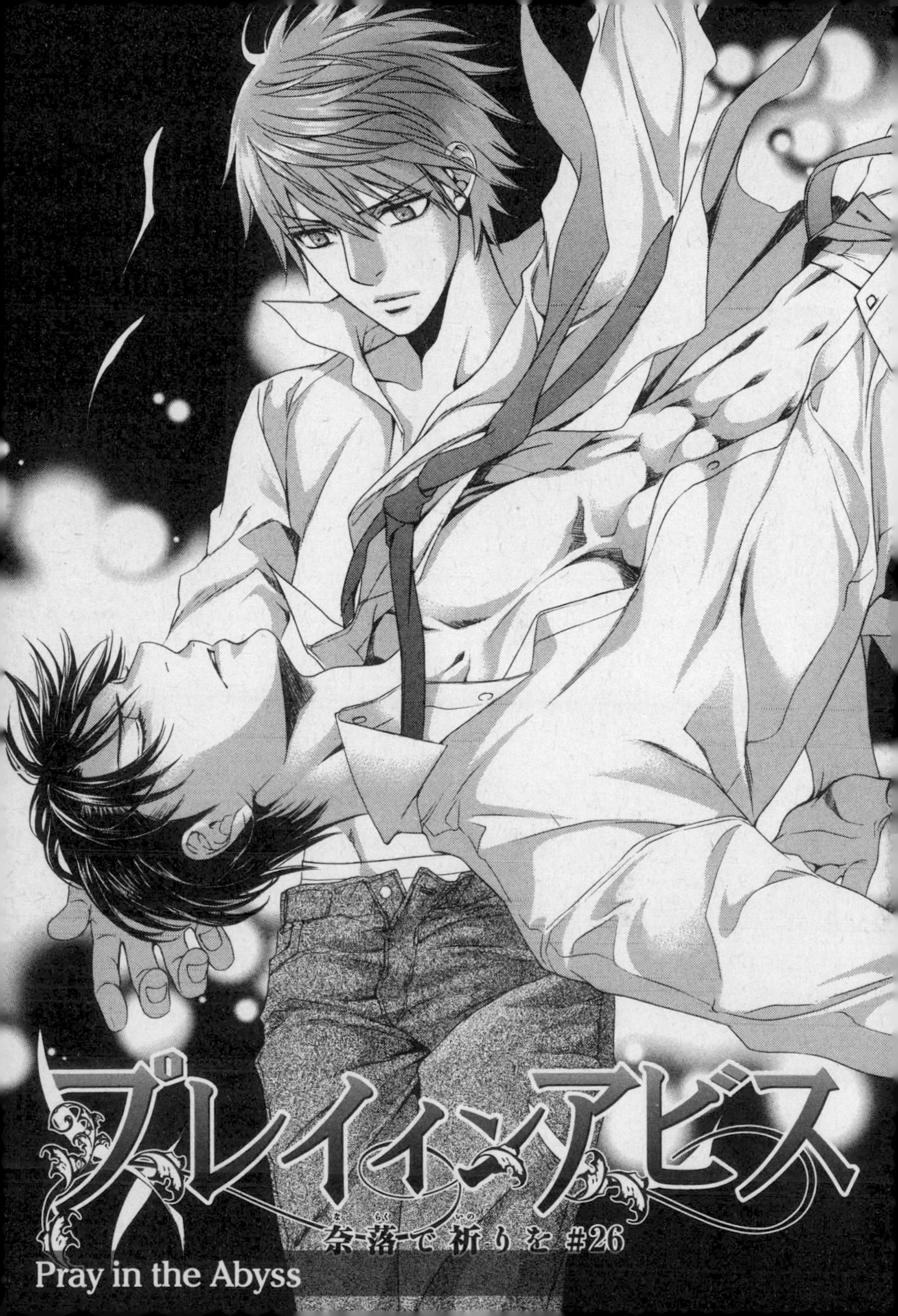
プレイインアビス
奈落で祈りを #26
Pray in the Abyss

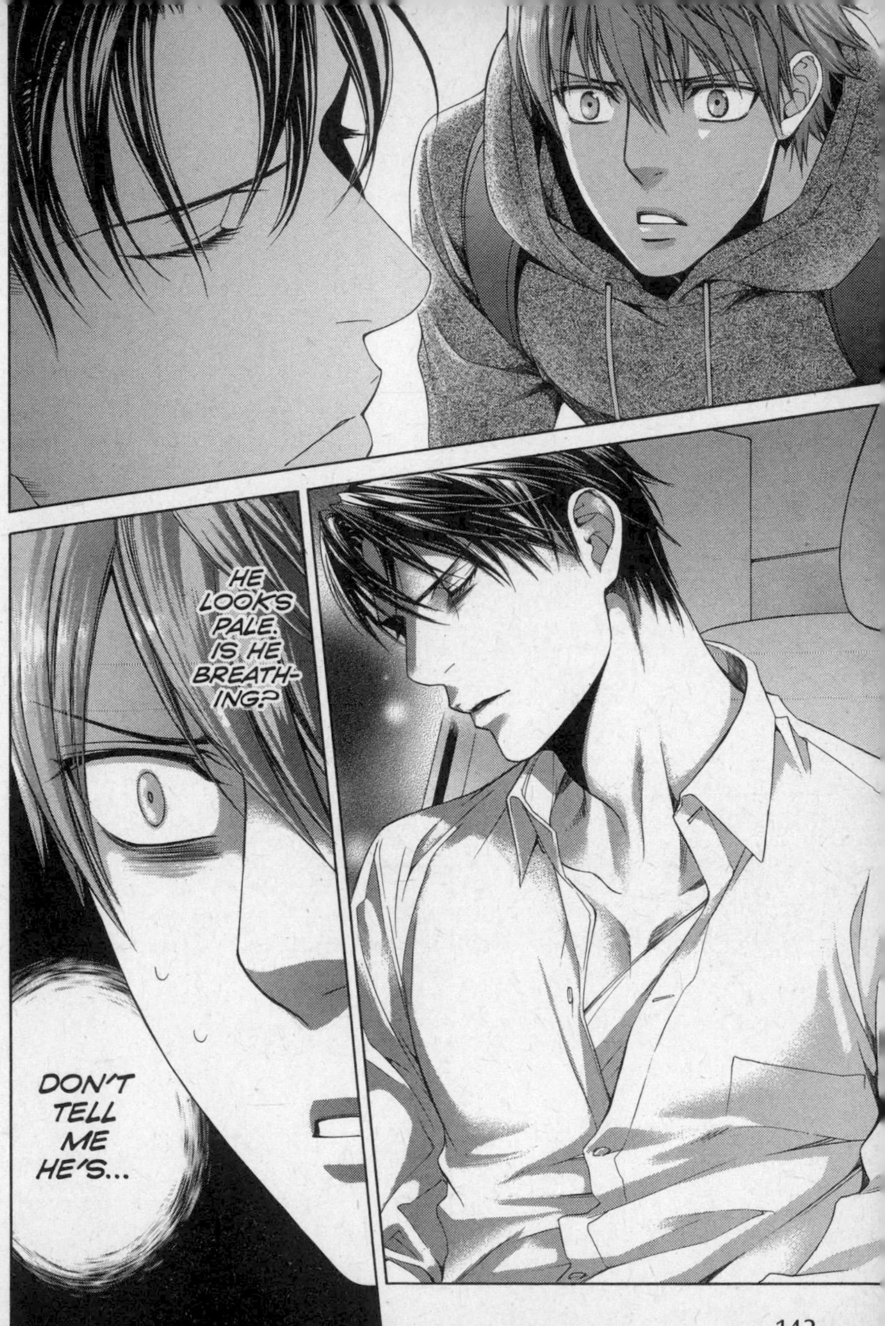
HE LOOKS PALE. IS HE BREATHING?
DON'T TELL ME HE'S...

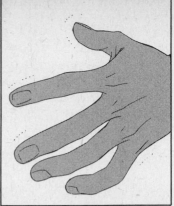

OH, THANK GOD... HE'S ALIVE.

HE'S WARM...

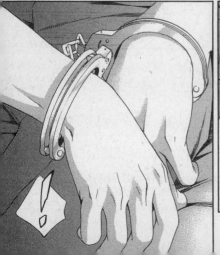

HEY, ASAMI. WAKE UP.

C'MON! WHAT DO YOU THINK YOU'RE DOING, HUH?

KLATTA

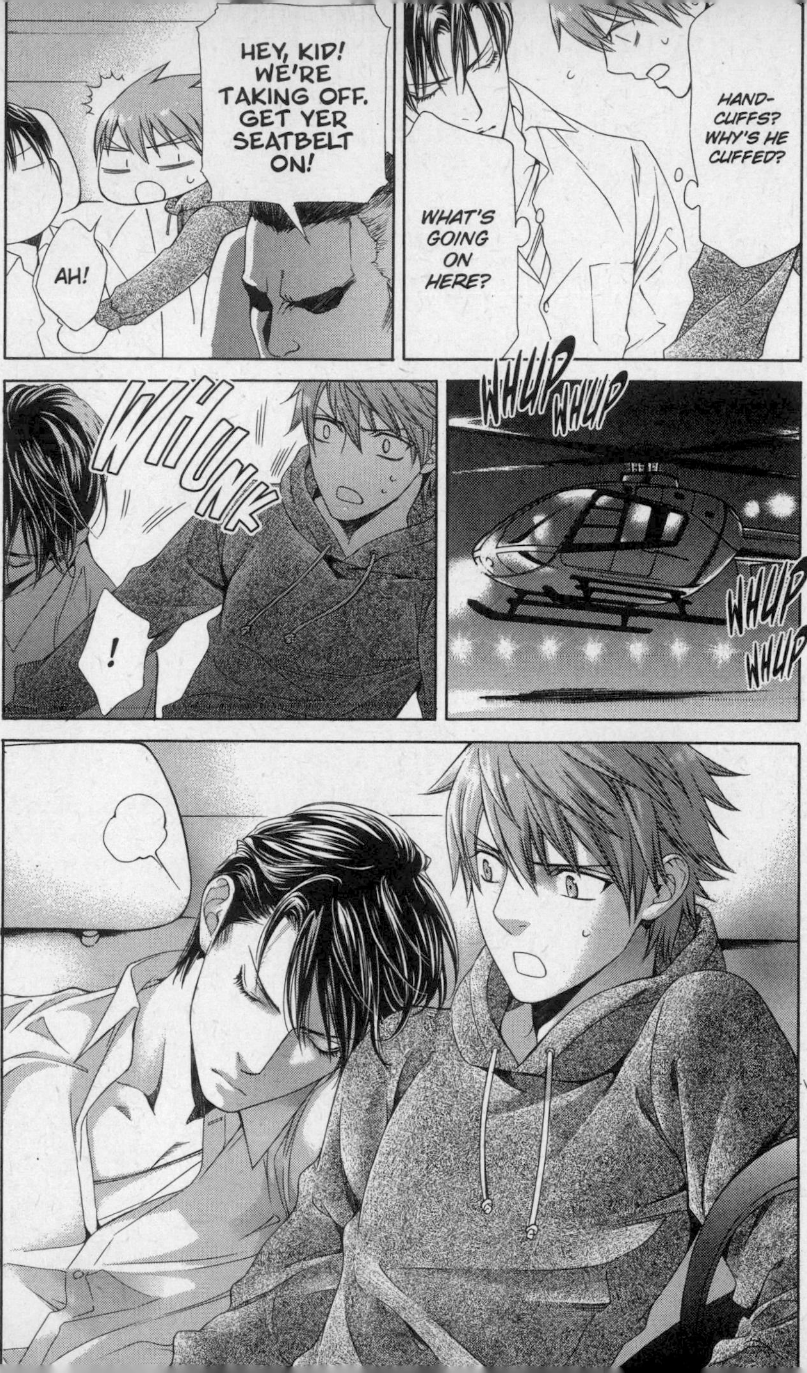
HAND-CUFFS? WHY'S HE CUFFED?
WHAT'S GOING ON HERE?
HEY, KID! WE'RE TAKING OFF. GET YER SEATBELT ON!
AH!
WHUP WHUP
WHUP WHUP
WHUNK
!

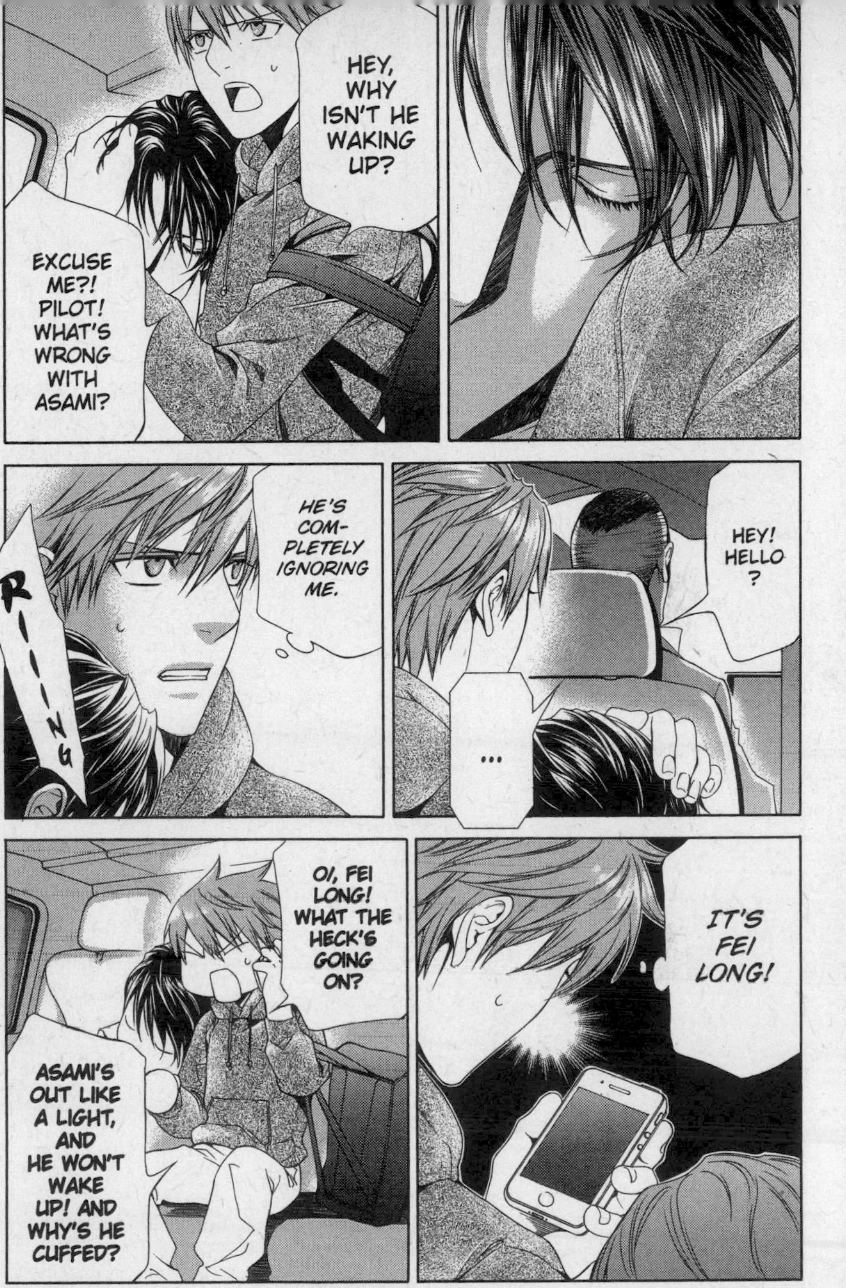
HEY, WHY ISN'T HE WAKING UP?
EXCUSE ME?! PILOT! WHAT'S WRONG WITH ASAMI?
HEY! HELLO?
...
HE'S COMPLETELY IGNORING ME.
RIIING
IT'S FEI LONG!
OI, FEI LONG! WHAT THE HECK'S GOING ON?
ASAMI'S OUT LIKE A LIGHT, AND HE WON'T WAKE UP! AND WHY'S HE CUFFED?

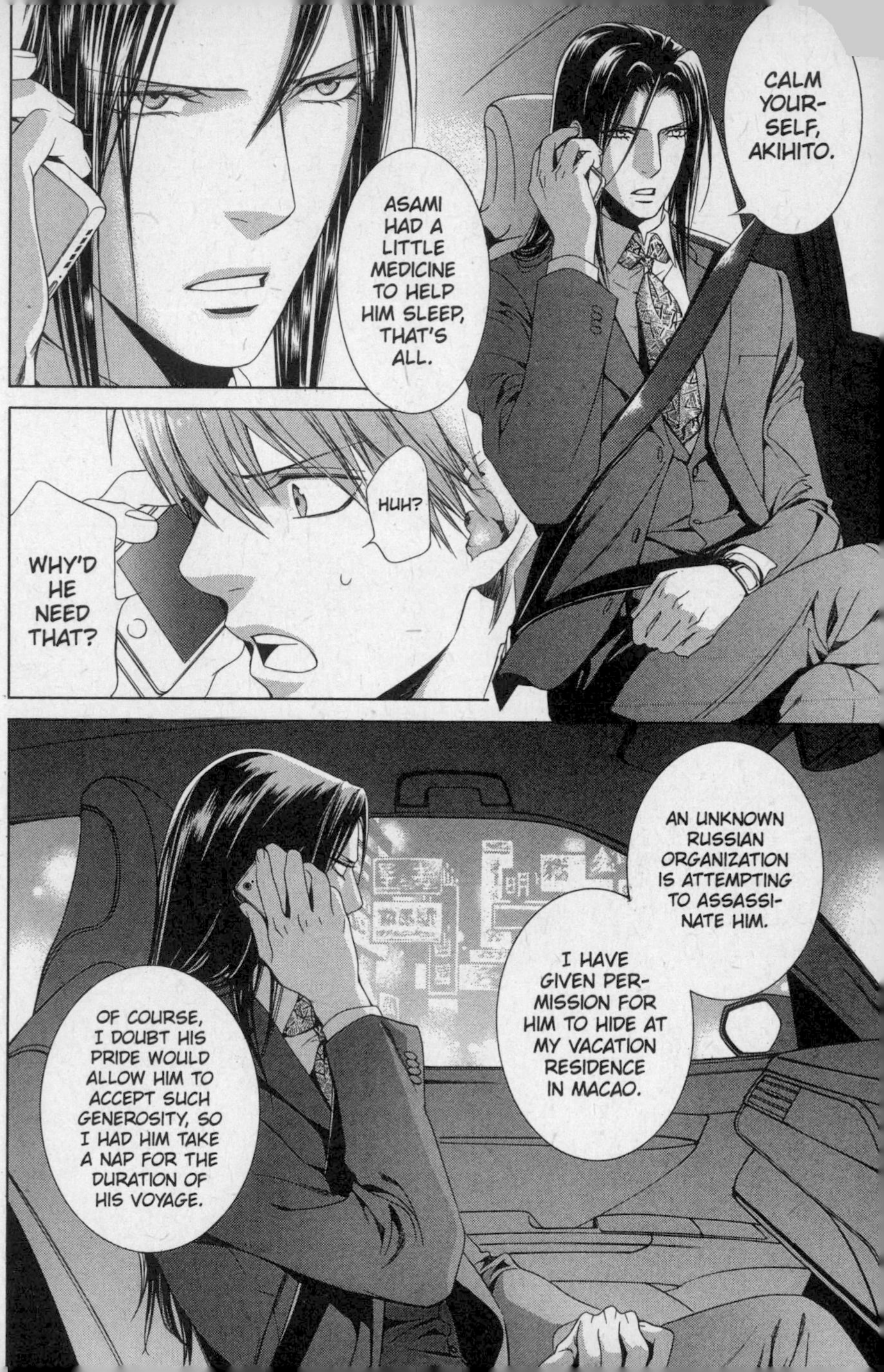
CALM YOURSELF, AKIHITO.
ASAMI HAD A LITTLE MEDICINE TO HELP HIM SLEEP, THAT'S ALL.
HUH?
WHY'D HE NEED THAT?
AN UNKNOWN RUSSIAN ORGANIZATION IS ATTEMPTING TO ASSASSINATE HIM.
I HAVE GIVEN PERMISSION FOR HIM TO HIDE AT MY VACATION RESIDENCE IN MACAO.
OF COURSE, I DOUBT HIS PRIDE WOULD ALLOW HIM TO ACCEPT SUCH GENEROSITY, SO I HAD HIM TAKE A NAP FOR THE DURATION OF HIS VOYAGE.

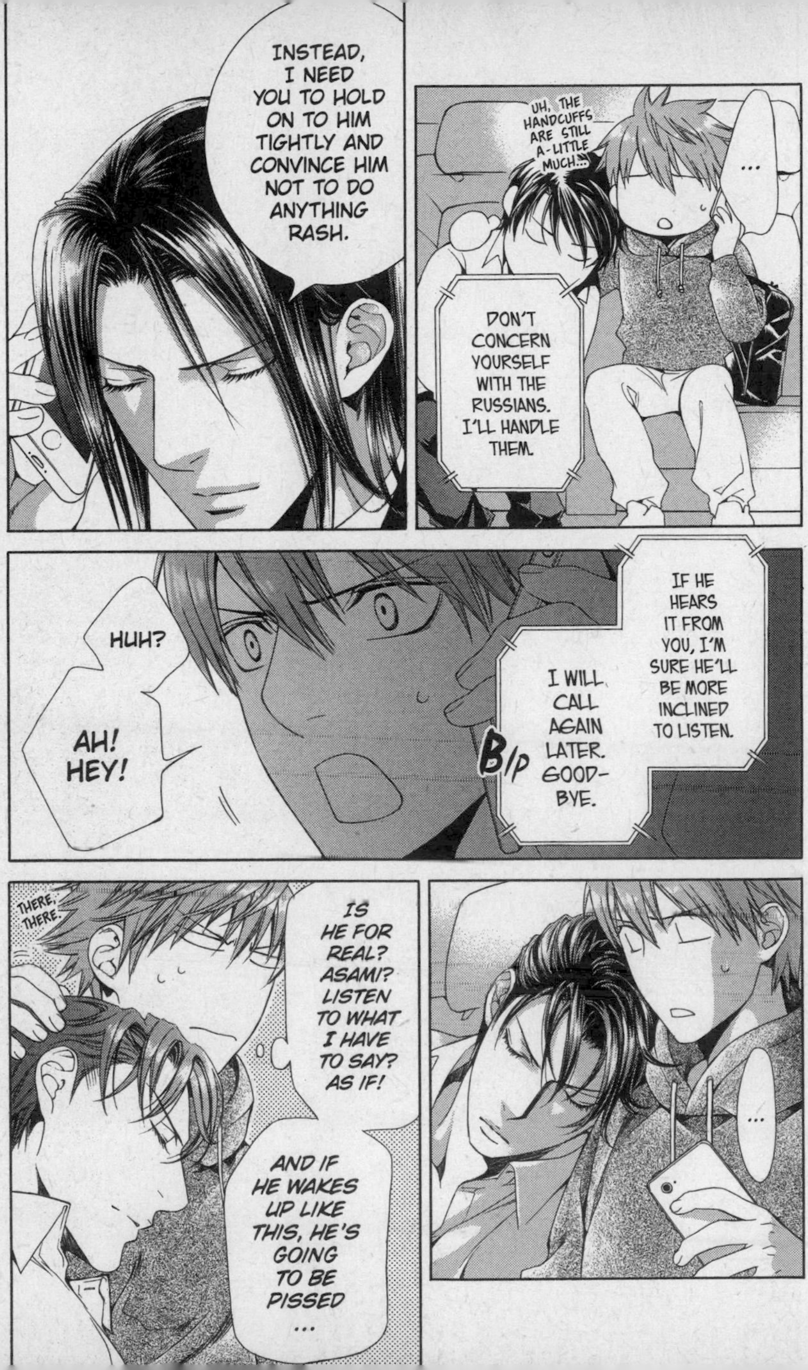
UH, THE HANDCUFFS ARE STILL A LITTLE MUCH...
...
DON'T CONCERN YOURSELF WITH THE RUSSIANS. I'LL HANDLE THEM.
INSTEAD, I NEED YOU TO HOLD ON TO HIM TIGHTLY AND CONVINCE HIM NOT TO DO ANYTHING RASH.
IF HE HEARS IT FROM YOU, I'M SURE HE'LL BE MORE INCLINED TO LISTEN.
I WILL CALL AGAIN LATER. GOOD-BYE.
BIP
HUH?
AH! HEY!
...
IS HE FOR REAL? ASAMI? LISTEN TO WHAT I HAVE TO SAY? AS IF!
AND IF HE WAKES UP LIKE THIS, HE'S GOING TO BE PISSED ...
THERE, THERE.

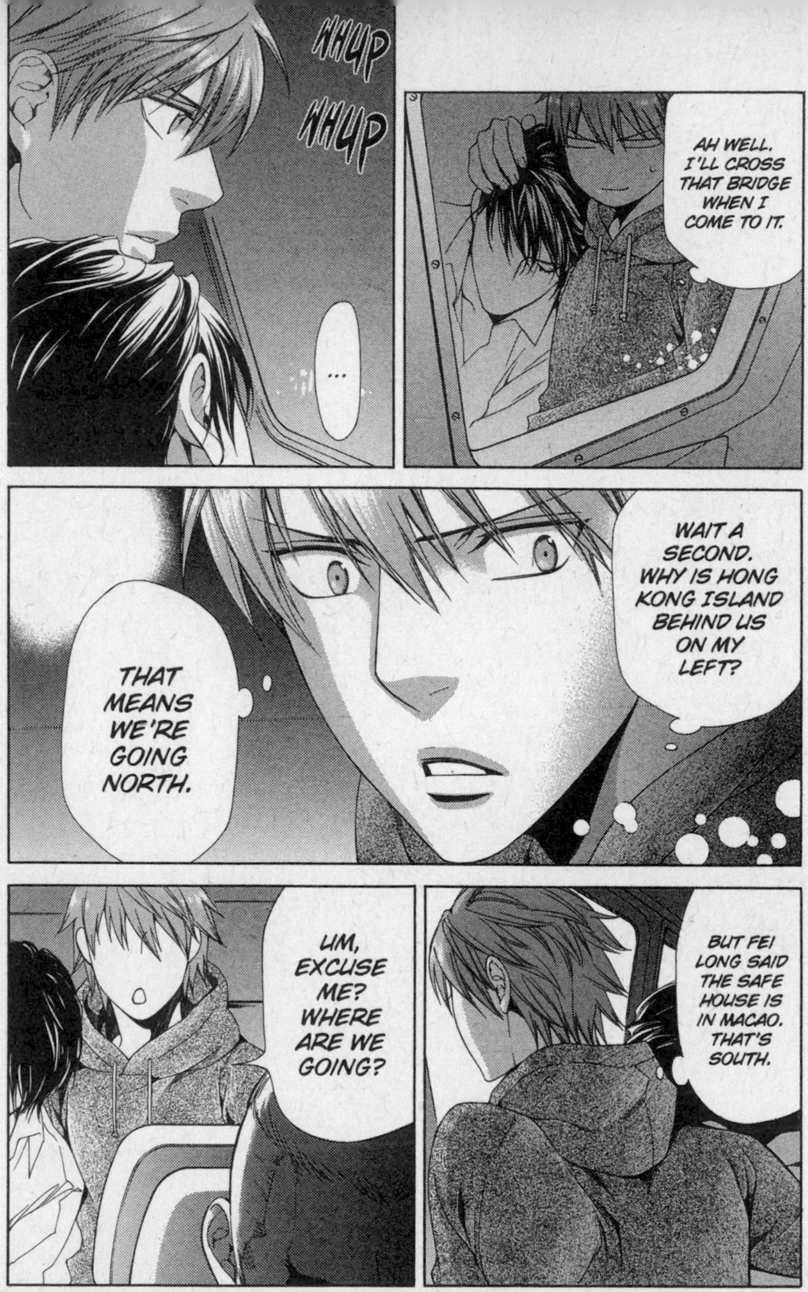
AH WELL. I'LL CROSS THAT BRIDGE WHEN I COME TO IT.
WHUP
WHUP
...
WAIT A SECOND. WHY IS HONG KONG ISLAND BEHIND US ON MY LEFT?
THAT MEANS WE'RE GOING NORTH.
BUT FEI LONG SAID THE SAFE HOUSE IS IN MACAO. THAT'S SOUTH.
UM, EXCUSE ME? WHERE ARE WE GOING?

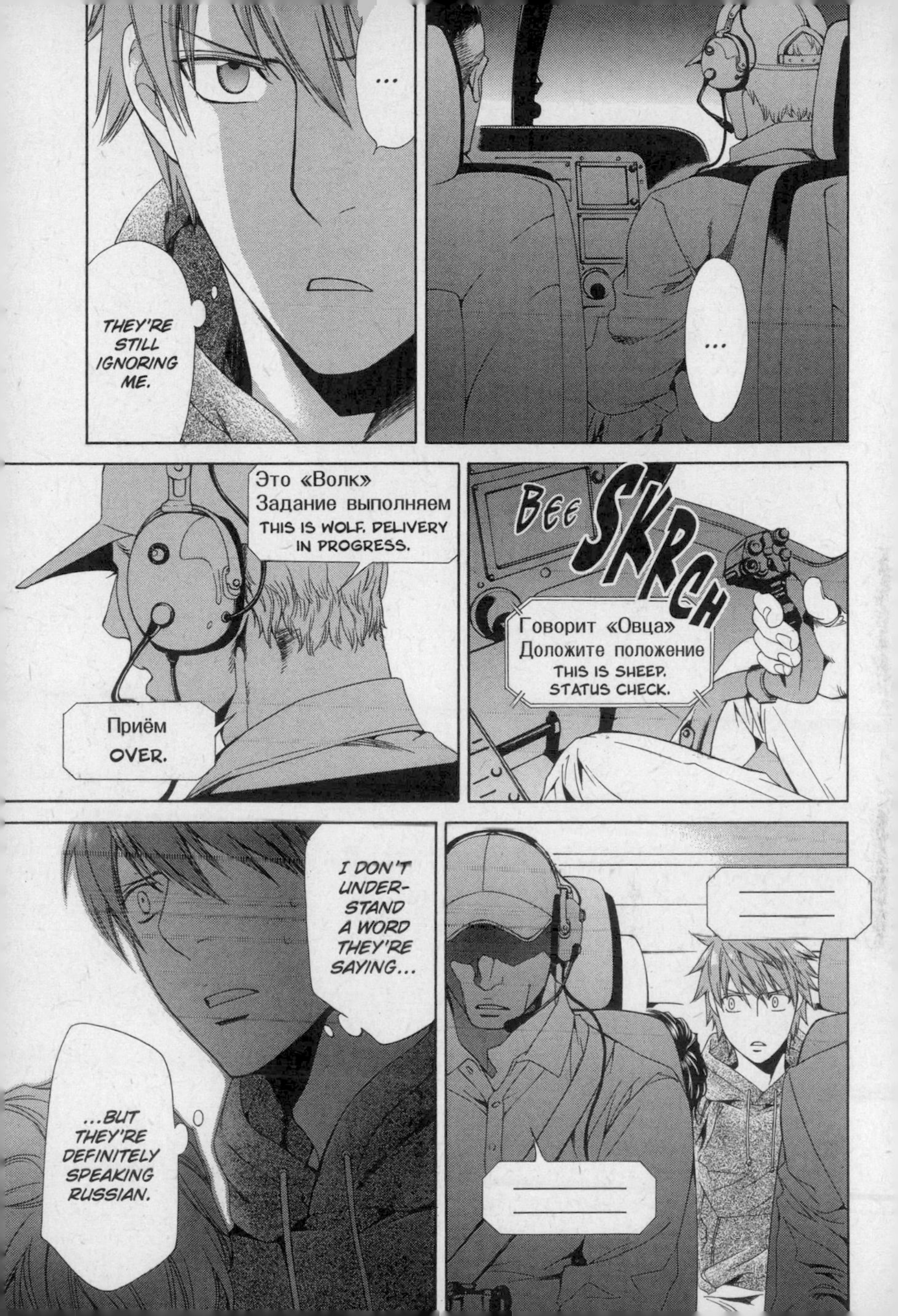
...
...
THEY'RE STILL IGNORING ME.
BEE SKRCH
Говорит «Овца» Доложите положение
THIS IS SHEEP. STATUS CHECK.
Это «Волк» Задание выполняем
THIS IS WOLF. DELIVERY IN PROGRESS.
Приём
OVER.
I DON'T UNDER-STAND A WORD THEY'RE SAYING...
...BUT THEY'RE DEFINITELY SPEAKING RUSSIAN.

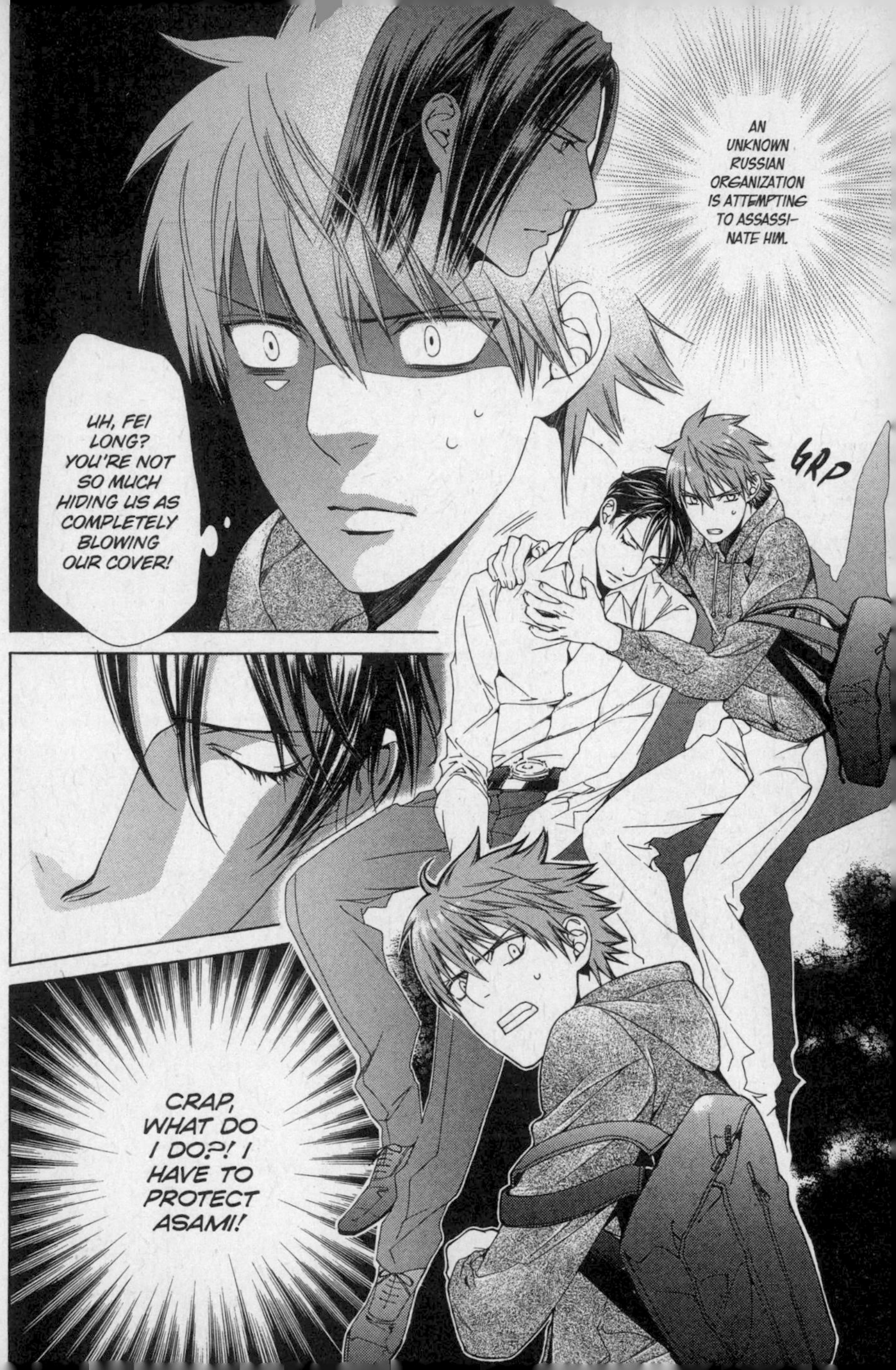
AN UNKNOWN RUSSIAN ORGANIZATION IS ATTEMPTING TO ASSASSI-NATE HIM.
UH, FEI LONG? YOU'RE NOT SO MUCH HIDING US AS COMPLETELY BLOWING OUR COVER!
GRP
CRAP, WHAT DO I DO?! I HAVE TO PROTECT ASAMI!

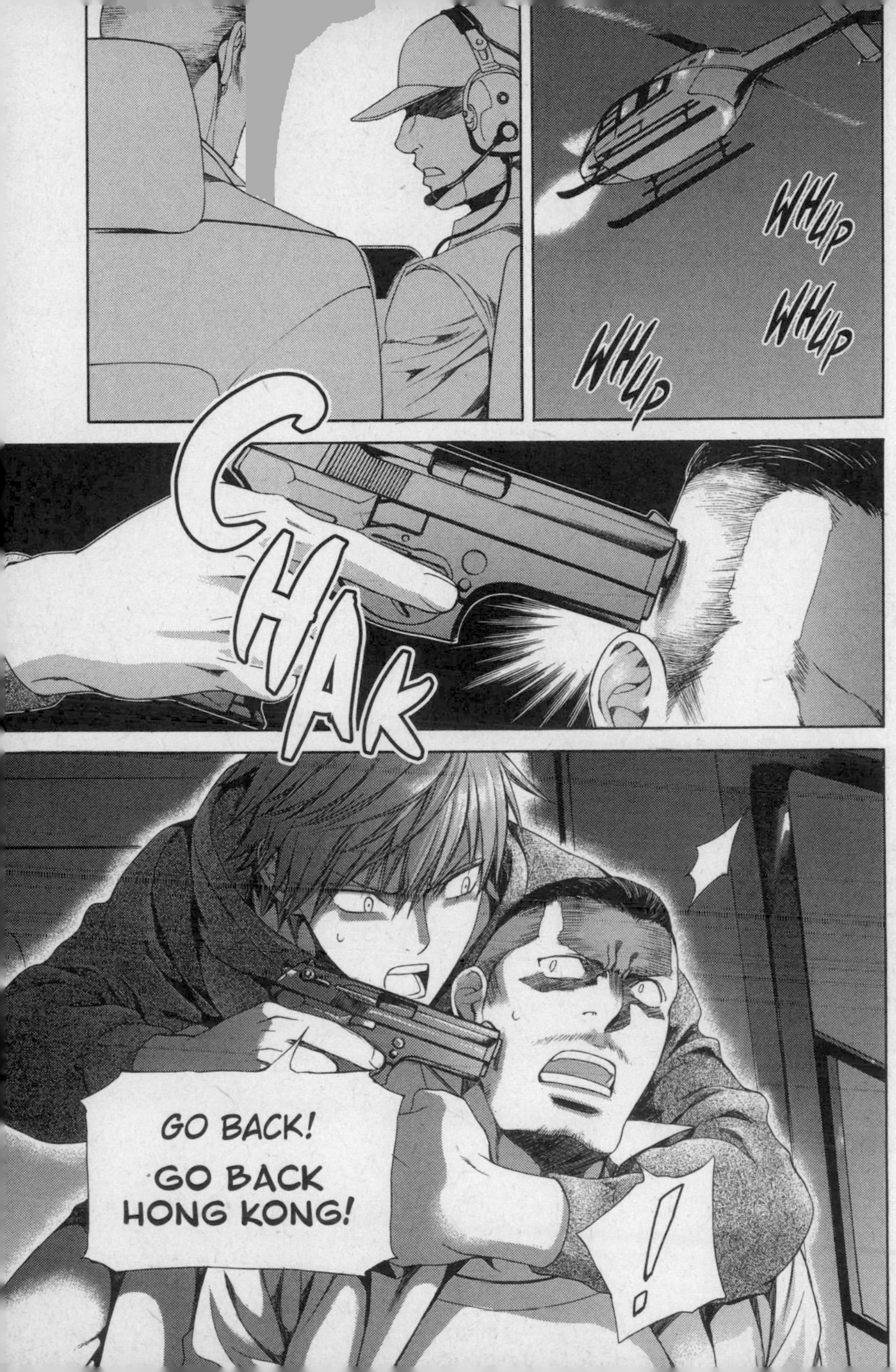
WHUP
WHUP
WHUP
CHAK
GO BACK!
GO BACK HONG KONG!
!

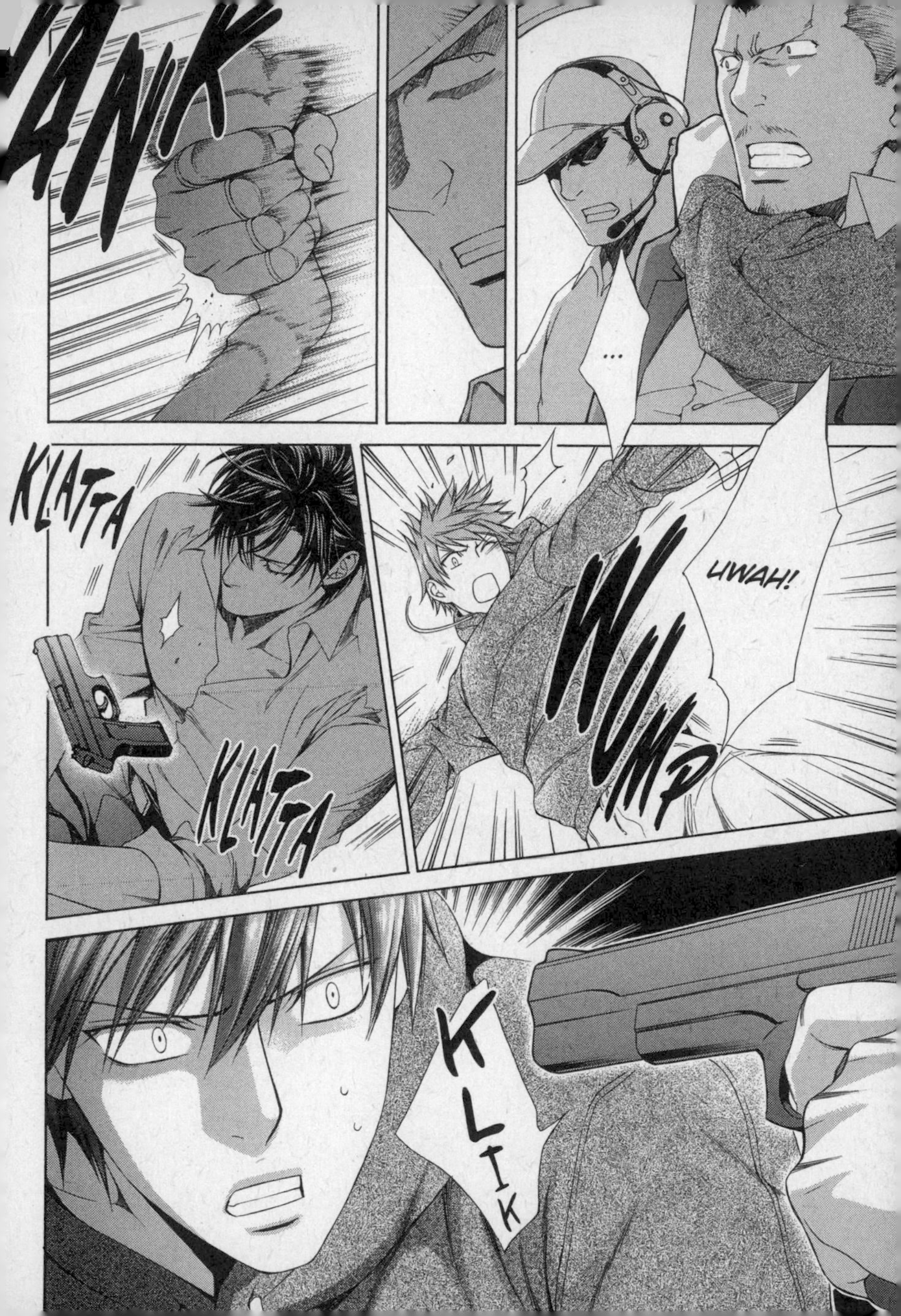
...
YANK
UWAH!
WUMP
KLATTA
KLATTA
KLIK

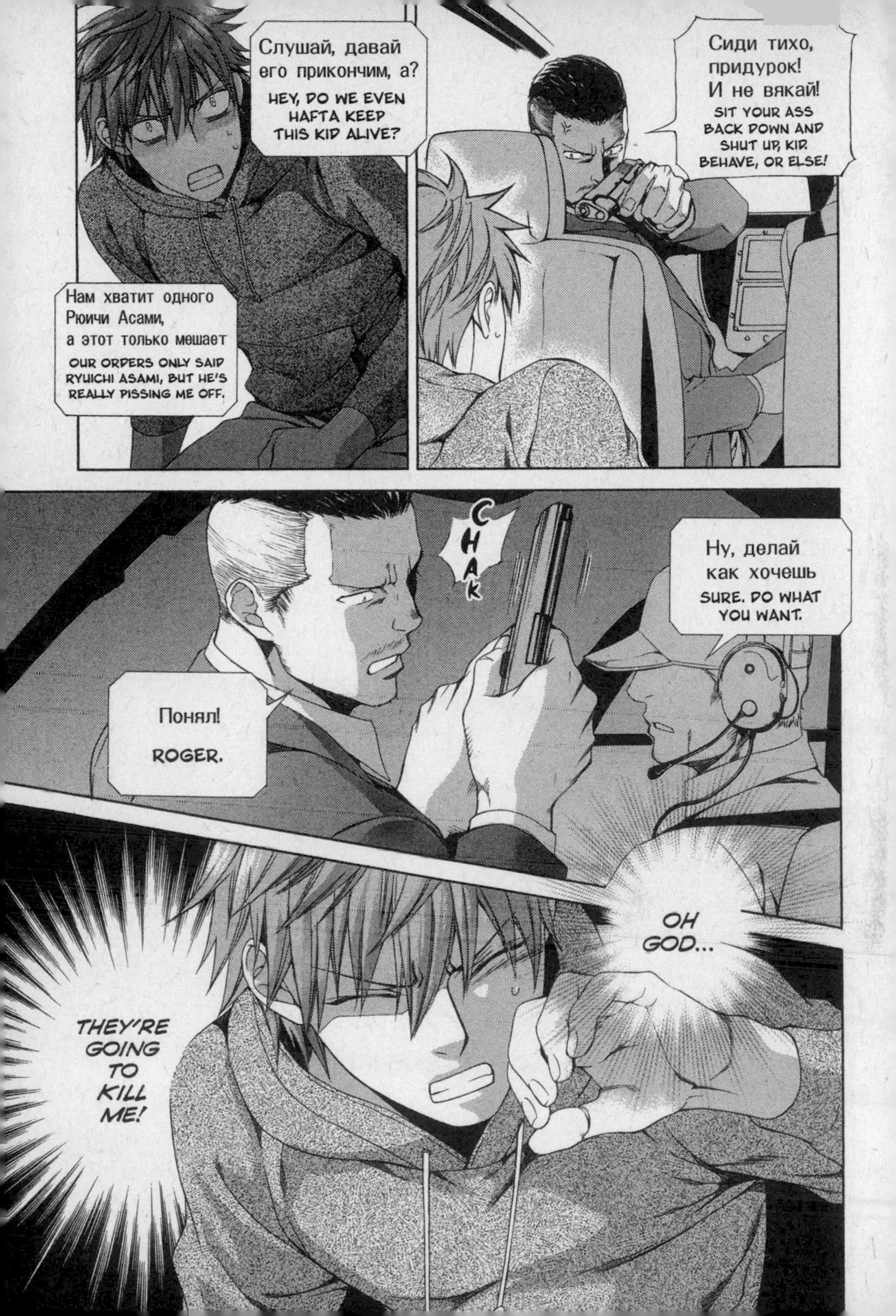
Сиди тихо, придурок! И не вякай!
SIT YOUR ASS BACK DOWN AND SHUT UP, KID. BEHAVE, OR ELSE!
Слушай, давай его прикончим, а?
HEY, DO WE EVEN HAFTA KEEP THIS KID ALIVE?
Нам хватит одного Рюичи Асами, а этот только мешает
OUR ORDERS ONLY SAID RYUICHI ASAMI, BUT HE'S REALLY PISSING ME OFF.
Ну, делай как хочешь
SURE. DO WHAT YOU WANT.
CHAK
Понял!
ROGER.
OH GOD...
THEY'RE GOING TO KILL ME!

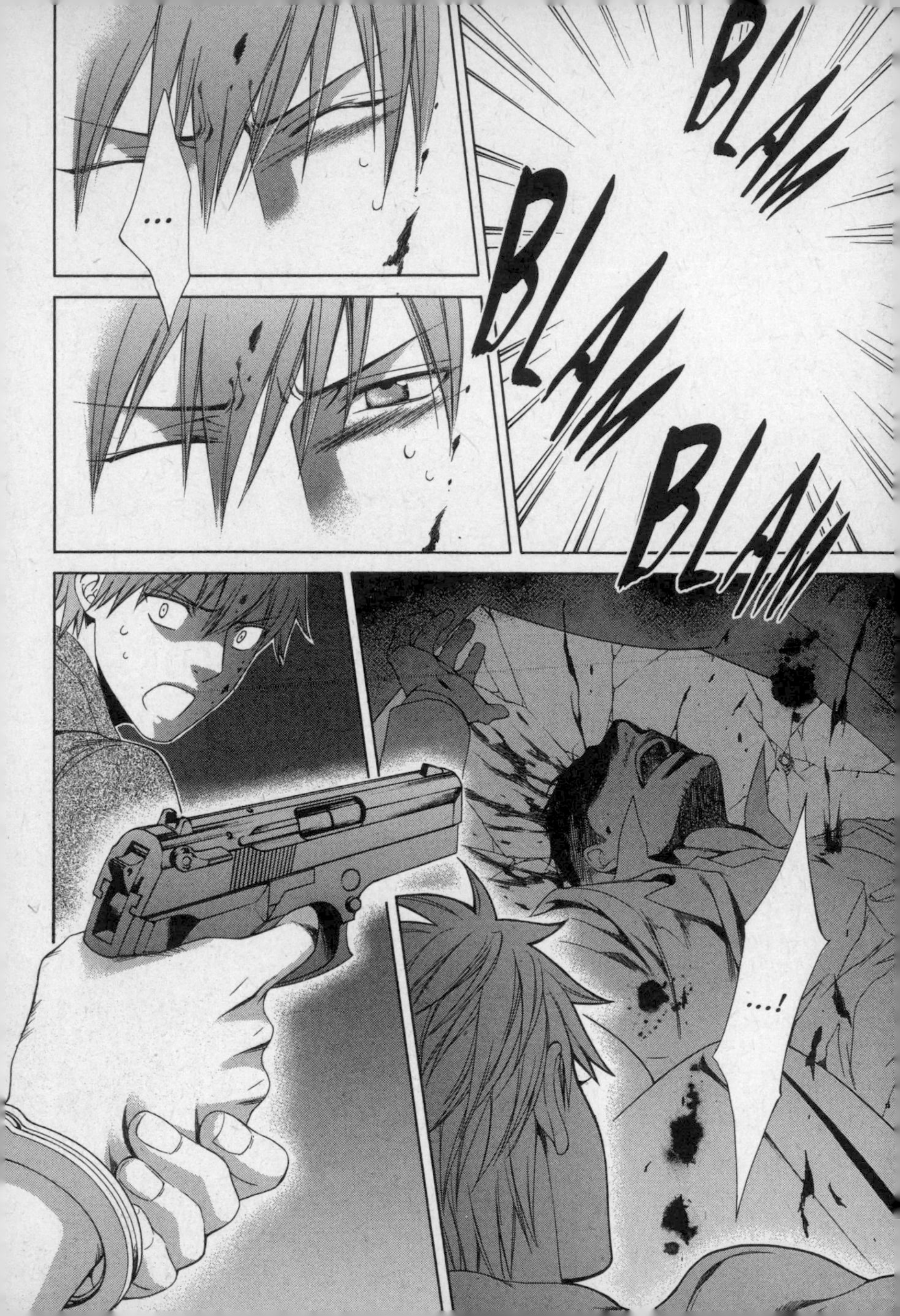
BLAM
BLAM
BLAM
...
BLAM
...!

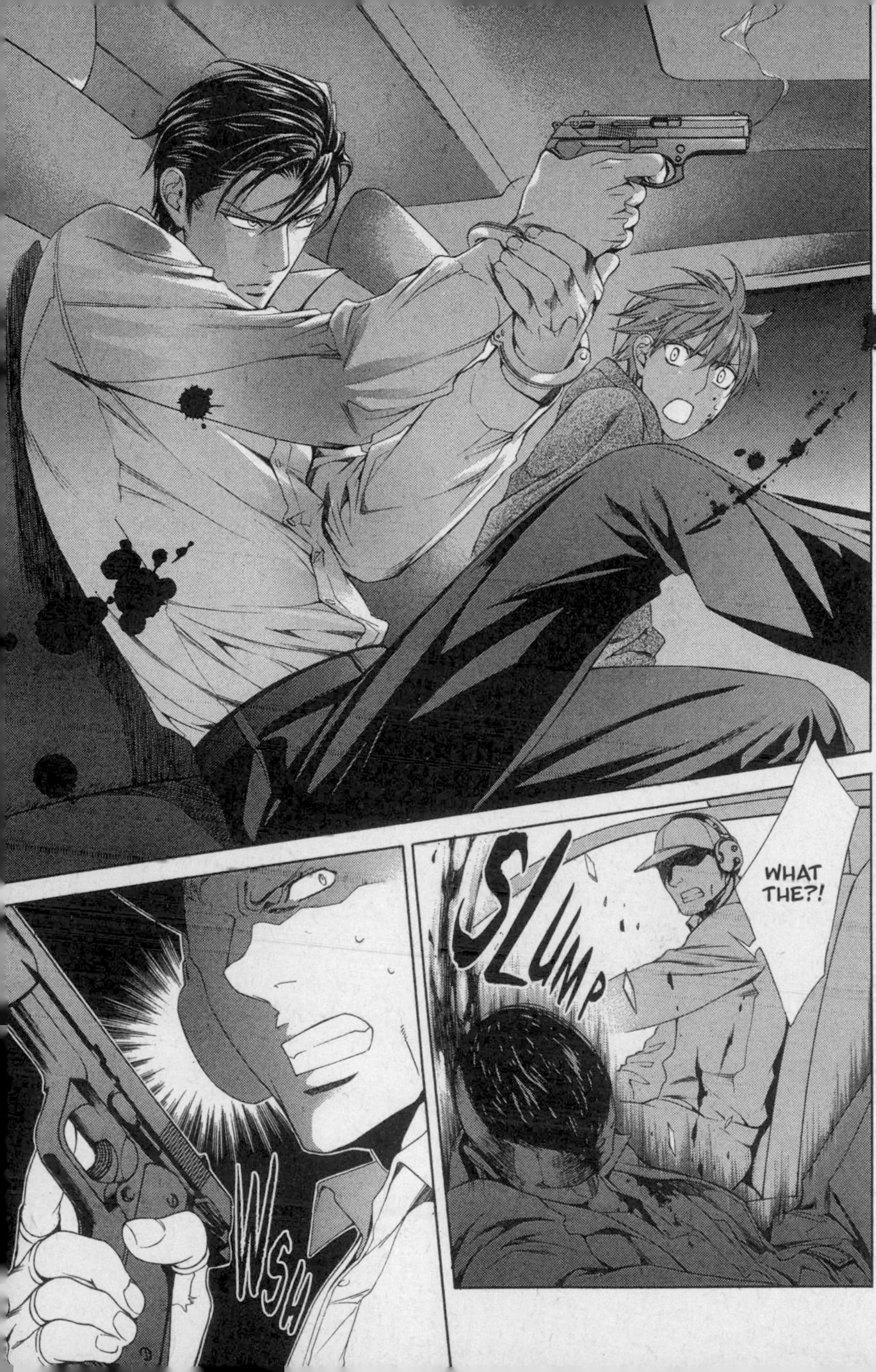
SLUMP
WHAT THE?!
WSH

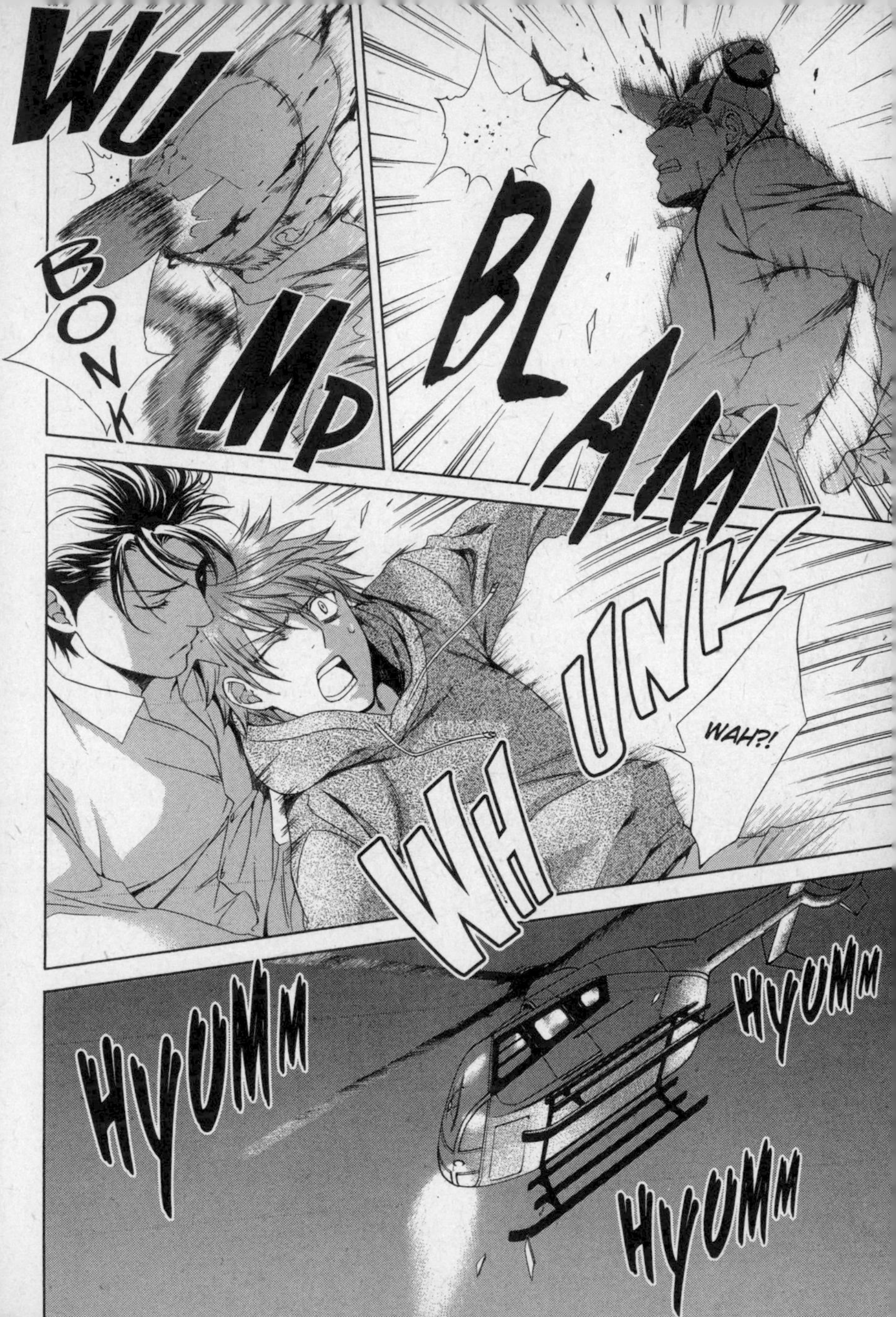
BLAM
WUMP
BONK
WHUNK
WAH?!
HYUMM
HYUMM
HYUMM

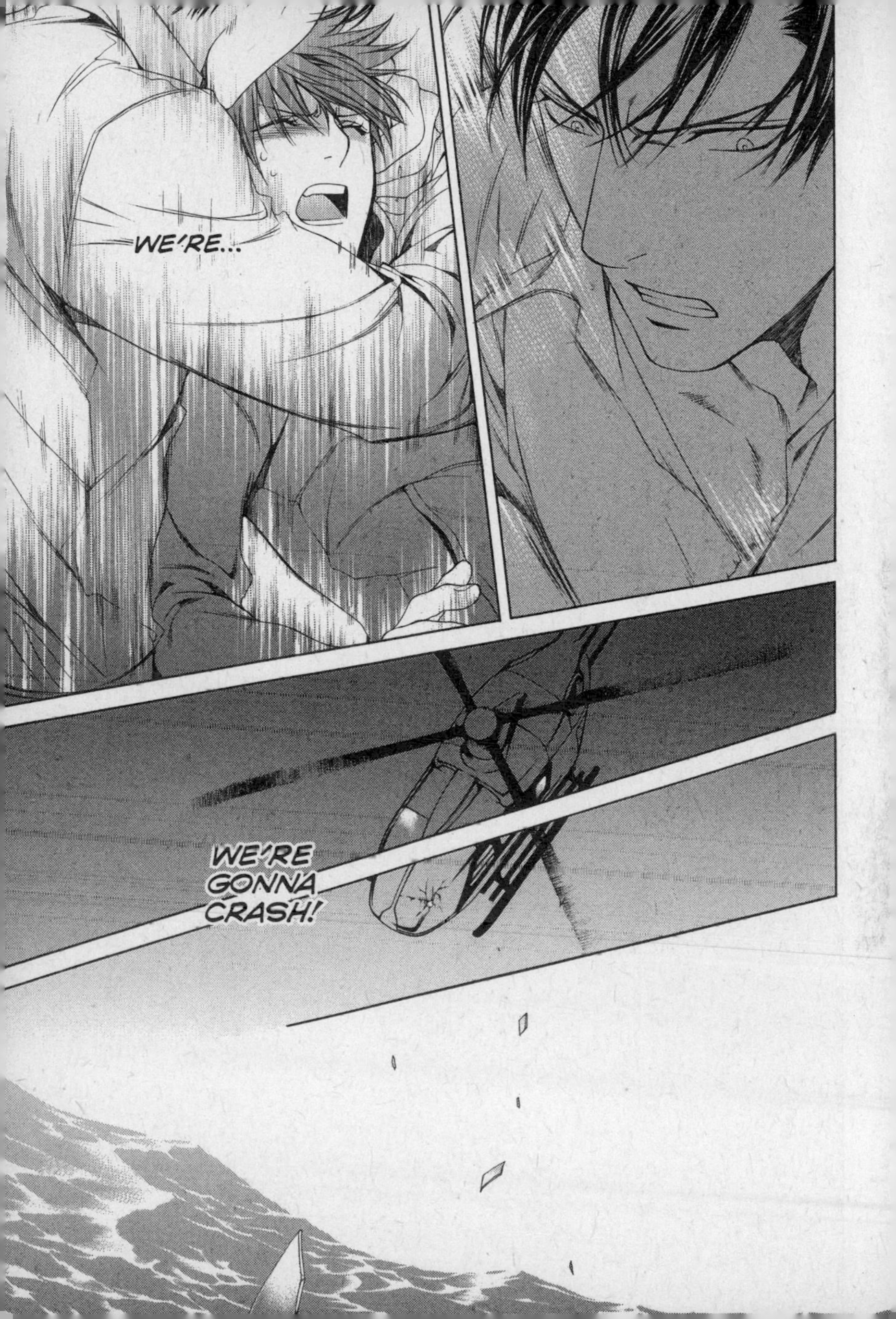
WE'RE...
WE'RE GONNA CRASH!

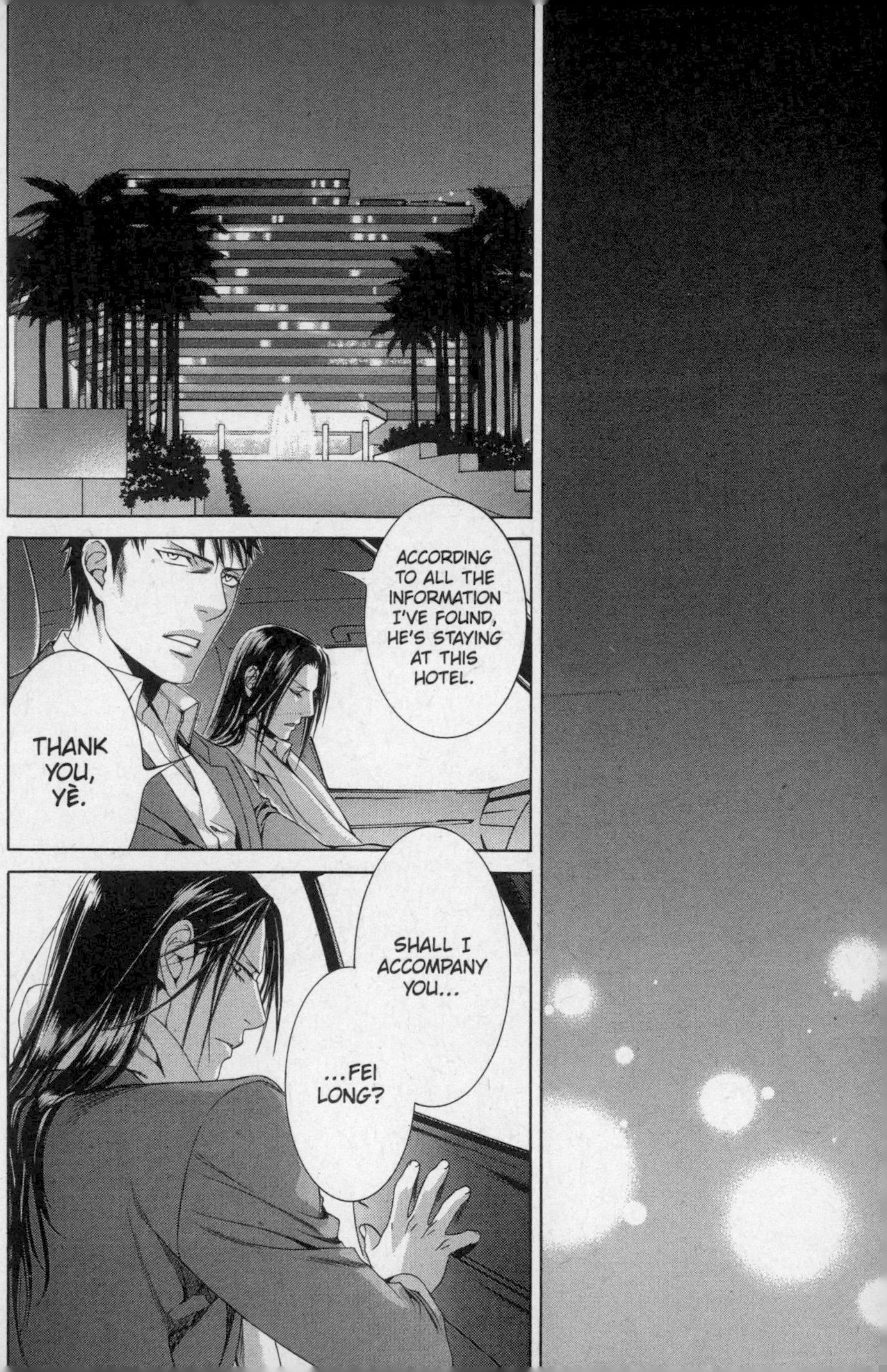
ACCORDING TO ALL THE INFORMATION I'VE FOUND, HE'S STAYING AT THIS HOTEL.
THANK YOU, YÈ.
SHALL I ACCOMPANY YOU...
...FEI LONG?

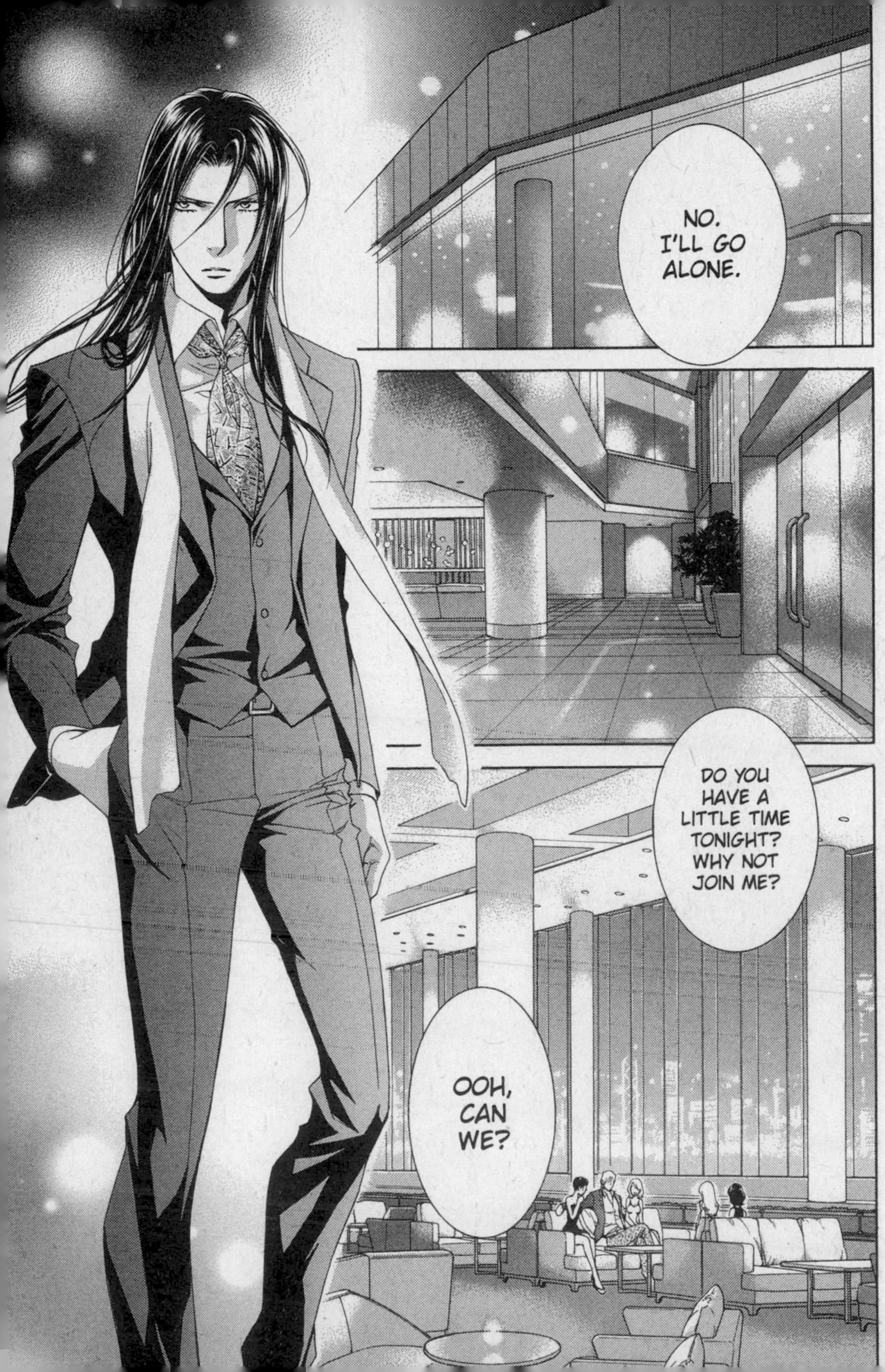
NO. I'LL GO ALONE.
DO YOU HAVE A LITTLE TIME TONIGHT? WHY NOT JOIN ME?
OOH, CAN WE?

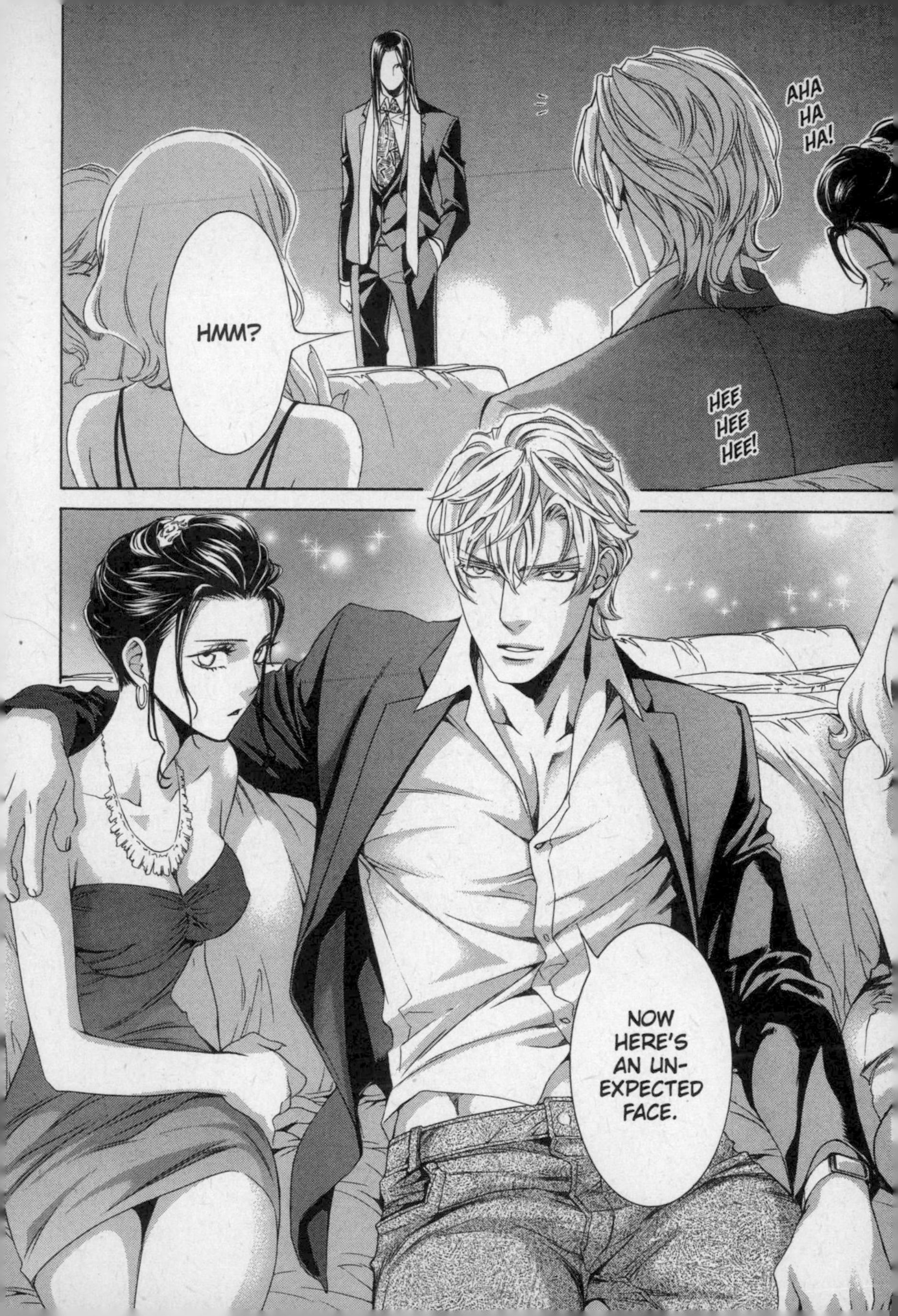
AHA HA HA!
HEE HEE HEE!
HMM?
NOW HERE'S AN UN-EXPECTED FACE.

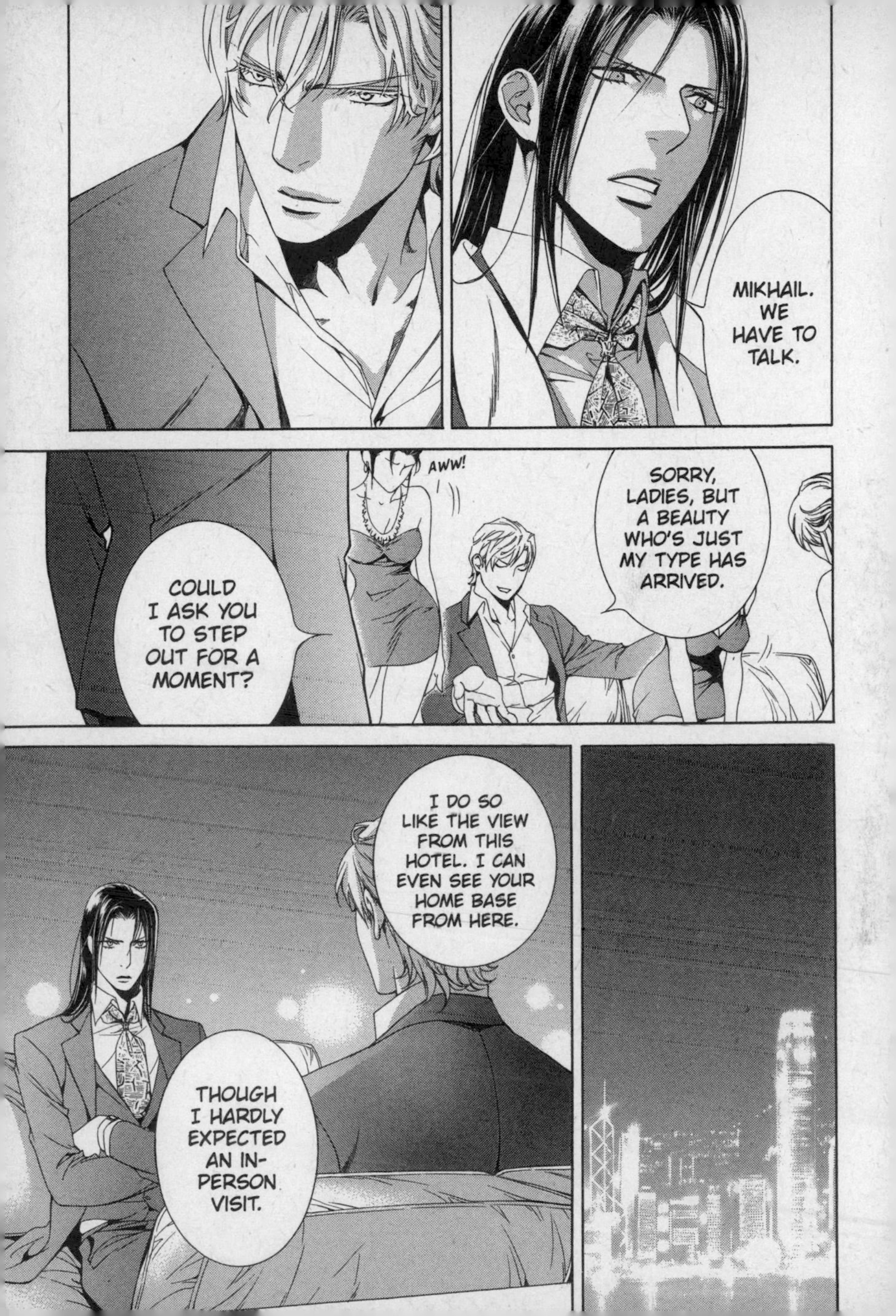
MIKHAIL. WE HAVE TO TALK.
SORRY, LADIES, BUT A BEAUTY WHO'S JUST MY TYPE HAS ARRIVED.
AWW!
COULD I ASK YOU TO STEP OUT FOR A MOMENT?
I DO SO LIKE THE VIEW FROM THIS HOTEL. I CAN EVEN SEE YOUR HOME BASE FROM HERE.
THOUGH I HARDLY EXPECTED AN IN-PERSON VISIT.

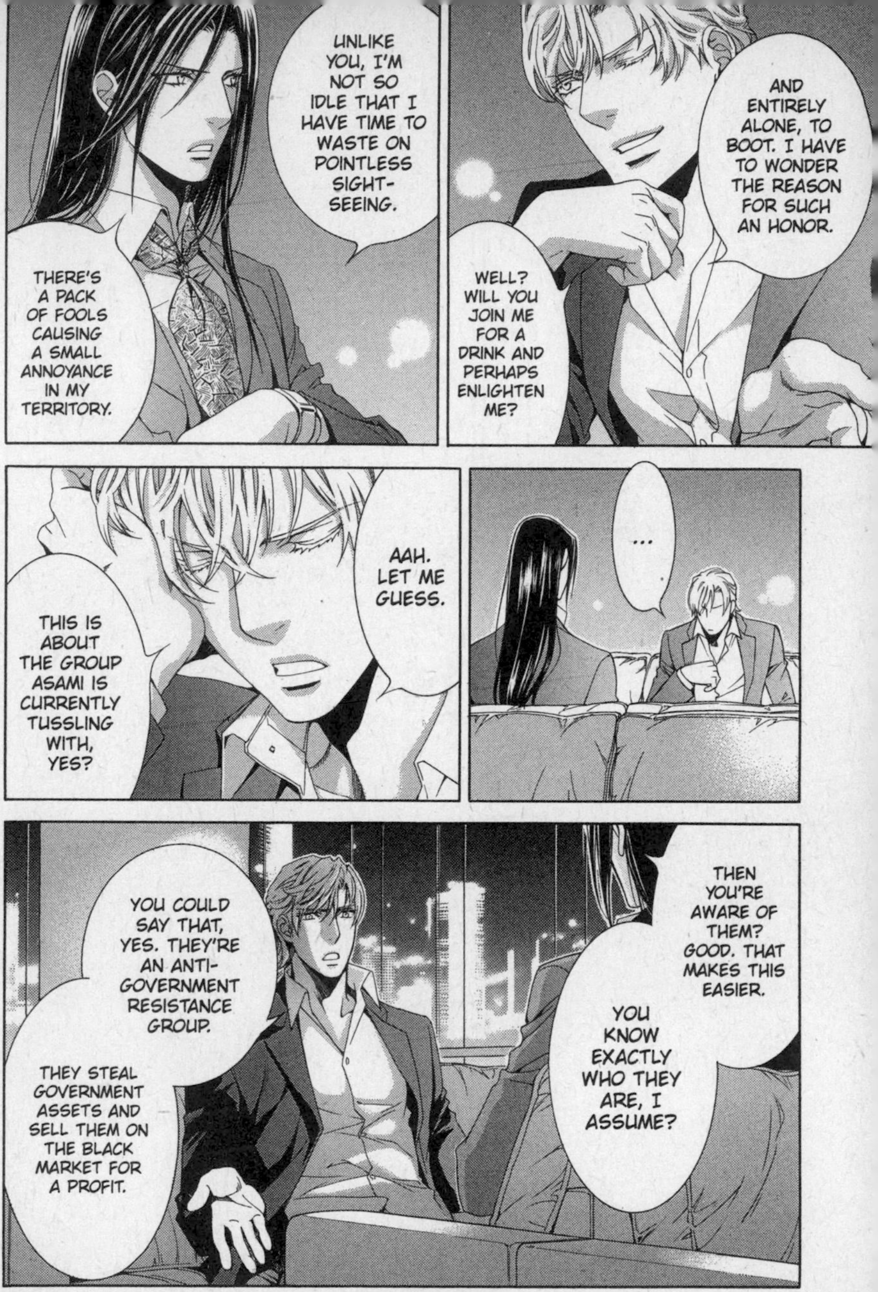
AND ENTIRELY ALONE, TO BOOT. I HAVE TO WONDER THE REASON FOR SUCH AN HONOR.
WELL? WILL YOU JOIN ME FOR A DRINK AND PERHAPS ENLIGHTEN ME?
UNLIKE YOU, I'M NOT SO IDLE THAT I HAVE TIME TO WASTE ON POINTLESS SIGHT-SEEING.
THERE'S A PACK OF FOOLS CAUSING A SMALL ANNOYANCE IN MY TERRITORY.
...
AAH. LET ME GUESS.
THIS IS ABOUT THE GROUP ASAMI IS CURRENTLY TUSSLING WITH, YES?
THEN YOU'RE AWARE OF THEM? GOOD. THAT MAKES THIS EASIER.
YOU KNOW EXACTLY WHO THEY ARE, I ASSUME?
YOU COULD SAY THAT, YES. THEY'RE AN ANTI-GOVERNMENT RESISTANCE GROUP.
THEY STEAL GOVERNMENT ASSETS AND SELL THEM ON THE BLACK MARKET FOR A PROFIT.

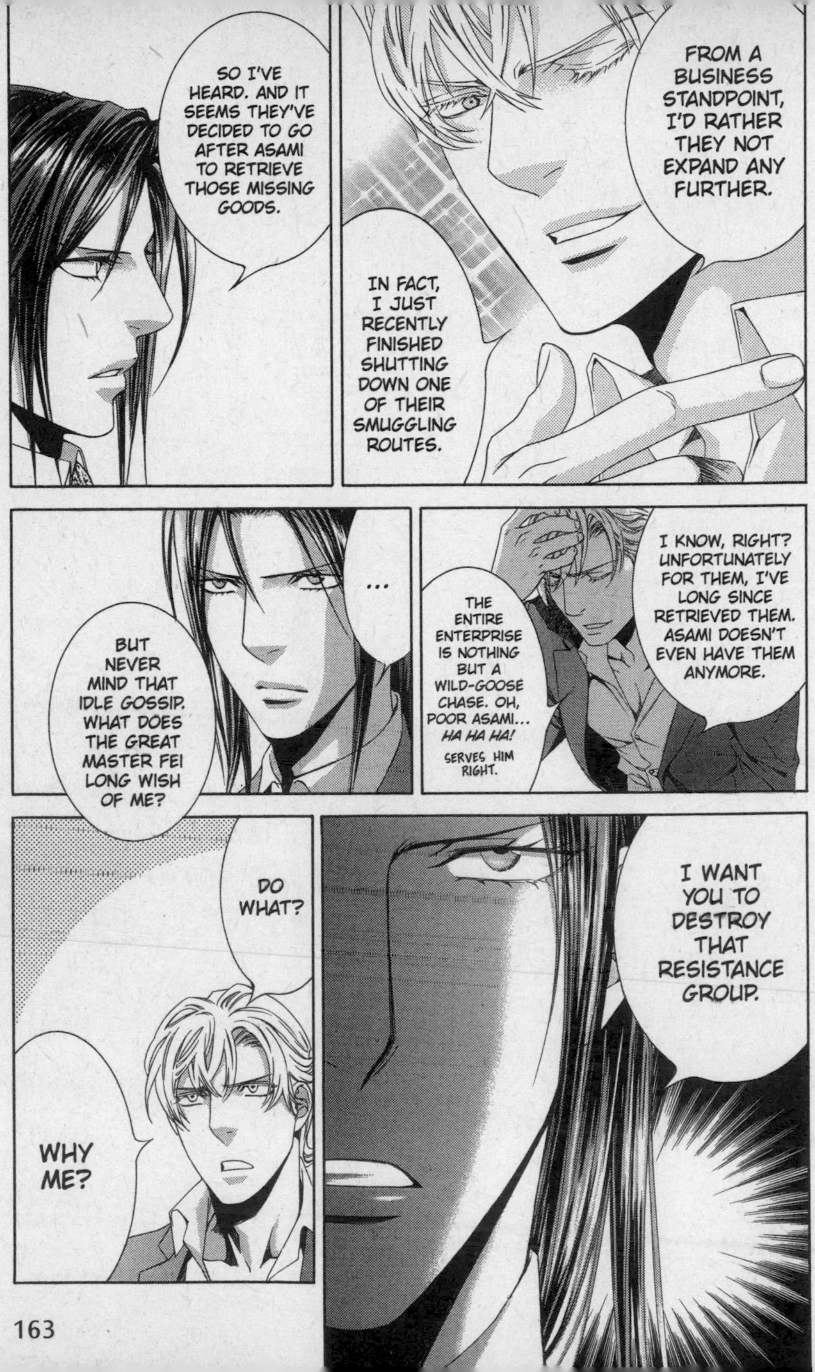
FROM A BUSINESS STANDPOINT, I'D RATHER THEY NOT EXPAND ANY FURTHER.
IN FACT, I JUST RECENTLY FINISHED SHUTTING DOWN ONE OF THEIR SMUGGLING ROUTES.
SO I'VE HEARD. AND IT SEEMS THEY'VE DECIDED TO GO AFTER ASAMI TO RETRIEVE THOSE MISSING GOODS.
I KNOW, RIGHT? UNFORTUNATELY FOR THEM, I'VE LONG SINCE RETRIEVED THEM. ASAMI DOESN'T EVEN HAVE THEM ANYMORE.
THE ENTIRE ENTERPRISE IS NOTHING BUT A WILD-GOOSE CHASE. OH, POOR ASAMI... HA HA HA!
SERVES HIM RIGHT.
...
BUT NEVER MIND THAT IDLE GOSSIP. WHAT DOES THE GREAT MASTER FEI LONG WISH OF ME?
I WANT YOU TO DESTROY THAT RESISTANCE GROUP.
DO WHAT?
WHY ME?

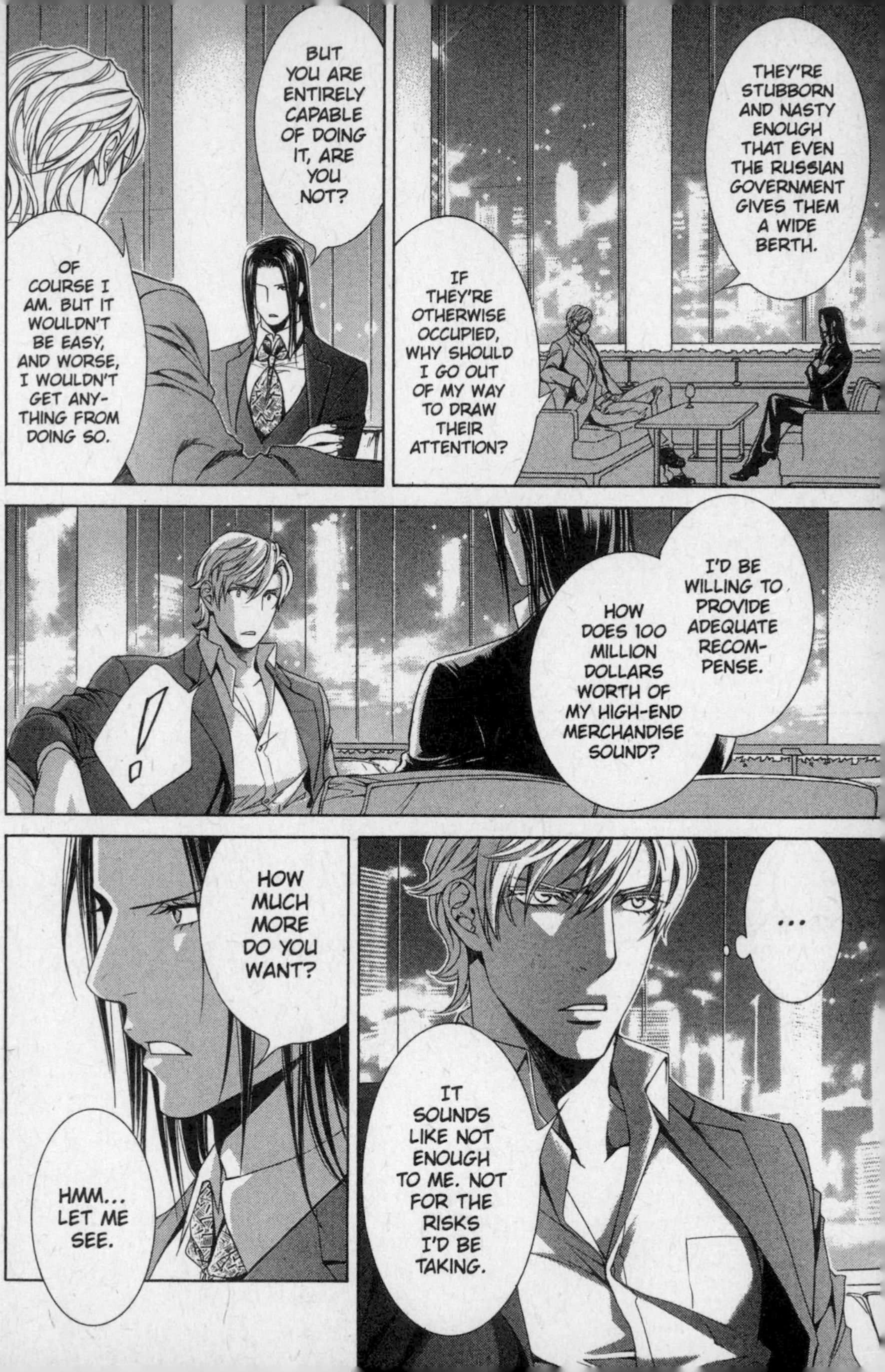
THEY'RE STUBBORN AND NASTY ENOUGH THAT EVEN THE RUSSIAN GOVERNMENT GIVES THEM A WIDE BERTH.
IF THEY'RE OTHERWISE OCCUPIED, WHY SHOULD I GO OUT OF MY WAY TO DRAW THEIR ATTENTION?
BUT YOU ARE ENTIRELY CAPABLE OF DOING IT, ARE YOU NOT?
OF COURSE I AM. BUT IT WOULDN'T BE EASY, AND WORSE, I WOULDN'T GET ANYTHING FROM DOING SO.
I'D BE WILLING TO PROVIDE ADEQUATE RECOMPENSE.
HOW DOES 100 MILLION DOLLARS WORTH OF MY HIGH-END MERCHANDISE SOUND?
!
...
IT SOUNDS LIKE NOT ENOUGH TO ME. NOT FOR THE RISKS I'D BE TAKING.
HOW MUCH MORE DO YOU WANT?
HMM... LET ME SEE.

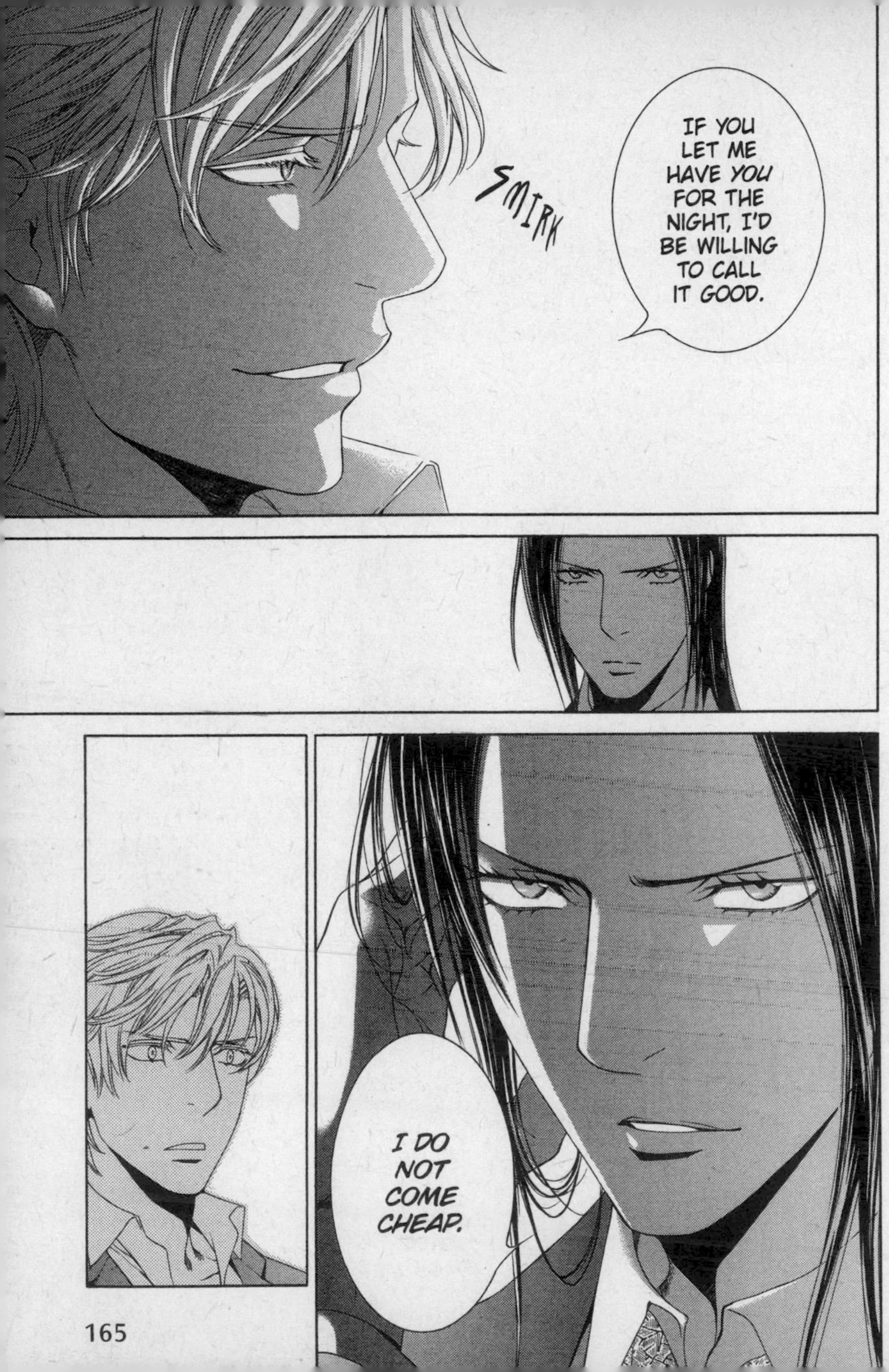
IF YOU LET ME HAVE YOU FOR THE NIGHT, I'D BE WILLING TO CALL IT GOOD.
SMIRK
I DO NOT COME CHEAP.

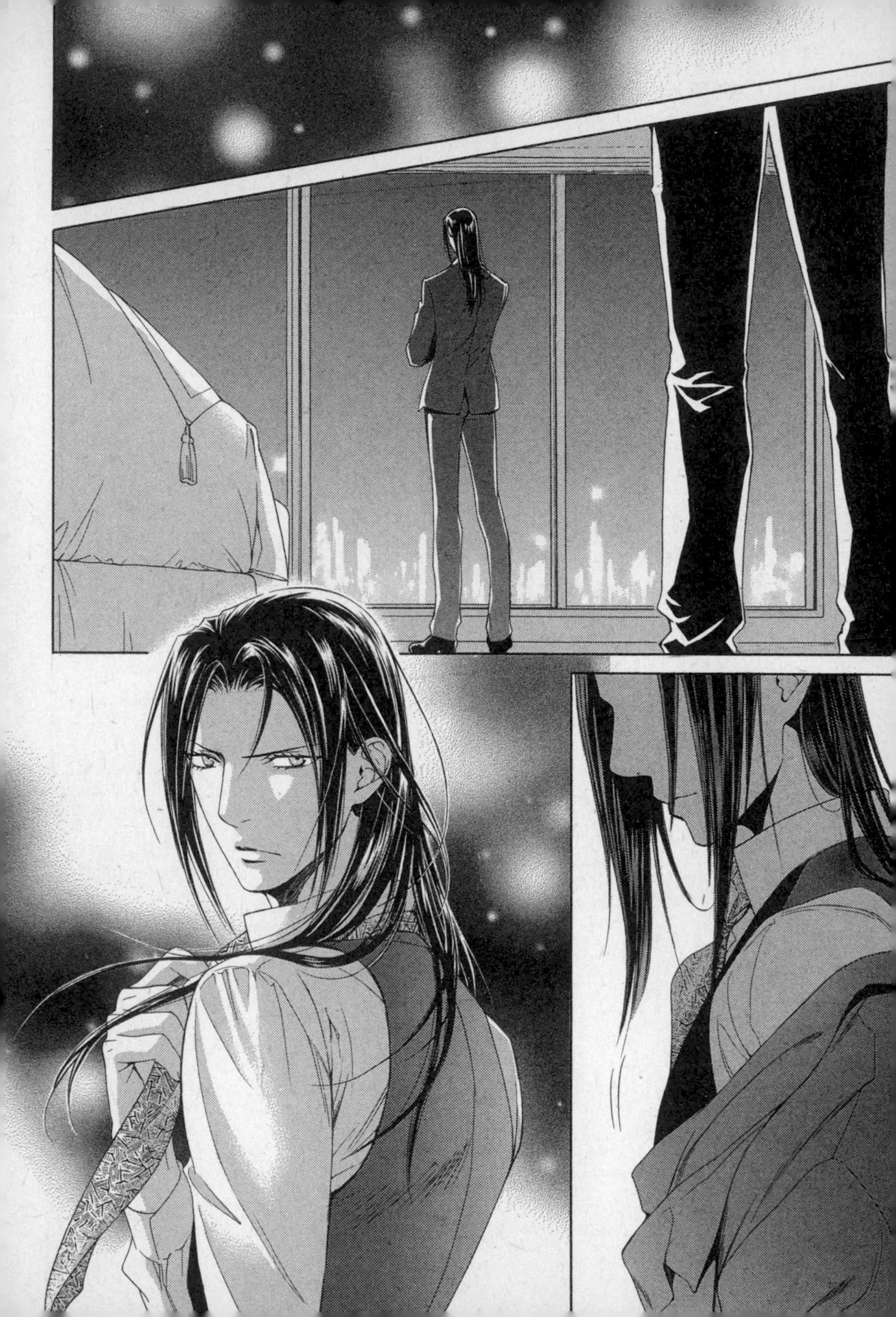

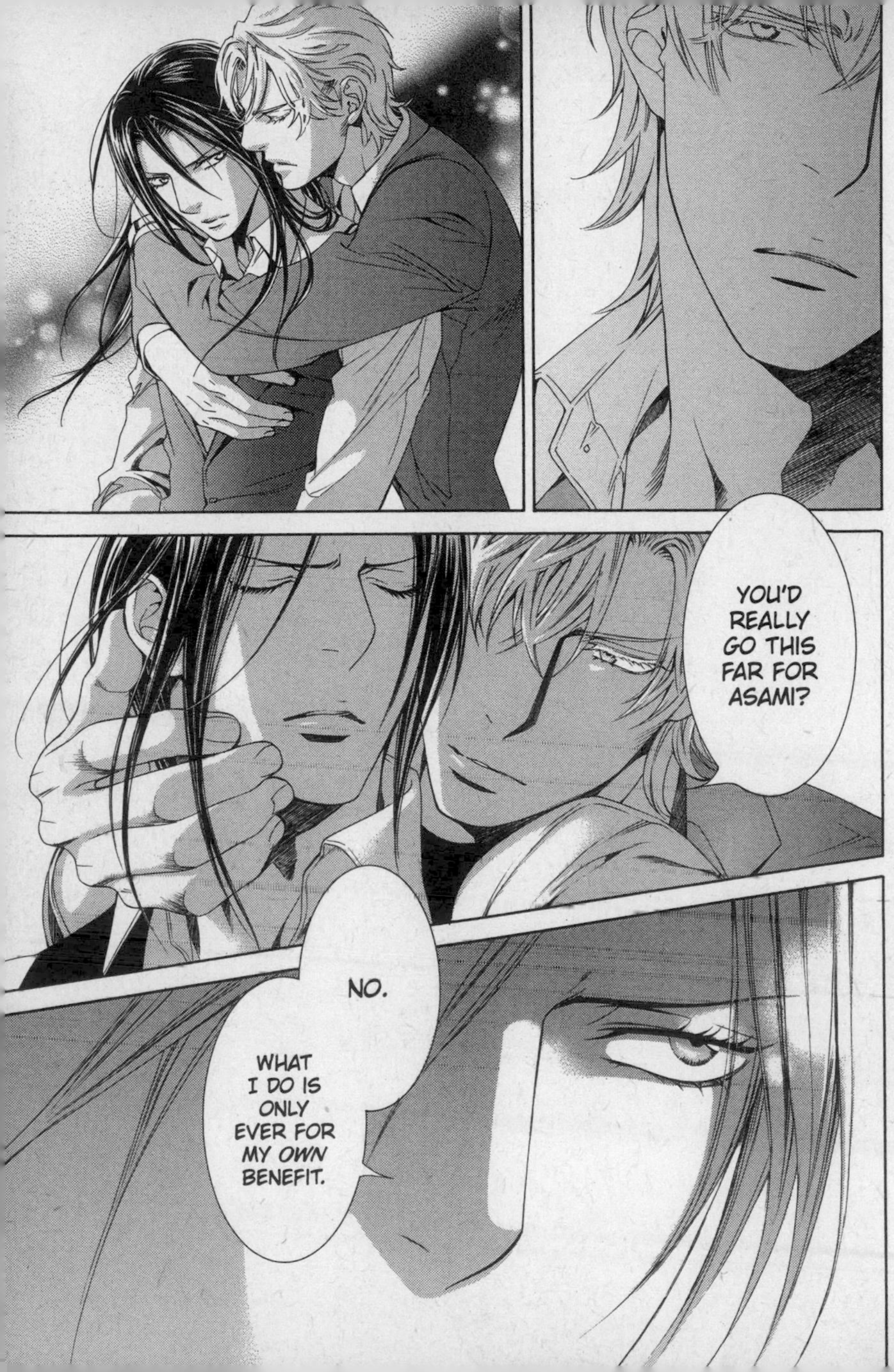
YOU'D REALLY GO THIS FAR FOR ASAMI?
NO.
WHAT I DO IS ONLY EVER FOR MY *OWN* BENEFIT.

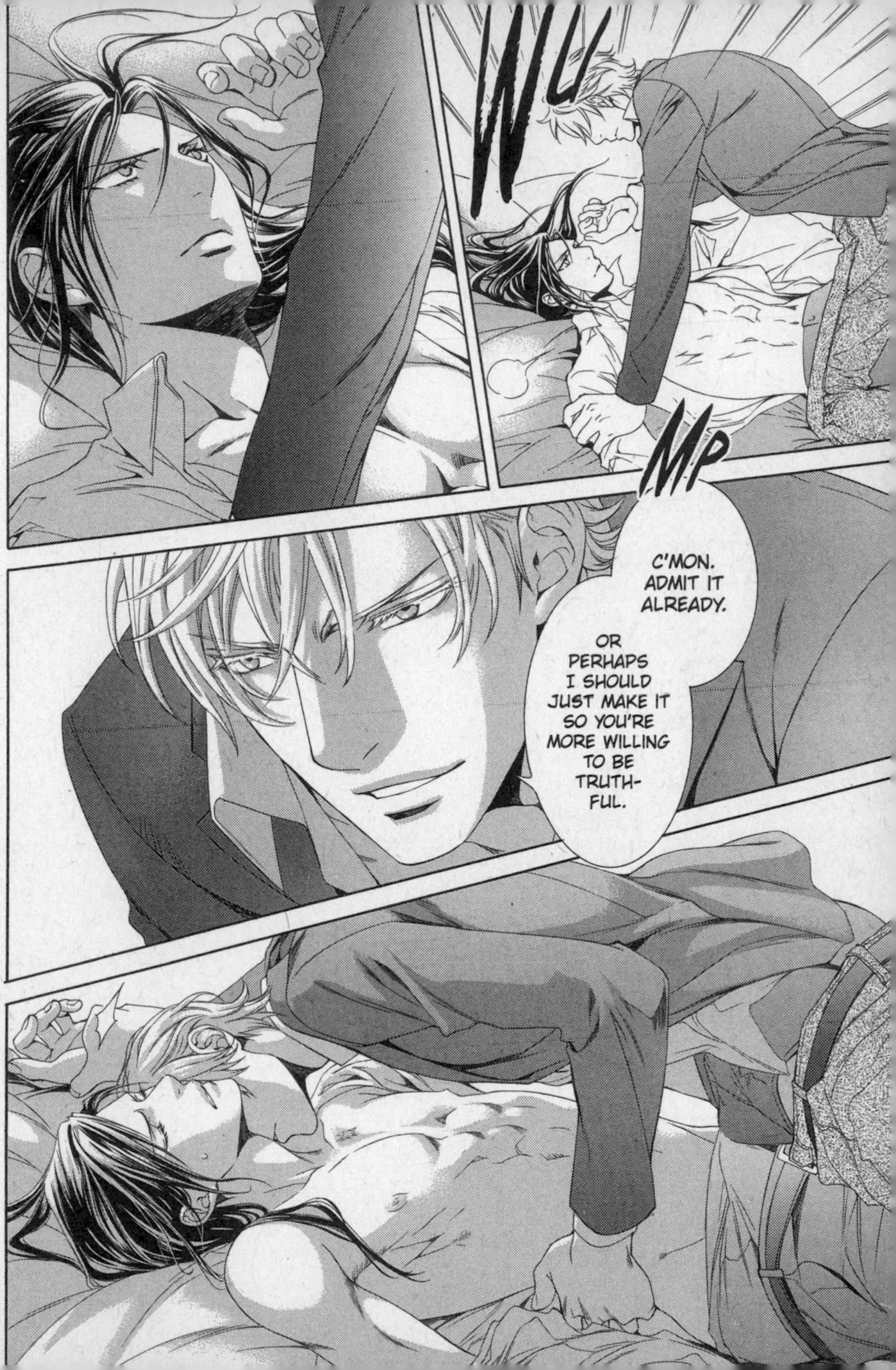
WU
MP
C'MON. ADMIT IT ALREADY.
OR PERHAPS I SHOULD JUST MAKE IT SO YOU'RE MORE WILLING TO BE TRUTH-FUL.

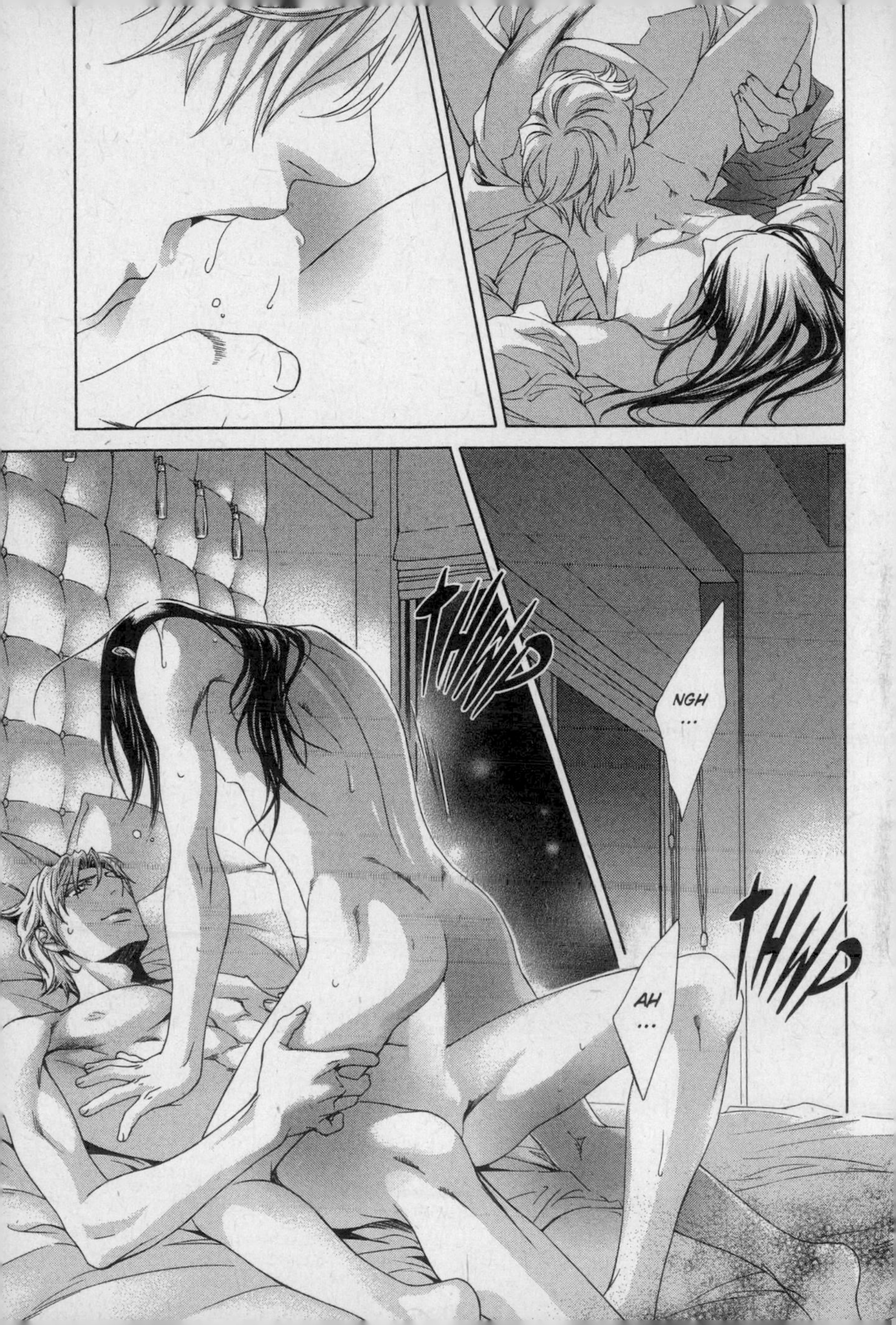
THWP
NGH …
THWP
AH …

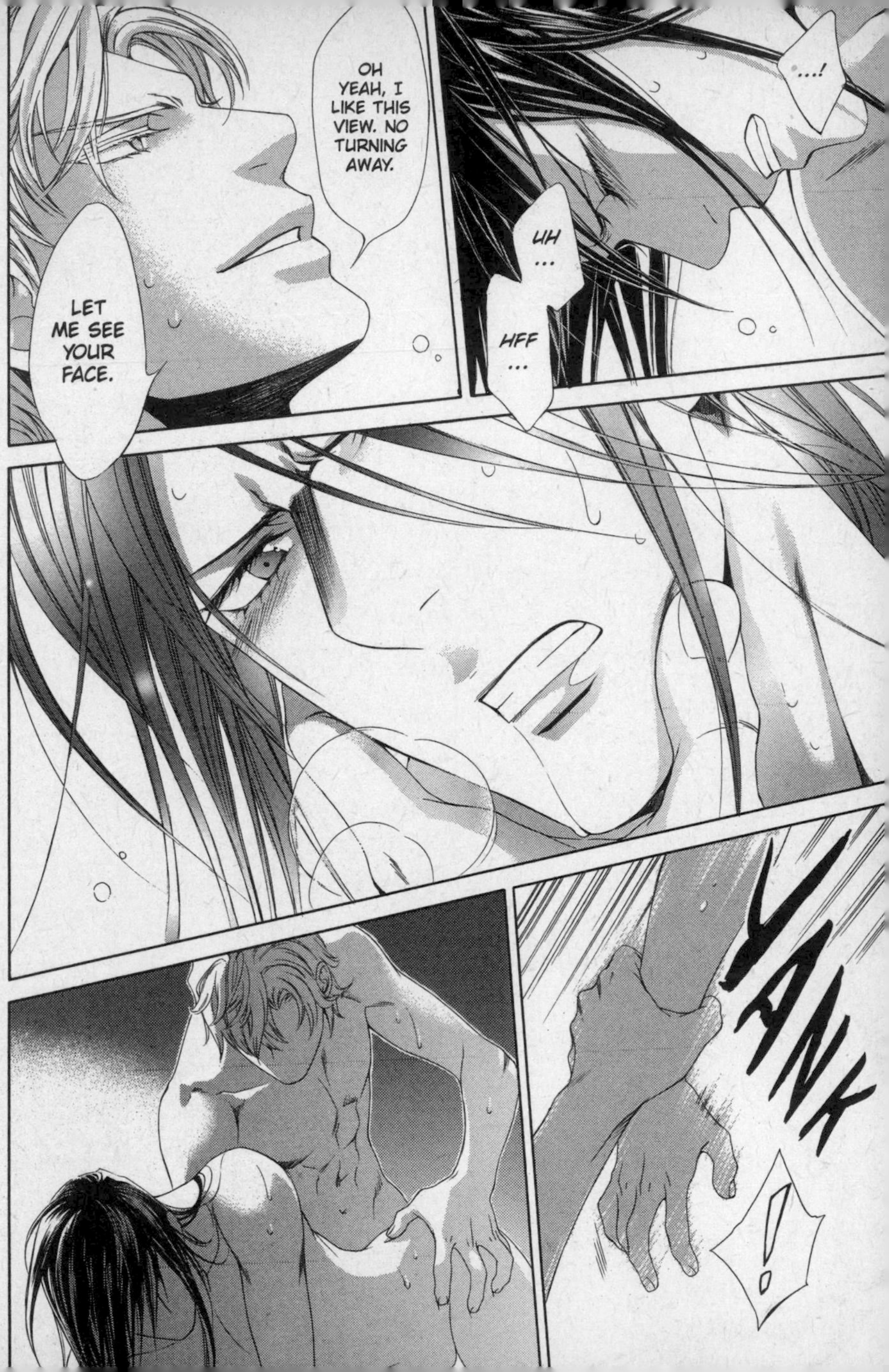
...!
UH ...
HFF ...
OH YEAH, I LIKE THIS VIEW. NO TURNING AWAY.
LET ME SEE YOUR FACE.
YANK
!

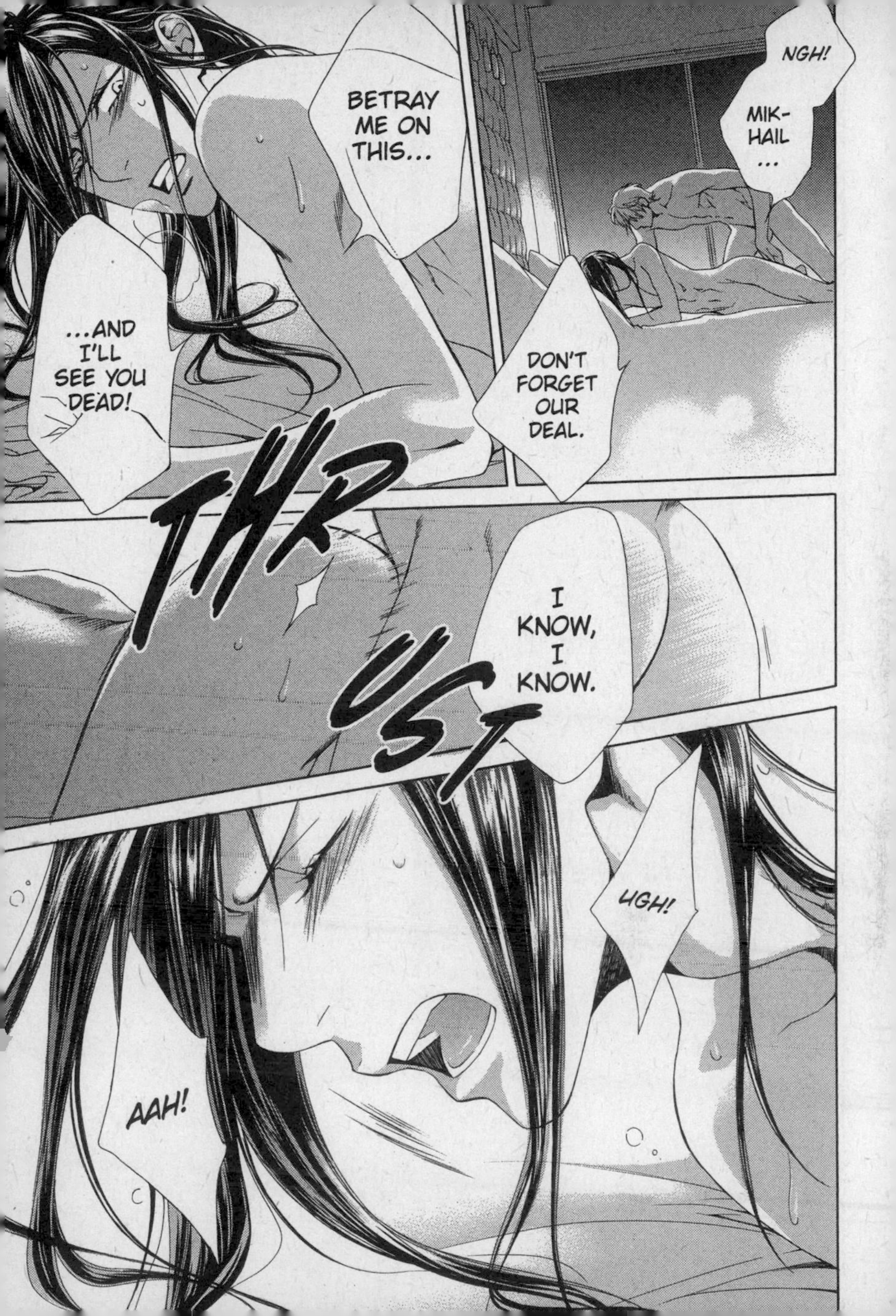
NGH!
MIK-HAIL...
DON'T FORGET OUR DEAL.
BETRAY ME ON THIS...
...AND I'LL SEE YOU DEAD!
THRUST
I KNOW, I KNOW.
UGH!
AAH!

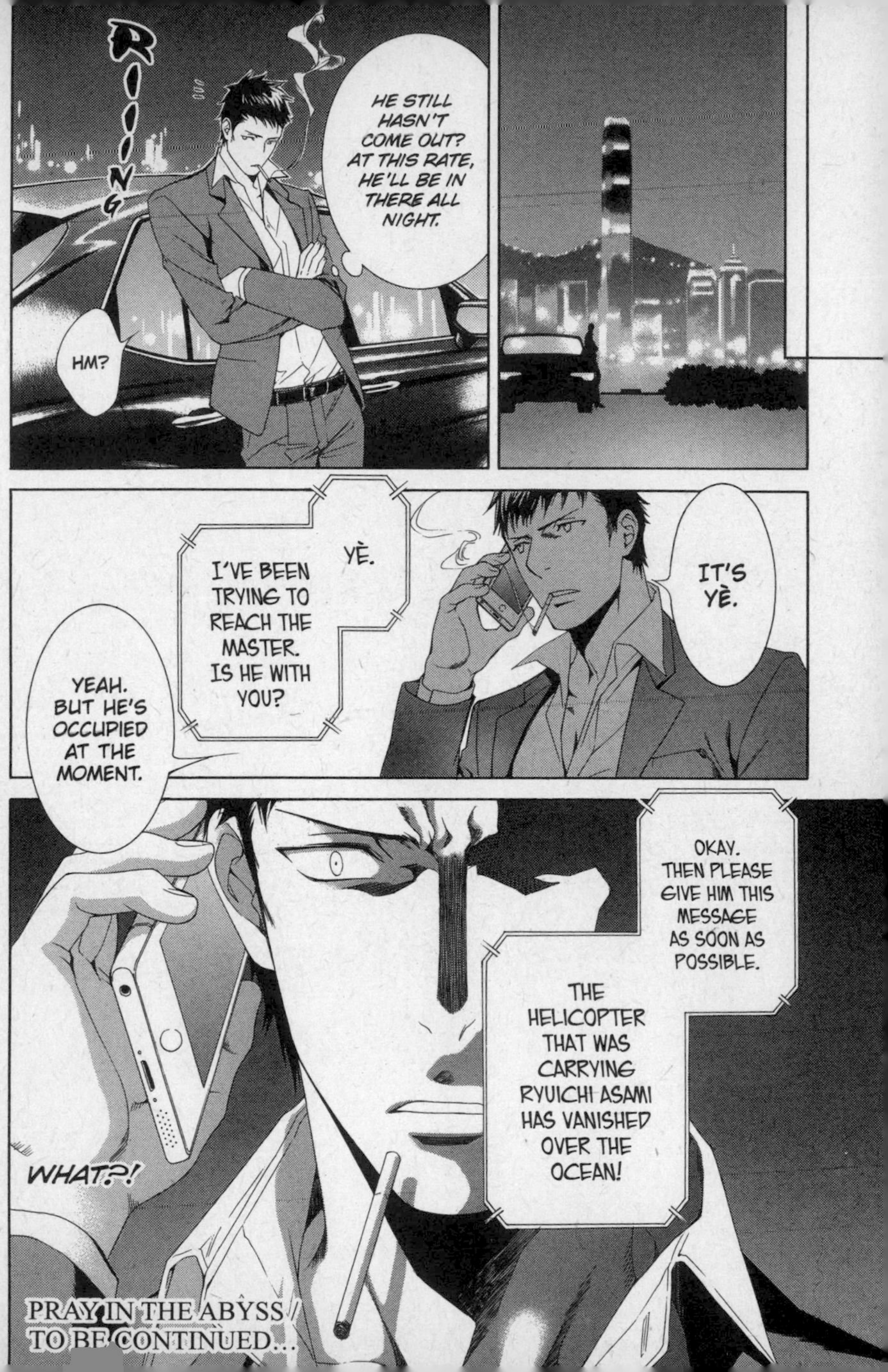
HE STILL HASN'T COME OUT? AT THIS RATE, HE'LL BE IN THERE ALL NIGHT.
RIIIING
HM?
IT'S YÈ.
YÈ.
I'VE BEEN TRYING TO REACH THE MASTER. IS HE WITH YOU?
YEAH. BUT HE'S OCCUPIED AT THE MOMENT.
OKAY. THEN PLEASE GIVE HIM THIS MESSAGE AS SOON AS POSSIBLE.
THE HELICOPTER THAT WAS CARRYING RYUICHI ASAMI HAS VANISHED OVER THE OCEAN!
WHAT?!
PRAY IN THE ABYSS / TO BE CONTINUED...

ブレイ　インアビス

Pray in the Abyss

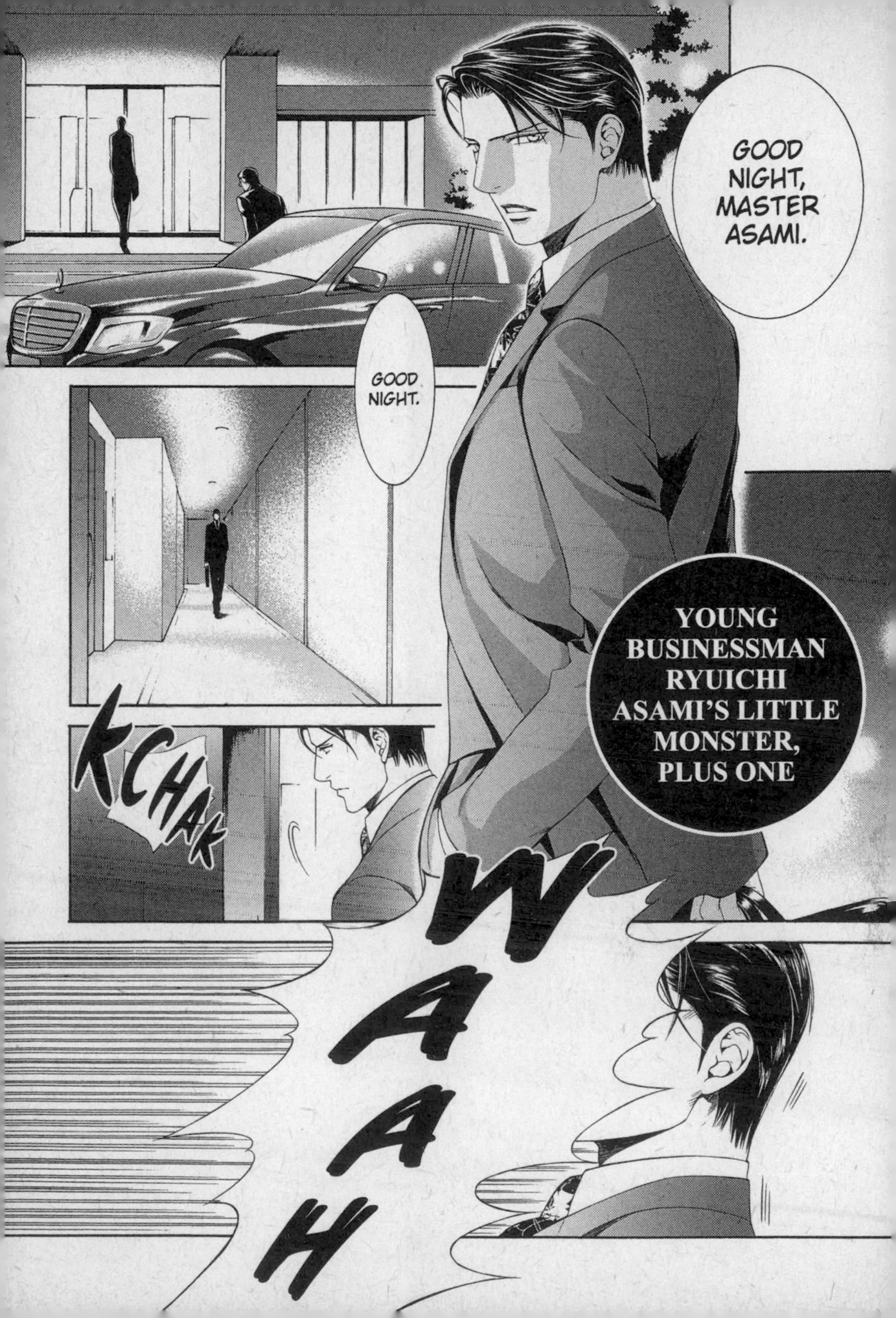
GOOD NIGHT, MASTER ASAMI.
GOOD NIGHT.
YOUNG BUSINESSMAN RYUICHI ASAMI'S LITTLE MONSTER, PLUS ONE
KCHAK
WAAAH

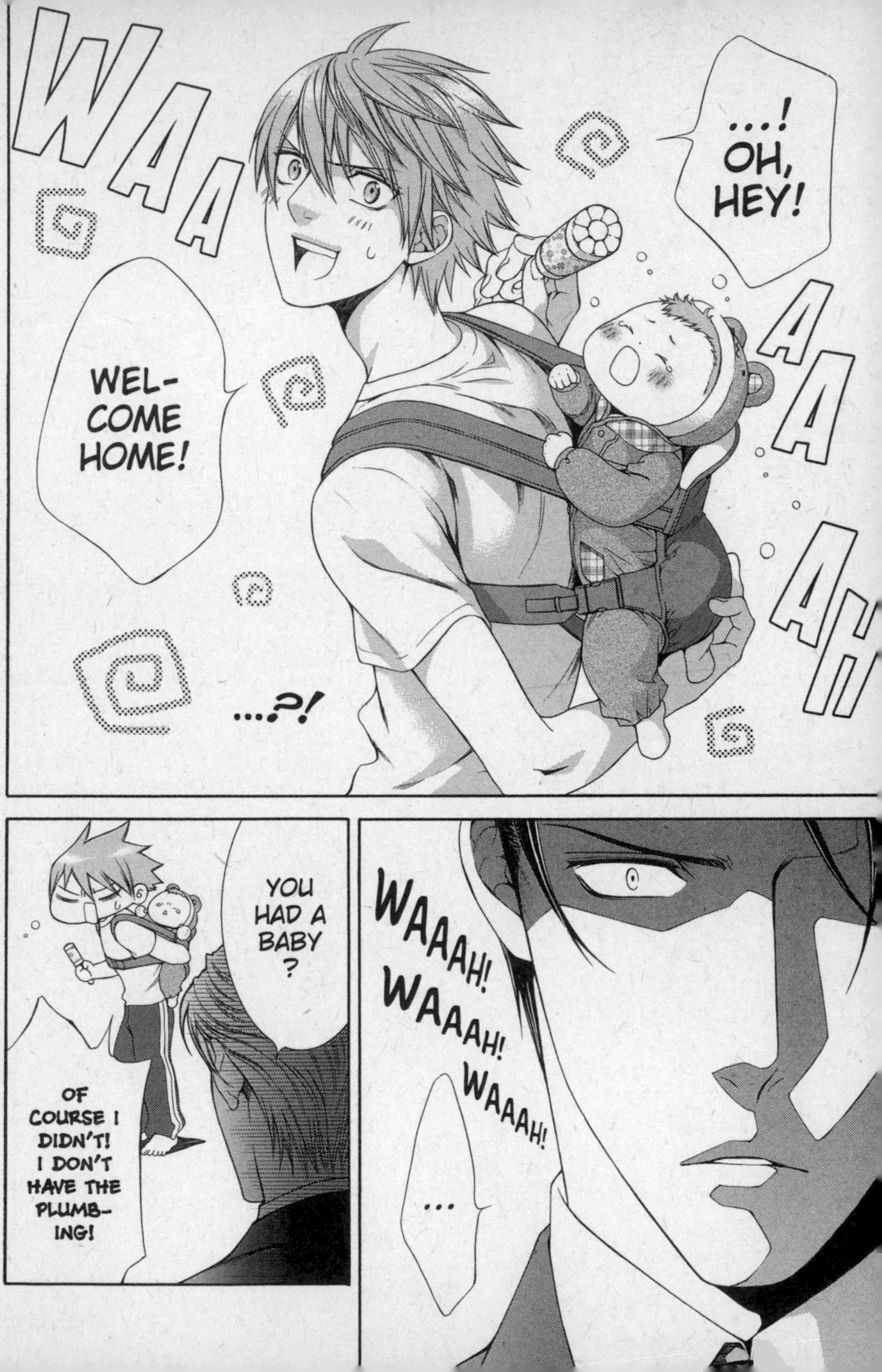
...! OH, HEY!
WAAA
AAAAH
WEL-COME HOME!
...?!
WAAAH! WAAAH! WAAAH!
...
YOU HAD A BABY?
OF COURSE I DIDN'T! I DON'T HAVE THE PLUMB-ING!

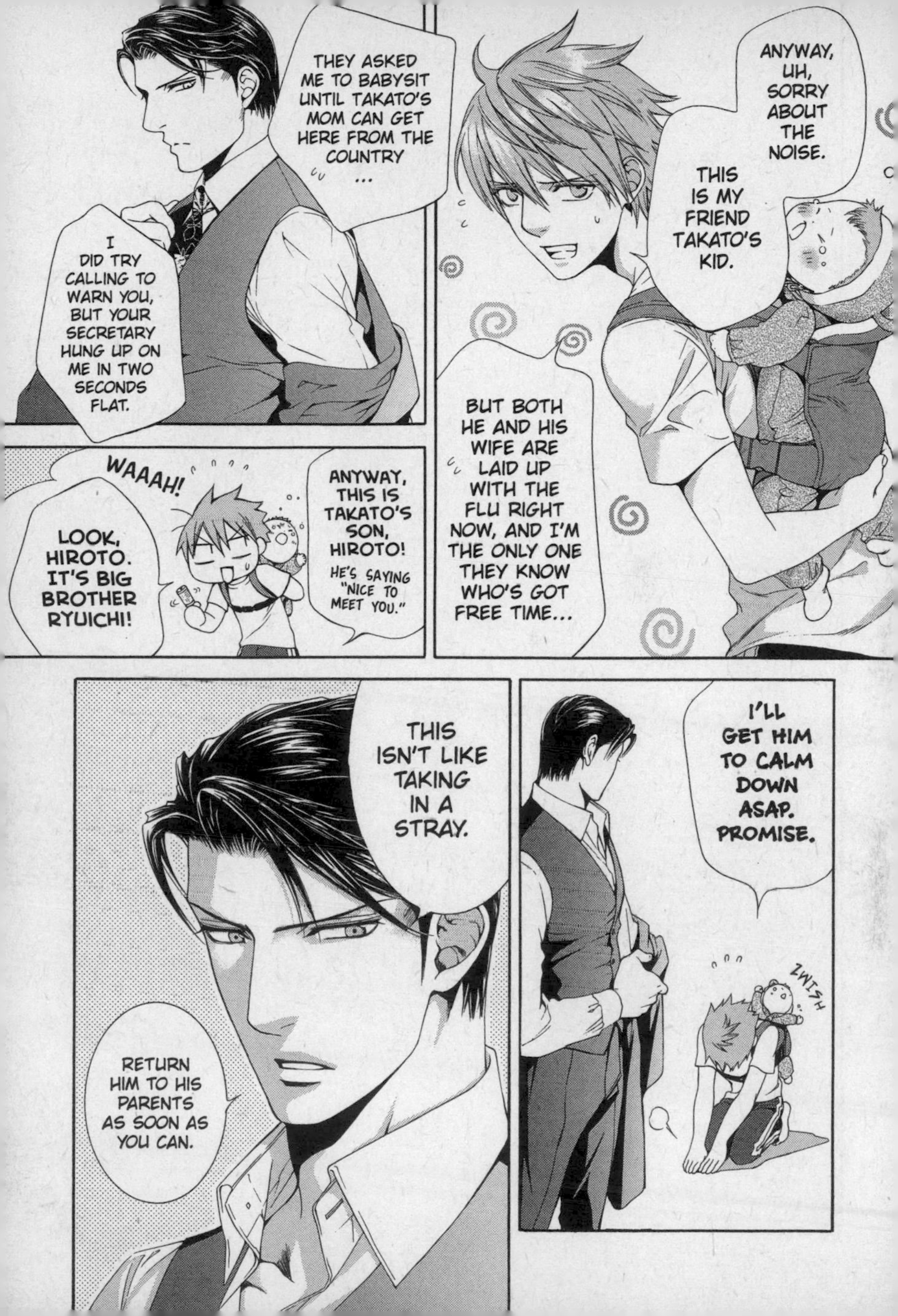
ANYWAY, UH, SORRY ABOUT THE NOISE.
THIS IS MY FRIEND TAKATO'S KID.
BUT BOTH HE AND HIS WIFE ARE LAID UP WITH THE FLU RIGHT NOW, AND I'M THE ONLY ONE THEY KNOW WHO'S GOT FREE TIME...
THEY ASKED ME TO BABYSIT UNTIL TAKATO'S MOM CAN GET HERE FROM THE COUNTRY ...
I DID TRY CALLING TO WARN YOU, BUT YOUR SECRETARY HUNG UP ON ME IN TWO SECONDS FLAT.
ANYWAY, THIS IS TAKATO'S SON, HIROTO!
HE'S SAYING "NICE TO MEET YOU."
WAAAH!
LOOK, HIROTO. IT'S BIG BROTHER RYUICHI!
I'LL GET HIM TO CALM DOWN ASAP. PROMISE.
ZWISH
THIS ISN'T LIKE TAKING IN A STRAY.
RETURN HIM TO HIS PARENTS AS SOON AS YOU CAN.

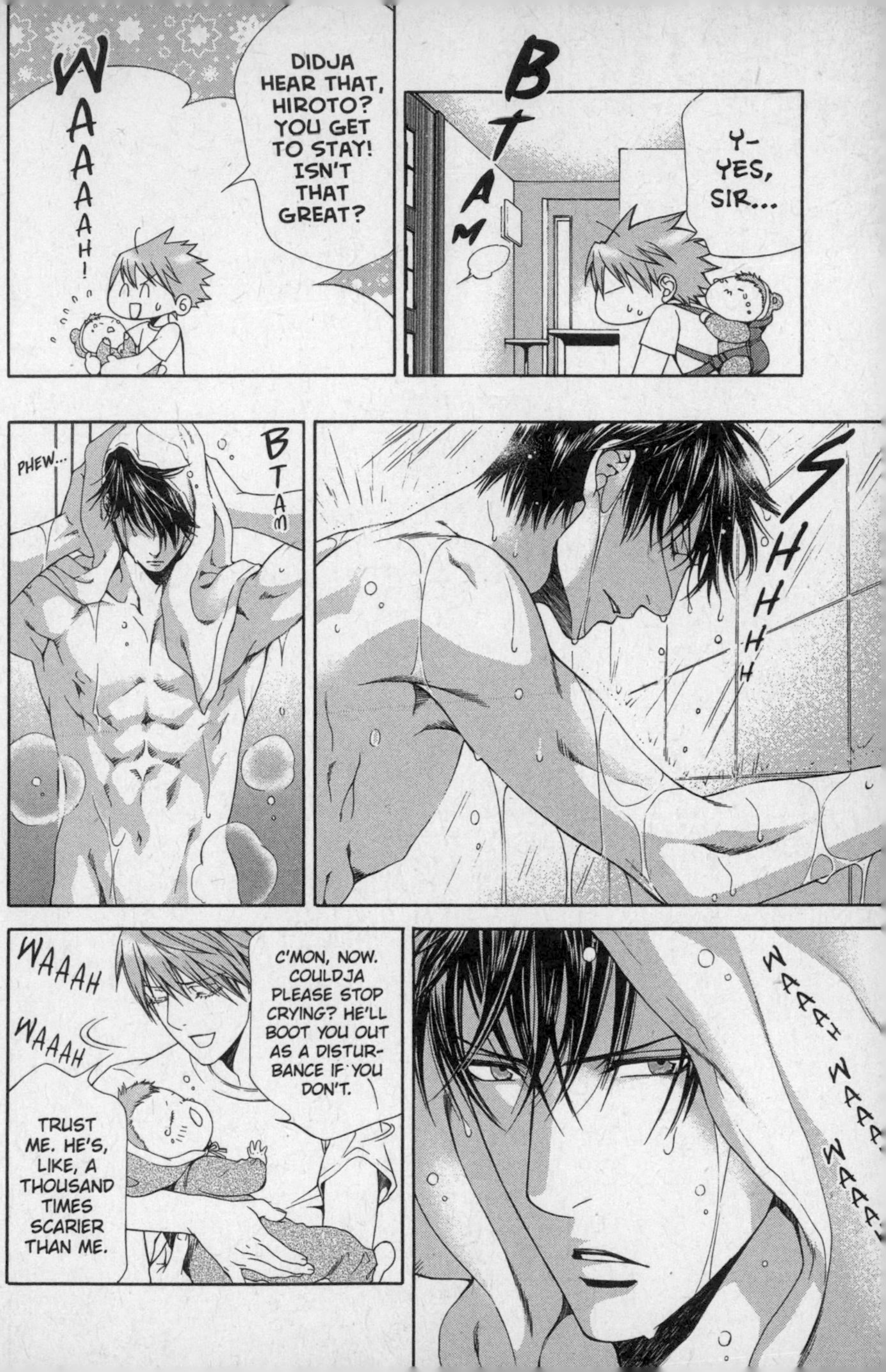
BTAM
Y-YES, SIR...
WAAAAAH!
DIDJA HEAR THAT, HIROTO? YOU GET TO STAY! ISN'T THAT GREAT?
SHHHHHH
PHEW...
BTAM
C'MON, NOW. COULDJA PLEASE STOP CRYING? HE'LL BOOT YOU OUT AS A DISTURBANCE IF YOU DON'T.
TRUST ME. HE'S, LIKE, A THOUSAND TIMES SCARIER THAN ME.
WAAAH
WAAAH

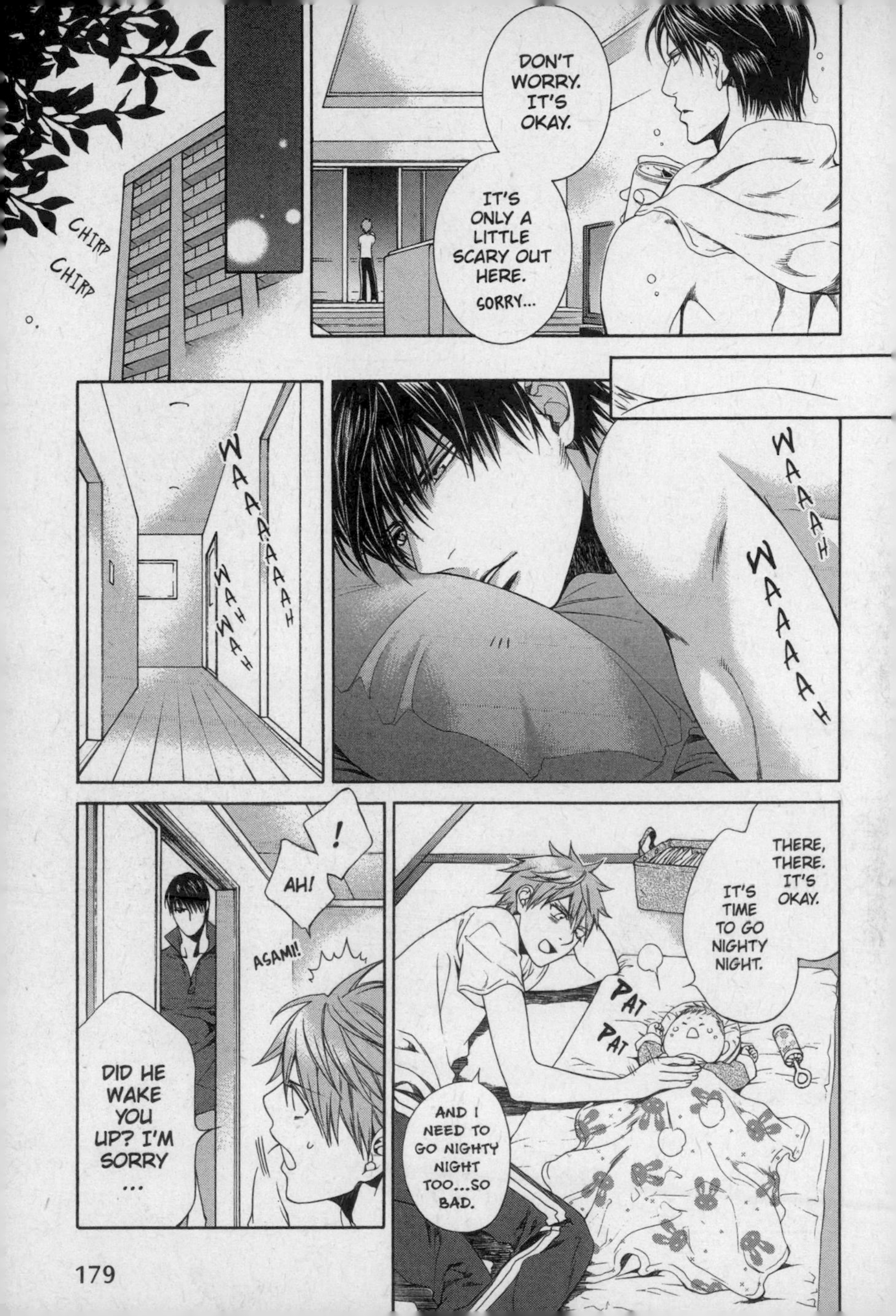
DON'T WORRY. IT'S OKAY.
IT'S ONLY A LITTLE SCARY OUT HERE.
SORRY...
CHIRP
CHIRP
WAAAAH
WAAAAAH
WAAAAAAAAH
WAH
WAH
THERE, THERE. IT'S OKAY.
IT'S TIME TO GO NIGHTY NIGHT.
PAT
PAT
AND I NEED TO GO NIGHTY NIGHT TOO...SO BAD.
!
AH!
ASAMI!
DID HE WAKE YOU UP? I'M SORRY ...

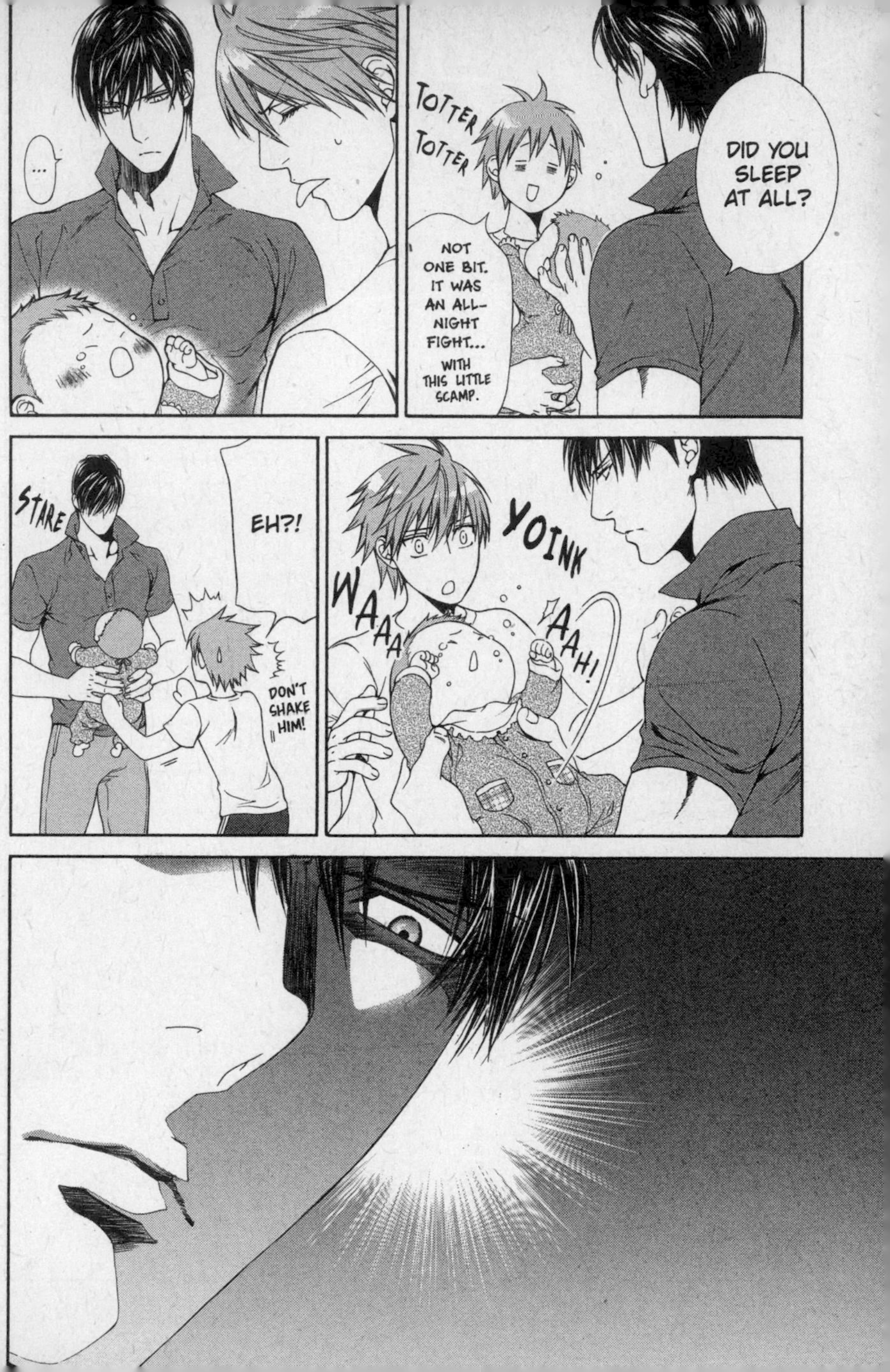
DID YOU SLEEP AT ALL?
TOTTER TOTTER
NOT ONE BIT. IT WAS AN ALL-NIGHT FIGHT...
WITH THIS LITTLE SCAMP.
...
YOINK
WAAA
AAH!
EH?!
STARE
DON'T SHAKE HIM!

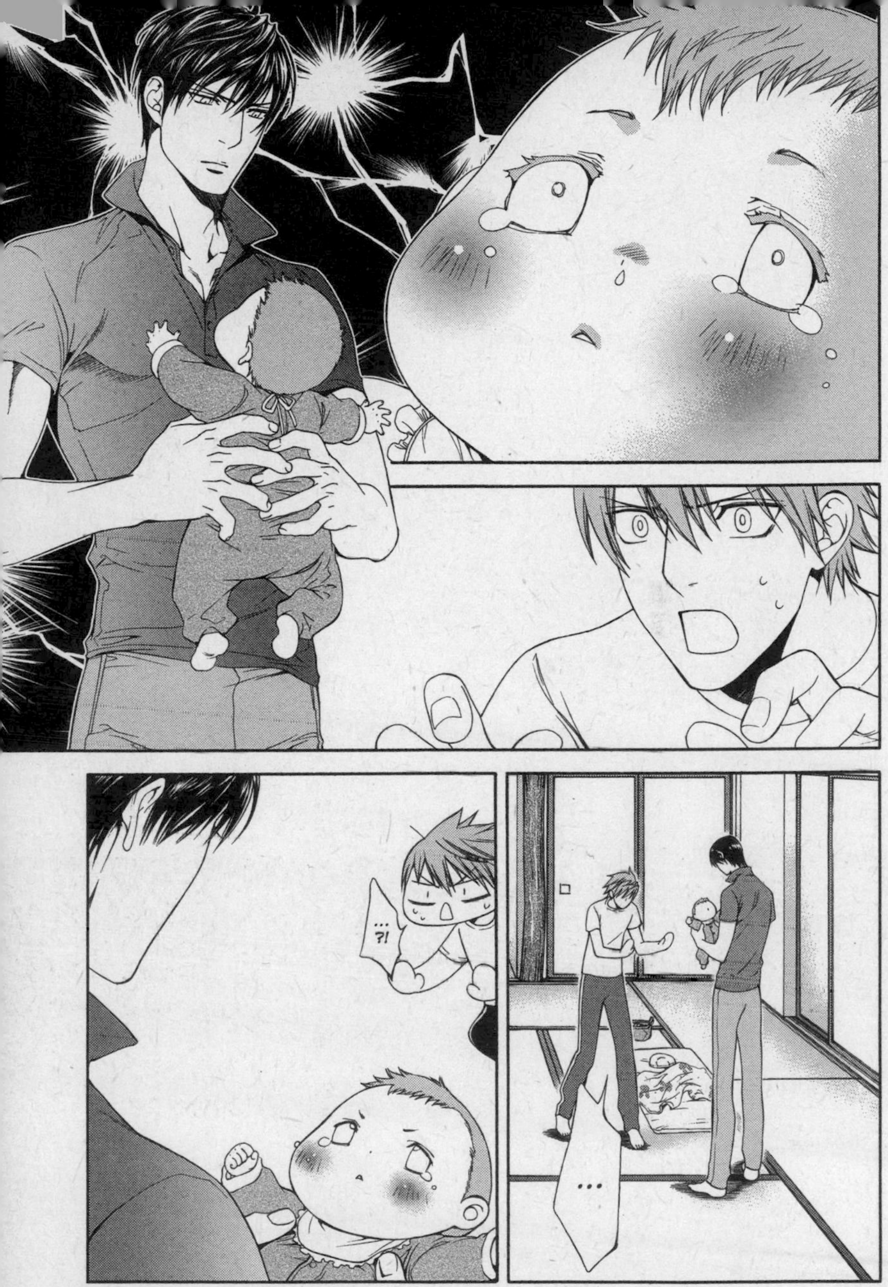
...
...
?!

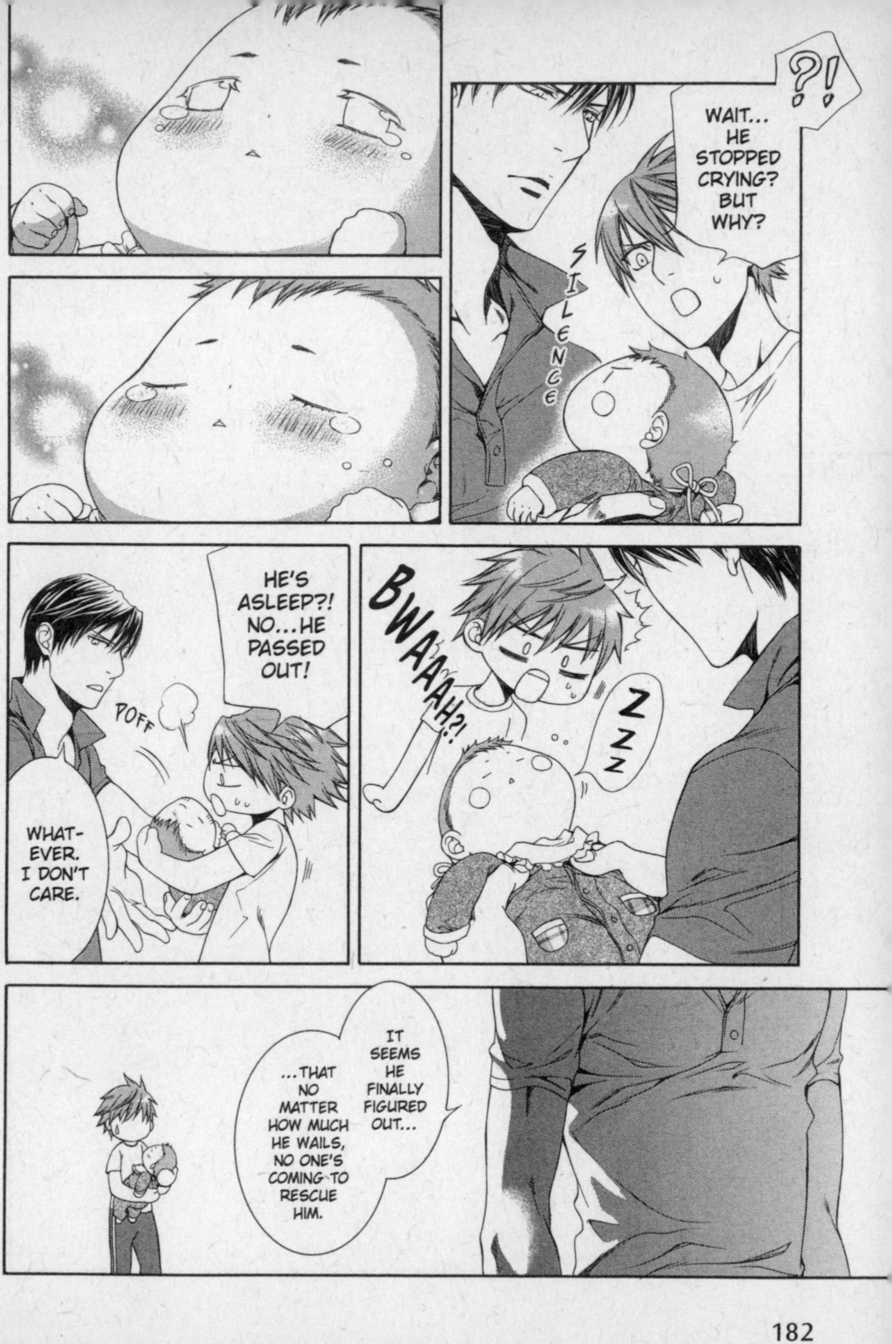
?!
WAIT... HE STOPPED CRYING? BUT WHY?
SILENCE
BWAAAH?!
ZZZ
HE'S ASLEEP?! NO...HE PASSED OUT!
POFF
WHAT-EVER. I DON'T CARE.
IT SEEMS HE FINALLY FIGURED OUT...
...THAT NO MATTER HOW MUCH HE WAILS, NO ONE'S COMING TO RESCUE HIM.

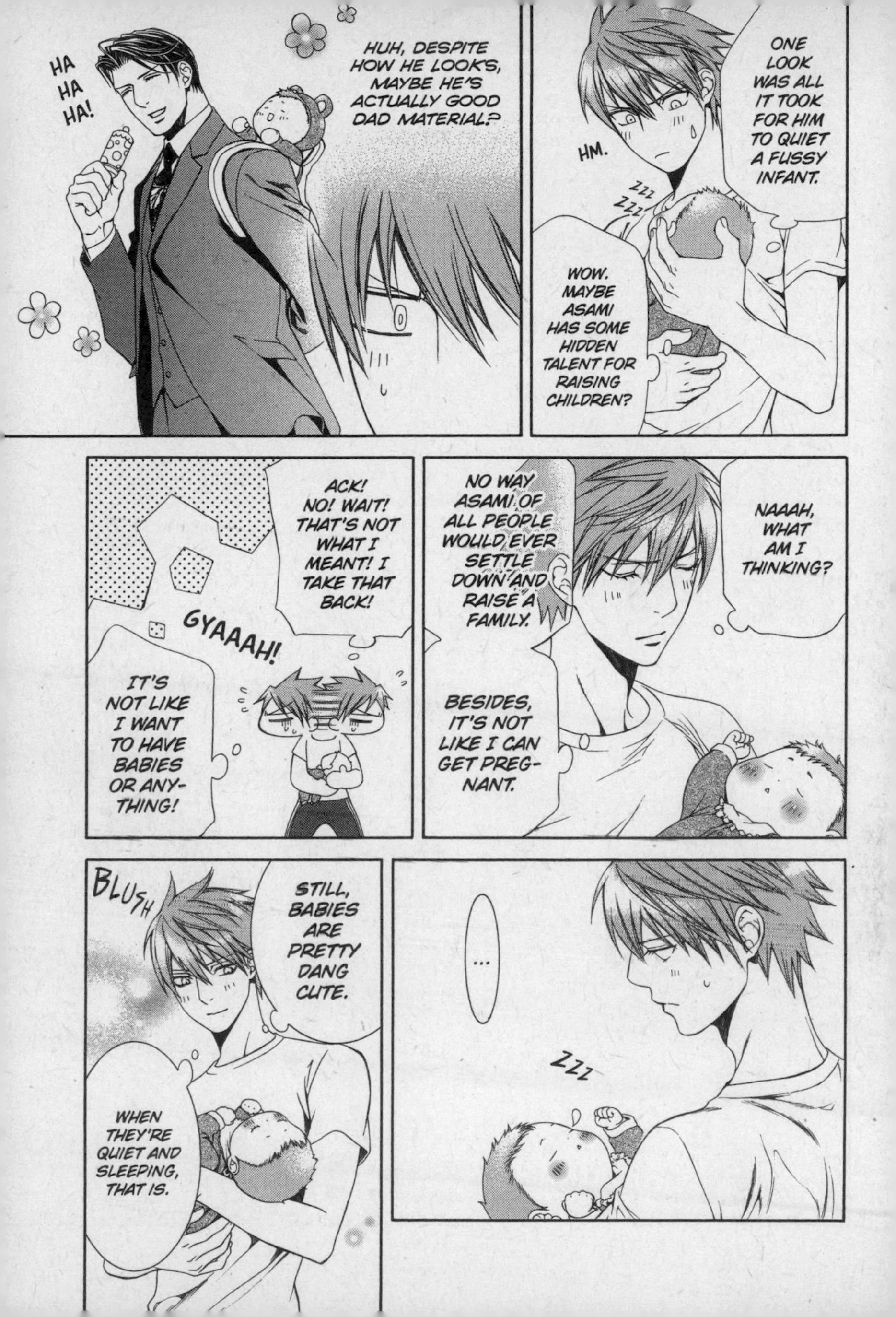
ONE LOOK WAS ALL IT TOOK FOR HIM TO QUIET A FUSSY INFANT.
HM.
ZZZ ZZZ
WOW. MAYBE ASAMI HAS SOME HIDDEN TALENT FOR RAISING CHILDREN?
HUH, DESPITE HOW HE LOOKS, MAYBE HE'S ACTUALLY GOOD DAD MATERIAL?
HA HA HA!
NAAAH, WHAT AM I THINKING?
NO WAY ASAMI OF ALL PEOPLE WOULD EVER SETTLE DOWN AND RAISE A FAMILY.
BESIDES, IT'S NOT LIKE I CAN GET PREG-NANT.
ACK! NO! WAIT! THAT'S NOT WHAT I MEANT! I TAKE THAT BACK!
GYAAAH!
IT'S NOT LIKE I WANT TO HAVE BABIES OR ANY-THING!
...
ZZZ
BLUSH
STILL, BABIES ARE PRETTY DANG CUTE.
WHEN THEY'RE QUIET AND SLEEPING, THAT IS.

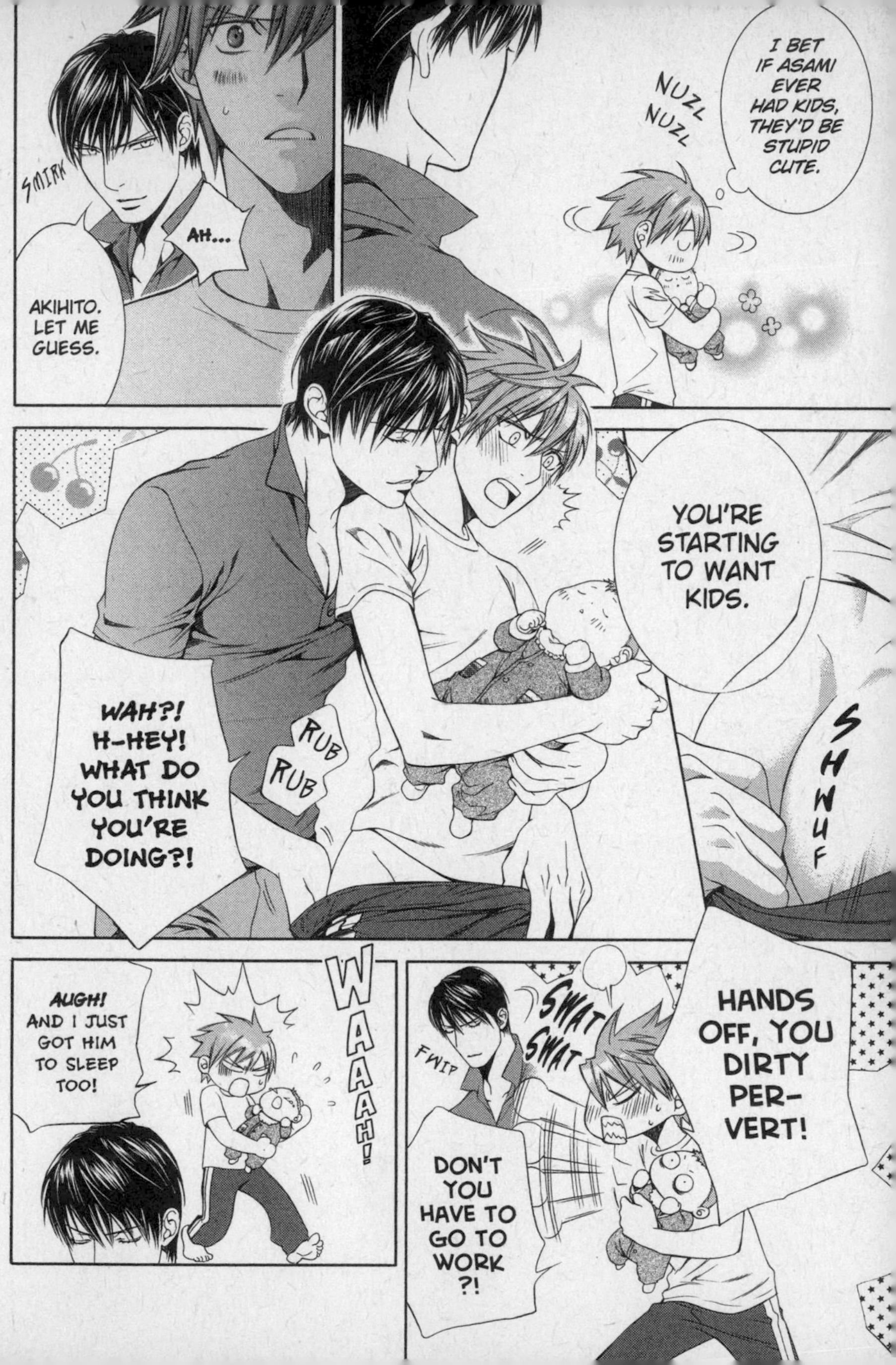

I BET IF ASAMI EVER HAD KIDS, THEY'D BE STUPID CUTE.
NUZL NUZL
SMIRK
AH...
AKIHITO. LET ME GUESS.
YOU'RE STARTING TO WANT KIDS.
SHWUF
RUB RUB
WAH?! H-HEY! WHAT DO YOU THINK YOU'RE DOING?!
HANDS OFF, YOU DIRTY PER-VERT!
SWAT SWAT
FWIP
DON'T YOU HAVE TO GO TO WORK?!
WAAAAH!
AUGH! AND I JUST GOT HIM TO SLEEP TOO!

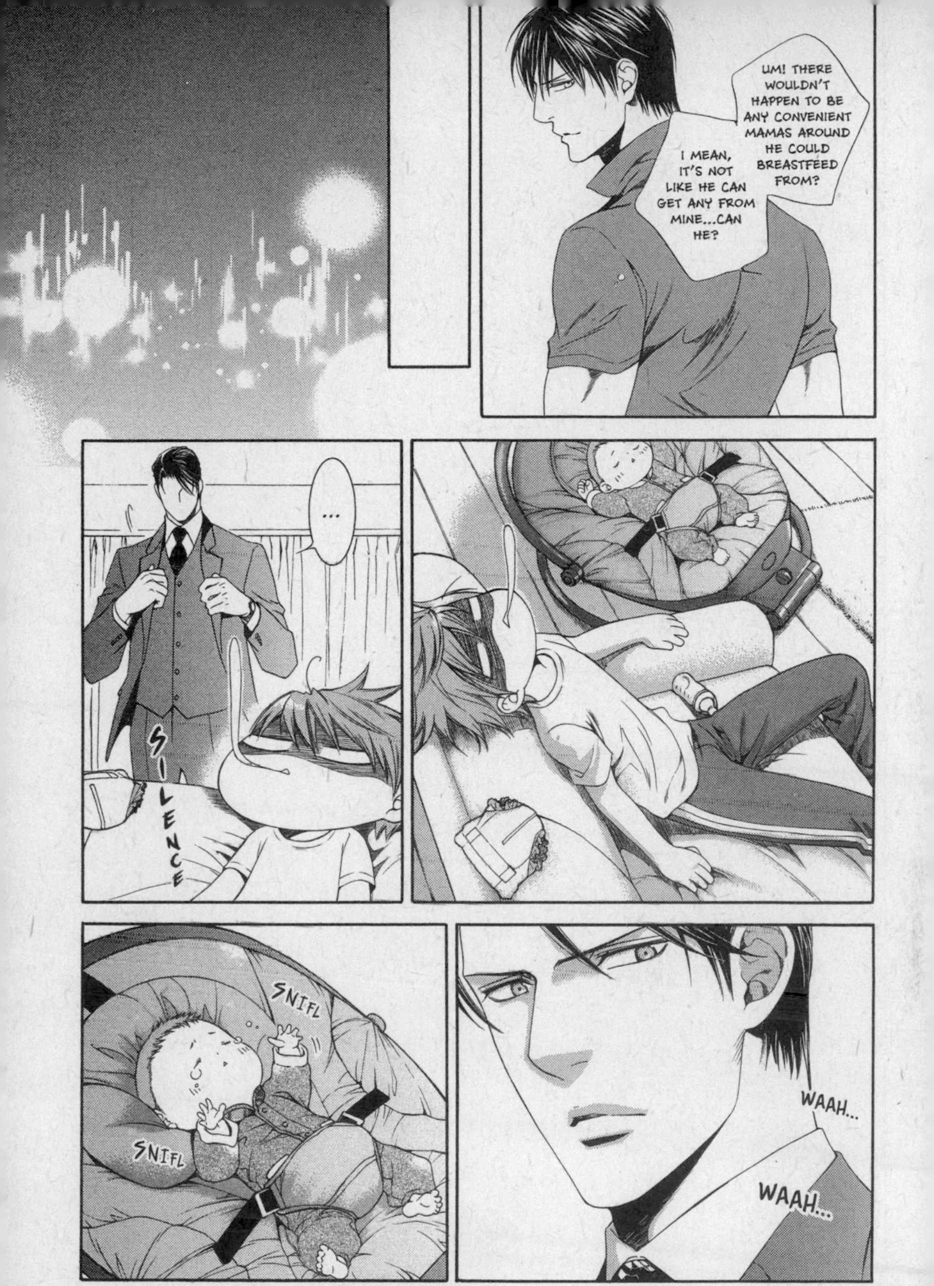
UM! THERE WOULDN'T HAPPEN TO BE ANY CONVENIENT MAMAS AROUND HE COULD BREASTFEED FROM?
I MEAN, IT'S NOT LIKE HE CAN GET ANY FROM MINE...CAN HE?
...
SILENCE
WAAH...
WAAH...
SNIFL
SNIFL

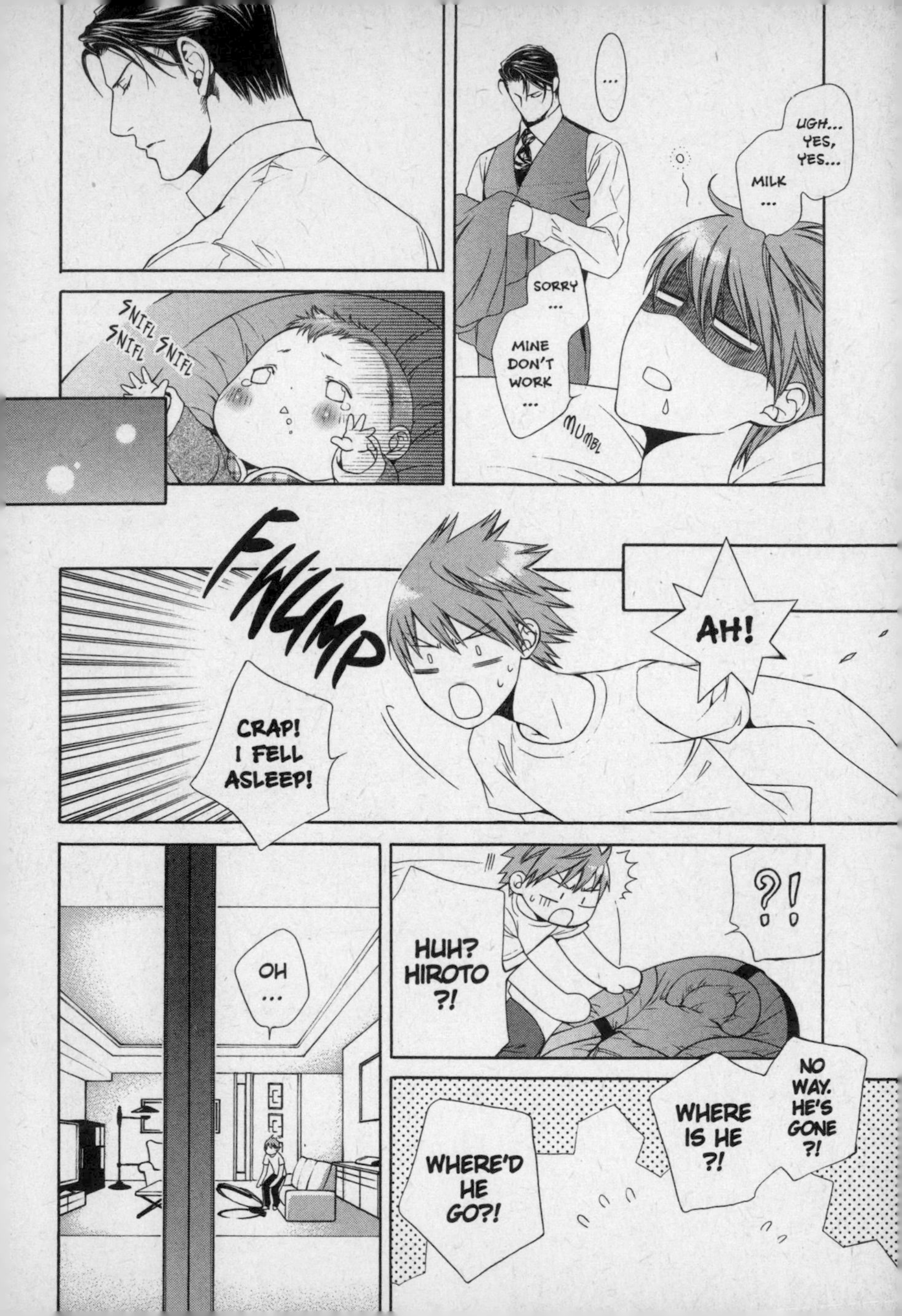
UGH... YES, YES... MILK ...
...
SORRY ... MINE DON'T WORK ...
MUMBL
SNIFL SNIFL SNIFL
AH!
FWUMP
CRAP! I FELL ASLEEP!
?!
HUH? HIROTO ?!
NO WAY. HE'S GONE ?!
WHERE IS HE ?!
WHERE'D HE GO?!
OH ...

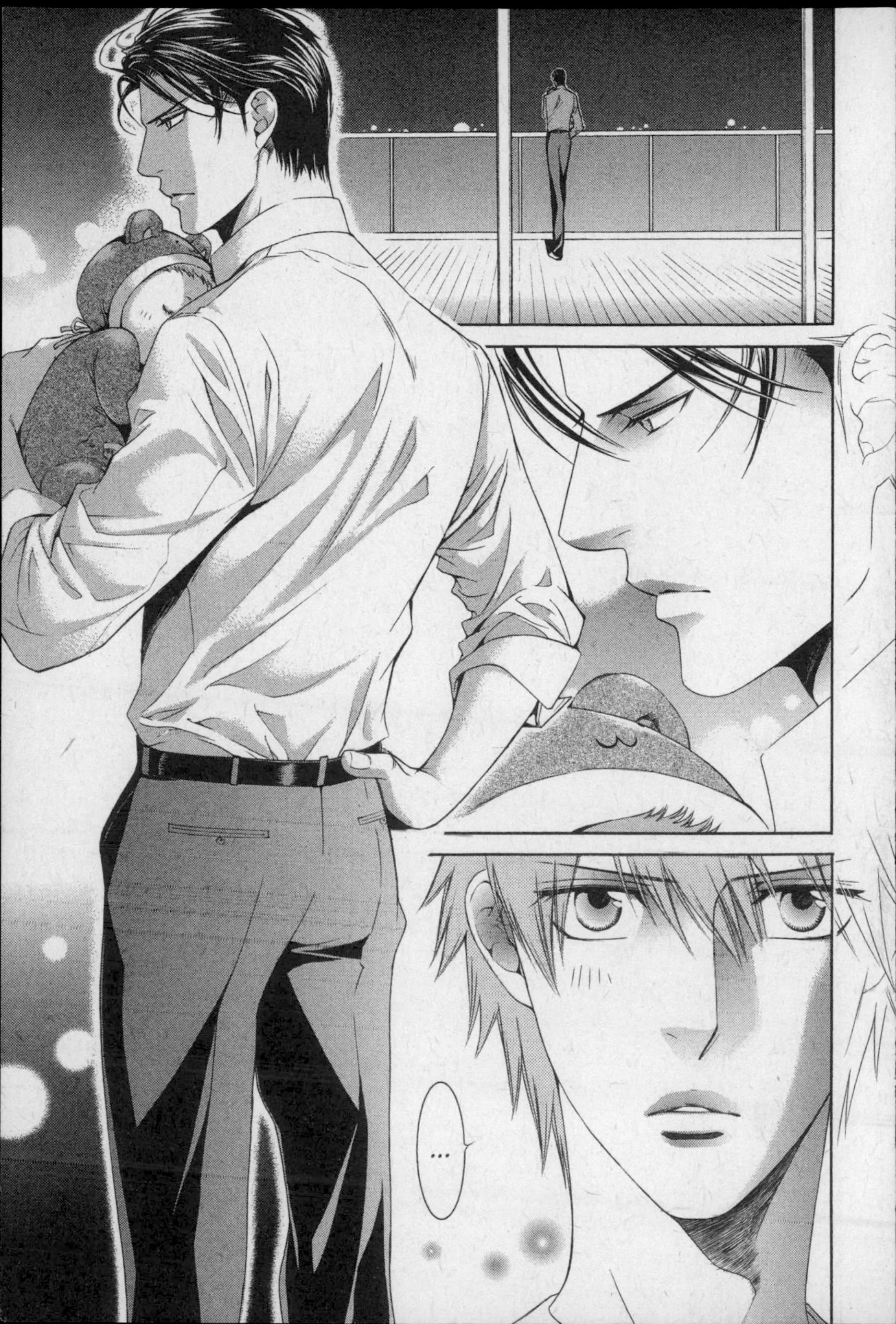
...

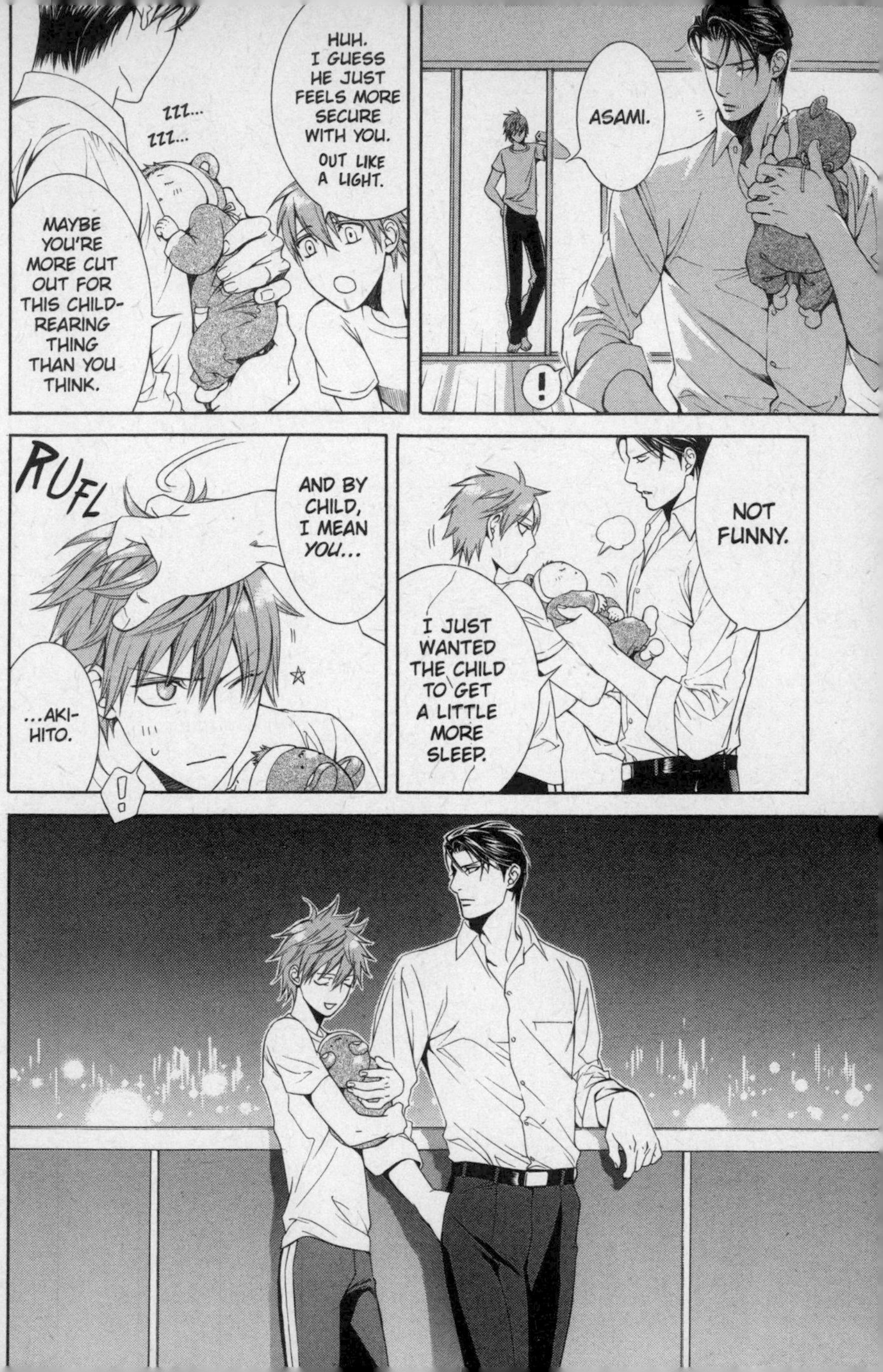
ASAMI.
!
HUH. I GUESS HE JUST FEELS MORE SECURE WITH YOU.
OUT LIKE A LIGHT.
ZZZ... ZZZ...
MAYBE YOU'RE MORE CUT OUT FOR THIS CHILD-REARING THING THAN YOU THINK.
NOT FUNNY.
I JUST WANTED THE CHILD TO GET A LITTLE MORE SLEEP.
RUFL
AND BY CHILD, I MEAN *YOU*...
...AKI-HITO.
!

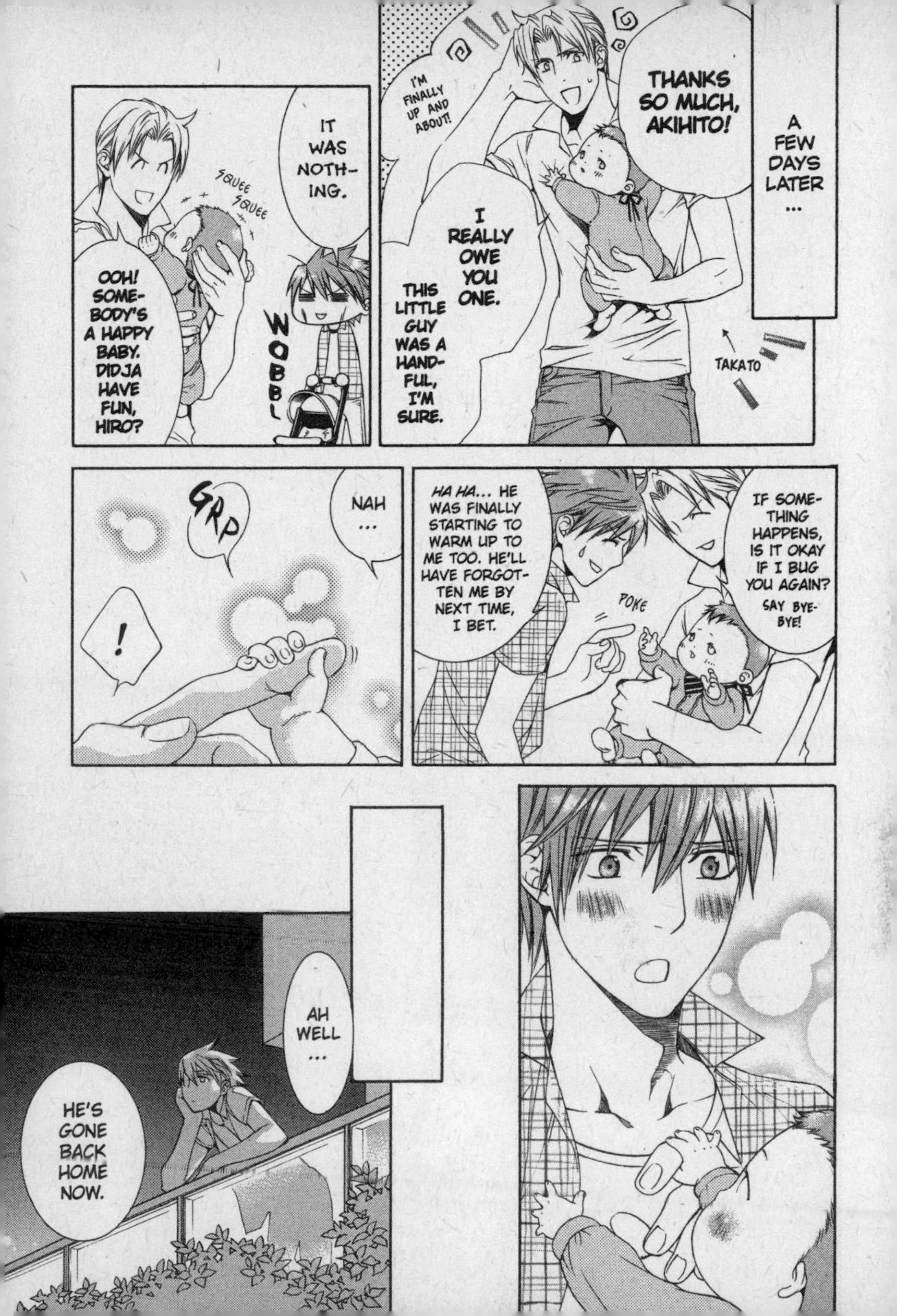
A FEW DAYS LATER ...
THANKS SO MUCH, AKIHITO!
I'M FINALLY UP AND ABOUT!
I REALLY OWE YOU ONE.
THIS LITTLE GUY WAS A HANDFUL, I'M SURE.
TAKATO
IT WAS NOTHING.
SQUEE SQUEE
OOH! SOMEBODY'S A HAPPY BABY. DIDJA HAVE FUN, HIRO?
WOBBL
IF SOMETHING HAPPENS, IS IT OKAY IF I BUG YOU AGAIN?
SAY BYE-BYE!
HA HA... HE WAS FINALLY STARTING TO WARM UP TO ME TOO. HE'LL HAVE FORGOTTEN ME BY NEXT TIME, I BET.
POKE
NAH ...
GRP
!
AH WELL ...
HE'S GONE BACK HOME NOW.

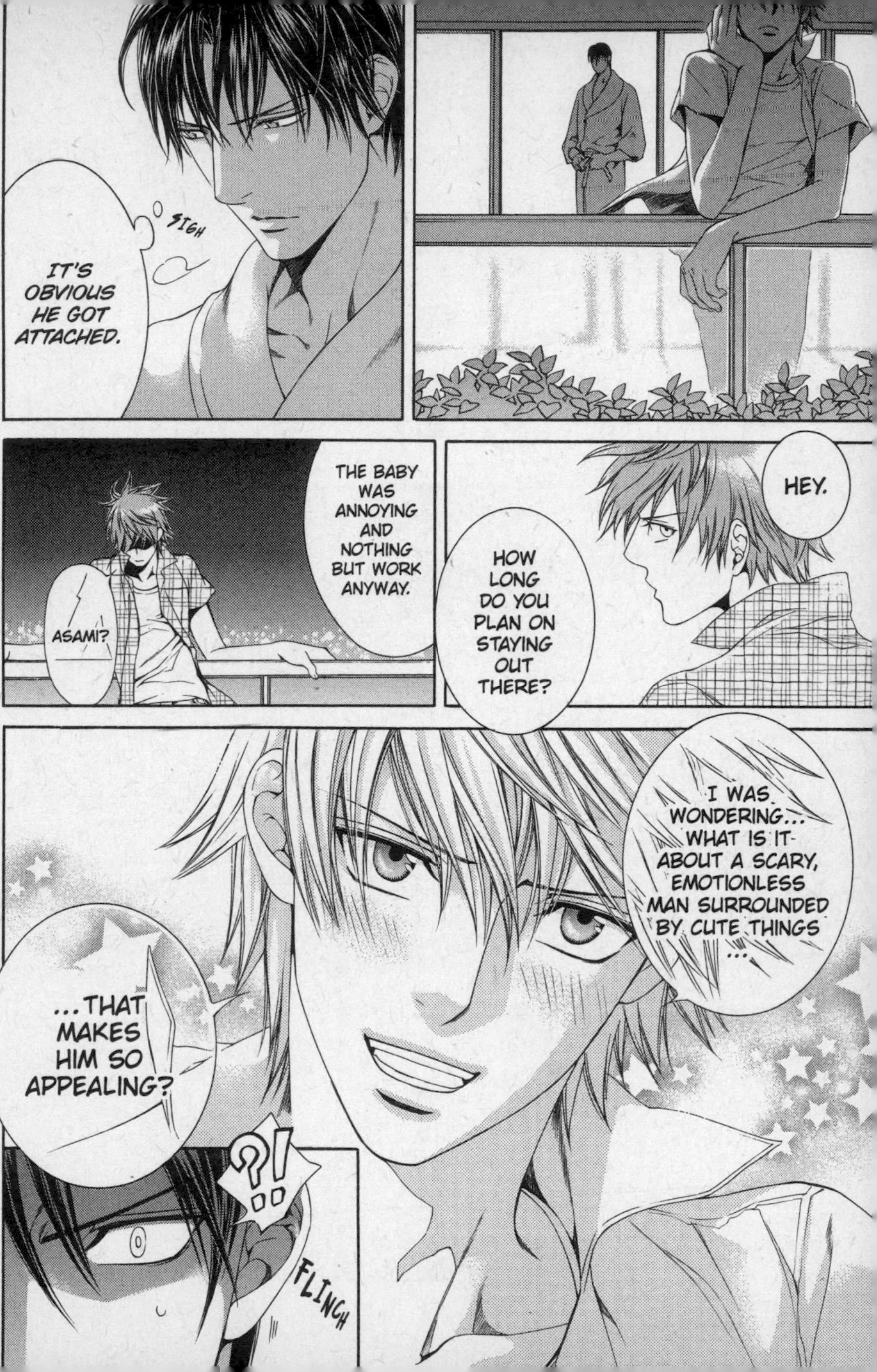
SIGH
IT'S OBVIOUS HE GOT ATTACHED.
HEY.
HOW LONG DO YOU PLAN ON STAYING OUT THERE?
THE BABY WAS ANNOYING AND NOTHING BUT WORK ANYWAY.
ASAMI?
I WAS WONDERING... WHAT IS IT ABOUT A SCARY, EMOTIONLESS MAN SURROUNDED BY CUTE THINGS...
...THAT MAKES HIM SO APPEALING?
?!
FLINCH

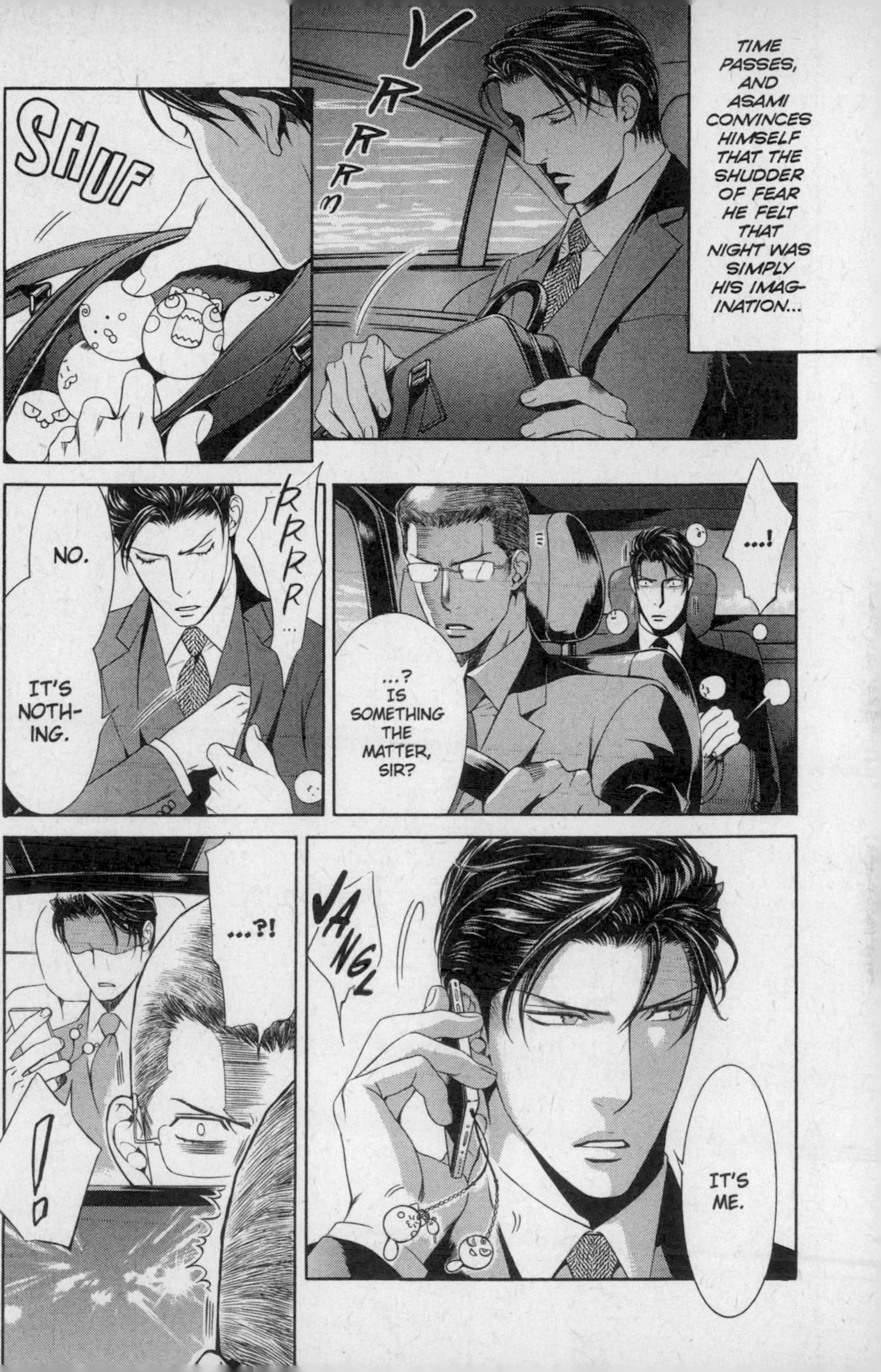
TIME PASSES, AND ASAMI CONVINCES HIMSELF THAT THE SHUDDER OF FEAR HE FELT THAT NIGHT WAS SIMPLY HIS IMAGINATION...
VRRRRn
SHUF
...!
...? IS SOMETHING THE MATTER, SIR?
RRRR...
NO.
IT'S NOTHING.
JANGL
IT'S ME.
...?!
!

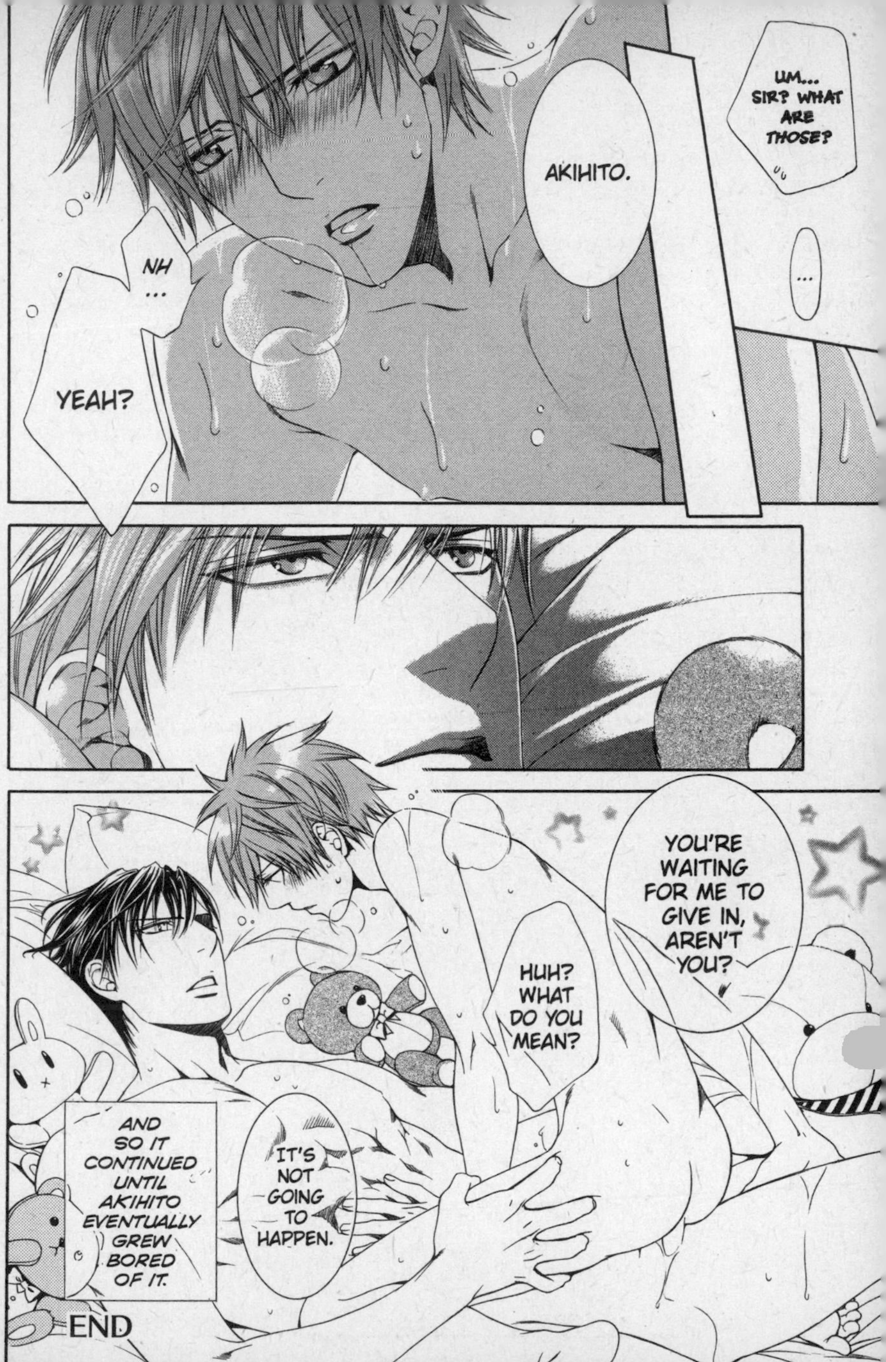
UM... SIR? WHAT ARE THOSE?
...
AKIHITO.
NH ...
YEAH?
YOU'RE WAITING FOR ME TO GIVE IN, AREN'T YOU?
HUH? WHAT DO YOU MEAN?
IT'S NOT GOING TO HAPPEN.
AND SO IT CONTINUED UNTIL AKIHITO EVENTUALLY GREW BORED OF IT.
END

AFTERWORD

HELLO! AYANO YAMANE HERE. THANK YOU VERY MUCH FOR PURCHASING VOLUME 9 OF THE *FINDER* SERIES! WILL ASAMI AND AKIHITO, NO MATTER HOW MANY BIRTHDAYS THEY HAVE, BE FOREVER A 30-YEAR-OLD AND A TEENAGER? AS FOR THE ONE BEHIND THE SCENES DRAWING IT ALL, YEAR AFTER YEAR SEES EVER WORSENING VISION AND EVER LESS ENERGY... ^-^; CASE IN POINT, IT'S BEEN OVER TWO YEARS SINCE THE PREVIOUS VOLUME CAME OUT. MY HUMBLEST APOLOGIES. I HAVE ALWAYS BEEN SLOW AT THE PLANNING AND DRAWING STEPS, BUT STARTING THIS YEAR I'VE FRESHENED UP MY WORK ENVIRONMENT, AND I INTEND TO PUT OUT MORE PAGES PER CHAPTER. I HOPE TO HAVE THE NEXT VOLUME READY TO GO ON SHELVES BY NEXT YEAR, SO PLEASE STICK WITH ME.

SPEAKING OF THIS NEW VOLUME, I CAN ALREADY HEAR VOICES CRYING, "WHERE'S ALL THE SMUT?!" I'M AFRAID THIS TIME IT JUST WORKED OUT SO THAT ASAMI SPENT HALF THE VOLUME MISSING OR PASSED OUT. HOWEVER, IF YOU WAIT JUST A LITTLE WHILE LONGER, THE NEXT VOLUME WILL BE *PERFECT* FOR A LITTLE SEASIDE STEAMINESS. HAVE PATIENCE! IN THIS VOLUME, INSTEAD OF AKIHITO, WE HAD FEI LONG STEP UP AND PROVIDE SOME EYE CANDY. "BUT WITH *HIM* OF ALL PEOPLE?!" I CAN HEAR YOU SAY. FOR SOME REASON, PEOPLE HAVE BEEN TREATING FEI LONG AS A VIRGIN, BUT TRUST ME, WHEN HE WORKED AS HIS ELDER BROTHER YAN'S HIT MAN, HE LEARNED TO TURN HIS WHOLE BODY INTO A WEAPON AND HAS STOCKPILED A LOT OF EXPERIENCE. MESS WITH HIM AND YOU'RE LIKELY TO GET BURNED. WILL POOR MIKHAIL, QUIETLY AND INNOCENTLY SPARKLING AWAY, COME OUT OF THIS ENCOUNTER ALIVE?! AS A SIDE NOTE, I ALSO LIKE HOW AMBIGUOUS OF A RELATIONSHIP FEI LONG HAS WITH YĒ.

IF YOU HAVE ANY COMMENTS OR SUGGESTIONS YOU'D LIKE TO MAKE, PLEASE FEEL FREE TO SEND A LETTER TO THE EDITORIAL DEPARTMENT. I HOPE YOU ALL ENJOYED VOLUME 9!

AYANO YAMANE
JULY 2018

LOOK AT ALL THOSE SPARKLES.

WHOA.

STAFF

UNO
ISU
IZAYA
PARUKO
UZUKI
SHIROE
MIKAN

SPECIAL THANKS
M. IRIE
M. E
LIBRE EDITORIAL DEPARTMENT,
IT CREW & SALES, THE BOOKSTORES,
ANIMATE, OUR CONTACT AT THE PRINTERS

THANK YOU SO MUCH TO ALL THE PEOPLE WHO HELPED PUT THIS VOLUME TOGETHER!

Akihito Takaba's
Sentai Warrior in
the Viewfinder

Deluxe Edition
Bonus

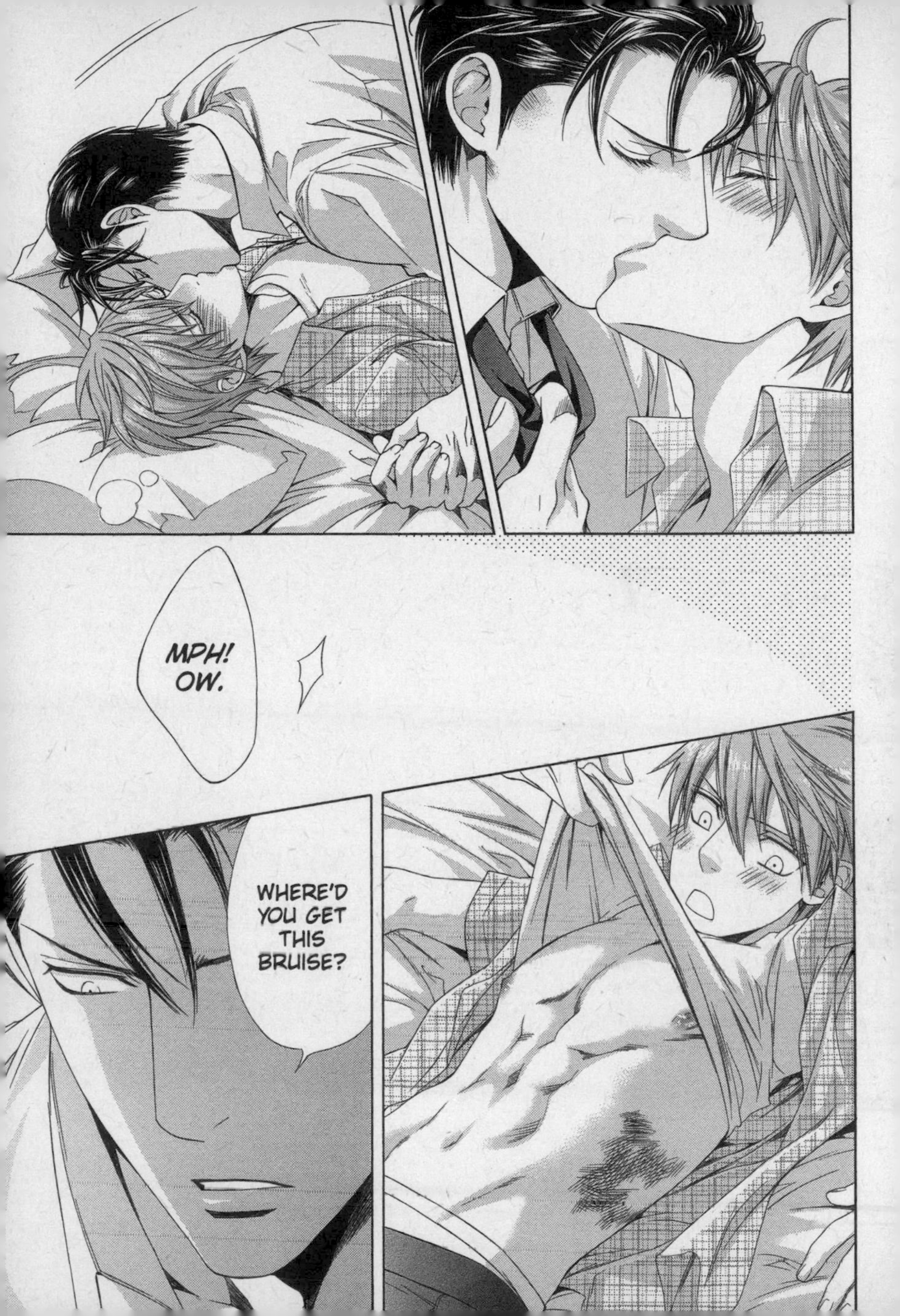
MPH! OW.
WHERE'D YOU GET THIS BRUISE?

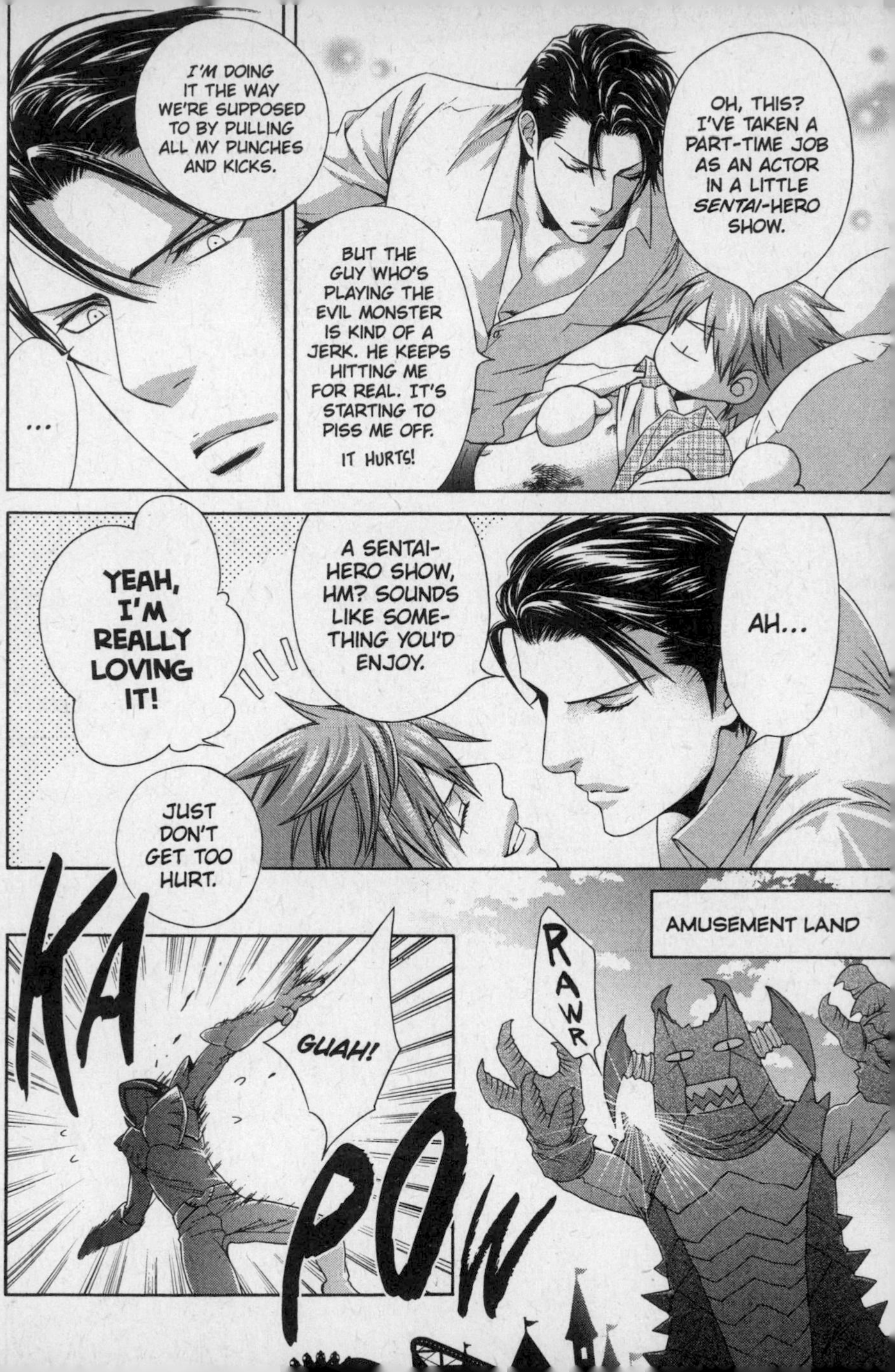
OH, THIS? I'VE TAKEN A PART-TIME JOB AS AN ACTOR IN A LITTLE *SENTAI*-HERO SHOW.
BUT THE GUY WHO'S PLAYING THE EVIL MONSTER IS KIND OF A JERK. HE KEEPS HITTING ME FOR REAL. IT'S STARTING TO PISS ME OFF.
IT HURTS!
I'M DOING IT THE WAY WE'RE SUPPOSED TO BY PULLING ALL MY PUNCHES AND KICKS.
...
AH...
A SENTAI-HERO SHOW, HM? SOUNDS LIKE SOME-THING YOU'D ENJOY.
YEAH, I'M REALLY LOVING IT!
JUST DON'T GET TOO HURT.
AMUSEMENT LAND
RAWR
GUAH!
KA
POW

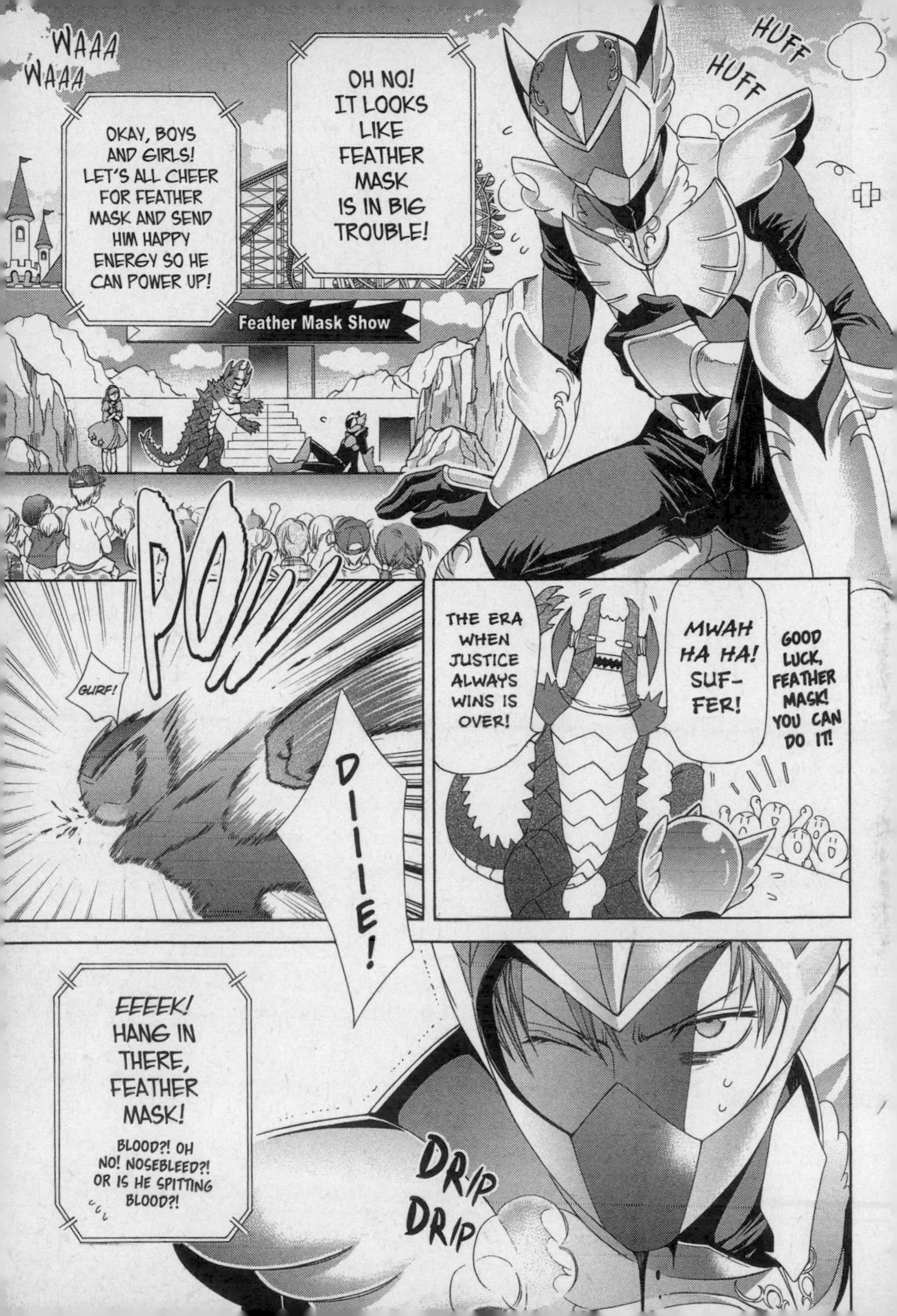
HUFF HUFF
OH NO! IT LOOKS LIKE FEATHER MASK IS IN BIG TROUBLE!
OKAY, BOYS AND GIRLS! LET'S ALL CHEER FOR FEATHER MASK AND SEND HIM HAPPY ENERGY SO HE CAN POWER UP!
WAAA WAAA
Feather Mask Show
MWAH HA HA! SUF-FER!
THE ERA WHEN JUSTICE ALWAYS WINS IS OVER!
GOOD LUCK, FEATHER MASK! YOU CAN DO IT!
POW
GURF!
DIIIIE!
DRIP DRIP
EEEEK! HANG IN THERE, FEATHER MASK!
BLOOD?! OH NO! NOSEBLEED?! OR IS HE SPITTING BLOOD?!

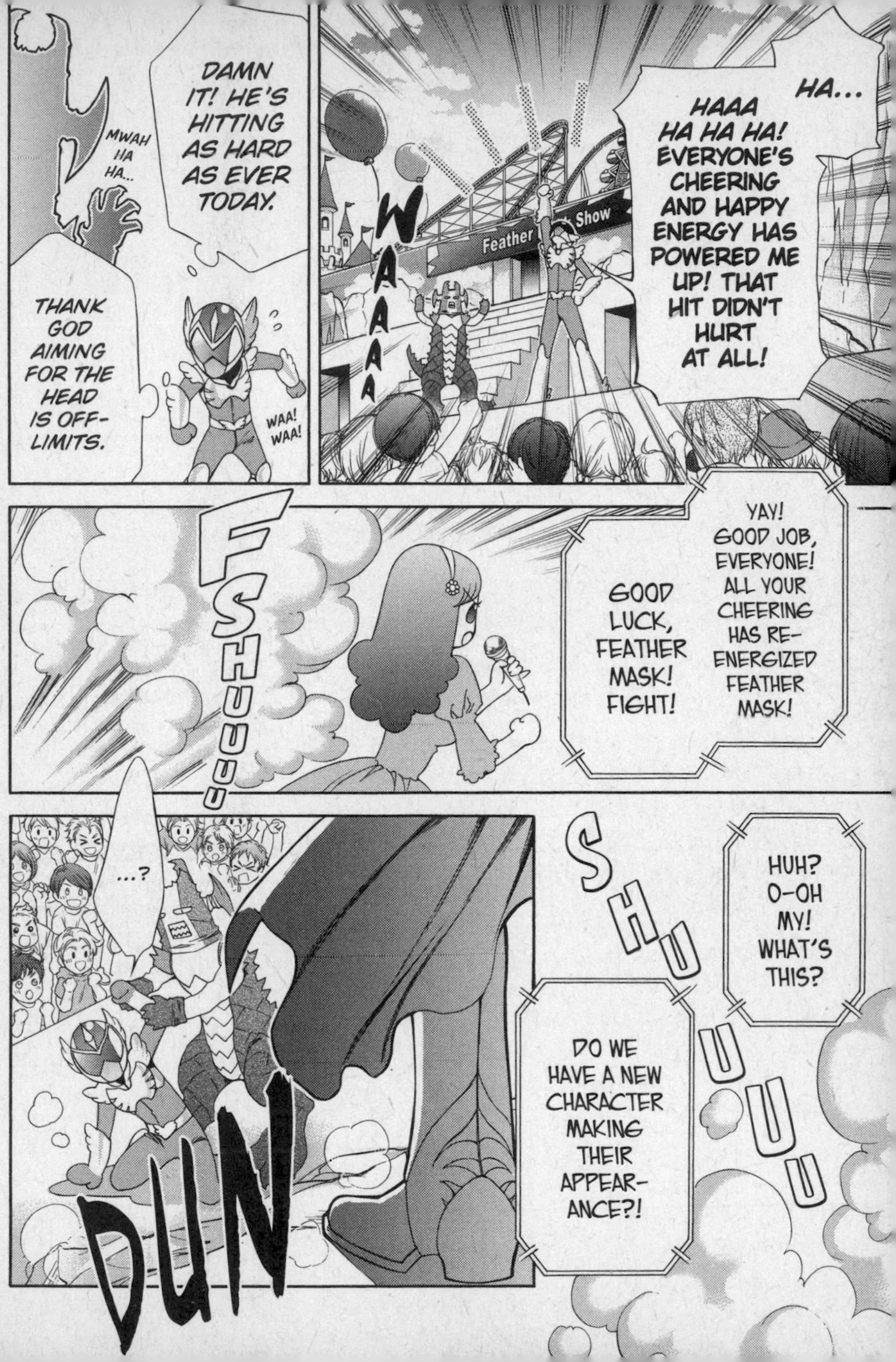
HA...
HAAAA HA HA HA! EVERYONE'S CHEERING AND HAPPY ENERGY HAS POWERED ME UP! THAT HIT DIDN'T HURT AT ALL!
Feather
Show
WAAAAA
DAMN IT! HE'S HITTING AS HARD AS EVER TODAY.
MWAH HA HA...
THANK GOD AIMING FOR THE HEAD IS OFF-LIMITS.
WAA! WAA!
YAY! GOOD JOB, EVERYONE! ALL YOUR CHEERING HAS RE-ENERGIZED FEATHER MASK!
GOOD LUCK, FEATHER MASK! FIGHT!
FSHUUUUUU
HUH? O-OH MY! WHAT'S THIS?
DO WE HAVE A NEW CHARACTER MAKING THEIR APPEARANCE?!
SHUUUUU
...?
DUN

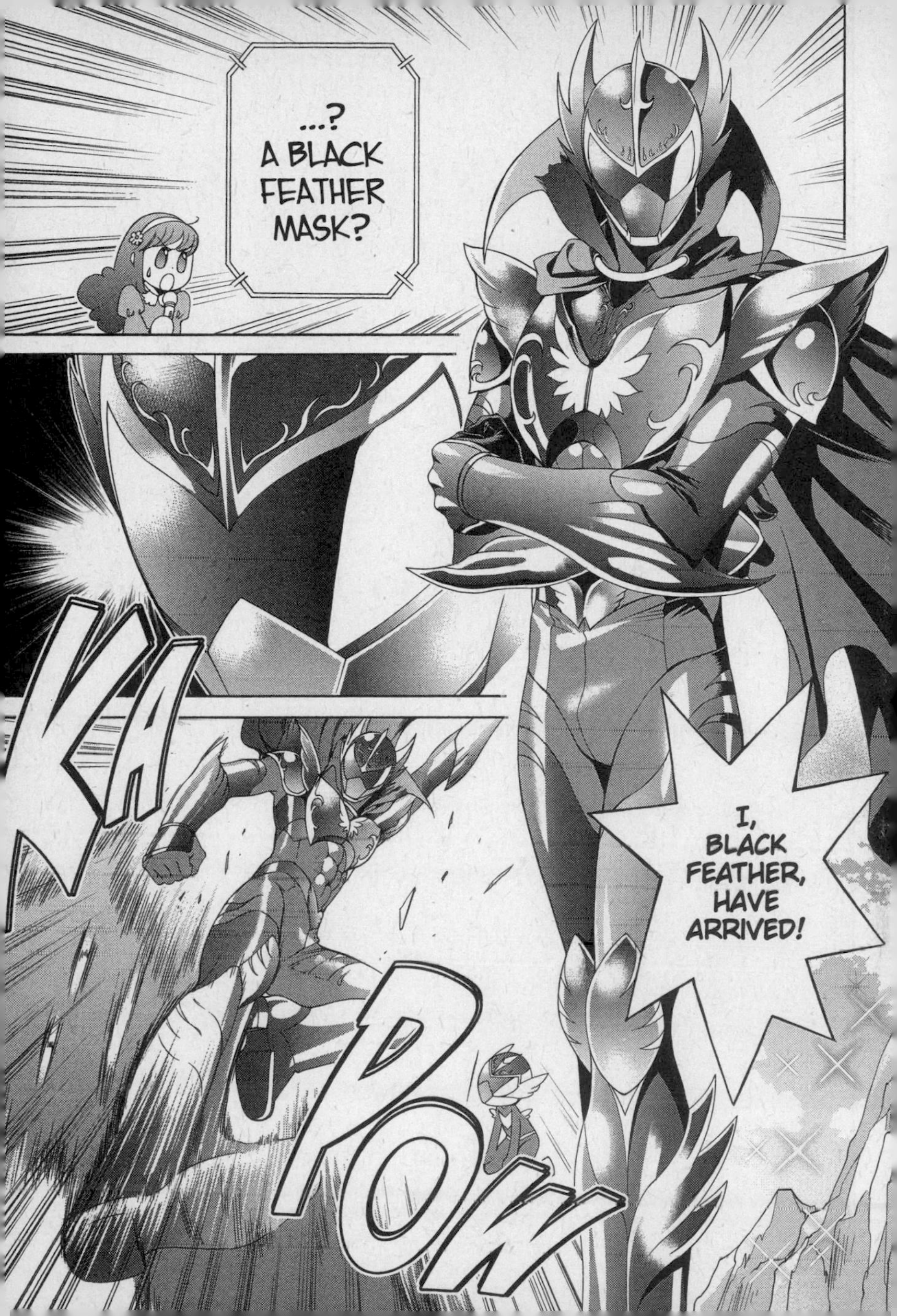
I, BLACK FEATHER, HAVE ARRIVED!
...? A BLACK FEATHER MASK?
KA
POW

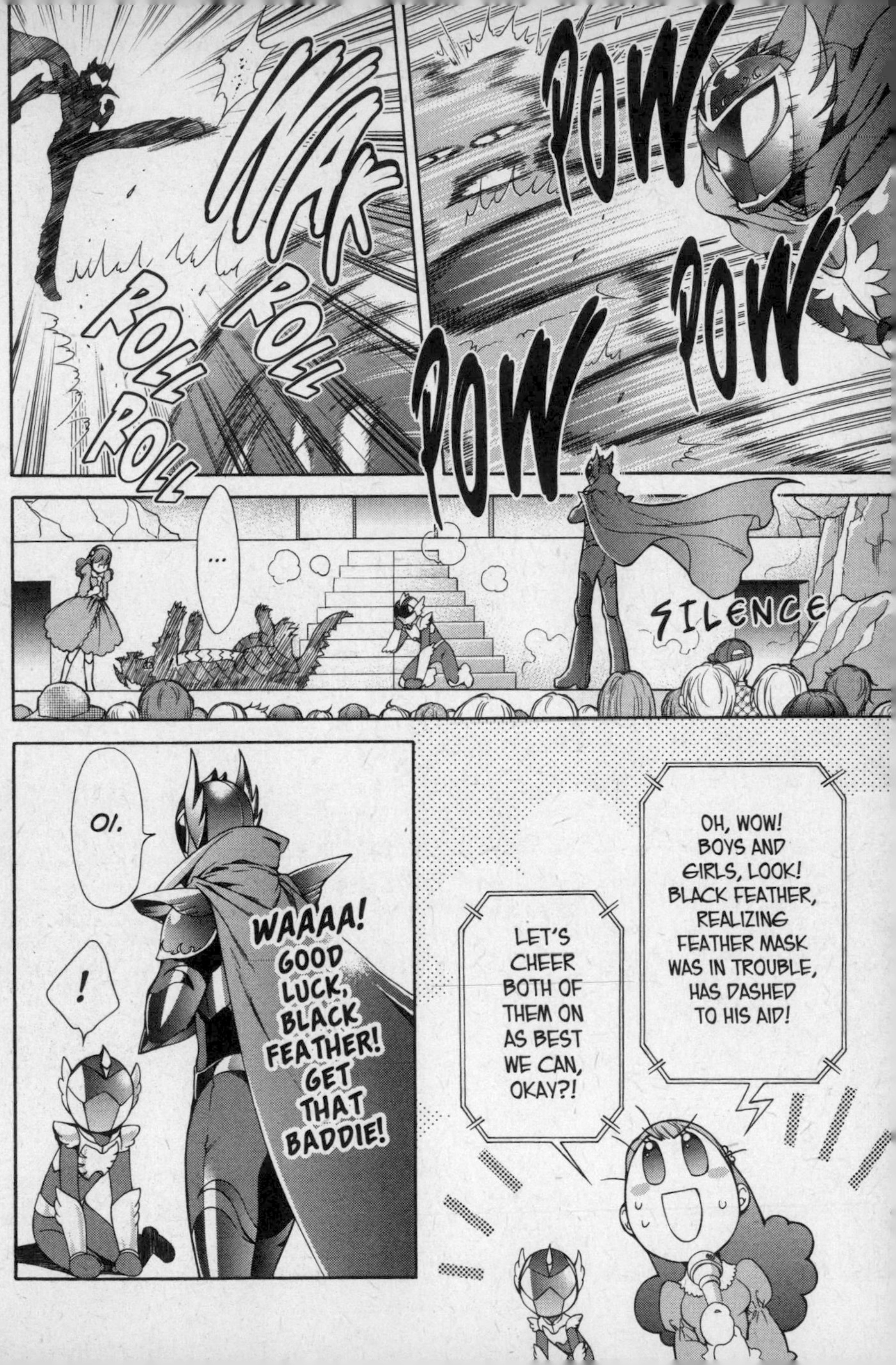
POW
POW
POW
POW
WAK
ROLL ROLL ROLL ROLL
SILENCE
...
OH, WOW! BOYS AND GIRLS, LOOK! BLACK FEATHER, REALIZING FEATHER MASK WAS IN TROUBLE, HAS DASHED TO HIS AID!
LET'S CHEER BOTH OF THEM ON AS BEST WE CAN, OKAY?!
OI.
WAAAA! GOOD LUCK, BLACK FEATHER! GET THAT BADDIE!
!

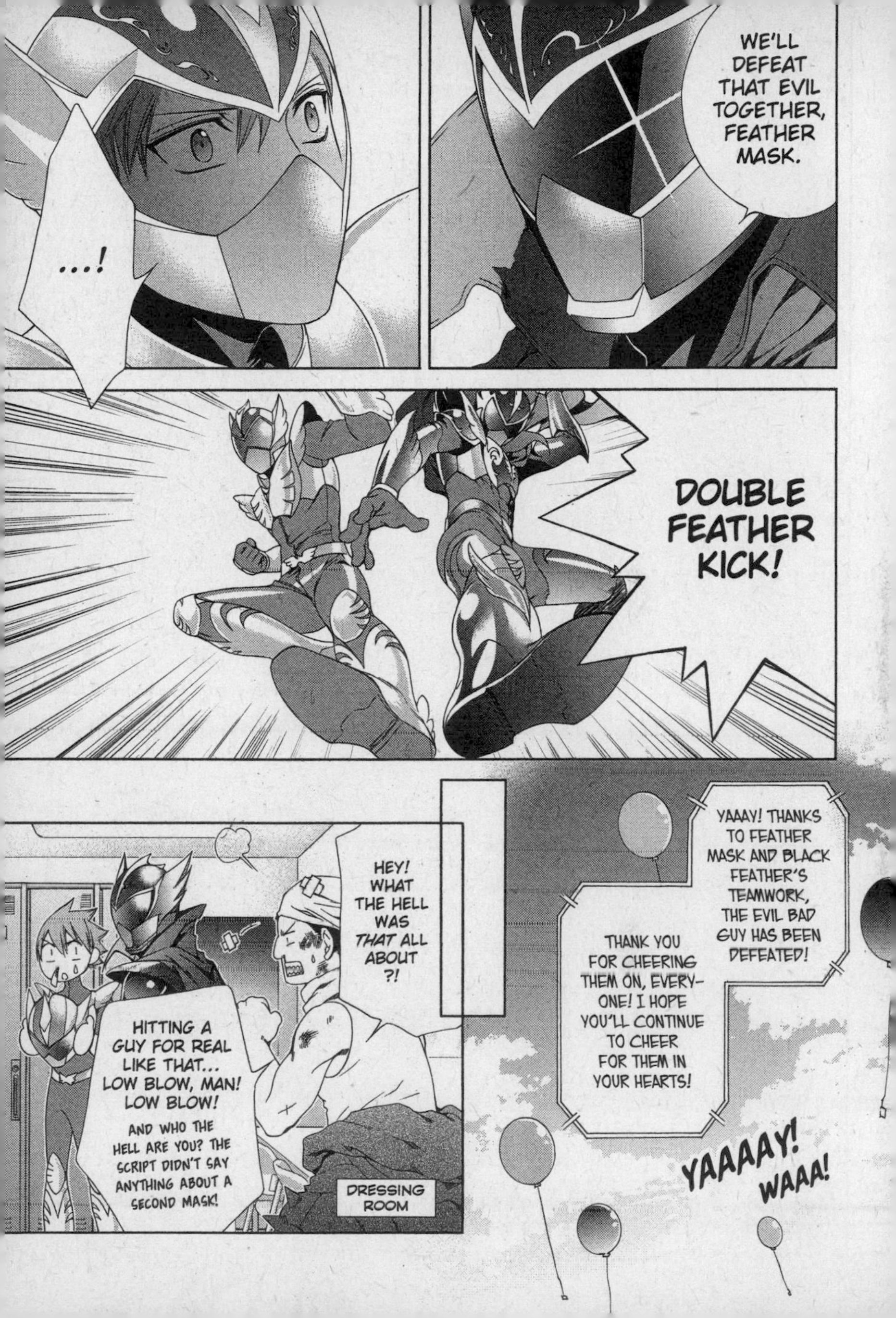
WE'LL DEFEAT THAT EVIL TOGETHER, FEATHER MASK.
...!
DOUBLE FEATHER KICK!
YAAAY! THANKS TO FEATHER MASK AND BLACK FEATHER'S TEAMWORK, THE EVIL BAD GUY HAS BEEN DEFEATED!
THANK YOU FOR CHEERING THEM ON, EVERY-ONE! I HOPE YOU'LL CONTINUE TO CHEER FOR THEM IN YOUR HEARTS!
YAAAAY!
WAAA!
DRESSING ROOM
HEY! WHAT THE HELL WAS *THAT* ALL ABOUT?!
HITTING A GUY FOR REAL LIKE THAT... LOW BLOW, MAN! LOW BLOW!
AND WHO THE HELL ARE YOU? THE SCRIPT DIDN'T SAY ANYTHING ABOUT A SECOND MASK!

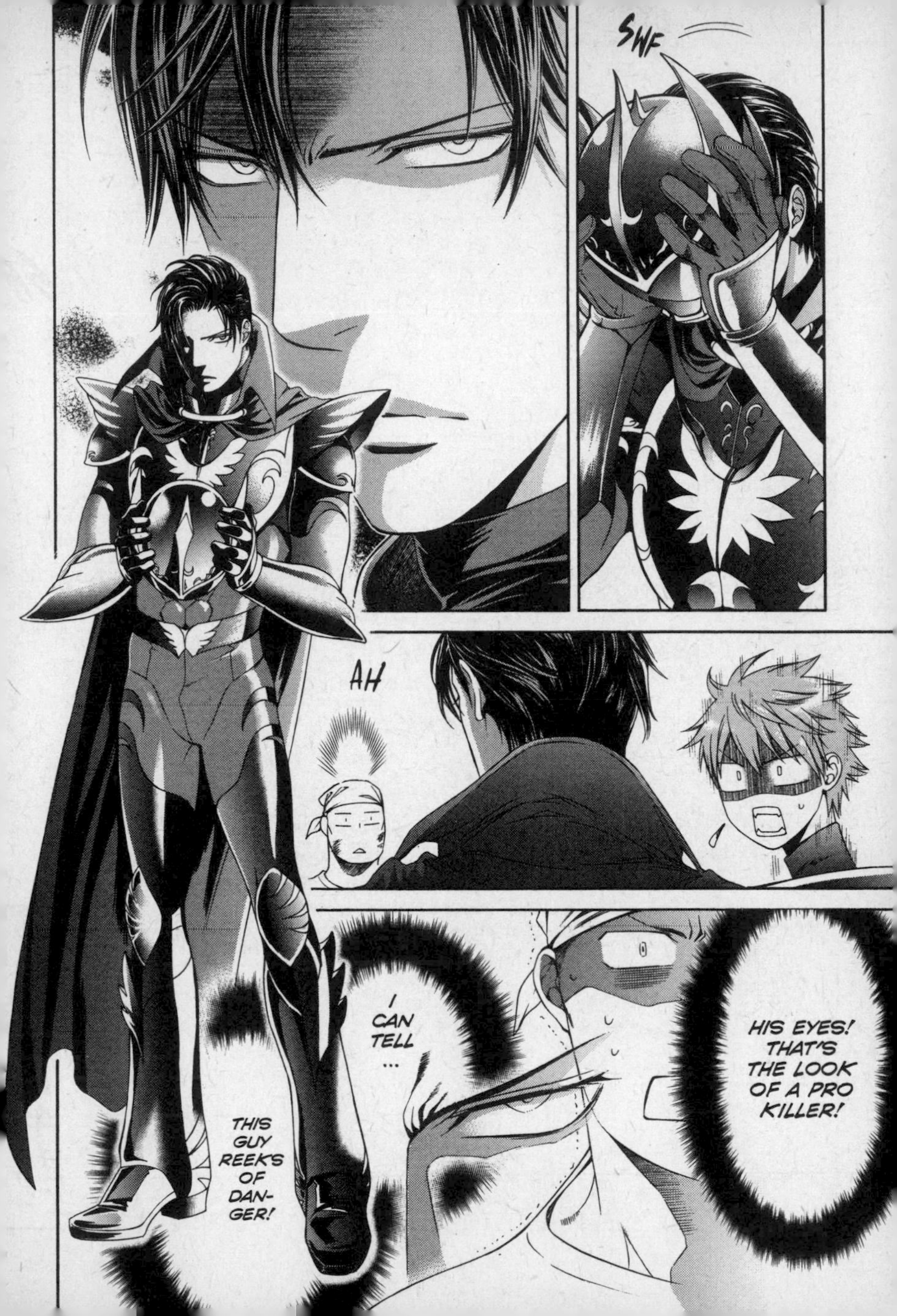
SWF
AH
HIS EYES! THAT'S THE LOOK OF A PRO KILLER!
I CAN TELL ...
THIS GUY REEKS OF DAN-GER!

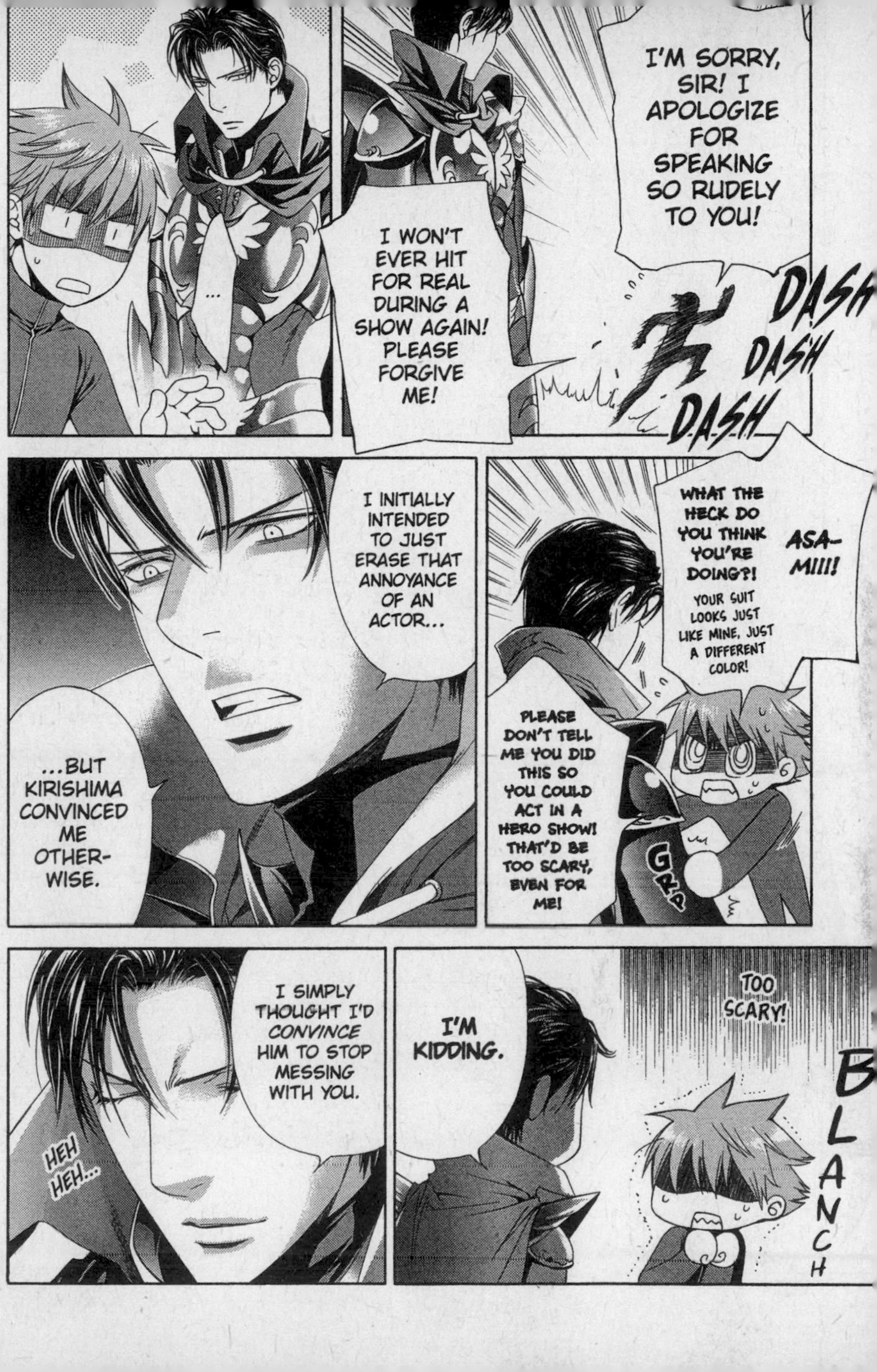
I'M SORRY, SIR! I APOLOGIZE FOR SPEAKING SO RUDELY TO YOU!
I WON'T EVER HIT FOR REAL DURING A SHOW AGAIN! PLEASE FORGIVE ME!
DASH DASH DASH
...
ASA-MIII!
WHAT THE HECK DO YOU THINK YOU'RE DOING?!
YOUR SUIT LOOKS JUST LIKE MINE, JUST A DIFFERENT COLOR!
PLEASE DON'T TELL ME YOU DID THIS SO YOU COULD ACT IN A HERO SHOW! THAT'D BE TOO SCARY, EVEN FOR ME!
GRIP
I INITIALLY INTENDED TO JUST ERASE THAT ANNOYANCE OF AN ACTOR...
...BUT KIRISHIMA CONVINCED ME OTHERWISE.
TOO SCARY!
BLANCH
I'M KIDDING.
I SIMPLY THOUGHT I'D *CONVINCE* HIM TO STOP MESSING WITH YOU.
HEH HEH...

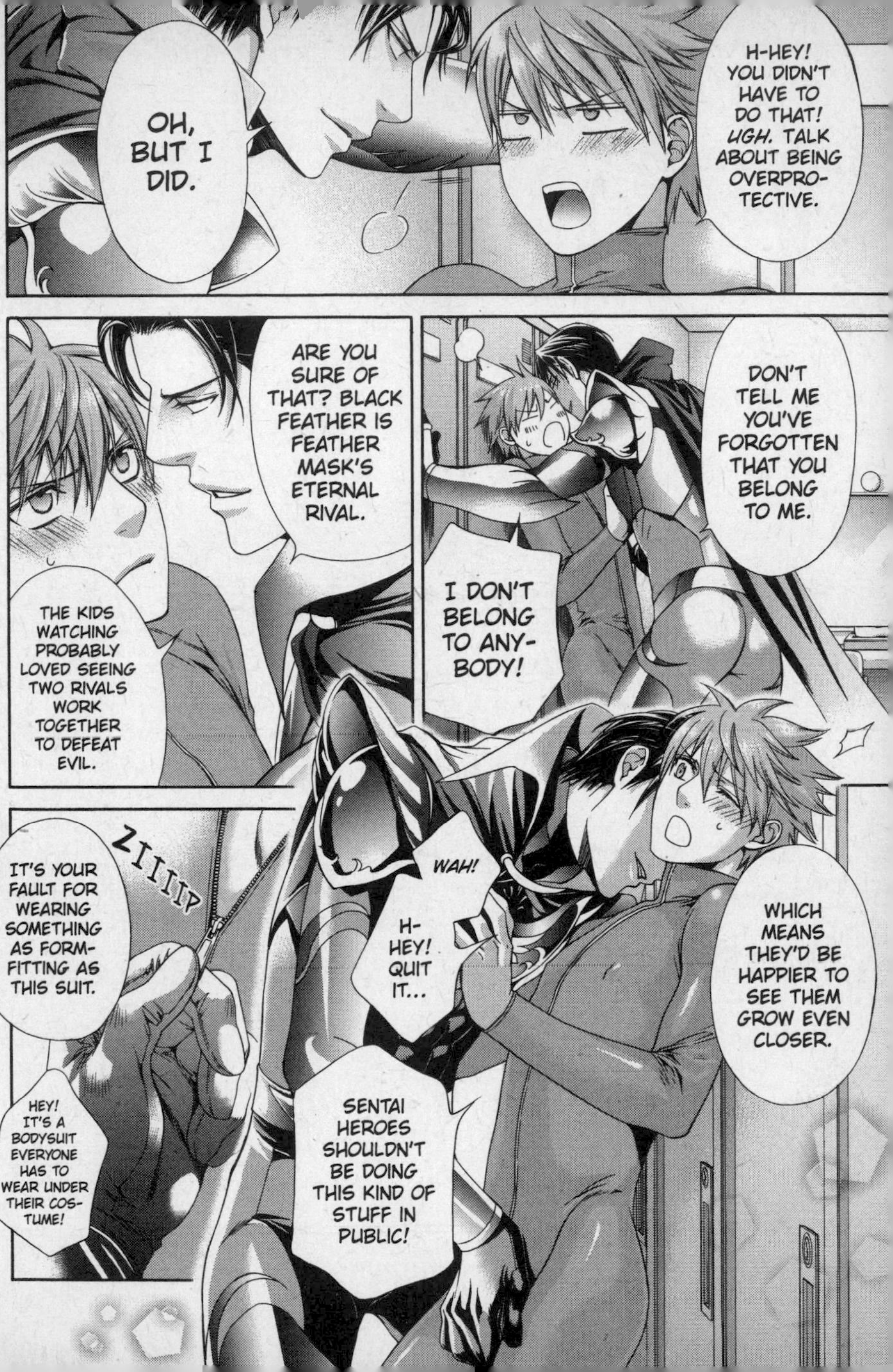
H-HEY! YOU DIDN'T HAVE TO DO THAT! *UGH.* TALK ABOUT BEING OVERPROTECTIVE.
OH, BUT I DID.
DON'T TELL ME YOU'VE FORGOTTEN THAT YOU BELONG TO ME.
I DON'T BELONG TO ANYBODY!
ARE YOU SURE OF THAT? BLACK FEATHER IS FEATHER MASK'S ETERNAL RIVAL.
THE KIDS WATCHING PROBABLY LOVED SEEING TWO RIVALS WORK TOGETHER TO DEFEAT EVIL.
WHICH MEANS THEY'D BE HAPPIER TO SEE THEM GROW EVEN CLOSER.
WAH!
H-HEY! QUIT IT...
ZIIIIP
IT'S YOUR FAULT FOR WEARING SOMETHING AS FORM-FITTING AS THIS SUIT.
SENTAI HEROES SHOULDN'T BE DOING THIS KIND OF STUFF IN PUBLIC!
HEY! IT'S A BODYSUIT EVERYONE HAS TO WEAR UNDER THEIR COSTUME!

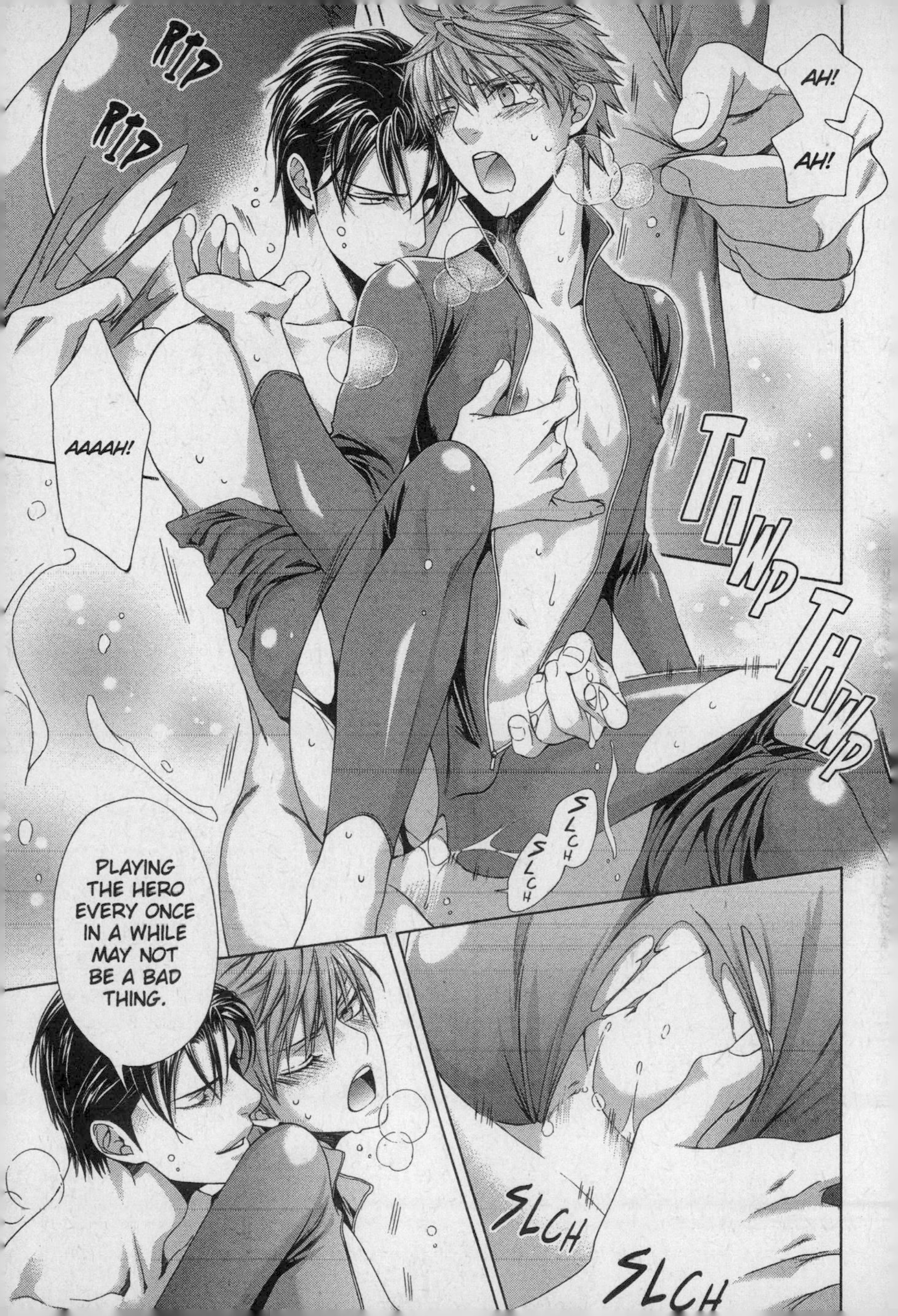

AH!
AH!
RIP
RIP
THWP THWP
AAAAH!
SLCH SLCH
SLCH
SLCH
PLAYING THE HERO EVERY ONCE IN A WHILE MAY NOT BE A BAD THING.

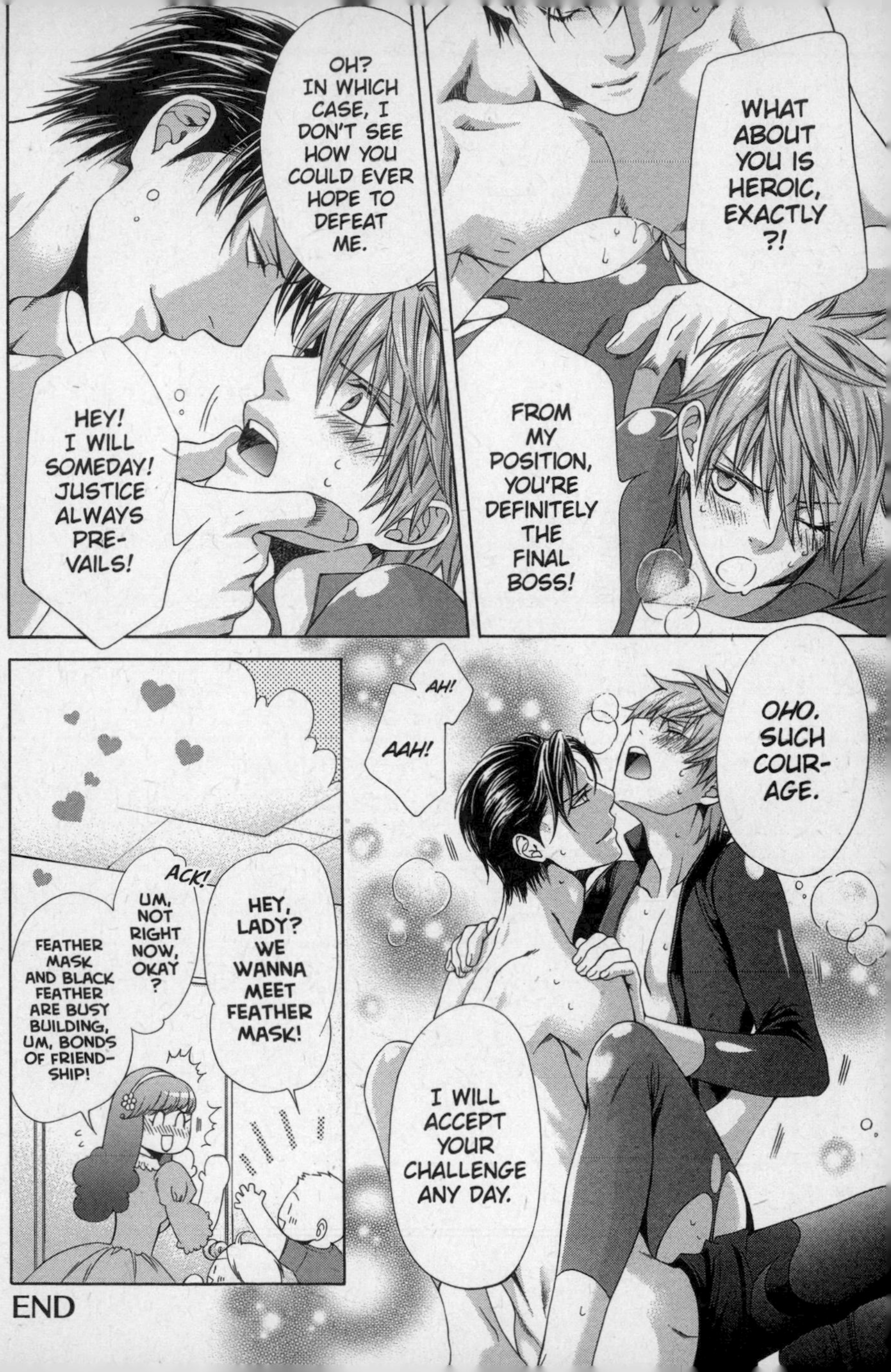
WHAT ABOUT YOU IS HEROIC, EXACTLY ?!
FROM MY POSITION, YOU'RE DEFINITELY THE FINAL BOSS!
OH? IN WHICH CASE, I DON'T SEE HOW YOU COULD EVER HOPE TO DEFEAT ME.
HEY! I WILL SOMEDAY! JUSTICE ALWAYS PRE-VAILS!
OHO. SUCH COUR-AGE.
AH!
AAH!
I WILL ACCEPT YOUR CHALLENGE ANY DAY.
HEY, LADY? WE WANNA MEET FEATHER MASK!
ACK!
UM, NOT RIGHT NOW, OKAY?
FEATHER MASK AND BLACK FEATHER ARE BUSY BUILDING, UM, BONDS OF FRIEND-SHIP!

END

THANK YOU FOR READING THE SPECIAL

LIMITED EDITION BOOKLET THAT GOES WITH THE

FIRST PRINTING OF VOLUME 9 OF THE *FINDER*

SERIES! I'M AYANO YAMANE. UM...I HOPE YOU

AREN'T TOO FED UP WITH ME. FOR SOME

REASON I HEAR VOICES SAYING "AGAIN WITH

THIS?!" IN THE DISTANCE. YES, AS YOU CAN SEE, I

WENT WITH ONE OF MY PERSONAL PREFERENCES...

AGAIN. *(WOOHOO!)* IT SURPRISED ME JUST HOW

MUCH LONGER IT TOOK THAN I EXPECTED.

(I TOTALLY UNDERESTIMATED HERO SHOWS.)

ANYWAY, IT'S YET ANOTHER STORY INVOLVING

COSTUMES. I HOPE YOU LIKED IT!

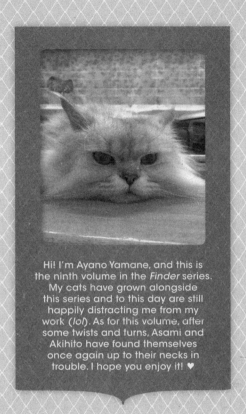

Hi! I'm Ayano Yamane, and this is the ninth volume in the *Finder* series. My cats have grown alongside this series and to this day are still happily distracting me from my work (*lol*). As for this volume, after some twists and turns, Asami and Akihito have found themselves once again up to their necks in trouble. I hope you enjoy it! ♥

About the Author

One of the most popular boys' love mangaka to come out of Japan, **Ayano Yamane** is the creator of *A Foreign Love Affair* and the *Crimson Spell* series. She has also published *doujinshi* (independent comics) under the circle name GUN MANIA. A native of Awaji Island, she was born a Sagittarius on December 18th and has an A blood type. You can find out more about Ayano Yamane via her Twitter account, **@yamaneayano**.

Finder
Volume 9
SuBLime Manga Deluxe Edition

Story and Art by **Ayano Yamane**

Translation—**Adrienne Beck**
Touch-Up Art and Lettering—**Deborah Fisher**
Cover and Graphic Design—**Natalie Chen**
Editor—**Jennifer LeBlanc**

Finder no Kodo © 2018 Ayano Yamane
Original Cover Design: Mamiko Saitou (Asanomi Graphic)
Originally published in Japan in 2018 by Libre Inc.
English translation rights arranged with Libre Inc.

libre

Printed in the U.S.A.

Published by SuBLime Manga
P.O. Box 77010
San Francisco, CA 94107

10 9 8 7 6 5 4 3 2 1
First printing, September 2019

PARENTAL ADVISORY
FINDER is rated M for Mature and is
recommended for mature readers. This volume
MATURE   contains graphic imagery and mature themes.

SUBLIME
www.SuBLimeManga.com

For more information

on all our products, along with the most up-to-date news on releases, series announcements, and contests, please visit us at:

 SuBLimeManga.com

 twitter.com/**SuBLimeManga**

 facebook.com/**SuBLimeManga**

 instagram.com/**SuBLimeManga**

 SuBLimeManga.tumblr.com

Downloading is as easy as:

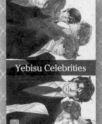